The Australian Film Revival

The Australian Film Revival

1970s, 1980s, and Beyond

Susan Barber

BLOOMSBURY ACADEMIC
NEW YORK • LONDON • OXFORD • NEW DELHI • SYDNEY

BLOOMSBURY ACADEMIC
Bloomsbury Publishing Inc
1385 Broadway, New York, NY 10018, USA
50 Bedford Square, London, WC1B 3DP, UK
29 Earlsfort Terrace, Dublin 2, Ireland

BLOOMSBURY, BLOOMSBURY ACADEMIC and the Diana logo
are trademarks of Bloomsbury Publishing Plc

First published in the United States of America 2023
Paperback edition published 2024

Copyright © Susan Barber, 2023

For legal purposes the Acknowledgments on pp. viii–ix constitute an extension of this copyright page.

Cover design by Eleanor Rose and Susan Barber
Cover image: ElenVD, iStock / Getty Images Plus

All rights reserved. No part of this publication may be reproduced or transmitted in any form or by any means, electronic or mechanical, including photocopying, recording, or any information storage or retrieval system, without prior permission in writing from the publishers.

Bloomsbury Publishing Inc does not have any control over, or responsibility for, any third-party websites referred to or in this book. All internet addresses given in this book were correct at the time of going to press. The author and publisher regret any inconvenience caused if addresses have changed or sites have ceased to exist, but can accept no responsibility for any such changes.

A catalog record for this book is available from the Library of Congress.

ISBN: HB: 978-1-5013-9002-9
PB: 978-1-5013-8999-3
ePDF: 978-1-5013-9000-5
eBook: 978-1-5013-9001-2

Typeset by Integra Software Services Pvt. Ltd.

To find out more about our authors and books visit www.bloomsbury.com and sign up for our newsletters.

*To my husband Joseph Lee for his unwavering faith
and encouragement*

*In memory of
Joan Long—mentor and guiding light*

Contents

Acknowledgments — viii

Introduction — 1

1 The Ocker: Chauvinistic and Oedipal — 45
2 Alternate Masculinities of Paul Cox and John Duigan — 71
3 Historical Women and the Bush — 93
4 Negligent, Runaway, and Abject Mothers — 121
5 The Indigenous Road Film — 145
6 Australian Gothic — 203

Index — 253

Acknowledgments

Some of the material in this book has appeared in other publications. Versions, revisions, and/or extensions appear in this work. Permission has been granted by the following publications:

- *Film Quarterly*, 50: 2, Winter, 1996–7, 41–5. "The Adventures of Priscilla, Queen of the Desert."
- *Metro*, 163, December 2009, 130–4. "Affairs of the Heart: The Oedipal Films of Paul Cox."
- *Screen Education*, 62, February 2011, 100–11. "Growing up in the 1960s: *The Year My Voice Broke* and *Flirting*."
- *Quarterly Review of Film and Video*, 37: 7, February 25, 2020. "*Walkabout*: A Timeless Cross-Cultural Journey." https://www.tandfonline.com/

I first wish to thank two very special long-time friends, Sue Murray and David Desser.

Sue provided valuable feedback on early drafts of my manuscript, and also generously shared her expertise of the Australian film industry on many occasions. David read many earlier versions of chapters and provided very helpful suggestions. To you both, my deep gratitude.

A sincere thanks to Marsha Kinder, my professor and dissertation advisor in the School of Cinematic Arts (SCA) at the University Southern California (USC). With her wisdom, Marsha guided me through the formative stages of my study of Australian film.

I took several wonderful classes from Richard Jewell and Drew Casper, also professors in the SCA at USC. Through these courses, I acquired an avid appreciation of a fascinating array of genres and directors. Each professor gave me a foundation for film history and analysis. Thank you both for your expertise, enthusiasm, and countless enchanting hours in Norris Theater.

Also I wish to express my gratitude to Bruce Kawin and James Palmer who taught film classes at the University of Colorado, Boulder, when I first began my formal study of film.

Acknowledgments

Thank you to my research assistants Erin Rodman, Ana Ávila, Anastasia Shulepova, Todd Stuart, Ryan Meyer, Rob Dunn, and Nancy Blevins.

My gratitude to my Word Processing "Wizard," Terrie Barna.

At Loyola Marymount University (LMU) I offer my sincere thanks to Bob Berman, Theater Manager, Mayer Theater, who found and ordered Australian titles (many difficult to find) for my Australian film classes over the years so my students could see the best of the film revival via a theatrical format experience.

Also at LMU, thanks to my wonderful friend Renee Harrangue for her wisdom, as well as to Joseph Jabbra for his support and encouragement. In the LMU School of Film and Television, my heartfelt gratitude to my colleagues Marilyn Beker, Carla Marcantonio, Richard Hadley, Karol Hoeffner, Steve Duncan, Mark Schwartz, and especially Stephen Ujlaki for his support of my work and flexibility during the writing process. Also I wish to acknowledge the pleasure of working with Howard Lavick, Thomas Kelly, and Warren Sherlock.

My appreciation to the Australian filmmakers/producers/writers who took the time to talk to me about their films: Michael Thornhill, Joy Hruby, John Duigan, Fred Schepisi, Rolf de Heer, Gillian Armstrong, Paul Cox, Phillip Noyce, and Tony Buckley.

My thanks to Australians in Film (AIF) in Los Angeles for their many screenings and filmmaker forums which enhanced my understanding and expanded my repertoire of Australian films.

To the hard-working Librarians at the Australian Film, Television and Radio School Library: Margaret Gwynne, Elisabeth McDonald, and Debbie Sander, my gratitude for all their enthusiastic help with my research. Also, my thanks to Simon Drake at the National Film and Sound Archive for his expertise and assistance.

My thanks to Susan Dermody for her Sydney hospitality and for providing helpful contact information during my first visit to Australia.

To Georgia Wallace-Crabbe—my appreciation for her Melbourne hospitality.

I wish to express my sincere thanks to the Bloomsbury Academic team: Editor Katie Gallof, Assistant Editor Stephanie Grace-Petinos, as well as Deputy Head of Production Ian Buck; and also to Sudhagaran Thandapani, Project Management Executive at Integra. My appreciation for your guidance.

Introduction

Rough and tumble men work long hours shearing sheep, living for that elusive Sunday when they can rest. A group of adolescent boarding-school girls embark on an outing to Hanging Rock at the turn of the century; three of them disappear along with their teacher. During the same time frame, a mixed-race Indigenous man goes on a killing spree in a murderous reprisal to the ugly racism that pervades his life; a young woman turns down an offer of marriage to a man she loves in order to maintain her sense of self in pursuit of a writing career. At the peak of the Great Depression a woman struggles to earn a living and support her two children by working in a pub. And in modern day a lawyer comes to grips with powerful Aboriginal myths, when he defends a group of young Indigenous men accused of murder.

Anyone with an interest in international cinema of the 1970s will recognize at least some, and perhaps all, of these landmark films from Australia based on this brief précis. What is most striking about this group of works, all of which were released in the period 1975–9, is not only that they range across temporality—from 1900 right up to the present—but that they also clearly derive from the specifics of Australian history and culture. And most striking of all is that they seemed to emerge from out of the blue in terms of global film history, many receiving international distribution and enthusiastic critical acclaim with strong box office results.

Prior to the 1970s, Australia did not have a continuous, full-fledged feature film industry, despite a robust silent film period and a range of comedies and dramas produced by a bona fide working studio, Cinesound, throughout the 1930s.[1] In the post–Second World War period during the 1950s and 1960s, only a small number of locally produced features were made, with an occasional export to Britain. Australia frequently served as a backdrop for films by American- or British-based film companies. Both countries (in particular Hollywood) had well-established distribution channels and exhibition houses which favored their own films in their "host" country. By the time the Australian film revival was in full swing in the mid-1970s, not only did Australian audiences flock to theaters to see "homegrown" films, but the quantity of Australian films on overseas screens was so high that ardent critics declared this outpouring an Australian "New Wave." The eyes of the world had turned to a compelling and largely unknown culture.

Yet how did it come about that such a large number of films of quality, richness, and resonance came to be produced by a previously nonexistent film industry? How could films such as *Sunday Too Far Away* (Ken Hannam, 1975), *Picnic at Hanging Rock* (Peter Weir, 1975), *The Chant of Jimmie Blacksmith* (Fred Schepisi, 1978), *My Brilliant Career* (Gillian Armstrong, 1979), *Caddie* (Donald Crombie, 1976), and *The Last Wave* (Peter Weir, 1977) emerge onto the international scene to so much acclaim? The work of this book is to understand and examine the matrix of forces—artistic, cultural, economic, political, governmental, and ideological—that gave rise to, shaped, and sustained this remarkable film movement.

The film renaissance was fueled by a surge of national pride in the 1960s, coined "The New Nationalism," bucking the country's tradition of cultural cringe—its deep-seated sense of inferiority. Activists from the documentary and television sectors, unions, guilds, and film societies rallied together and lobbied Parliament repeatedly for full government support and protection of a local industry. As Graeme Turner noted about this critical time frame, "an increasingly powerful nationalist mythology came to recognize film as the most desirable medium for projecting an image of the new confidence and maturity seen to mark contemporary Australian culture and society" (Turner, 1989, 101). In other words, popular and successful films could boost national morale. This push for government patronage and support of a film industry was initially linked to the sheltering of local television programming amidst the predominance of American shows on Australian television. A major part of activists' arguments was the dearth of Australian films to fill local television screens.

Activists' questioning of American sovereignty over Australian media had its counterpart in the political arena; a large contingent of the population protested an unpopular American war in Vietnam where Australian troops supported the country's post–Second World War ally, the United States, as per Pacific defense agreements. Though still a member of the British Commonwealth (and founded as a penal colony in 1788), Australia's political alignment with a superpower introduced a new era in its defense strategies as Australia became a key player in

United States' policies amidst the East–West Cold War. For film activists, years of campaigning paid off. With the blessing of and a financial commitment from the government in 1970, as well as the support of prime ministers John Gorton (1969–71) and Gough Whitlam (1972–5), or as producer Phillip Adams noted, "Gorton the progenitor" and Whitlam "the munificent benefactor," the first government funding agency, the Australian Film Development Corporation (AFDC), was created in 1970 (and in operation until 1975) with an initial government endowment of $1 million.[2] (All dollar figures in this chapter are in Australian dollars unless otherwise noted.) The revival had been launched. We can encapsulate the revival into five phases. During the first two phases the majority of films were funded by the federal government (essentially based upon a European model), some with the assistance of state corporations. The third phase, the "10BA period," was supported primarily by private financing, or open market funding, with the last two phases representing a combination of private and government-supported films. The following sections give an overview of the five industry phases with respect to financing structures, trends, notable films, and prominent filmmakers in order to contextualize and construct a framework for the primary focus of this study, the 1970s and 1980s, with several selected 1990s and new millennium films. Filmmakers' "Visions of Australia" break new ground and reflect innovation in a variety of ways.

The Australian Film Development Corporation

In the first phase, the AFDC funded primarily commercially oriented films to kick-start the industry. This period was dominated by the infamous, outrageous, and highly commercially successful ocker comedies. The ocker, which also refers to the male protagonist, was a unique and genuine Australian genre derived from a strong tradition in popular culture, including literature and television. Films such as *Stork* (Tim Burstall, 1971), *The Adventures of Barry McKenzie* (Bruce Beresford, 1972), and *Petersen* (Tim Burstall, 1974) featured vulgar and hedonistic males misbehaving in the company of their mates in pubs, at sporting events, or in a public place for maximum exposure. The ockers were enormously popular with local audiences (*Barry McKenzie* was even a minor hit in Britain), and significantly, their success demonstrated that Australians would seek out and attend local films in theaters heretofore dominated by Hollywood. *Stork* was singled out and received a best picture award from the

Australian Film Institute (AFI), an organization created in 1958 (and modeled on the British Film Institute), to develop and support an active film culture in Australia. As the industry matured, the AFI increasingly recognized artistic and technical excellence, in 1976 creating a full-fledged award system based on the American Academy of Motion Picture Arts and Sciences. (In 2011 the AFI initiated The Australian Academy of Cinema and Television Arts—AACTA—an organization that continues to honor outstanding work in these media forms.)

However, despite the success of the AFDC in launching popular films and kick-starting a local film industry, the AFDC was criticized for encouraging "culturally debased" films deemed too gauche for export. What was the problem? As industry activists, filmmakers, critics, and even members of Parliament (many of whom had lobbied for a government-subsidized industry) pointed out, the ockers were an embarrassment. They were frequently laden with coarse phallocentric language and behavior, crude bathroom humor, and the tawdry sexual objectification of women. The ocker genre clearly and consistently took advantage of the easing of censorship in the early 1970s with full frontal nudity and the depiction of sex. The range of criticism directed toward the ocker genre implied and pointed to a particularly sensitive issue for a country interested in making a bid for international recognition with a revived national cinema. Established and burgeoning filmmakers wished to expand the parameters of Australian films, and looked to overseas markets and festivals as venues for the serious presentation and exploration of Australian culture and history in order to develop a more reputable and less crass image of the country and its people.

After a series of hearings throughout 1972, the AFDC instituted a new policy in support of more serious-minded and reflective films with "exceptional artistic potential ... which would previously have been rejected on commercial requirements ... in the interest of developing individual Australian filmmakers and the industry as a whole" (*Lumiere*, 1973, 4). For example, the AFDC funded *Between Wars* (1974), written by novelist Frank Moorhouse and directed by first-time feature director, Michael Thornhill. *Wars* was a compelling drama which focused on a young doctor at the end of the Second World War in Britain, not only caring for shell-shocked veterans, but also later pioneering a psychoanalytic practice back in Australia. *Sunday Too Far Away*, and set in 1956, paid tribute to working-class sheep shearers with their indelible camaraderie or "mateship" (the strong and close bond of friendship and loyalty between men) in remote rural areas. Experimental and documentary filmmaker Peter Weir made his first feature with AFDC support after new guidelines were put into place. His *Cars That Ate Paris* (1974) was a deliriously gothic vision of a bloodthirsty and carnivorous town obsessed with cars. *Cars* tapped into the Australian passion for motor vehicles, and served as a prelude to the *Mad Max* films in the late 1970s and 1980s. Weir's subsequent *Picnic at Hanging Rock* (discussed in more detail later) was partially made with AFDC monies, though it was released during the second phase, the reorganized Australian Film Commission or AFC in 1975. The AFC was the principal source of investment in the majority of approximately sixty films released within the time frame of 1975–81 (including many of the aforementioned classics noted at the beginning of this introduction). This body was in operation until 2008 with the creation of Screen Australia, when the funding role of the AFC changed.

The Australian Film Commission

During this second phase, the AFC financed a good share of production costs and, if requested and approved, funding for marketing, both through grants and loans, often in tandem with state corporations such as the New South Wales Film Corporation (NSWFC) and the South Australian Film Corporation (SAFC). The AFC funding policy was derived from AFDC Act: "made wholly or substantially in Australia by Australians, with significant Australian content." The majority of films funded by the AFC, and as realized by filmmakers, aspired toward world-class standards: sophisticated narratives, complex characters, rich imagery, and high-quality sound design (frequently including original music). Rather than comic exaggerations and send-ups, the majority of AFC films were thoughtful representations of Australian history, culture, and society. Whereas AFDC-funded filmmakers intended their films primarily for local audiences, AFC-supported filmmakers had their eyes on international festivals and markets, not, of course, overlooking or ignoring Australian audiences. Since a good number of AFC films were selected for Cannes screenings in and out of competition, the second half of the 1970s was a critical time frame for the new industry, as noted at the beginning of this introduction. Cannes was the venue that had screened two seminal pre-revival films (funded by private sources): *Walkabout* (Nicolas Roeg, 1971) and *Wake in Fright* (Ted Kotcheff, 1971). Though not officially part of the revival, that is, the government funding of works by Australian filmmakers, these films were stunning precursors to the quality films that followed. The former was Nicolas Roeg's first foray into directing solo; at the time he was one of Britain's top cinematographers. *Walkabout* was a major contribution to the forthcoming legacy of Indigenous films with its exploration of the close relationship that evolves between a young Aboriginal man (richly characterized, and deviating considerably from prior non-Indigenous-ethnocentric depictions of Indigenous males) and two lost British children—a teenage girl and her younger brother—in the outback. The gothic *Wake in Fright*, a precursor to the *Max* films, is a nightmarish odyssey of a young male teacher on holiday, who is seduced by the deceptively amiable camaraderie of a group of boozing and gambling ockers.

In addition to Peter Weir, Ken Hannam, and Donald Crombie, the first wave of directors from the AFC period included Fred Schepisi, Gillian Armstrong, and Phillip Noyce (whose *Newsfront*, 1978, followed the career and personal life of a post–Second World War, pre-television newsreel cameraman). Armstrong and Noyce were both graduates of the first class from the Australian Film, Television and Radio School (established in 1973, and originally known as the Australian Film and Television School). Also in this group was Bruce Beresford, shifting to other subjects set at the turn of the century after his auspicious debut with *The Adventures of Barry McKenzie*. The first was the female-centered *The Getting of Wisdom* (1977), set in a boarding school for young women, the second *Breaker Morant* (1980), which focused on Australian soldiers fighting on behalf of Britain during the Boer War in Africa. With respect to recognition at Cannes, *Career*, *Blacksmith*, and *Morant* were each selected for official competition with a special supporting actor award given to Jack Thompson in *Morant*. *Newsfront*, given an exclusive screening, was a "minor sensation" at Cannes, according to critic/writer David Stratton, and was subsequently invited to the London and New York Film Festivals. *Caddie* became the showcase film for the International Women's Year Celebration, bringing acclaim to Australia, this recognition dovetailing nicely with the heyday of the Australian Women's movement. As a result of its Cannes screening, *Picnic at Hanging Rock* was sold to thirty-seven territories all over the world by distributor Atlantic Releasing. Highly popular among Australian audiences, its box office $5.1 million, *Picnic* held the number one box office position among Australian viewers until *Mad Max* in 1979. Weir's subsequent *Gallipoli* (1981) also found favor with local audiences, with a box office $11.7 million. This film featured the brave and earnest Australian soldiers fighting in Turkey on behalf of the British Empire during the First World War, and served as an appropriate companion film for *Breaker Morant*, as both films explored the historical Imperial British/colonial Australia relationship. *Gallipoli* was one of the few films from this era funded independently, in this case, by Associated R&R Films, owned by newspaper/media mogul Rupert Murdoch and partner Robert Stigwood. *Newsfront*, *Career*, *Sunday*, and *Caddie* all did very good business in Australia, reigning in the top ten films by the end of the decade, thus reinforcing the attraction of "locally grown" films to Australian audiences.

Significantly, two time frames were frequently (though not exclusively) tapped and explored during the AFC period. The first period was the turn of the century—1901 to be precise—when Australia was granted "Federation" status, giving the country a greater measure of independence and autonomy as it transitioned from a colonial to commonwealth standing (with a sovereign head, the Queen of England). Federation marked significant growth and maturity for Australia as a nation. *Picnic*, *Blacksmith*, *Career*, *Morant*, and *Gallipoli* (set a little later) are situated during these years. All of these films in various ways explore the dynamics and ironies of freedom of choice and self-determination in the larger context of an authoritarian power structure.

The second most commonly utilized period was the 1950s, post–Second World War. During this decade, Australia achieved increasing prominence in the world, for example, hosting the Olympics in Melbourne in 1956. Moreover, the country acquired the status as a full political, trade, and defense partner in the Pacific region as it aligned itself with the United States, as well as with other Asian nations, including its membership in the SEATO alliance. *Newsfront* and *Sunday* are situated in this decade. Accordingly, the news stories dramatized within *Newsfront* draw not only upon local events, but international ones. *Sunday* swells with national pride (as opposed to historical cultural cringe) in its tribute to the strong Australian work ethic. (Wool had historically been one of Australia's primary industries and served as a bedrock of the Australian economy.) Interestingly, *Between Wars* bridges these two time frames commencing in 1918 and ending in the late 1930s, when the world was on the brink of another world war. (Only *Caddie* is set in another time frame, the 1930s, the actual years the real-life Caddie lived and worked.)

Filmmakers' decisions to investigate the turn of the century and the more recent past (as well as the years in between) suggested that they saw the need to address and understand Australia's history, rarely explored in local films prior to 1970. These films gave audiences, Australian and overseas, insights into the country's unique origins. Clearly filmmakers were fortifying a formidable cinema heritage, building on the foundational body of works from filmmakers who made silent and sound films: Raymond Longford, the McDonagh Sisters, Charles Chauvel, and Ken G. Hall.

10BA

In 1980, with the industry on its feet and the reputation of Australian films firmly established locally and abroad, the Liberal government under PM Malcolm Fraser introduced a new financing scheme, "10BA" (in place until 1988), which encouraged private financiers to invest in films through generous tax concessions. Though the AFC still invested in films, it shifted to more modest amounts for script development and marketing. This strategy was consistent with a new era of deregulation and privatization, as the "Australian economy ... [entered] the international marketplace ... [and] foreign banks were encouraged to enter Australia" (Falconer, 1997, 252). 10BA opened up production funding to outside investors (local and overseas). Ideally, this scheme was intended for investors and producers with expertise in the business side of filmmaking (though this did not always turn out to be the case). As Falconer noted (quoting Sam Rohdie), the industry shifted from "'production values to market values'" (Falconer, 1997, 252), which had its benefits and downside, though not all 10BA films put the box office first. Many did not. According to this plan, Australian investors would receive substantial tax concessions which started out at 150 percent. Thus, for every $100 spent, an investor could claim a $150 deduction, and for every $50 earned on an outlay, this amount would be tax-exempt. These amounts were reduced to 133/33 and then to 120/20 (in 1983 and 1985, respectively). However, whereas the AFDC and AFC periods had clearly defined cultural and aesthetic criteria, no such standards were articulated with 10BA. Despite the drawbacks and problems associated with this strategy (discussed later in this section), 10BA, however, facilitated the production of heretofore unexplored stories rooted in Australian society in its larger cultural context often set in contemporary areas of Australia, such as suburbs and coastal areas.

Two tiers of films operated during this period: those budgeted at $3 million and above, and those more modestly budgeted, $500,000 to $3 million. The first group includes three very successful films that captured the hearts and minds of Australian audiences who lined up at theaters, often for repeat screenings: *The Man from Snowy River* (George Miller, 1982), *Phar Lap* (1983, Simon Wincer), and *"Crocodile" Dundee* (Peter Faiman, 1986). *Snowy River* and *Dundee* dramatized the allure of the Australian landscape: the mountains and the bush (respectively), incorporating the Australian mythology of rugged masculinity. *Phar Lap* paid tribute to a beloved Depression-era racehorse, the film's namesake.

Snowy River was one of the most popular films of the decade, and was based on the A. B. "Banjo" Paterson 1890 poem, which dramatized the rites of passage for a determined young mountain man who proves himself a worthy horseman in a dazzling roundup of "brumbies" (horses). Television director Miller (not to be confused with *Dr.* George Miller of the *Mad Max* series) cast veteran Hollywood actor Kirk Douglas in two roles, as station (ranch) owner and gold prospector, thus demonstrating an eye for the American market with a classic American star. The film turned out to be a rich and lucrative balance of Australian legends, history, and American Western iconography. *"Crocodile" Dundee*, based upon an original story by television personality Paul Hogan, who stars as Mick Dundee, is featured as a bush hero (touting trumped-up crocodile hunting skills) not only in the Australian wilds, but also in New York City. This film was a huge hit in Australia, achieving blockbuster status, making an astonishing $47.8 million, an unprecedented record. This figure was three times the box office of *Snowy River*, which had held the lead as Australia's most popular local film. Released in the States over the summer, *Dundee* captured the US market, and was number one for six weeks with US$175 million in sales. (Its budget was $8.8 million.) Another boost for Australia beyond the film itself was a huge shot in the arm for the tourist industry. The number of visitors quadrupled, with everyone seeking a "'*Crocodile' Dundee*" holiday. Both Jim Craig (*Snowy*) and Dundee represented a new kind of masculinity: strong, confident, resilient, and victorious, as opposed to the (nevertheless brave) colonial scapegoats in *Gallipoli* and *Breaker Morant*. *Phar Lap* also garnered much acclaim throughout Australia. Fresh off the success of *The Man from Snowy River* (as executive producer), Simon Wincer took on the directing helm of *Phar Lap*, Australia's cherished and celebrated horse—a true inspiration for a country crushed by hard times. Phar Lap boldly emerged as an Aussie battler, often performing against tremendous odds, winning race after race between 1929 and 1932, including the prestigious Melbourne Cup in 1930. *Phar Lap* exuberantly captures the exhilaration of the massive and majestic horse as he gallops down the racetrack amidst passionately cheering crowds, nostrils flaring, chest heaving, powerful legs propelling him to the finish line. This film received

AFI awards for its technical expertise in editing and sound design, with AFI nominations for best picture and director.

Mad Max, directed by George Miller with producing partner Byron Kennedy, deserves mentioning, though this film was made in 1979 before inauguration of 10BA, and was not funded by any government bodies but wholly by private investors. *Mad Max* is an audacious, brutally nihilistic road picture set "a few years into the future," featuring murderous scoot jockeys (motorcycle gangs) at war with equally bloodthirsty outback police (the "Bronze") in a bleak "civilization"—irony intended—on the brink of collapse. The same easing of censorship that opened the way for the flaunting of nudity and sexuality in the ocker films (with the R Certificate in 1971) also unleashed an aggressive display of violence in *Max*, both graphic and implied. *Mad Max* was clearly a radically different film than the preceding AFDC and AFC projects. Its success locally and internationally contributed to a new financial climate, as the film's funding plan became a precursor for 10BA. With the proceeds from *Max*, Kennedy and Miller set up Kennedy Miller Productions in Sydney, generating sequels *Mad Max II* (1981, US title, *Road Warrior*) and *Mad Max Beyond Thunderdome* (1985), both made with 10BA monies. Roughly modeled on classical Hollywood studios, KM also produced high-caliber television programs and modestly budgeted quality features, along the lines of the best of the AFC films, including John Duigan's enchanting and wistful coming-of-age film, *The Year My Voice Broke* (1987), and its sequel, *Flirting* (1991). Both these films are discussed in detail in Chapter 2. KM studios also produced internationally oriented films, such as *Dead Calm* (Noyce, 1989), a high seas suspense thriller with a stowaway stalking a vacationing couple. This film featured Nicole Kidman on her way to global stardom. *Babe* (Chris Noonan, 1995) broke new ground with special effects: animatronic animals blended with live action, and more recently, fully animated films, *Happy Feet* (George Miller, 2006) and *Happy Feet II* (2011, George Miller, US funding with KM productions holding creative control). KM studios was renamed KMM (Kennedy Miller Mitchell) studios in 2009.

10BA also opened the way for a second tier of more moderately budgeted films from respected and experienced producers such as John Maynard (*Sweetie*, 1989), Penny Chapman (*High Tide*, 1987), and Joan Long (*Puberty Blues*, 1981), with the budget norm between $1 and 3 million. Inherent in these and other works were refreshing new takes on femininity, motherhood, and the family, utilizing locations in innovative ways. Jane Campion's *Sweetie*, alternatively comic and tragic, and imbued with a dark and wry sensibility, featured a suburban dysfunctional family under the thumb of a delusional daughter. *Sweetie* competed at Cannes (to which Campion would return with *The Piano* a few years later in 1993, winning the Palme d'Or). Gillian Armstrong teamed up again with Judy Davis in *High Tide*. (Davis had made an impressive feature debut in Armstrong's *My Brilliant Career*.) Amidst a seaside trailer park in winter, a mother meets up with the teenage daughter she gave up to her paternal grandmother thirteen years ago. Set in another beach locale, *Puberty Blues* (with Bruce Beresford directing) was an intimate look at Sydney summer surf culture from the perspective of two bold, teenage women surfers who challenge the all-male clique. This film was a qualified success and caught on with the lucrative 15–25-year-old audience, its box office $3.9 million (on a budget of $800,000). Another noteworthy film, *Fran* (1985), written and directed by Glenda Hambly, is in a more rigorous social realist mode. It focuses on a single welfare mother torn between her three children and her shaky love life. Breaking new ground in exploring the lives of troubled, yet sympathetic mothers, both *High Tide* and *Fran* won an array of awards from the AFI, including acting for the leads (Noni Hazelburst in *Fran* in addition to Davis in *Tide*), best screenplay for Laura Jones (*High Tide*), and directing honors for Hambly. Both films are discussed more fully in Chapter 4. Amidst this stimulating climate, writer/director Paul Cox made some of his best and most mature work, all semi-autobiographical (and funded by a combination of 10BA and government financing, in addition to support from a group of European investors): *Lonely Hearts* (1981), *Man of Flowers* (1983, selected for *Un Certain Regard* at Cannes), and *My First Wife* (1984, with a strong Cannes reception facilitating, as with *Man of Flowers*, sales in Europe and the United States). Cox's male characters broke new ground in the representation of Australian masculinity: recessive loners worlds apart from rambunctious ockers, as well as the rough-hewn bush and outback heroes. *Man of Flowers* and *My First Wife* are discussed in more detail in Chapter 2.

Even though the 10BA period produced an array of critically acclaimed, ground-breaking works, many achieving popularity locally and abroad, thus preserving the momentum of film production with increased employment opportunities for Australian creative and technical personnel, several problem areas surfaced. First, one-year limits on the money raising and production period imposed real stress on producers and creative teams for many projects. Filmmakers had to rush the writing, and often the result was underdeveloped scripts as well as a hurried shooting and post-production period. These factors put a strain on the limited pool of writers, actors, and crews. Secondly, control of a project was often not in the hands of filmmakers but the financiers, including stock brokers, merchant bankers, and film management companies. Whereas the AFDC and AFC periods were project-driven, with government backing and approval, the 10BA period could often be finance-driven with investors more interested in the tax write-off. These exploitation "quickies" (more recently coined "ozploitation," a category which can also cover the ocker films) included *Turkey Shoot* (Quentin Masters, 1982) and *Midnite Spares* (Brian Trenchard-Smith, 1983).

The Australian Film Finance Corporation

Even though many ground-breaking films were made during the 10BA period, the shortcomings and excesses of an open market system amidst increasing (and urgent) requests from filmmakers for reinstituted government subsidies and backing—ideally to bring back cultural and fiscal accountability—convinced the government to establish two funding agencies. The first was the Australian Film Finance Corporation—FFC (1988–2008, the fourth industry phase), with an initial pledge of $70 million; the second, Screen Australia, the most recent and fifth phase, which commenced in 2008 and continues into the present. Unlike 10BA guidelines, both these organizations designated a cultural framework. The FFC brief articulated "significant Australian content" with the addition of the phrases "national 'interest' and 'quality,'" as Lisa French noted (Craven, 2001, 20). The guidelines of Screen Australia were more broadly defined: "Australian creative control" and "developed by Australians," to reflect more flexible interpretations of Australianness.

The FFC operated as a "film bank," providing government-backed loans at preferred rates (with profit participation), supporting approximately fifteen to twenty films per year. Budgets for most films were between $3 and 6 million. Production funding, as approved by the FFC board of directors (composed of experienced producers, directors, and writers), would be granted *after* the procurement of a distribution guarantee or pre-sale amounting to one-third to one-half of the budget from private financiers, thus, an assurance of market potential. (A project could be funded by several private sources in addition to a combination of federal and state financing.) During the FFC period, the AFC continued to assist with the financing of low-budget features. At this point in the development of the industry, it was crucial to maintain global connections (i.e., from multinational companies) from which most of the pre-sales and guarantees came. The board's intention was to attract established companies with track records and expertise in production, distribution, and marketing which could best finance, handle, and promote Australian films at home and abroad.

During the FFC period, a new generation of talented and innovative filmmakers emerged, thus opening up new areas in the exploration of ethnicity, indigeneity, masculinity, femininity, and sexuality, as well as novel modes and styles, thus presenting fresh and distinctive visions of Australia. (This is not meant to devalue or denigrate films made earlier in the revival.) Filmmakers were able to benefit from more flexible financing structures and take risks on otherwise marginalized, uncharted, or even taboo aspects of Australian history and culture, and included Jocelyn Moorhouse, Geoffrey Wright, John Ruane, Ana Kokinos, P. J. Hogan, Stephan Elliott, Scott Hicks, Baz Luhrmann, Rolf de Heer, and Rachel Perkins. The initial generation of 1970s filmmakers, who had helped to shape the early years of the renaissance, often worked abroad in Hollywood or Europe (though not exclusively): Peter Weir, Gillian Armstrong, Fred Schepisi, Phillip Noyce, Bruce Beresford.

The FFC years demonstrated significant maturity and growth for the film industry. The best of the FFC films had the class, narrative richness, and complexity of AFC films. Further, as with AFDC and 10BA films, a significant number of FFC films boldly expressed a breakout larrikin sensibility. (Larrikin is an Australian term for mischievous, irreverent, and/or rowdy, often with undertones of anti-authoritarianism.) The "glitter cycle," discussed later in this section, is a prime example of this Australian phenomenon. Moreover, FFC films exuded the entrepreneurial and enterprising spirit of 10BA. Lastly, with a longer development period (versus a constraining time frame during the 10BA period, wherein filmmakers had to finish a film in the year of investment for the tax deduction), FFC-financed scripts, often developed with support from the AFC and state film agencies, benefited from a more ample time frame, which provided the opportunity for careful, thoughtful, and nuanced writing. In addition to box office popularity, extra clout for this was distinction at film festivals around the world. Cannes continued as the gold standard for prestige recognition, though the Sundance, Berlin, and Toronto Film Festivals, for example, certainly held merit, as did the British Independent Film and British Academy of Film and Television Arts Awards (BIFA and BAFTA, respectively). Hollywood Academy Award nominations and wins were a hallowed honor and an artistic boost for filmmakers. And locally, nominations and awards from the AFI enhanced the visibility and renown of FFC-financed films and filmmakers, as well as featured screenings at the Sydney, Adelaide, and Melbourne International Film Festivals. (Not all releases were FFC-financed.) Clearly, the tricky part for government and private financiers was the balancing of cultural breakthroughs with commercial success locally and abroad—ideally in the same film. Highlights of this period follow with special attention to noteworthy films and trends.

First, contemporary working-class, underclass communities and neighborhoods in contemporary Melbourne came to the fore in two very different ways. *Proof* (Jocelyn Moorhouse, 1991) focused on a blind photographer in a love triangle, exploring mateship and sexual allure amidst undertones of motherly love. *Romper Stomper* (Geoffrey Wright, 1992) was based on actual viciously racist and sadistic neo-Nazi gangs perpetrating attacks on a Vietnamese community. *Stomper* alluded to disturbing white Australian racism in the wake of increased Asian Pacific immigration in the early 1970s, as more flexible government policies relaxed a heretofore predominantly white European immigrant policy. Both these films featured up-and-coming actor Russell Crowe in two very different roles, compassionate and easygoing versus hateful and vicious. Whereas *Proof* explores the subjective viewpoint of an isolated man with elegance and subtlety, Wright, in his dynamic mise en scène and explosive montage style accented by rock music, lays bare the deep-seated hostilities in an urban battlefield. *Proof* was selected for the Directors Fortnight at Cannes, with Moorhouse receiving a Special Mention in the Camera d'Or category. This film was also voted best picture by the AFI, and had solid runs in major Australian cities, London, Los Angeles, and New York. *Stomper* was lauded by the AFI for its superb technical attributes, and singled out Crowe as best actor of the year. Despite its disquieting subject, *Stomper* found an audience, playing for fourteen weeks in Sydney and Melbourne, and becoming the second highest grossing Australian film in 1992 behind *Strictly Ballroom*.

Secondly, a group of noteworthy films focusing on Greek communities, also set in Melbourne, was released throughout the 1990s. Along with an Italian enclave, Greeks constitute one of the largest ethnicities in Australia, and the country itself houses an array of immigrant populations, one of the most varied in the world. The financial and thematic openness of the FFC period opened up the ethnic diversity of modern Australia, or, as Stephen Crofts commented, a "pluralist multi-cultural ethic" (Crofts, 1999, 730). This new ethnicity was in contrast to the primarily (but not exclusively) Anglo-Celtic milieu for the AFDC and AFC periods. John Conomos notes the "important aesthetic, cultural, exilic, gendered, historical and political complexities ... presented by certain filmmakers of Greek-Australian descent" (Conomos, 2009, 115). For example, *Death in Brunswick* (John Ruane, 1990) is a black comedy focusing on a romance between a young Greek woman and her Anglo lover amidst the hilarious possessiveness of his mother and the overbearing demeanor of her father. *The Heartbreak Kid* (Michael Jenkins, 1993) and *Head On* (Ana Kokkinos, 1998) explore the travails of two young men under the thumbs of their domineering fathers and the allure of forbidden relationships—in the former with an Anglo-Celtic woman (who happens to be his high school teacher) and the latter with another young man who is not of Greek nationality. These three films found eager audiences among Greek and other communities within Melbourne as well as in Sydney. Like *Proof*, *Head On* was chosen for *Un Certain Regard*, and both films certainly filled the festival's criteria for this venue: the recognition of young talent through innovative and audacious works. *Head On* won the AFI award for adapted screenplay for Kokkinos, Mira Robertson, and Andrew Bovell (who would go on to write *Lantana*, discussed later in this section). In the States, *Head On* also received the LA Outfest Grand Jury Award and best first feature in San Francisco International Lesbian and Gay Film Festival.

Thirdly, a wide range of Indigenous films flourished. The full momentum of the Aboriginal civil and land rights movements, which surged in the 1960s and 1970s, had brought Indigenous history into public awareness, infusing filmmakers (Indigenous and non-Indigenous) with an array of timely subjects well into the new millennium. As noted at the beginning of this introduction, Fred Schepisi bravely and boldly broached vicious racism at the turn of the century in 1978 with *The Chant of Jimmie Blacksmith*, just as Peter Weir positioned a group of urban Indigenous males at the heart of his suspense thriller *The Last Wave*, adding an aura of mysticism as he did with *Picnic at Hanging Rock*. Several years later, Bruce Beresford manifested his dexterity and skill in yet another mode and directed *The Fringe Dwellers* (1986), which featured a contemporary working-class Indigenous family resettling in a non-Indigenous middle-class neighborhood. Part comedy and part serious drama, the film presented tensions and conflicts of two races in an uncomfortable existence side by side. Like *Blacksmith*, *Dwellers* was selected for competition at Cannes. Rachel Perkins' *Radiance* (1998) was a rare and unique project: Australia's first Indigenous feminist feature film, directed by an Aboriginal woman, its focus three Aboriginal sisters, estranged and wary of each other, who convene after the death of their dysfunctional mother. Through this contentious trio, the film dramatizes racial self-hate and the plight of mixed-race children. *Radiance* was selected as the most popular feature film at the Melbourne International Film Festival and, after a solid run in major cities, was sold to television with very high ratings, a post-theatrical practice for many Australian films in the 1990s. (*Radiance* is discussed in detail in Chapter 4.)

A key Indigenous film at the beginning of the new millennium was *Rabbit Proof Fence* (Phillip Noyce, 2002); set in 1931, it put "The Stolen Generations" on the cinematic map. This phrase refers to the hundreds of mixed-race children who were taken from their families from the 1930s through the 1970s. These "pale" children were relocated within white foster families as per the government-sanctioned process of "assimilation," a practice which devastated Aboriginal communities, and amounted to forced integration into white society. For *Fence* Noyce returned to Australia from Hollywood after directing several high concept 1990s action thrillers. Screenwriter Christine Olsen based her screenplay on the book by Doris Pilkington-Garimara, *Follow the Rabbit Proof Fence* (1996), an account of the trek by Pilkington-Garimara's mother, her sister, and cousin, who walked a thousand miles back home after being kidnapped. *Fence* was the first feature film to focus on the Stolen Generations not readily in the public eye until the 1990s with the publication of Pilkington-Garimara's account. *Fence* crossed over into the mainstream. As Felicity Collins and Therese Davis note, it "reversed the historical lack of interest by Australian audiences in films about Aboriginal people" (Collins and Davis, 2004, 133). The film played in major Australian cities, becoming the second highest grossing film for 2002. It also won many top honors at a variety of international film festivals, including the audience award at the Edinburgh International Film Festival. Moreover, the National Board of Review endowed *Fence* with its Freedom of Expression Award. Fence is discussed in detail in Chapter 5.

The Tracker (Rolf de Heer, 2002) is another ground-breaking film set in the period preceding assimilation at the end of the Frontier period (1788–early 1930s), when police hunted Indigenous individuals for sport and/or fabricated crimes against them. David Gulpilil (who made his debut with *Walkabout*) plays a wily tracker forced by outback police to find an allegedly guilty Aboriginal man. For his body of work, climaxing with *The Tracker*, Gulpilil received a best actor award from the AFI. Like *Fence*, *The Tracker* opened up a relatively unknown area in Australian history. de Heer continued his collaboration with Gulpilil in *Ten Canoes* (2006), which they co-wrote, with de Heer directing. Narrated by Gulpilil, who inflects his lines with a delightful and ironic sense of humor, the film was based on Indigenous mythologies set in pre-colonial times, approximately one thousand years ago, long before the first landing by British colonizers. *Ten Canoes* was in the top ten grossing films screening in Sydney during its release, and as one producer commented, it was an Indigenous film that *did not* induce guilt. At Cannes, de Heer received the *Un Certain Regard* Special Jury Prize, and *Canoes* was honored for artistic excellence by the International Press Academy (IPA). De Heer's/Gulpilil's latest works are discussed in the Screen Australia section.

Fourth, another salient group of films produced during the FFC period amidst much fanfare and avid local popularity was the "glitter cycle" (a term coined by Emily Rustin). Films such as *The Adventures of Priscilla, Queen of the Desert* (Stephan Elliott, 1994), and *Strictly Ballroom* (Baz Luhrmann, 1992) feature "Aussie battlers," a legendary term for an individual, usually, but not always, male, struggling against the odds, such as a repressive social system and/or an authority figure(s). The battlers in each film boldly challenge the status quo in satirical send-ups of Australian life. Further, these narratives are characterized by a wildly vivid and colorful visual style, as Rustin points out (Craven, 2001, 133). The humor in the glitter cycle is more sophisticated than that of the ockers, incorporating irony and parody. *Priscilla* (with, however, a display of crude ocker banter) charts the road journey of two gay male transvestites and one male to female transsexual performing outrageous and creative nightly drag shows in various outback towns. *Priscilla* had a smashing debut at Cannes, followed by screenings in the United States to establish a track record, with a subsequent release in major Australian to already eager audiences. This successful exhibition pattern would be used by other filmmakers. *Priscilla* also received an Academy Award for best costume design, with co-winner Lizzie Gardiner accepting her award in a "dress" made of American Express credit cards, a clever and much publicized allusion to the film's bountiful box office, an event certainly not lost on loyal Australians back home. In Chapter 1, Priscilla is explored as a neo-ocker film.

Strictly Ballroom was the Australian film revival's first full-fledged musical infused with an imaginative and good-natured dose of Australian lampoon-style humor and camp. *Ballroom* centers on a talented young male dancer, who defies the strict rules of Federation Ballroom Dancing and wins the final competition, as well as the adulation of family and friends, along with the heart of his Spanish dance partner. *Ballroom* achieved immense popularity within Australia (often among young males who had great admiration for "the wild colonial boy," Scott Hastings, the film's protagonist), and held the title of one of the most popular films in the 1990s, along with *Priscilla* and another glitter cycle film, *Muriel's Wedding* (P.J. Hogan, 1994). The namesake of this latter film is an insecure young woman in an obsessive quest for marriage; *Wedding* deftly balances hilarity and tragedy. All three films went into profit, giving the FFC and the films' investors a boost. *Ballroom* in particular was selected for a midnight *Un Certain Regard* screening at Cannes, and also received a special "Youth Film" award. The musical format was a genre to which Luhrmann would return several years later with *Moulin Rouge!* (2001, co-financed by the FFC and 20th Century Fox), which put him firmly on the international map (with US$179.2 million global box office), establishing his trademark mode: flamboyant spectacle-style mise en scène, high melodrama, and romantic love cut through with heartbreak. However, rather than flaunting its Australianness as *Ballroom* had, *Moulin* effaced all traces of "native" culture (beyond the presence of international star Nicole Kidman and a variety of Australian actors). Australian accents, recognizable settings, cultural milieus, and reverberations were nowhere to be heard or seen. Along this line, George Miller's *Babe*, mentioned earlier, foregrounded the film's namesake, an orphaned pig which is adopted by a kindly farmer. Babe perceives itself to be a sheep dog, even going so far as to compete in a herding contest. Beyond the bush setting, which could be linked to any pastoral environment, there were no identifiable Australian characteristics. Both these films stretched the definition of Australianness, as local filmmakers maintained "Australian creative control," with, however, no direct or obvious Australian traits, that is, specific events drawn from history or culture that characterized prior Australian films. *Rouge* and *Babe* were films shot in Australia, but were not really *about* Australia. Nonetheless, these were intelligent, well-directed films with local and global appeal that revealed Australian filmmakers' savvy, craft, and originality. *Babe* made over US$246 million worldwide.

Fifth, a pair of films, *The Castle* (Rob Sitch, 1997) and *Shine* (Scott Hicks, 1996), featured different kinds of "Aussie battlers" than those featured in the glitter cycle. "Soft masculinity" was a new area in these two bull's-eye local hits. *The Castle* was a witty and touching saga of a tight-knit family—headed by a loving, stubborn, and ethical father—whose property is encroached upon by an expanding airline company. Made for under a million dollars, *The Castle* topped $10 million after a several-month run in Australia, also receiving acclaim in Britain as Best Independent Film. Another kind of battler, David Helfgott, was featured in *Shine*, based on Helfgott's life as a piano protégé, often crippled by mental illness and physical frailty. A brilliant performer, he achieved fame within Australia and also around the world. Featuring Geoffrey Rush in an Academy Award-winning performance, *Shine* was a breakthrough international triumph (with a budget of $6 million, it grossed $64 million). Just as *"Crocodile" Dundee* was the "feel-good" film for the 1980s with its iconic bush hero, who civilized and charmed New York, *Shine* was the Australian darling of the 1990s—a troubled artist overcoming adversity and triumphing the world over. This film's success could be read as a metaphor for the industry itself in the 1990s: talent proudly stepping out on a highly visible global stage.

Sixth, a fascinating group of films with criminal themes proliferated from the late 1990s into the new millennium. The representation of the lives and social milieu of "crims"—the Australian abbreviation for criminals—may be linked in part to the publication of the widely revered *The Fatal Shore* (1987), Robert Hughes' history of the first landing by British colonizers at the end of the eighteenth century. Men and women were involuntarily removed from overflowing prisons, in line with Britain's desire to relocate lawbreakers as far away from the mother country as possible. Hughes' work was based on the perspectives, letters, diaries, etc., of "felons" (whose crimes ranged from petty and desperate—stealing food—to more serious—forgery and breaking into homes). Transportation lasted until the last ship disembarked in 1868, and was consistent with Britain's extensive exploration and colonization of the world as part of the creation of the British Empire. The word "Australia" was based on the Latin word, "austral," meaning south. The British warden/Australian prisoner hierarchy has been linked to "historical stain," allegedly fueling (in part) Australia's tradition of cultural cringe, though not all Australian settlements were initially prisoner-populated. In the 1990s and new millennium, Australia confidently flaunted its lawbreakers in mainstream cinema via complex and compelling characters—street- or bush-wise criminals not altogether unsympathetic with law-breaking instincts and desires who lived by their own moral code (or lack thereof). *Two Hands* (1999, Gregor Jordan) kicked off this cycle of harder edged, social realist cinema featuring an urban mobster (played by Bryan Brown from *Breaker Morant*), recruiting a young henchman, played by Heath Ledger in one of his first feature roles. Its local appeal and success led to other underworld stories. *Chopper* (2000, Andrew Dominick) and *Ned Kelly* (2003, also directed by Gregor Jordan) in particular fascinated Australian audiences. The wildly popular *Chopper* was based on the tongue-in-cheek, sardonic biography by

"Chopper" Mark Read, one of Australia's most notorious, violence-prone, and eccentric modern criminals (with a tour de force performance by then stand-up comedian, Eric Bana). *Ned Kelly* dramatized the life of Australia's most infamous historical bushranger with Heath Ledger in the title role. (Bushranger refers to a frontier outlaw in the 1880s time frame, and was a popular genre during Australia's silent film era.) Both films swept the AFI awards in their respective years. Though resonating with Australian audiences, "heroes" Chopper and Ned Kelly did not engage American viewers or global viewers, these crims too parochial, too steeped in Australian mythology perhaps. A few years later, *The Proposition* (2005, John Hillcoat), set in the approximate lifetime of Ned Kelly, focused on a (fictionalized) family of bloodthirsty, sadistically violent, and predatory bushrangers. This film was the dark flip side of comparatively "civilized" film, *The Man from Snowy River*, situated in the same time frame.

Two unique films from the FFC period deserve brief discussion: *Lantana* (2001, Ray Lawrence) and *The Dish* (2000, Rob Sitch). *Lantana* was a breakthrough film in a genre not often associated with Australia, the suspense thriller. A suburban mystery presented through a "de-centered, multiple strand narrative" (Collins and Davis, 2004, 34), and in a class with other multi-layered films in the same time frame such as *Amores Perros* (Mexico, 2000), *Crash* (US, 2004), and *Babel* (US, 2006), *Lantana* explores the turbulent intersecting lives of several middle-aged couples. (The film's title aptly refers to a tangled thicket of brush native to Australia.) Sophisticated and intricately written, *Lantana* presents a range of complex characters amidst desire, betrayal, and lies. It took the majority of the AFI awards for that year and set the standard for subsequent thrillers, including *Jindabyne* (2006, also directed by Ray Lawrence) and *The Square* (2008, Nash Edgerton). The prestigious London Critics Circle selected Andrew Bovell as screenwriter of the year, and *Lantana* was the most popular feature film at the Melbourne International Film Festival. Overseas, it received the British Independent Film Award for Best Foreign Independent Film (English language). *The Dish*, set in the late 1960s, was a wry and genial work harking back to a thrilling milestone in space exploration history: the US Apollo landing on the moon in 1969. Australia played a crucial role in the televising of this event to the world through one of its satellites (a fact not widely known within or outside of Australia). Within the narrative framework, cultural cringe (the inhabitants of a rural isolated town are meek and overly polite) turns to the "strut," as Australian technicians confidently create the crucial link to the landing (solving an equipment malfunction that threatens to shut down the moon broadcast), making Australia a key player in this world event. The town, and by implication, Australia, beams with pride. Taken in its larger new millennial context in the wake of 1990s cinematic successes, *The Dish* metaphorically dramatizes Australia's savvy and distinction.

Australia (2008) deserves mention at this point. This film was Baz Luhrmann's extravagant, epic vision of the country on the brink of its entry into the Second World War. It was released during the Screen Australia period, but funded over a three-year, pre-production and production time frame through a combination of state government funding—Screen West of Western Australia—and private financing, primarily 20th Century Fox, in addition to generous Location Offsets, an incentive plan detailed later. With a budget of $130–150 million, this adventure–romance featuring international stars Nicole Kidman and Hugh Jackman stood at the time as the most expensive Australian film ever made, exploring on a large canvas and in an almost three hour-length, every social/political issue Luhrmann could squeeze in, often within an unwieldy narrative: Australia's isolation in the first decades of the twentieth century; its entry into the Second World War after an attack on its northern shores by the Japanese; Aboriginal–non-Indigenous tensions; station life in rural Australia. As with a good number of AFC films, *Australia* looked back upon the nation's history during a critical period when a young nation was on the brink of a new age in the second half of the twentieth century. Aiming for blockbuster status, and grossing $37.5 million in Australia, *Australia* eventually broke even with global sales. Consistent with Luhrmann's prior films, the style of *Australia* was lavish: highly expressive camerawork and opulent mise en scène with great care placed on detailed period recreation.

Though *Australia*'s budget was *huge* in comparison to the financing for other Australian films, this amount was comparable to the budgets for a variety of high-profile Hollywood films being shot in Australia during the first half of the new millennium. The stronger US dollar translated into more buying power in Australia. With state-of-the-art production and post-production facilities, special effects houses, and highly trained technicians, including cinematographers, sound experts, and a range of technicians, Australia was an enticement for Hollywood filmmakers to work in a more cost-effective location. The country certainly filled the bill for a lucrative and desirable location. Facilities included the Fox Studios in Sydney, the Warner Center/Village Roadshow Studios in Queensland, and the Docklands Studios in Melbourne. Apart from Australia's legacy of homegrown films, Hollywood productions shot in Australia brought a different kind of prominence to Australia. As Matt Hearn, executive producer of the gothic film *Wolf Creek* (2005), noted at the time, "As long as people ... [were] looking at Australia as a place where good movies come from, it ... [didn't] matter *what kind* of movie it ... [was]" (Kroenert, 2007, 28; emphasis mine). Hollywood films shot in Australia included the following: *Dark City* (directed by an Australian, Alex Proyas, but funded by Hollywood, 1998), *The Matrix* (1999), *Mission Impossible 2* (2000), *Star Wars: Episode II—Attack of the Clones* (2002), *Matrix Reloaded* and *Matrix Revolutions* (both 2003), *Star Wars Episode III: Revenge of the Sith* (2005), and *Superman Returns* (2006). Concurrently, a recession caused a downturn in local productions between 2001 and 2004. Total investment dropped from $28.9 to $10.1 million, as wary investors held on to their money. In 2004, only fifteen films were made, even though the 2001–4 time frame included key works such as *Rabbit Proof Fence* and *Ned Kelly*. New strategies were needed to (1) assist and boost locally based productions; (2) maintain a healthy level of overseas productions in Australia, as it was already in competition with Canada, Germany, and later in the decade, New Zealand, all of which offered attractive incentives.

Screen Australia: The Australian Production Screen Incentive

Realizing that facilities could not survive on local productions alone, and that "[a]ttracting international dollars [primarily from the US] in the form of film expenditure ... [held] a positive effect on growth" (Bodey, 2013), in 2007 the government introduced two offset schemes under the Australian Production Screen Incentive—an umbrella term for the Producer Offset, Location Offset, PDV Offset, and Location Service. The first offset, the Producer Offset, was intended to benefit Australian producers and allowed them to claim 40 percent of the QAPE (Qualifying Australian Production Expenditure) back from the ATO (tax office) for feature film productions with at least a $1 million budget (later reduced for $500,000). For this offset, the project had to meet the Significant Australian Content (SAC) guidelines: subject matter of the film, place, nationalities, and residences of personnel. The PDV (Post, Digital, and Visual Effects) provided a 30 percent rebate for post-production regardless of where a film was shot with the stipulation that a foreign company was operating through a permanent Australian company. The PDV was available for local producers who did not wish to access the Producer Offset, with these available percentages: 40 percent, 30 percent, and 16.5 percent. If the producers selected the Producer Offset, they could not use the PDV, though stage agencies made provisions for a 10 percent rebate on post-production done within the state. The second offset, the Location Offset, was available for overseas-based companies, with a rebate of 16.5 percent. These companies could use the Location Offset or the PDV, but not both. To qualify for either offset, the budget would need to be at least $15 million. Both of these schemes were put into place shortly after the restructuring and renaming of the FFC to Screen Australia (SA) in 2008. This agency, established in 2008, consolidated several government media agencies, including the Australian Film Commission and Film Australia (the documentary division). The AFC continued to provide marketing and script development monies, a role it had maintained during the 10BA and FFC periods, in addition to investing in low-budget features.

Screen Australia continued with FFC financing practices, that is, requiring outside funding to kick-start a project in the form of a distribution guarantee, pre-sale, a local distribution arrangement or private investment before SA's consideration, evaluation, and decision to provide equity investment. Screen Australia's equity investment was capped at $2.5 million (now $2 million). Screen Australia also invested in projects that qualified for the Producer Offset, and provided grants up to $500,000. As noted earlier, funding guidelines were more flexible according to the following: "Australian creative control" and "developed by Australians." Also inherent in the SA guiding principles was special consideration of films that had strong national interest, as retiring FFC Chief Executive Brian Rosen noted (Bulbeck, 2007, 17). But as Ruth Harley, chief executive of SA, emphasized, "commercial viability and attract[ing] audiences" were crucial for this new age which included "a greater emphasis on growth, sustainability and commercial returns, rather than subsidization of purely cultural expression with commercial imperatives" (Ryan, 2010, 86). The SA board also made further provisions for the funding of projects by new feature filmmakers, in light of criticism directed at the board for favoring established directors. At the time of this writing, SA has been in existence for fourteen years with the agency providing partial financing for approximately twelve to fifteen films per year, some years higher. The average time frame from the onset of production (with funding in place) until release is from one to two years for Australian production and release, and sometimes up to three years before the film is distributed internationally. Under SA guidelines, a number of remarkable and strikingly original films have been made which break new ground; other films have courageously and audaciously put new spins on Australian generic conventions, but nonetheless have proven to be critical and popular successes. Several observations can be made.

Crime and gothic films continued to capture the imagination of filmmakers. For example, writer/director David Michod made a name for himself with *Animal Kingdom* (2010), which added a noir dimension to prior Melbourne-set gangster films. *Kingdom* centers on a tight-knit family of crime-addicted and self-serving sons dominated by a savvy and seductively controlling matriarch (who has an ironically innocent-sounding name, "Smurf"). This film was Michod's first foray into feature filmmaking, and his rich narrative featured multifaceted and compelling characters. In addition to being a popular box office attraction for three months, *Kingdom* was singled out by the AFI as the best picture of the year, with acting awards for the leads, as well as for best original screenplay. Overseas, it received the Grand Jury Prize for World Cinema at Sundance, and played for several weeks in Los Angeles and New York. Moreover, Jacki Weaver (Smurf) received an Academy Award nomination for best actress in a supporting role. The popularity and acclaim accorded *Kingdom* enabled Michod to continue his fascination with violent men in his next film, *The Rover* (2014), which he also wrote and directed. A bleak vision of psychic and social instability, brutality, and anarchy—which shifts the film into Australian Gothic territory—this film focuses on one man's ferocious and ruthless pursuit of carjackers in the outback as well as his unlikely bond with one of the bandits. *The Rover* conjures up *Mad Max* with its dangerous outback setting, obsession with fast cars, and savage violence. However, it was a little too derivative of *Max* and lacked the fully realized characters and ominous atmosphere of *Kingdom*.

Wolf Creek 2 (2013, Greg McLean), the sequel to the original *Wolf Creek* (2005), also set in the remote outback, continued the saga of a pathological sadist–killer waiting for innocent and lost young backpackers to accidentally stumble into his turf. The original outdid most horror films released globally at the time with its gruesome torture, graphic and implied. Both films aptly fit into a group of torture–porn films (non-Australian), such as *Last House on the Left* (2009) and the *Hostel* trilogy (2005–11). Mick, the villain-monster in both *Wolf Creek* films, is imbued with a laconic sense of dark humor, and emerges as an amalgam of the most horrific traits of the vicious bikers from *Mad Max* and barbaric predators from *Max II*. The Australian predilection for the darker side of Australia helped to make *Wolf Creek* a big hit in Australia (especially among male audiences eighteen to thirty), locally and globally. Made on a budget of $1.4 million, it earned $6.2 million in Australia and US$27.8 million worldwide. *Wolf Creek 2* did not do as well as the original, lacking the suspense and fever pitch that made *Wolf Creek* so arresting.

More recently, Jennifer Kent's *The Nightingale* (2018) depicts the criminal and monstrous in a different context and time frame: the early years of British colonization of Tasmania, 1825. Kent had started her feature film career with the highly imaginative and inspired *Babadook* (2014), which focuses on a mother and her young son living in the suburbs, who are paid visits by an eerie and frightful creature. In *The Nightingale*, the monsters are British soldiers who lord over and abuse the Irish convicts, specially a young Irish woman named Clare and her husband Aiden. After her husband and baby are viciously killed by a sadistic British Lieutenant, who also repeatedly raped and beat her, Clare sets upon a vengeful hunt to find and kill him. Her quest takes place in dense forests, replete with all kinds of hazards, including menacing male itinerants, bitter cold rainy weather, and dangerous quick-moving rivers. At first, Clare treats her Indigenous tracker, Billy, like a slave, barking orders and angrily insulting him, playing out her own power hierarchy. Billy and his community have had to contend and live with the violent imposition of British Imperialists, who have seized and desecrated Aboriginal land, killing off their families. Billy reluctantly indulges Clare for his much-needed payment of two shillings. However, a strong bond of support, friendship, and mutual aid evolves between them throughout their grueling journey. *The Nightingale* is bold and unsparing in its graphic depiction of fierce, brutal sexism and racism. Kent took great care in her historical accuracy, consulting with Indigenous Tasmanian elders with respect to the treatment of Aboriginal people at the time, as well as researching the plights of transported Irish convicts whose crimes were often petty thievery of food in order to stay alive. *The Nightingale* received local and global recognition, winning top honors from the AACTA for the following: best film, direction, and screenplay (Kent also wrote the screenplay), lead actress Aisling Franciosi, with a nomination for Baykali Ganambarr, who played Billy. This film also received a Special Jury prize, the Golden Lion Award, at the Venice Film Festival, and won a top honor in the independent film category by the New York-based National Board of Review.

A second area within the SA phase includes new works in Indigenous cinema. Rolf de Heer, along with Molly Reynolds and Peter Djigirr, continued exploring Indigenous culture and history with *Twelve Canoes* in the wake of the success of

Ten Canoes, as de Heer resumed his collaboration with David Gulpilil. *Twelve Canoes* (2009) is a website documentary exploring the complexities of sacred land and ancestral Indigenous communities in Ramingining, Northern Territory, home to generations of Aboriginal tribes (where *Ten Canoes* was filmed). The film is composed of an array of unique oral histories told by tribal storytellers as well as Gulpilil himself. As with *Ten Canoes*, *Twelve Canoes* goes a long way in dramatizing a heretofore unknown society in a remote Aboriginal community. Another project by Gulpilil is *Charlie's Country* (2013), which he co-wrote. This film is roughly based on recent events in Gulpilil's life and features an Indigenous man (Gulpilil) caught between his home community and non-Indigenous communities. This film was invited to Cannes in 2014, where Gulpilil was awarded best actor in *Un Certain Regard* division. de Heer produced Indigenous-themed documentaries such as *Still Our Country* (2014) and *Another Country* (2015), both films directed by Molly Reynolds. Most recently, *My Name Is Gulpilil* (2021), a documentary written by de Heer and directed by Reynolds, features Gulpilil reflecting upon his career in film in the wake of his diagnosis of terminal lung cancer. (Gulpilil died in November 2021.) Another Indigenous film, *Samson and Delilah* (2009), a film directed and co-written by Warwick Thornton, features two alienated teenagers living in a remote Central Australian community. They seek refuge in each other as they travel in an often perilous land. *Samson and Delilah* was honored at Cannes with the Camera d'Or, and is discussed in more detail in Chapter 5.

The Sapphires (2012, Wayne Blair) is a different kind of Indigenous-themed film and features four feisty and talented women. Significantly, it is the third Aboriginal film to foreground a primarily female cast (the first two *Radiance* and *Rabbit Proof Fence*, mentioned earlier). *The Sapphires* is based on an actual 1960s group: a Supremes-style troupe invited to Vietnam to entertain deployed Australian troops amidst resounding popularity. *The Sapphires* is smartly written to reflect the pride and bold spirit of the 1960s Indigenous rights movement, as the acclaimed group proudly transcends the boundaries of their racist country. At Cannes, it was eligible for a Camera d'Or award, and like *Rabbit Proof Fence*, *The Sapphires* entered the mainstream, playing for several months in Australia, as well as in Los Angeles and New York.

Recent releases include *Sweet Country* (2017), Thornton's second feature after *Samson and Delila*, and *High Ground* (2020), directed by Stephen Johnson, set in 1929 and 1919 (respectively), during the "Frontier Stage" (from the first landing in 1788 through the early 1930s). Along with *The Tracker*, these films break new ground in investigating the vicious impact of colonizer dispossession upon Indigenous peoples as they imposed their own brand of law and order, initiating vicious attacks on and massacres of Aboriginal families and communities, including random shootings and the killing of innocent children and women (who were frequently raped). Aboriginal reprisals quickly followed. Both films explore the later years of this period.

In *Sweet Country* (set in the MacDonnell Ranges in central Australia), an Indigenous man, Sam, who works and lives on a station, shoots his violent and abusive non-Indigenous boss in self-defense. He and his wife Lucy run away, fearing for their lives. They continually and successfully elude the search party made up of ex-soldiers and local townspeople, clearly out of their element and ill-suited to the outback desert. Hoping for the best outcome, and terrified of being slaughtered, the couple eventually give themselves up. They are tried by a unfair non-Indigenous judge who, however, is under enormous pressure to convict. Nevertheless, the vengeful racist community has the last word, for shortly after being released, the Aboriginal man is shot and killed by an unseen sniper while on his way home. *High Ground* covers several years of bloody conflicts in the Northern Territory, prompting a military company assigned to "civilize" the land and locate the Indigenous leader Baywara and his band of followers, who have been attacking isolated colonizer settlements. (In the film's early scenes, Baywara almost dies from wounds suffered during an unprovoked attack by bush soldiers.) A fair-minded officer, Travis, befriends and mentors Baywara's young nephew Gutjuk, a sensitive, intelligent, and proud young man, who was orphaned after the bloodbath that opens the film. He has been raised by the camp's nurse and her pastor brother; yet, he has maintained strong spiritual and family ties to his people. Travis promises Gutjuk that Baywara will be brought in alive for an impartial trial.

Both films feature finely drawn characters, Indigenous and non-Indigenous: the hardworking, hunted man and his wife as well as the aforementioned judge in *Sweet Country*; in *High Ground*, Gutjuk, in addition to Darrpa, the wise and seasoned elder (and Baywara's father), who understands the menacing power of the soldiers, and, protective of his community, encourages a peaceful retreat and distance from the vengeful Baywara. Also noteworthy are the compassionate nurse and her decent and respectful brother, who are appalled at the treatment of Indigenous people, and finally Travis, who ultimately sacrifices his life so that Gutjuk can be free of military retaliation. Both films received local and international acclaim. *Sweet Country* was awarded Best Feature at the Adelaide

Film Festival, and was the recipient of AACTA awards for best film, direction, and original screenplay. It was also honored with a Special Jury Prize at the 2017 Venice Film Festival, and voted Best Feature at the 2017 Asia Pacific Screen Awards. *High Ground* was recognized by the Film Critics Circle of Australia for Best Director and Screenplay (Chris Anastassiades), with Jacob Junior Nayinggul (Gutjuk) honored for his supporting role. This film premiered at the 70th Berlin International Film Festival on February 23, 2020, with a gala screening, and was selected for the Berlinale Special section.

A third salient area could be called "The Asia–Pacific connection": films foregrounding characters and themes in narratives giving insight into cultures and societies beyond Australian shores. Some of these films were shot in Australia, or in Asia (partly or wholly), or in the Southwest Pacific. Geographically, Australia is close to Indonesia (with Bali a popular vacation retreat for Australians) and Southeast Asia (including Vietnam, Cambodia, and Laos), with Japan and China further to the north. To the east are a myriad of islands in the Pacific. As noted earlier, Australia has been a destination for Asian immigrants since the 1970s. These films are significant as they provide critical insights into neighboring countries with respect to their histories, cultures, and politics and the ways these areas interface with Australia.

Though released during the FFC period several years before Screen Australia was established, *Japanese Story* (Sue Brooks, 2003) merits discussion, as it broke new ground for subsequent features addressing the Asian context. Though the film subtly alludes to Australia's wariness toward Japan in the context of the Second World War, when Japanese fighter planes attacked Darwin (1942–3) and submarines invaded Sydney and Newcastle (1942), modern Australia has strong economic ties to Japan, and Australia is a tourist destination for Japanese visitors.

This film focuses on the unlikely friendship that develops between a visiting Japanese businessman Hiromitsu, and the young woman geologist, Sandy, who is assigned to take him to visit the Pilbarra iron ore region in Western Australia to investigate mining operations. Arrogant and racist—Sandy refers to Hiromitsu as a "Japanese prick" even before she meets him—she takes on this responsibility reluctantly. When Sandy first meets him, she is curt and condescending. Hiromitsu also expresses his own share of sexism, making disparaging remarks about Sandy in Japanese to a friend over the phone when they begin their journey together. However, over the long drive through the desert terrain, they both open up and learn much from each other about their respective countries and cultures. For example, Hiromitsu delights in the expansive splendor of the landscape, noting with joy that it is very different from the crowded urban area where he and his family live. Sandy, clearly touched, begins to see the picturesque Australian desert environment through his eyes. Mutual respect evolves as well as their attraction to each other. After Hiromitsu's accidental and tragic death while diving into a pond, Sandy is devastated; yet during their journey she has been transformed, opening up her heart and mind to welcome and appreciate an Asian visitor. *Japanese Story* was honored with international recognition, selected for the prestigious Un Certain Regard at the 2003 Cannes Film Festival. It also won several AFI awards, including best film, director, screenplay by Alison Tilson and lead actress Toni Colette.

Tony Ayres' semi-autobiographical *Home Song Stories* (2007) was FFC-financed, but released during the FFC/SA transition period. Taking the Asian link back several decades, the film features a Chinese woman, who meets and marries an Australian soldier stationed abroad during the Second World War. As a wife and mother, she faces a difficult life adjusting to Australia. *Stories* was the first film in the revival to acknowledge war brides in the post-war period, and Ayres' original screenplay was honored in Taiwan at the Golden Horse Film Festival. Further, Joan Chen (who plays the troubled mother) was nominated for Asian Pacific and Asian Film Awards. In Australia, the Australian Critics Circle awarded *Stories* a prize for best screenplay, and the film was Australia's official entry to the Oscar Foreign Language film category.

Like *Stories*, *Mao's Last Dancer* (2009, Bruce Beresford) was also based on actual characters and events. *Dancer* features the brilliant career of a gifted Chinese dancer, Li Cunxin, who grew up during Mao's repressive Cultural Revolution period, and who ultimately sought asylum in Australia. For authenticity, Beresford shot much of the film in China, often secretly without official government permission. Enhanced by beautifully staged dance sequences, the film explores the complexities of growing up in China in this 1960s/1970s time frame. *Dancer* was the top Australian film at the box office in Australia in 2009, and was nominated for best film, screenplay, and director by the AFI. *Wish You Were Here* (2012, Kieran Darcy-Smith), set in Cambodia and Sydney, features an initially pleasurable and fun vacation for two couples in an exotic land abroad. However, the holiday turns tragic when one of the men mysteriously disappears in a remote village. The past haunts the present throughout the narrative, which is full of mystery and revelation. *Wish* received AFI award for best screenplay, awarded to Darcy-Smith and Felicity Price.

The Rocket (Kim Mordaunt, writer and director, 2013), shot completely in Laos, centers on a determined boy who uses his ingenuity to win the annual village rocket building and launching contest—a unique and unusual film by any standard. Interestingly, this film is not about Australia, as it features Laotian villages with resident villagers (most of them non-actors) speaking Lao. There are no Australian characters, and there is no exploration of Australian history and culture. The "home country," that is, Australia, is represented by the writer/director and producer only. Yet these filmmakers from a post-colonial country boldly and sympathetically examine a more recent, post-colonial nation across the Asian sea, exposing a serious dilemma left over from the Vietnam War in the second half of the 1960s and early 1970s: unexploded rockets and bombs buried in former war zones. Accordingly, *The Rocket* received the Amnesty International prize at the Berlin Film Festival along with the Crystal Bear Generation K Plus award for best feature. Moreover, the New York-based Tribeca Festival, which selects a wide range of innovative and distinctive works, often with a humanitarian bent, named *The Rocket* as its best narrative feature, while back in Australia this film received the audience favorite award at both the Sydney and Melbourne Film Festivals. Finally, and as a show of Australian pride, *The Rocket* was submitted as Australia's official entry to the Oscar Foreign Language film category for 2014.

More recently, two films based on actual events and people were released. *Tanna* (2015, Martin Butler and Bentley Dean), financed by SA and the state corporation Film Victoria, is set on Tanna. Two young lovers, Wawa and Dain, each belong to a different tribe in a culture where young women are frequently promised in a patriarchal system of arranged marriages. Despite their requests to marry, they are refused by their elders. They run away and commit suicide by eating poisonous mushrooms, causing great distress to their communities. *Tanna* was shot in a variety of locations in a social realist style, while all roles in the film were played by members of the Yakel tribe, who contributed substantially to the script. *Tanna* was honored for best direction by the Australian Directors Guild, also receiving the prestigious International Critics Award at the Venice Film Festival. Moreover, it was nominated for an Academy Award for best foreign language film.

Lion (2016, directed by Garth Davis), an Australian, US, and UK production, features Australian actors Nicole Kidman, David Wenham, and British/Indian actor Dev Patel. It begins in 1986, where a five-year-old, Saroo, living in a rural town in India, accidentally takes the wrong train and is transported 1,500 miles away from his home, ending up in Calcutta. Saroo lives hand to mouth on the streets, then in an orphanage, and is eventually selected for adoption by an Australian couple living in Tasmania. They raise him in a loving and comfortable, middle-class home. However, Saroo increasingly feels estranged from Australian society and culture, and longs for his home and blood ties in India. As a young man, he returns to India to visit his mother and older brother, who welcome him with open arms. Based on the book by Saroo Brierley, *A Long Way Home*, *Lion* respectfully captures the texture of underclass, Indian rural life, which is vastly different from Australian culture in the 1990s. Dev Patel, who played the adult Saroo, received best supporting actor honors from BAFTA, which also awarded Luke Davies the best-adapted screenplay award. The AACTA recognized Nicole Kidman as well as Patel for best supporting roles. The US Directors Guild awarded Davis for outstanding achievement from a first-time feature director, and the film was nominated for several Academy Awards, including best picture, adapted screenplay, cinematography, and original score.

A recent film, *The Furnace* (2020), written and directed by Roderick MacKay, shot in the Mid West region of Western Australia, and set in 1897, focuses on immigrant Asian settlers—including Afghans, Sikhs, Hindus, and Persians—working as cameliers for British soldiers who oversee mining for gold during the end of the century gold rush. Another group is a family of Chinese miners/smelters—hence the film's title, which also refers to extreme heat across the vast desert. The film focuses on several harrowing days of the life of a young Afghan man, Hanif, who is learning to tend to the camels which carry freight across the region. However, he is soon on the run from a company of menacing British soldiers, who see Hanif as a thief, for he is in the unlikely and certainly unplanned company of a renegade bush ranger, who has stolen the Queen's gold bullions. Throughout his trek, Hanif is protected and mentored by members of an Indigenous community, which is under the constant specter of British occupation of and imposition on sacred land. For historical authenticity in an array of scenes, MacKay meticulously incorporates the Indigenous tribal dialect "Badimaya," as well as two languages spoken by Afghans at the time, "Pashto" and "Dari." He has noted that the work and lives of historic cameliers—clearly strangers in a strange land—felt like a huge historic omission, which fueled his motivation for making *The Furnace*. Significantly, this film was the first revival feature film to explore the lives of these immigrant communities. *The Furnace* played worldwide, including Europe, Asian countries, and North America, with a wide release in Australia. It was nominated for the Venice Horizons Award at the

Venice Film Festival, also receiving several nominations from the AACTA, not only for Ahmed Malek's performance as Hanif, but also for best film, direction, screenplay, and supporting Aboriginal actor Baykali Ganambarr ("Billy" from *The Nightingale*), who plays Woorak, Hanif's chief protector and friend.

Along with this variety of eclectic subjects and themes discussed within these categories, the hugely popular family fare *Red Dog* (Kriv Stenders, 2011) was released. *Red Dog* was based on accounts of an actual beloved kelpie from the early 1970s, adopted by a remote, tight-knit mining community, a virtual melting pot of Italians and Eastern Europeans. Red Dog became everyone's ideal "mate": amiable, loyal, and trustworthy, and subsequently gained mythical status during and after his long journey to find his missing master. Like *Phar Lap*, this film exudes a warm shimmer of nostalgia, with the added twist of rowdy, yet good-natured pub humor. The enormous success ($21 million) of *Red Dog* positioned it as the eighth most popular film in the revival's history, inspiring a "prequel," *Red Dog: True Blue* (2016).

In the area of Hollywood-based productions, two notable films released in 2013 need to be discussed. *Wolverine* (directed by American James Mangold) and *The Great Gatsby* (directed by Baz Luhrmann) were produced by high-powered Australians: Hugh Jackman, who plays the namesake of the first film, and Luhrmann for *Gatsby*. Both men hold local as well as global clout and prestige. Even though these films were not Australian-themed, each was granted the Producer Offset (40 percent) *and* Location Offset (16.5 percent). Government agencies bent over backwards to secure these productions, especially with respect to *Gatsby*, which was originally scheduled to film in New York City. The combined government incentives for *Gatsby*, including state rebates (from New South Wales) and federal, totaled $80 million. *Wolverine* was granted an additional 13.5 percent location offset, or $25 million. Both films had very large budgets by Australian standards: approximately $135 million for *Wolverine* and $125 million for *Gatsby*.

With respect to the Location Offset, since 2008 a variety of films (financed by Hollywood-based companies) have been shot in Australia and/or had post-production or visual effects work done in local facilities. For example, *San Andreas* (2015) received an offset of $26.5 million and *Pirates of the Caribbean: Dead Men Tell No Tales* (2017), the fifth in the *Pirates* franchise, was granted $26.6 million. Other franchise films included *Spiderman: No Way Home* and Marvel's *Shang-Chi and the Legend of the Ten Rings* (both released in 2021). Clearly, the benefits reaped from overseas-based productions such as these boost the local economy, keep facilities up and running, employ Australian creative and technical personnel, and maintain world awareness of Australia as a prime filming location. However, SA has been open to criticism that overseas productions are being subsidized with Australian taxpayer dollars in the form of rebates. Additionally, SA has been criticized for favoring established filmmakers, although many of the aforementioned filmmakers were new to feature filmmaking, their productions made possible with monies from SA as well as rebates through the Producer and Location Offsets.

The revival is now over fifty years old. Since its inception, a number of studies have been devoted to the film revival, many of them written at least twenty years ago. With the benefit of more historical hindsight, we can begin to see just which genres, cycles, films, and filmmakers proved to be the most innovative, thought-provoking, and influential. This study brings fresh perspectives and applies new theoretical approaches to overlooked and undervalued films and filmmakers. I build upon the scholarship of other authors, opening up further areas of inquiry and analysis. My study also identifies compelling and original categories and trends, in some cases challenging other writers' assumptions and arguments. My areas of focus include the complex and contentious subjects of masculinity, femininity and feminism, the maternal, as well as the Indigenous road film and Australian Gothic, all analyzed in their larger cultural, political, and historical contexts. To date, there have been few studies written within the past two decades that re-examine the 1970s and 1980s—the critical time frame of Australia's production of popular and acclaimed films, which appealed to domestic and world audiences as the industry expanded and matured. These two decades are the primary area of concentration of this book. Included are detailed and extended analyses of approximately thirty films from this period, in addition to discussions of selected films from the 1990s and new millennium. My study is in the spirit of and consistent with the strategy and focus of *Australian Cinema in the 1990s* (2001, Ian Craven, editor). Within this work, authors apply original and insightful methodologies and models to a variety of key films and filmmakers from this decade, often identifying new motifs, for example, "Romance and Sensation in the 'Glitter' Cycle," "Vulnerable Bodies: Creative Disabilities in Contemporary Australian Film," and "Unhappy Endings: The Heterosexual Dynamic in Australian Film."

Other studies published later in the new millennium are *The Directory of World Cinema: Australia and New Zealand*, volume 3, Ben Goldsmith and Geoff Lealand, editors (2010) and volume 19 (same title), Goldsmith, Mark David Ryan, and Lealand, editors (2015). The first book covers an array of films that encompass a broad timespan: pre-revival films from the silent era, early sound films of the 1930s, 1940s, and 1950s, the first three decades of the revival, and into the new millennium. The second work focuses primarily on revival films and topics. The organization of each is generic, and within each genre, several films are discussed with a synopsis and short critique. For instance, in volume 3, the bushranger, ozploitation, prison films, and horror are discussed, including a section on different representations of disabilities; for volume 19, examples include action/adventure, thriller, Australian Gothic, and science fiction. Each volume includes short essays on selected directors. Volume 19 adds new areas of inquiry: "Festival Focus: Brisbane International Film Festival," "Australian Film Locations," and "Marketing Mix"—acknowledging and exploring increasing international influences and pressures on Australia in the new millennium, areas outlined earlier in this introduction.

Two additional new millennium studies, the first, *Diasporas of Australian Cinema*, edited by Catherine Simpson, Renata Murawska, and Anthony Lambert (2009), and the second, *Companion to Australian Cinema*, edited by Felicity Collins, Jane Landman, and Susan Bye (2019), expand areas of inquiry. The former focuses on "diasporic hybridity": filmic explorations and representations of Australia's diverse, multicultural society—immigrant and refugee cultures in feature films (as well as documentaries), including pre-Revival works. Chapters include, for example, Turkish, Polish, Lebanese Muslims, as well as Korean and Japanese communities. The latter work takes an eclectic approach to the new millennium, including the following: different approaches to Indigenous culture, such as "The Blak Wave of Indigenous Women Shaping Race on Screen" and the semi-autobiographical film *Charlie's Country*, which features Indigenous actor David Gulpilil; a focus on "auteurs," such as the internationally renowned writer/director Jane Campion, in addition to producer/writer/director Robert Connolly; the new Australian production company business model, Matchbox Pictures. Also included are essays on other contemporary media with respect to television and multiple digital platforms.

Earlier works are important foundational studies written when the revival was evolving. The studies noted below are organized according to a range of approaches and methodologies, including generic, topical, individual film analyses, and film reviews: Susan Dermody and Elizabeth Jacka's *The Screening of Australia: Anatomy of a Film Industry* (v. I, 1987; v. II, 1988); their subsequent *The Imaginary Industry: Australian Film in the Late 80's* (1988); Albert Moran and

Tom O'Regan's *The Australian Screen* (1989); Neil Rattigan's *Images of Australia: 100 Films of the New Australian Cinema* (1991); and *Australian Cinema*, edited by Scott Murray (1994). Jonathan Raynor's later work, *Contemporary Australian Cinema* (2000), includes analyses of not only the 1970s and 1980s, but the 1990s as well. The scope of each of these books is ambitious, the intentions of the authors and editor to cover as many films as possible, while providing cultural, historical, and financing contexts for the dynamics of the evolving film revival.

Another work which covers 1970s and 1980s films is Brian McFarlane and Geoff Mayer's intriguing *New Australian Cinema: Sources and Parallels in American and British Film* (1992). Rather than a survey format, the authors encompass, compare, and contrast these three English-speaking national cinemas with respect to narrative design, style, and character analysis within the authors' designated "boom" periods: for Britain, the 1940s and 1950s; and for the United States, classical Hollywood cinema, with an emphasis on melodrama as well as range of paradigms from each country. Albert Moran and Errol Vieth in their study, *Film in Australia: An Introduction* (2006), also use Hollywood-designated generic categories to organize and discuss selected films from the 1970s, 1980s, 1990s, and the first half of the new millennium, including for example, the detective film, the suspense thriller, and the musical. The authors further identify and discuss sub-categories that can be specifically applied to Australian culture and history, for instance, fugitives and street life in the Crime genre, and within the Adventure film, Australian men at war and female heroes. An interesting and noteworthy addition is a chapter covering the influence of European Art Cinema on a group of Australian Art Films.

My approach differs. Rather than basing my analyses on outside models, I identify and apply new models and frameworks detailed later in this introduction. One of the underlying assumptions in my work is that Australian filmmakers created *their own* Australian genres and/or selected specific areas of interest, utilizing and experimenting with modes and distinctive styles in their interpretations of masculinity, femininity, feminism, motherhood, race, and ethnicity. Or in the case of the *Mad Max* trilogy, Hollywood genres *were* appropriated to launch a whole new perspective of Australia in the creation of an original prototype.

McFarlane and Mayer, and Dermody and Jacka are critical of films from the 10BA period. I disagree with McFarlane and Mayer's contention that there was a "perceived decline in Australian film standards" during this third industry phase (McFarlane and Mayer, 1992, 238). Moreover, I disagree with Dermody and Jacka, who argue that "[t]he greater commercialization of its base [the infrastructure set up by 10BA] has not liberated its filmmakers or thrown open [Australian cinema's] field of aesthetic possibilities" (1988, 232). Despite abuses of this scheme, as detailed earlier, 10BA opened up creative opportunities for filmmakers so they could realize their bold and novel visions of contemporary Australia (and in one case, Australia's recent past), thus breaking new ground with respect to gender, race, and class. Several films included in my study were financed wholly or in part by 10BA, and are worth reiterating: *Fran*, *Lonely Hearts*, *Man of Flowers*, *My First Wife*, *The Year My Voice Broke*, *High Tide*, *Sweetie*, *Flirting*, and *Mad Max II*.

In my study, I break down two categories: (1) the "male ensemble film," designated by Dermody and Jacka, a term also used by Raynor; (2) the "period film"—an appellation used by Dermody and Jacka, Raynor, and O'Regan and Moran (*The Australian Screen*). Thus, I focus specifically on the ocker male and women at the turn of the twentieth century (respectively). With respect to the ocker, I apply a different level of analysis, taking a closer look at this genre's depiction of women. Though the ocker narrative frequently reduces females to sexualized objects of male desire, as Dermody and Jacka and O'Regan note, I argue that women are central to the ocker male's unstable and insecure identity, which is critically shaped through his strong and dependent bond with a maternal figure, who can be sexualized. Interestingly, this relationship alludes to the crucial historical role of mothers in Australian society—ironically in a traditionally staunchly patriarchal culture. Rather than discussing the ocker in the context of the company and activities of his mates, as Dermody and Jacka do, or in the context of a work/sports ethos or from an anti-authoritarian stance, as Raynor does, I explore the ways in which the adolescent ocker (and adolescent-acting) male has conflicting desires—to be in control of females who are perceived as threats, yet attracted and often deferential to a motherly character.

Further, I dissect Dermody and Jacka's "AFC genre," their term for films funded by the Commission, many of them set in the past (hence the term "period film"), to open up a fuller, more comprehensive understanding of the dynamics and specifics of gender at the turn of the twentieth century. I single out and focus on the complexities of unique women circa 1900, in addition to discussing their critical bonds with the landscape, applying two illuminating models. The first is Liz Ferrier's "Vulnerable Bodies: Creative Disabilities in Contemporary Australian Film." According to Ferrier, a good number of Australian films feature at least one embattled and/or isolated individual suffering from a disability (which can be physical, psychological, and/or social). An individual, however, finds social recognition and acceptance by way of creative performance. This is a significant dynamic in *Picnic at Hanging Rock, The Getting of Wisdom*, and *My Brilliant Career*. The second model is Kay Schaffer's *Women and the Bush: Forces of Desire in the Australian Cultural Tradition* (1988). Schaffer argues that the Australian land/landscape or "bush" has traditionally been perceived as the body of a woman, a feminized entity which is essential to the construction of Australian male identity. The aforementioned films problematize this ideology, using the bush in highly expressive ways in the construction of *female* identity. Dermody and Jacka take the position that AFC films in general often feature "bland" characters that invite "gentle nostalgia" (Dermody and Jacka, 1988, 33–4). Further, with respect to *My Brilliant Career* in particular, Rattigan comments that this film "teeters dangerously close to being little more than a stunningly beautiful film that gives visual pleasure but not much intellectual substance" (Rattigan, 1991, 221). In my analysis of the aforementioned films, I discuss the ways in which dynamic and complex women have an organic connection to the Australian bush, a multidimensional entity in rich and multifaceted narratives. In a more recent study, *Girls' Own Stories: Australia and New Zealand Women's Film* (1997), Jocelyn Robson and Beverley Zalcock do acknowledge the impact of the settings—indoors and outdoors—upon protagonist Sybylla Melville in *My Brilliant Career*. I take their visual analysis further, exploring Sybylla's bond with the bush appropriating Schaffer's model. By designating a special category which features historical women, I focus on a more specific feminist analysis by way of Ferrier's and Schaffer's models. The films in question do not conform to the tradition of cloyingly sentimental, steeped-in-the-past, "heritage-style films." The featured young women exude a fresh modern sensibility, which ties in nicely with the films' mid-to-late 1970s release dates in the wake of the Australian Women's Movement, which paralleled a prior age of independence—1900—a new era of self-determination for the young country as it moved away from a colonial to commonwealth status.

Another new area I discuss is the Indigenous road film: a bold and innovative version of the broader category, the Australian road film. These films diverge from white, male-centered films within this genre (such as *The Cars That Ate Paris* and the *Mad Max* trilogy), which foreground a fierce and aggressive masculinity revved up and intensified by high-powered vehicles. Films such as *The Chant of Jimmie Blacksmith, Wrong Side of the Road* (1981), and *Rabbit Proof Fence*, for example, rework the road picture, linking the journey—often on foot and within a variety of settings—to bold defiance of and proactive challenges to invasive and destructive colonizing forces, as if, on one level, to (re)cover and reclaim lost Indigenous land and a usurped cultural identity. The Indigenous road film thus appropriates a popular and protean model to specify and explore Aboriginal struggles and achievements, past and present. While other writers, including Felicity Collins and Therese Davis (*Australian Cinema after Mabo*, 2004) and Karen Jennings (*Sites of Difference: Cinematic Representations of Aboriginality and Gender*, 1993), feature insightful discussions on individual Indigenous road pictures in their studies, this section of my book is the first to acknowledge and examine Indigenous road films as a unique body of work. *Australian Cinema after Mabo*, which discusses selected 1990s and early new millennium films, is noteworthy in its distinctive and enlightening approach. The Mabo decision refers to the 1992 Supreme Court overturning of the founding myth of Australia—"terra nullius"—land belonging to no one, the creed of entitlement by which British colonizers forcefully stole Indigenous land. Mabo was a crucial decision in the Land Rights Movement, preparing the way for native land title claims. In light of this historical underpinning, the authors explore the dynamic of "trauma cinema," which reflects direct, indirect, or metaphorical aftershocks of the Mabo decision. (Collins/Davis discuss non-Indigenous as well as Indigenous and ethnic cinema.) Under the rubric of trauma cinema may be found the following themes that the authors identify: traumatic memory, loss and mourning; new configurations of the land on a personal, social, political level with respect to national identity (race, gender, and class) and history. I incorporate these areas in various sections of my study. Among others, two Aboriginal films, *The Tracker* and *Rabbit Proof Fence*, are discussed by the authors. These films are also included in my study, which benefits from the authors' arguments and insights, but my methodology is different, as my discussion approaches and analyzes these ground-breaking films as dynamic and critical road journeys.

With respect to the *Mad Max* trilogy, I apply the cultural transfer theories of semiotician Yuri Lotman in order to more fully examine these films, which were wildly popular in Australia and overseas. However, *Mad Max* was accused of selling out to Hollywood by a substantial number of local writers and filmmakers. As they argued, this film undermined, even negated, Australian uniqueness by using Hollywood generic conventions. Worse, *Mad Max* betrayed one of the revival's crucial ideals at its forefront: the creation and showcasing of films *that stood proudly apart from overseas models*. As I argue, director George Miller and his filmmaking team flaunt Australian culture through deliberate and deft appropriation of Hollywood genres (which include the Western and the road film, among others) in *Mad Max* and its sequel *Max II* (American title, *The Road Warrior*). The result? Highly original works. My application of Lotman's theories opens up a discussion of the uniqueness and richness of these two films as well as the fourth film in the Max series, *Mad Max: Fury Road* (2015). Lotman argues that "transmitting" and "receiving" cultures are components of a "semiosphere," a synchronic space where transmitting and receiving cultures interact with and impact each other via permeable borders. Hollywood has traditionally served as a transmitting culture, playing a dominant global force in sending out models, stylistics, and modes to other receiving cultures. (Fred Schepisi once quipped that Hollywood was the "Roman Empire" of film.) *Mad Max* and *Max II* reverse the direction of the "signals," demonstrating that Australia can be a transmitting culture too, thus initiating a new historical position. *Mad Max* and *Max II*, then, break new ground as a vibrant brand, the apocalyptic "crash and burn" genre (a term coined by David Chute), catapulting a bold vision of futuristic Australia to eager world markets, and inspiring a host of spin-offs and imitations from other countries. I argue that *Mad Max* and *Max II* in particular transcend value judgments about the "correctness" or integrity of adopting and assimilating outside models. Though other writers, such as Christopher Sharrett in *Crisis Cinema: The Apocalyptic Idea in Postmodern Narrative Cinema* (1993) and Delia Falconer, in her chapter "We Don't Need to Know the Way Home" from *The Road Movie Book* (1997), have noted the variety of international sources for these two films, no one has detailed the ways in which the *Max* filmmakers skillfully and with great panache blend together and "customize" (to use Tom O'Regan's term) imported texts to create authentic Australian works that present Australia and Australian culture in innovative and novel ways, including landscape, characters, and ideology. O'Regan's inclusion of Lotman's models in discussing an array of films in his *Australian National Cinema* (1996) stimulated my thinking to explore in greater detail the originality of the first two *Max* films. In this work, O'Regan discusses Australian cinema as a case study vis-à-vis other national cinemas (primarily European) in the larger global context. His time frame is more extensive than a number of the aforementioned studies, as he includes an overview of pre-revival years in addition to post-1970 films. The organizational strategy of his work is also different, for he applies structuralist as well as semiological models in addition to paradigms from cultural and media studies to selected films and groups of films.

The chapters in this book are organized as follows. In Chapter 1, "The Ocker: Chauvinistic and Oedipal," I bring a new perspective to the ocker films. I discuss the ocker male as an adolescent boy/man drawn to an often sexualized maternal female, who protects and nurtures him. I also explore the ironies and complexities of the ocker male's attraction to and fear of women and female sexuality in the larger context of the women's movement, which challenged Australia's traditional patriarchal society. The constant phallic references, the celebration of the male libido, and the subsequent sexual objectification and marginalizing of women serve as a smokescreen for male fears of women's political and sexual power, as well as fears over loss of their own authority. Yet, ironically, despite the ocker's anxieties over women, he seeks the companionship of a maternal figure in a dependent Oedipal bond. In specifically noted films, I contextualize this relationship in terms of its (1) chauvinism: proud and aggressive Australian difference in defiance of British culture and authority as well as internal antiestablishment sensibilities; (2) racist posturing (in the context of Australia's white patriarchal society) fueled by the end of the white Australian policy in the early 1970s. This event opened up Australia's primarily white society to a more diverse ethnic mix. The following films are discussed: *The Adventures of Barry McKenzie*, *Stork*, *Alvin Purple* (1973), *Petersen* and *Don's Party* (1976). I also update this genre to include the neo-ocker *The Adventures of Priscilla, Queen of the Desert*, which explores gender and race, as it features a male to female transsexual, gay males, lesbians, and a Filipino stripper.

In Chapter 2, "Alternate Masculinities of Paul Cox and John Duigan," I discuss selected 1980s and early 1990s works by Paul Cox and John Duigan, filmmakers whose best films from this period have not been thoroughly investigated. Cox and Duigan are often given a few paragraphs or pages in other studies. The middle-aged and young men featured in their semi-autobiographical films differ from the flamboyant ockers, as well as the men in action-oriented works (the *Max* films, Mick "Crocodile" Dundee, and men at war in *Gallipoli* and *Breaker Morant*), which dominated the end of the 1970s and into the 1980s. Cox's and Duigan's recessive males are recluses, often without the benefit of mateship, a prevailing dynamic in many male-centered films. They have strong interior lives and their "mental landscapes" are revealed through voice-overs, dreams, and flashbacks. The protagonists in Cox's *Lonely Hearts*, *Man of Flowers*, and *My First Wife* feature middle-age Oedipal males and the beloved women at the centers of their lives; yet, these Oedipal men are very different than those in the ocker comedies. Duigan's *The Year My Voice Broke* and *Flirting* draw on his adolescent years living in small towns and in a boarding school, both environments insular and alienating. These two films explore the pleasures, mysteries, magic, as well as the pain and disappointments of teenage years.

As outlined earlier, I re-evaluate the representation of women from the past in Chapter 3, "Historical Women and the Bush." I argue that *Picnic at Hanging Rock*, *The Getting of Wisdom*, and *My Brilliant Career*, which focus on vibrant and talented, yet eccentric female "misfits," who have strong attachment to and relationships with the Australian bush, boldly challenge the traditional patriarchal notion of a feminized landscape necessary for the construction of male identity. Thus, featured young women appropriate the bush in the formation of *their* unique female identities. Protagonists counter the reigning mores of respectability, gentility, and demureness in narratives critical of oppressive, British-modeled boarding schools situated in the Australian bush (*Picnic*) and (*Wisdom*), and/or the limited life roles for women as defined by a patriarchal hierarchy (*Career*). This chapter also includes shorter sections on *The Man from Snowy River* and "*Crocodile*" *Dundee*. These two films were made after the release of *Picnic*, *Wisdom*, and *Career*, and dramatize a "reversion" to the traditional construction of male identity through the feminization of the landscape. Thus, *Snowy River* and *Dundee* recoup and claim the landscape as male (rather than female) territory. At the end of the chapter, modern counterparts to historical women, Sweetie (*Sweetie*) and Muriel (*Muriel's Wedding*), are briefly discussed.

Chapter 4, a radically different focus on motherhood, is entitled "Negligent, Runaway, and Abject Mothers." I identify a group of mother–daughter dramas set in the present which break new ground by presenting a dark side of the maternal with special attention to class and race. *Fran*, *High Tide*, and *Radiance* feature irresponsible and/or abusive mothers, who are deeply ambivalent about their roles. These films explore difficult and distressed mother–daughter relationships characterized by estrangement, mistrust, even child endangerment, but also love, devotion, and commitment in a pressure cooker of personal, social, and political forces. This group of films is unusual and unique, for it deviates from a large number of Australian melodramas which examine, on the one hand, loving, unproblematic mother and daughter bonds, and, on the other, the maturing daughter's rites of passage into womanhood under the guidance of her devoted mother. This chapter explores the unthinkable—what if a mother abandons her daughter(s) and/or relinquishes her role as a stable, nurturing figure? Significantly, these women are not monsters, nor are they entirely unsympathetic. They live in the "perfect storms" of the consequences of their own choices within situations and events often outside their control.

"The Indigenous Road Film," a subgenre of the road film, is the focus of Chapter 5. I discuss a range of cutting-edge films spanning over three decades: *Walkabout, Backroads* (1977), *The Chant of Jimmie Blacksmith, Wrong Side of the Road, Rabbit Proof Fence,* and *The Tracker*. These films dramatize a range of journeys: quests for manhood, searches for home and family (established or new), escapes from the law, adventures on the high road, political activism through performance, and hunts for fugitives. All films exude an acute sensitivity to racial politics, historical and contemporary, directly or indirectly exploring critical issues and events for Aboriginal and Torres Strait Islander peoples, including frontier violence, the Stolen Generations, reconciliation, land rights, and the Mabo decision. At the end of the chapter, I include short analyses of new millennium road films directed by Indigenous filmmakers: *One Night the Moon* (2001), *Beneath Clouds* (2002), and *Samson and Delilah* (2009). As David Callahan has argued, the historical (and ongoing) discord between colonizers and Indigenous peoples is "the original and psychically most significant conflict on which the nation is based" (Callahan, 2001, 96).

Chapter 6, entitled "Australian Gothic," focuses on a genre which, along with the ocker, kicked off the film revival. Australian Gothic reveals the dark side of Australia and the Australian psyche: fantasies and nightmares of madness, dysfunction, chaos, anarchy, destruction, and death. Whereas the ocker revealed deep-seated male anxieties about women, Australian Gothic reveals an underworld of psychic and social instability and disturbance, arguably a reaction to the myriad of changes socially and politically that impacted women as well as men in post–Second World War society as Australia entered the modern age. Australian Gothic emerged as a highly imaginative and complex hybrid incorporating the horror and science fiction genres, melodrama, the road picture, and/or the Western in bold, insightful, and disturbing visions of Australia. I advance the scholarship on Australian Gothic, detailing the mixing and balancing of these genres throughout this chapter, exploring the political and social underpinnings. As noted earlier, I apply the cultural transfer theories of Yuri Lotman to the *Mad Max* trilogy. Included in my analysis is also a section on *Mad Max: Fury Road*, which takes the series to new heights and international power. This chapter also examines another gothic film, *The Cars That Ate Paris*, which explores a remote town's ferocious and rabid fixation on cars, violence, and sadism. Last but not least, I discuss two important female-centered works,

Shirley Thompson Versus the Aliens (1972) and *The Night the Prowler* (1978). Both are directed by Jim Sharman (most famous for the British–American co-production *The Rocky Horror Picture Show*, 1975). *Thompson* and *Prowler* are compelling investigations into the psyches of disturbed, yet proactive women in the context of the family and their societal milieus. These two films are often overlooked and marginalized in favor of male-centered gothic films.

It is my intention and hope that my study will open up and illuminate neglected and understudied areas, put a new spin on others, while encouraging a higher level of understanding and appreciation of what I consider to be one of the great waves in world cinema.

Notes

1 Cinesound was a division of Greater Union, Australia's largest exhibitor which began operations during the silent period. The last feature made by Cinesound was in 1940, but the studio continued to make newsreels up until the early 1970s.
2 The Bill also made provisions for a film and television school.

Sources

Australian Film Development Corporation (1973), *Lumiere*, 26, August.
Bodey, Michael (2013), "In a Flap Over the Great Subsidy," *The Australian*, May 22. http://www.theaustralian.com.au/arts/in-a-flap-over-the-great-subsidy/news-story/55d34fe5c8a580d6d5152da3235a2804 (accessed April 12, 2014).
Bulbeck, Pip (2007), "Project Greenlight," *Inside Film*, 100, July.
Callahan, David (2001), "His Natural Whiteness: Modes of Ethnic Presence and Absence in Some Recent Australian Films," in Ian Craven (ed.), *Australian Cinema in the 1990s*, London: Frank Cass Publishers, 96.
Collins, Felicity and Therese Davis (2004), *Australian Cinema after Mabo*, Cambridge, England: Cambridge University Press.
Conomos, John (2009), "Other Shorelines, or the Greek–Australian Cinema," in Catherine Simpson, Renata Murawska, and Anthony Lambert (eds), *Diasporas of Australian Cinema*, Bristol, UK: Intellectbooks, 115–24.
Crofts, Stephen (1999), "New Australian Cinema," in Geoffrey Nowell-Smith (ed.), *Oxford History of World Cinema*, London: Oxford University Press, 722–30.

Dermody, Susan and Elizabeth Jacka (1988), *The Screening of Australia*, Volume II, Sydney: Currency Press.

Falconer, Delia (1997), "'We Don't Need to Know the Way Home': The Disappearance of the Road in the Mad Max Trilogy," in Steven Cohan and Ina Rae Hark (eds), *The Road Movie Book*, London: Routledge, 249–70.

French, Lisa (2001), "Patterns of Production and Policy: The Australian Film Industry in the 1990s," in Ian Craven (ed.), *Australian Cinema in the 1990s*, London: Frank Cass Publishers 15–36.

Kroenert, Tim (2007), "Reign of Terror," *Inside Film*, 101, August.

McFarlane, Brian and Geoff Mayer (1992), *New Australian Cinema: Sources and Parallels in American and British Film*, London: Cambridge.

Rattigan, Neil (1991), *Images of Australia: 100 Films of the New Australian Cinema*, Dallas: Southern Methodist University Press.

Rustin, Emily (2001), "Romance and Sensation in the 'Glitter' Cycle," in Ian Craven (ed.), *Australian Cinema in the 1990s*, London: Frank Cass Publishers, 133–48.

Ryan, Mark David (2010), "Film, Cinema, Screen," *Media International Australia*, 136, August: 86.

Turner, Graeme (1989), "Art Directing History: The Period Film," in Albert Moran and Tom O'Regan (eds), *The Australian Screen*, Victoria, Australia: Penguin, 99–117.

1

The Ocker: Chauvinistic and Oedipal

In retrospect, who could have foreseen that a renowned and prestigious, world-class national cinema that became firmly established during the mid-1970s—revered internationally and equally popular at home—would be launched at the beginning of the decade with exploitation comedies, the "ockers," a term which refers to the genre as well as featured males. Early films such as *Stork* (1971) and *The Adventures of Barry McKenzie* (1972), which featured phallocentric, raunchy, and raucous males in hedonistic pursuits, appealed instantly to a broad spectrum of Australian viewers, who had long favored overseas films and shunned local productions. This is precisely what happened with the ocker films. Their commercial success endorsed two new government organizations, both established in 1970, The Experimental Film Fund, which provided seed monies for *Stork*, and the Australian Film Development Corporation (AFDC), which completely underwrote *Barry McKenzie*, thereby positioning the fledgling industry on the map, and paving the way for subsequent ockers, including *Alvin Purple* (1973), *Petersen* (1974), and *Don's Party* (1976). With roots in television, theater, literature, and popular journalism,[1] the clever and crassly commercial ocker defied Australian cultural cringe or the "crouch" in its presentation of cocky, headstrong, and very Australian males. As Harry Oxley succinctly noted, the ocker is "a self-satisfied vulgarian, a beer sodden slob, uncouth in behavior and thought ... a loudmouth obsessed by his own plastic masculinity, a conceited braggart" (Oxley, 1984, 193). At the time, filmmakers took advantage of relaxed censorship codes, eagerly incorporating female and male nudity into numerous sex scenes, in addition to lacing their films with crude and vulgar language. The ocker had enormous appeal in particular for sexually liberated younger viewers, who also embraced the ocker's inherently antiestablishment attitude.

The ocker films deliberately avoided British and American models in their presentation of cultural difference from an aggressive white male viewpoint. For the first time in many years, as Tom O'Regan points out, characters spoke in the vernacular: "'strine' ... an aggressively ... Australian accent" (O'Regan, 1989, 76), using local idioms for enthusiastic and receptive audiences. Distributors and exhibitors, who had traditionally ignored Australian films in favor of the American and British product, took notice with the success of the ocker, and began to invest in local productions. The ocker, then, was a critical beginning for local industry development, and its commercial success served as an incentive for the creation, production, and distribution of a variety of other later works, many funded by the new government agency, the Australian Film Commission (AFC, established in 1975). Filmmakers continued to explore Australia's unique culture as well as its history in a more serious dramatic format, many of their works funded by the AFC, which set forth a revised set of criteria aimed at achieving international standards.

An important precursor to the ocker genre was *Wake in Fright* (1971, aka *Outback*), made before the official start of government funding for local feature films and before the Australian Film Development Corporation was active. Written by Evan Jones, based on the novel by Kenneth Cook, and directed by Ted Kotcheff, this film was financed by the private Australian company NLT and the American company Group W. *Wake* featured a group of violent and self-destructive boozers on a several-day binge in the isolated outback. This film was not in the comic mode that characterized the ocker genre in the first half of the 1970s, but played as a riveting psychological odyssey, spilling over into the nightmarish and pathological territory of Australian Gothic. *Wake* dramatized the darker side of mateship, as a group of ockers entice and awe a young schoolteacher with their drinking contests, fistfights, and a horrific kangaroo hunt. This film tapped into the ocker's overindulgence, self-destructive tendencies, self-reproach, sexism, and misogyny, characteristics that became increasingly salient as the genre evolved, climaxing in the mid-1970s with *Don's Party*.

However, a short time after the first wave of ockers, this genre was accused of cultural debasement. Its raunchiness—initially regarded as a strength and a strong Australian statement—was increasingly viewed as an embarrassment by industry activists, filmmakers, critics, and even members of Parliament (many of whom had pushed for a government-subsidized industry). This was a particularly sensitive issue for a country interested in presenting a more respectable national image abroad, as well as for filmmakers making a bid for global recognition and distinction through festivals and overseas sales. The Tariff Board Hearings (which commenced in late 1972) assessed the first years of the AFDC. As a result of these proceedings, where the commercial aims and uneven funding policies of the AFDC were criticized, the AFDC financed or co-financed a group of non-ocker films, which broke new ground over the next two years, such as Peter Weir's gothic *The Cars That Ate Paris* (1974, examined in Chapter 6), Weir's turn of the century, female-centered *Picnic at Hanging Rock* (1975, discussed in Chapter 3), as well as Michael Thornhill's *Between Wars* (1974), which explored the dynamics of Australian politics and psychiatry in the tenuous post-First World War period. But the ocker was initially regarded as industry gold. And its legacy survived in a subsequent wildly successful, neo-ocker film twenty years later in *The Adventures of Priscilla Queen of the Desert* (1994).

As a way into understanding the complexities of the ocker films, a logical place of introduction and discussion is its two-tiered chauvinism. The focus of my analysis will then shift to a new and unexplored area with respect to the ocker's depiction of women: a maternal character in various incarnations, who plays a vital role in the ocker male's life, someone with whom he forms a close bond. This is an intriguing and insightful dynamic that adds another dimension to the genre's frequently sexist depiction of women as dramatized from *Stork* and *Barry McKenzie* to *Petersen, Alvin Purple, Don's Party*, and *Priscilla*, all explored later in these contexts.

The first component of chauvinism is zealous patriotism: proud and aggressive proclamation of Australian difference from and defiance of the British—its authority, culture, and society. In the case of Barry McKenzie (Barry Crocker), he flaunts his pride wildly for his mates and the Brits, and in his mind, he demonstrates ingenious creativity. Directed by Bruce Beresford, written by Beresford and Barry Humphries, *Adventures* is a tongue-in-cheek saga of a young upstart colonial on holiday abroad. British stereotypes are sent up (the cheating cabbie, "poofters" in the pub), in a "repudiation of the old desire to win the mother country's approval," as Dermody and Jacka have commented (Dermody and Jacka, 1988, 88). Barry outsmarts the British with ingenious yet base acts which play out his "superiority," frequently through phallic expression. For example, during a studio fire, Barry comes up with the idea of dousing the flames by urinating on them after he and his mates down can after can of Fosters. One of the producers sardonically deadpans, "a cultural breakthrough." Throughout the film, Barry comes up with a myriad of names for urinating, including "shaking hands with my wife's best friend" (an expression which can also mean masturbating) and "draining the dragon." Barry's crass and unselfconscious Australianness becomes a cause for celebration. Australian self-esteem is presented ironically through this ocker's behavior, which ranges from the ridiculous to the outrageous.

Another example is Jock Petersen, featured in *Petersen* (1974, written by David Williamson, directed by Tim Burstall), who flirts with British culture. *Petersen* plays out a different kind of Australian/British dynamic, balancing comedy with somber, rigorous drama. Rather than an Australian brandishing his distinctiveness abroad, this film focuses on a working-class electrician and former football star (several years older than Barry, married, with a family), trying to better himself through a British-modeled university education system (within Australia). Jock (Jack Thompson) has an affair with his former English professor, Patricia Kent (Wendy Hughes). The British-modeled Patricia, who has aspirations to teach at Cambridge University in England, gives the rugged and virile Australian man class and a pedigree. Jock's attraction to her implies Australia's continued fascination with and attraction to a "superior" culture and intellectual atmosphere. (This was a subject that Burstall explored in his first feature made in 1969, *2,000 Weeks*. A young writer in a professional crisis ultimately decides not to work in England, but to stay in Australia to grow, thus endorsing his/Australia's cultural/intellectual worth.)

Petersen discovers that higher education in Australia is hardly challenging or exciting, and as Meaghan Morris has suggested, university is a "breeding ground of hypocrisy" (Morris, 1980, 140). Kent's husband flunks Petersen (partly as payback for the affair with his wife), even though Kent himself crosses the professional line by dating his students. To add insult to injury, Patricia accepts a job abroad, leaving Petersen behind, her decision suggesting that successful academia pursuits necessitate leaving Australia for England (clearly the antithesis of *2,000 Weeks*). Petersen's plans for their life together are dashed. He becomes the embittered lover left behind, and to punish Patricia, he brutally rapes her. Subsequently, Petersen drops out of university, abandoning his studies, resuming his tradesman job, still making house calls and still the philanderer. However, he adapts the veneer of an educated man, quoting Shakespeare to the women he beds, using British-based literacy to present a superficial intellectual façade, suggesting an ambivalence about himself and his Australianness, whereas Barry McKenzie's pride about Australia is quite clear. So despite the ocker's "culturalist nationalist push," as Stephen Crofts has noted (1997, 723), Petersen is haunted by cultural cringe.

As the films discussed later in the chapter demonstrate, not all the ockers incorporated the British Other in their narratives. However, Australia's colonial past with respect to Britain became a key area to mine as the film revival developed and flourished in the latter part of the 1970s and into the 1980s and beyond—a genre unto itself. For example, Australian soldiers serve on behalf of Britain in *Gallipoli* (1981) in the First World War, as well as in South Africa during the Boer Wars in the early twentieth century in *Breaker Morant* (1980). Set at the turn of the century, *Picnic at Hanging Rock* (1975) features young women seeking independence from an oppressive British-modeled boarding school, a similar setting in *The Getting of Wisdom* (1977), where a working-class teenager from the bush pursues her interest in music. During the same time frame, *My Brilliant Career* (1979) focuses on a female protagonist, Sybylla Melville, who confidently resists and rejects her persistent British suitor. In different ways, each of these films and many others delve into the complexities of the ties between the young nation and Imperial England.

The second component of chauvinism refers to the ocker genre's representation of women, who are frequently reduced to sexual objects, often partially or completely nude. Women are also patronized and disparaged by the ocker male. As noted earlier, the ocker films celebrate the male libido and ego amidst a hyperinflated, macho bravado. Other writers have noted the ocker males' aggressive sexism (Dermody and Jacka, Meaghan Morris, Neil Rattigan), a dynamic that is clearly a function of the "entrenched misogyny" of Australian culture, as O'Regan has stated (O'Regan, 1989, 81).

The depiction of women in the ocker films may be attributed to profound internal changes within Australian society from the early 1960s forward in the wake of the women's movement, when feminists challenged the culture and ideology of sexism in a traditionally patriarchal Australian society.[2] Within a decade, women achieved more equal status by law, including antidiscrimination legislation, equal opportunity in the work force, and anti-sexual harassment laws.[3]

Ocker male posturing and aggression, verbal and physical, reflects not only a backlash to women's political and sexual power, but also deep-seated male fears about the loss of their traditional authority and dominance—essentially their terror of emasculation. Morris speaks of the tradition of "hysteria" about the body in Australian cinema in general, but this condition is perfectly applicable to the ocker perspective of and reaction to an empowered female. The sex and toilet jokes that Morris notes (1980, 134) allude to a full male body reaction to women: men are not necessarily aroused by the presence of women, but anxious and apprehensive.

Further, and notably, an overlooked dynamic with respect to the ocker genre's representation of women is the presence of at least one maternal female character, who becomes an integral part of the life of the ocker male. He gravitates toward, and even favors the company of a nurturing, motherly woman, who provides physical, emotional, and/or psychological comfort and companionship, an attraction that can also be sexualized. This connection conjures up the Oedipal relationship and trajectory from a psychoanalytic perspective: a pre-Oedipal male bonded to his mother and threatened by castration from the father ultimately separates from her on his way to achieving his own identity in order to continue the patriarchal line with a different female and a family of his own, thereby functioning as an adult member of society. Given that fathers and father figures are frequently and largely absent in the ocker genre (as well as in many Australian films), the ocker's relationship with a maternal figure is intensified. A separate and mature adult identity is compromised or not possible. Ocker males then have contradictory desires: first, desiring a woman or women, craving a sexual relationship, perhaps attempting to control a woman or women in order to reinforce his male identity and masculinity; second, experiencing anxieties over and fear of women and/or women's power; third, dependent upon a sought-after, motherly figure to nurture him in a close attachment and state of dependency. Rather than maturing into an adult, the ocker remains "stuck" in an immature, adolescent status.

The rest of this chapter discusses the complexities of the roles and representations of women vis the ocker males with a special emphasis on the maternal in *The Adventures of Barry McKenzie*, *Stork*, *Alvin Purple*, *Petersen*, and *Don's Party*, as well as *The Adventures of Priscilla, Queen of the Desert*. This last film opens up another component of chauvinism—racism.

The Adventures of Barry McKenzie

As discussed earlier, Barry frequently reduces all conversations to his penis. Barbara Creed has aptly commented that this obsession is evidence of his pathological refusal to accept sexual difference, which stunts his growth and keeps him in a pubescent phase (Creed, 1992, 19). Thus, in spite of his macho posturing, he is a virgin and is unable to comfortably be in the company of women. In the presence of women, he backs off, suggesting his fear of women's bodies and female sexuality. This is dramatically demonstrated when he goes over to the flat of Caroline, a British woman whom he met earlier after his arrival in Britain. She is dressed provocatively in a gauzy, see-through outfit as she greets him at the door, and seductively leads him to her bed. While Caroline puts the moves on him, Barry lies in bed next to her, wide-eyed and motionless, his body seemingly frozen in place, as if he is trying to keep himself from having a panic attack. He quickly excuses himself to dump prawn and beef curry down his drawers because he has heard that British women "like it hot." Yet this is a tactic that seems intended to turn *him* on, and to bolster *his* confidence. He never does find out, because he is saved by the sudden appearance of Caroline's beau, who summarily kicks (a greatly relieved) Barry out.

Barry's Aunt Edna Everage (played with panache by comedian and co-writer Barry Humphries) is a mother substitute to watch over Barry while abroad. Though not present at all his gross-out events, she does hear about the fire-dousing trick, which prompts her to gather Barry up for a return trip home to Australia. Fussy and overbearingly maternal, Edna wants Barry *out* before he can do even more damage. Tucked back under her wing, he is still an adolescent needing her approval. Though Barry has established his own unique Australian identity abroad as a mock celebrity Aussie superstar, Edna must chaperone Barry back to the homeland. Rather than growing and maturing, he is still the sexual naïf, certainly in no position to choose a female companion, yet happy to remain bonded to and dependent on Edna in a pre-Oedipal state.

Stork

Written by David Williamson and directed by Tim Burstall, *Stork* features the film's namesake, who, like Barry, enjoys acting out in public. For example, at a posh restaurant, he crams an oyster up his nose, proudly and defiantly checking out the astonished stares from the upper-crust customers. Also similar to Barry, Stork (Bruce Spence) is a virgin and also terrified of women, perceiving them as threats to his masculinity. When confronted by an aggressive, young woman at a party whom his roommates have convinced to seduce him, Stork takes one look at her, and quickly retreats, wailing, "I'm about to be castrated." Further, in the presence of Anna (the woman who shares a flat with Stork and his roommates), Stork experiences a "hysterical" attack, though different from that of Barry McKenzie with Caroline. In order to create "modern art," Stork guzzles beer and cheese and then throws up on the canvas. On the surface, this is a typical ocker gross-out, chunder scene, but significantly, Anna (Jacki Weaver) is present, watching him. It's as if Stork is so uptight and upset that his body freaks out, the ironies of a six-and-one-half-foot man scared of a woman two feet shorter than he notwithstanding!

Yet Anna proves to be gentle, kind, and very different from the ballbuster he encountered earlier; she patiently guides him through his first sexual encounter. Rather than remain his lover, however, Anna marries one of Stork's roommates, Clyde. But she becomes a maternal figure for Stork (and her pregnancy reinforces this role, though it's not clear who the father is from among the four roommates). Anna and Clyde become Stork's new parents, and he takes on the role of the slaphappy, larrikin son, accompanying them on their honeymoon after crashing the wedding reception. Rather than growing up and forging out on his own, with his own wife and possible family, Stork rejects marriage. His choice guarantees his perpetual and carefree adolescence, just like Barry McKenzie.

Alvin Purple

Though frequently included in discussions of the ocker genre, *Alvin Purple* (written by Alan Hopgood and directed by Tim Burstall), the saga of a young man irresistible to women, is clearly not an ocker male. Rather than boorish and antisocial like Stork, and phallocentric like Barry McKenzie, Alvin (Graeme Blundell) is well-mannered and passive, though his initial timidity around women is reminiscent of Stork and Barry. But like a good number of the ocker films, as O'Regan points out, *Alvin Purple* has the same "'fantasy' fascination with sexuality and the body" (O'Regan, 1989, 85). This film boasts many sex scenes, flaunting full frontal male and female nudity, as well as simulated sex. Further, female sexuality is the film's primary obsession. It's as if the wall-to-wall sex is making up for the lack of sex in *Barry McKenzie* and *Stork*. (Stork's sexual initiation takes place off-screen.)

Graeme Blundell, who plays Alvin, also played a shy male in *The Naked Bunyip* (1970, written and directed by John B. Murray), an important precursor to the ocker films in terms of its obsession with females and female bodies. Blundell is cast as a young journalist doing a feature on sex for his newspaper, and conducts actual unscripted and unrehearsed interviews. Throughout the film a variety of people are polled, ranging from politicians to members of The Welfare and Decency League to a pharmacist and psychologist, for example. Though the film features straight and gay men, its primary center of attention is women—single mothers, pregnant women, prostitutes, and strippers—as well as the issue of female sexuality, abortion, contraceptives, and childbirth. *Bunyip* has the same prurient fascination with the female body that the ocker has.

Alvin goes through three phases—innocent teenager, experienced stud, and chaste male. As the film begins, the women are the sex-starved ones and Alvin is *their* object of desire. Thus the film turns the tables on the myth of "the male's boundless sexual appetite," as Dermody and Jacka point out (Dermody and Jacka, 1988, 90), while setting up females as sexual predators. Further, like *Stork* and *Barry McKenzie*, *Alvin* plays out male fear of female sexuality, but in very different ways.

Part I features schoolboy Alvin as a shy and reluctant "victim" pursued by a group of overeager, horny teenage girls. He is "rescued" by the wife of his high school teacher, who introduces Alvin to sex. Subsequent housewives also find Alvin irresistible. This section of the film suggests that uncontrolled female lust can be fun. Part II, however, implies that female sexuality needs to be managed, even controlled, as if the oversexed females in Part I had too much fun and male control needs to be established. In this section, a more confident and enterprising Alvin sets himself up as a sex therapist, clearly a fraudulent choice, for he is not licensed. He is the "expert," who treats sexually dysfunctional women, many of whom are repressed. Alvin is essentially a stud to draw out their sexuality—as if using all the savvy and technique he learned from his lovers earlier in Part I. Female sexuality is now a *problem* and must be regulated by a male—an antidote for the freewheeling days of unbridled female sexuality from the first part of the film.

Alvin's relationship with Dr. Liz Sort (Penne Hackforth-Jones), a psychiatrist, ups the ante. Though Dr. Sort is initially his mentor and a maternal therapist, guiding Alvin toward "mental health," which is a new developmental phase for him in order to fend off horny women, she crosses the professional line, ultimately playing the castrating female. From the film's perspective, this is the worst kind of sexuality—aggressive *and* uncontrollable *and* linked to women. (At least Alvin could control his female "patients.") As O'Regan comments, "Dr. Sort's attempt to 'cure' Alvin entails both his emasculation and her accompanying sexual frustration. As she equips him to resist female overtures, she also enables him to resist her. [Ironically, Alvin has become an object of infatuation for Dr. Sort.] Thus [Alvin] incurs her unforgiving wrath as a woman" (O'Regan, 1989, 85–6). Dr. Sort turns into a voracious harridan, who incessantly demands sex; thus, the film links the mental health profession to a sexually monstrous woman. Ultimately, Dr. Sort tries to punish Alvin for refusing her by exposing him as a fraud, hoping to criminalize *his* behavior when the film clearly suggests that her aggressive, sexual overtures constitute the crime. The comic court proceedings dissolve into a circus, as the judge and court (primarily male) become duly titillated with footage of Alvin's lovemaking sessions with his "patients," which essentially re-masculates him, re-objectifies women, and reinforces Dr. Sort's role as a repulsive and vengeful female.

In Part III, Alvin enters into a final phase, introducing another version of motherhood, settling down with a chaste, non-aggressive, and non-sexual maternal figure—his "girlfriend" Tina (Elli Maclure), who has no sexual interest in Alvin at all (nor he for her). Tina functions as a "mother confessor," one to whom he can confide about his past of sexual escapades, and one who provides a refuge and safe haven. It's as if the filmmakers have decided that the only way to manage female sexuality is to turn both male and females into model celibates. Alvin and Tina both retreat to a neutral convent, she as a nun, he as a gardener. There are two implications of this ending, which imply the best of all worlds for Alvin and give him a way around his vow of chastity (and suggest that he isn't ready to stop sowing his wild oats). First, the film suggests that this is the ideal place for women from a male viewpoint where female sexuality is repressed, that is, there are no libidinous females to tempt the newly chaste Alvin. A second implication, hinted at by Alvin's slightly leering glance at the women at the convent, is that *he* will take the prerogative to initiate the sex, not they, so the nunnery potentially functions as his own personal harem, a situation similar to part II of the film where he managed female sexual desire.

Petersen

Like Alvin, Petersen's view of women is twofold, as either caretaker (Petersen's wife) or lovers—from the casual (Petersen having sex on campus as a protest) to more serious (his aforementioned affair with Patricia Kent). Clearly, with an abundance of liberated females, Petersen's initial educational aims for entering university are sidetracked. Yet, an intriguing Oedipal triangle is played out among Petersen, Patricia Kent, and her husband (Arthur Dignam), who plays the avenging and punitive Father when he learns of the affair between Petersen and his wife, essentially castrating Petersen by failing him. Patricia defers to Kent's patriarchal law, not challenging her husband's decision, even when Petersen asks her to intervene. When Patricia leaves to go to England, it's as if she is cutting Petersen loose from her apron strings, affording him the opportunity to achieve his own identity on his own, without Patricia's nurturing, that is, returning to fidelity with his wife, and functioning as a proper father to his children. Petersen has the opportunity to finish his education and teach as planned. By dropping out of university, however, Petersen sabotages his career, and reverts to typically self-destructive, ocker behavior: getting stinking drunk and goading the police into attacking him. Petersen shows up at home, bloodied and beaten. Unaware of his affairs, Petersen's wife consoles him, enacting the comforting maternal to her little boy who has been beaten up.

As noted earlier, Petersen regresses to his old identity and job as electrician, having abandoned his intellectual pursuits. But rather than asserting himself as the head of his own household, and reassuming the role of father and husband (responsibilities shirked during his affair with Patricia) that would mark his maturity and the success of his Oedipal journey, he resumes his life as a philanderer, bedding women on house calls. Petersen has the best of both worlds: a wife to take care of him at home, and lovers to service him on the road.

Don's Party

Don's Party, directed by Bruce Beresford and written by David Williamson (his third scripted ocker after *Stork* and *Petersen*), is clearly in the ocker tradition and mode with its brash and broad visual comedy, including nude frolics in a swimming pool and rowdy chases within and outside of Don's home. This film also conjures up ocker excesses: macho posturing, crass dialogue (sexual innuendos, sexual come-ons), drunken bouts, sex scenes (primarily acrobatic and reminiscent of those in *Alvin Purple*), all in the larger context of a pointed satire of male behavior. We laugh at the antics of the boy–men under Beresford's deft direction, and are duly impressed with Williamson's smart and droll dialogue. However, whereas Barry McKenzie celebrates proud Australian difference in ironic, self-deprecating ways for his cheering mates, and Stork launches bold and raunchy tirades, *Don's Party*, like *Petersen*, exposes the vicious and spiteful side of males: bad tempers, hostility toward women, rancorous self-doubt, especially with respect to vocational and professional choices. A biting social commentary, *Don's Party* is much more rigorous as it explores the darker undertones of suburban life, exposing the "shibboleths" of Australian middle-class lives, as Brian McFarlane notes (2007, 106). This film also dramatizes the deep cultural divisions between men and women only hinted at in earlier ockers that surface in unhappy marriages, some of which have turned into battlefields with Don's house staging bitter exchanges. Moreover, *Don's Party* also dramatizes more forcefully than prior ockers the impact on men and women of the changing status of women in Australian society in the wake of the women's movement. Finally, *Don's Party* continues the through line of the maternal with intriguing and revealing variations.

Don's Party was the last major film of the ocker genre, and in many ways can be considered the "grand finale," though ocker characters appeared in subsequent films, for example, the troop of soldiers in *The Odd Angry Shot* (1979), Peter Handcock in *Breaker Morant* (1980), Barry Fife in *Strictly Ballroom* (1992), Tic and Adam in *The Adventures of Priscilla, Queen of the Desert*.

Rather than one primary ocker character, *Don's Party* features an ensemble: Don (John Hargreaves), teacher, former aspiring novelist; Mal (Ray Barrett), psychological consultant, Don's mate and former professor at university; Mack (Graham Kennedy), photographer; and Cooley (Harold Hopkins), lawyer. There are two characters who do not fit into the ocker mode: Evan (Kit Taylor), a dentist; and Simon (Graeme Blundell), an industrial accountant. All of the above, except Evan and Simon, see the evening as a chance to ogle and score with the women. Set during a key political moment—the eve of the 1969 election when Labor had a fighting chance of overturning twenty years of Conservative rule, and clearly sympathetic to Labor—*Don's Party* does not intend to analyze the election or explore in detail the specific political agendas of the two candidates, but uses the election as a backdrop to explore the party's sexual politics. However, the political emasculation of Labor PM Gough Whitlam (1972–5), who was sacked a year before *Don's Party* was released, hangs heavy in the air as the men experience their own levels of sexual frustration, even impotence, in the presence of women who turn them on and/or intimidate them.

Significantly, to Williamson's credit, and deviating from prior films discussed in this chapter, there are five major female characters: Kath (Jeanie Drynan), Jenny (Pat Bishop), and Jody (Veronica Lang), who are wives and mothers of Don, Mal, and Simon (respectively); Susan (Clare Binney), a university student and Cooley's girlfriend; Kerry (Candy Raymond), an artist/working professional and Evan's wife. These women give the film a robust, enlightened, female perspective. Each woman has a strong presence and voice. They are not relegated to the margins or cast as sex objects—with Susan the exception, to be discussed later. As Peter Fitzpatrick notes, the women's "directness throws into relief the hollowness of the male rituals" (Fitzpatrick, 1987, 55).

Unlike prior ockers, which primarily feature male space, such as pubs, *Don's Party* takes place mainly within the home, that of Don and Kath—the kitchen, living room, bedrooms—with some scenes set outside (the garden, the swimming pool next door). The home is usually associated with female space and melodrama, and is a place where the women maintain the house and raise children, while the men, the breadwinners, are at work, though clearly not all of the women are wives and mothers. This setting ties in nicely with Williamson's emphasis on the female viewpoint and experience, and in several scenes the women sit comfortably on the couch or in easy chairs contributing to conversations about the men in their lives and raising children, for example. Williamson's and Beresford's focus on the female experience—household, professional, personal—and female desire counterbalances the typical ocker male perspective, presenting brave new worlds. In many ways, the women come across as far more centered, mature, reflective, and poised than the men. Dermody and Jacka have noted that the women in *Don's Party* are characterized by their relationships to their men (Dermody and Jacka, 1988, 113), implying that they would not be at the party interacting if their husbands were not present. Nevertheless, the women act on their own volition and prove to be strong, assertive, and independent during the evening. For example, Kerry refuses to leave the party with her abusive and possessive husband, whose ill humor and childlike tantrums make him look downright silly. Kerry could probably survive on her own as a self-sufficient, successful artist. Moreover, Simon's wife, Jody, enjoys interacting with Mal and Mack in discussing politics, much to the chagrin of her husband Simon, who feels more and more out of place as the evening progresses. She stays, when he decides to leave early.

Susan and Kerry are clearly sexually liberated women; they both go to bed with Cooley at different times, and Susan comes on to Don. They are refreshingly assertive and just as randy as the men. Significantly, they are not punished for exercising their sexual ambitions. Thus, female sexuality does not become monstrous (like Dr. Sort in *Alvin Purple*), nor does it connote unhealthiness or require male management as in *Alvin Purple*. Unfortunately, nineteen-year-old Susan is set up right away as the token nude—in an early scene, she is barebreasted in a hotel room with Cooley, and then is playfully unclothed by the men who decide to take a late night swim, which puts the film temporarily back in *Alvin Purple* territory. Moreover, Williamson does not shy away from female perspectives on sex. There is a revealing scene where the women frankly discuss their attitudes toward sex with their husbands or partners—scenes inconceivable, even out of the question in prior ockers, where the point of view would, of course, be male. This scene even suggests the possibility of female bisexuality, as Kerry openly admits a sexual interest in women: "The female body is more infinitely more beautiful than a man's," she exclaims, smiling at Susan, who is clearly interested.

The host for the evening is Don, who has the boyish good looks of Alvin Purple, and a ready-for-anything-look in his eye. He fluctuates between the horny, juvenile lusting after and making out with nineteen-year-old Susan, and a guilty teenager in need of stern reprimanding from his maternal wife, who constantly admonishes him like a wayward, misbehaving son. Kath's dual role as mother is reinforced by her frequent carrying of their toddler son as she moves about the house, including the kitchen, living room, and child's bedroom with Don usually in sight. Frustrated by his inattention to his guests, and especially Don's preoccupation with Susan amidst his nude frolic in the neighbor's pool with her and his mates, Kath later explodes in an angry outburst in front of their guests, giving an account of her unanticipated maternal role throughout their marriage. As she tells it, she tended to Don—referring to him as an "adolescent genius"—when he was writing his novel (either never finished or never published), before she gave birth to their son. She exclaims, "I put him [Don] on an invalid's diet" (then looking directly at him), "hand washed all your clothes, cooked your meals, because your mummy hadn't told you that the world is a big fucking place!" At the film's end in the early daylight hours, when Don is wandering through his garden, hung over, he appears to be lost, outside the domestic protection of the house. Kath admonishes him to go to bed like a wayward child. The last we see of Don, he sits, cradled in a hanging bamboo chair.

Don is further linked to the maternal when he listens attentively and sympathetically to Jenny's sad, extended, touching, and very intimate confessional of despair over her body, as well as her miserable life with her husband—the type of scene unheard of in the ocker, and more consistent with melodrama in the best sense, for instance, the films of Gillian Armstrong. Yet Jenny is a devoted mother, and the film implies that she does a good share of the parenting. Her account presents a daring honesty from a female point of view, and she is arguably the most complex woman in the film. Jenny's middle-aged perspective of her body after four children is in stark contrast to her husband's callous attitude toward female bodies. This was demonstrated at the beginning of the film when Mal showed up at Don's door with a Playboy-style, pinup sketch. Predictably, Mal spends the evening leering at and making sexual overtures to most of the women. Jenny's marriage to Mal is in a state of cold war, and she desperately tries to keep up appearances; yet, she is dour, depressed, and suffers from migraines. Her form of payback for Mal's alternating inattention and hostility is to spend beyond their means, indulging their children. Her latest purchase is a swimming pool, which has drained their bank account and created a new set of creditors, Don and Kath, who recently bailed them out.

In response to Don's quite sincere solution for her depression—to have an affair—Jenny replies, "You try having an affair after four kids have made your tits droop, and your stomach looks like something's that got stuck into a soggy steam pudding with a fucking whip." Jenny's heartfelt outburst certainly enlists compassion. If one of the men had said this, it would have been another distorted male version of the female body. Coming from Jenny, who has gone through labor and childbirth multiple times, it bespeaks an emotional frankness: the psychological and physical challenges of pregnancy, the ways that pregnancy changes a woman's appearance and self-image, especially if her husband treats her with contempt.

Besides Don, Mal, Cooley, and Mack are the main male characters, who exhibit traits from Williamson's prior ockers in *Stork* and *Petersen*, but with more complexity. Mal is older, more jaundiced than prior ocker males (or anyone in the film's party of men). His name conjures up "malcontent" or "malaise," both equally applicable to his state of mind. Mal aggressively and nostalgically defends Labor ideals, "health, education, and social welfare." He once had aspirations to be prime minister, but is now in the fallback position of highly paid political consultant, a job economically rewarding but with nowhere near the clout nor fulfillment. His arch political stance is linked, however, to his reactionary and sexist attitudes toward women. He quickly sizes up Kerry and Jody as possible one-night sexual escapades. Yet, with his paunch, sneering face, and smirking condescension, he appears repulsive to the women he ogles at the party. He clumsily flirts with any woman within range as his drunken state intensifies. Like Petersen, Mal is much more interested in sex outside his marriage, the difference here that Mal comes on to women in front of his wife. Like the posturing of Stork and Barry McKenzie, Mal's macho bravado is a smokescreen for his deep sexual insecurity. At one point he confesses, "It's not small ... I just *think* it's small."

Mal's close friendship with Don goes back to college days when Mal was Don's professor. Mates ever since, their relationship is arguably the most emotionally satisfying one in the film. By the end of the evening, when just about everyone has left, Don and Mal lie drunkenly and endearingly in each other's arms with obvious affection, talking about the "bloody great days" at university together.

However, they are so enamored with each other, that they assume they are equally appealing to each other's wife. They offer to swap wives for the evening, the ultimate sexist gift from one mate to another. This mutually self-serving ploy elicits the expected disdain from both wives, obviously not interested, causing the men to look ridiculous with their pumped-up sense of sex appeal.

Cooley, brash and self-centered, is a younger and more sophisticated version of Mal (and the person Petersen would probably be if he had stayed in school). Cooley is as obsessed with sexual conquest as Mal, regarding it as a game or sport, as McFarlane has noted about the tenor of the evening (McFarlane, 2007, 104). He brags nonchalantly, "I scored with the national charity queen two years in a row." When Cooley is not boasting about his sexual feats, he flaunts his ribald tales with typical ocker coarseness. However, whereas Stork's version of bowel problems at least had shocking originality, in *Don's Party* Williamson makes the point that Cooley's scatological humor is tedious. It's as if Cooley is so desperate to be the center of attention that he resorts to the most graphic rendition of bodily functions. Whereas Stork pulled crude stunts to keep people at their distance, Cooley thinks his behavior is a turn-on for the women. Though he beds two willing women, these acts are never consummated, which speaks for the whole evening of frustrated sexual forays. The last we see of Cooley, he is running away from a furious Evan, who has discovered Kerry and Cooley in bed together.

At the other end of the sexual spectrum is the undersexed Mack, who arrives solo. Whereas Cooley tells vulgar stories, Mack presents crass and sexist "art" with a poster of a nude, which is an enlarged photograph of his estranged wife. Despite his apparent fascination with the opposite sex, Mack's only source of pleasure is at a distance as voyeur, secretly taking pictures of couples having sex, including his ex-wife, who apparently had a tryst with Cooley. Mack flirts with Simon's wife Jody, but conveniently passes out in the bedroom when she comes on to him, suggesting that his voyeurism is a safety valve. He is either unable to perform in the moment or may be impotent, or, like Barry McKenzie with Carolyn, he is too frightened to have sex, which may have been the case with his wife. Mack's fear of women is also graphically played out with his duck-hunting story. Duck is Australian slang for a woman. For example, it is used in *Sunday Too Far Away* (1974), when the station owner's daughter enters the shearing shed, and the men call out, "Ducks on the pond!" In *Don's Party*, as Mack acts out his story, he mimes the need to defecate almost simultaneously with the ducks arriving. His body goes into another kind of a "hysterical breakdown" in the symbolic presence of women, whereas Stork and Barry had real women with whom to contend.

Like Mack, Simon is sexually timid, but rather than drinking to excess and sounding off with crude language like the others, he is delicately polite, in contrast to the grotesqueries of the other men. Simon also votes Liberal (read conservative), and is therefore the brunt of Mal's attacks on his (Simon's) favored party. Simon is played by Graeme Blundell, who also played the irresistible Alvin Purple discussed earlier. The film makes an inside joke: Simon is staid, mild-mannered, and boring, the complete opposite of Alvin, and without a trace of sex appeal.

When the party is over, at the dawn of the next day, Don staggers about his garden, hung over, looking like a teenager who stayed up all night drinking with his mates. He blinks at the daylight, having to face up to the realities of the new day: his mate Mal has gone home and his garden is in shambles with all the human traffic from the night before. Kath, disgruntled with his inebriated state, gives him a good maternal scolding.

Don's party promised the ideal ocker fantasy—unlimited booze with mates, a ripe occasion to act out, women to flirt with and hopefully bed—held on an election night that many of the guests hoped would change the country. Yet the results—return of the status quo, coitus interruptus, and alienation among men and women, and in particular, between husbands and wives—leave behind a bitter, stagnant atmosphere of loss and disenchantment: Jody's indifference toward Simon; Mal and Jenny's unhappy, hopeless marriage; the hostility between Evan and Kerry; Don and Kath going through the motions of husband and wife. Though Nigel Spence and Leah McGirr are speaking of 1980s and 1990s films such as *Monkey Grip* (1982), *The Last Days of Chez Nous* (1992), and *Love Serenade* (1996) in "Unhappy Endings: The Heterosexual Dynamic," their assessment can apply to *Don's Party*. They write, "[T]here is some kind of unbridgeable gulf, some essential incomprehension, some incurable enmity, between Australian men and women. This feature is a bar or barrier, an obstruction whose outline only becomes visible through the richness, complexity and honesty of depiction which has developed in Australian filmmaking during recent decades" (Spence and McGirr, 2001, 54). Along these lines, *Don's Party* may be understood as a precursor to the discontent between men and women depicted in later films.

Don's Party is an appropriate end game to the ocker genre in the mid-1970s, when its males reached middle age as working professionals and husbands in suburbia, their hedonistic desires at odds with adult responsibilities. This film features at least one Oedipal male, Don, who is clearly in perpetual need of motherly care. With respect to Mal, we sense that he will remain with Jenny if only for the security of a family in name only: he disdains his wife, and either neglects or does not know his children. Though Don and Mal are best mates, deep down inside they need the stability of their wives and marriages: Jenny is a token mother, whom Mal may need more than he knows, and Kath an overbearing and fed-up mum. Ultimately, the wives and girlfriend are the stable ones, with the wives holding the family together and the other women pursuing successful professional/artistic and academic lives. *Don's Party* emerges as a strong feminist film.

Almost twenty years later, *The Adventures of Priscilla, Queen of the Desert* would resurrect ocker males with variations: gay transvestites befriended by a male to female transsexual, who introduces a new version of the maternal. This film also introduces a new component of chauvinism—racism directed at Asians.

The Adventures of Priscilla, Queen of the Desert

In *The Adventures of Priscilla, Queen of the Desert*, writer/director Stephan Elliott cleverly conjures up and reworks the ocker, but instead of a white male heterosexual milieu, the film features two drag queens, Tick (Hugo Weaving) and Adam (Guy Pearce), and a (male to female) transsexual, Bernadette (Terence Stamp), on an outback romp. For Adam, the trip is a lark; for Tick, a means to rendezvous with his estranged wife and young son; for Bernadette, a chance to ease the pain of her husband's death. *Priscilla* puts a new spin on sexual—and significantly, racial—politics with its gay male leads and an Asian stripper.

Unlike earlier ockers films that were mainly geared for Australian audiences, *Priscilla* was intended for international audiences first to establish a track record before playing in Australia. The film opened at Cannes in May 1994 and made a big splash; shortly thereafter, it premiered at the Gay and Lesbian Film Festival in Los Angeles, then opened in theaters across the United States. With strong word of mouth, it moved to Australia, doing extremely well. Worldwide, *Priscilla* achieved the coveted status of a crossover film, appealing to both gay and straight audiences with its sympathetic treatment of gay men.

Priscilla's gay setting would not have been possible as a mainstream film subject in the first part of the 1970s, when Australian culture via the ocker was more narrowly defined by a white male heterosexual perspective that initially repressed an increasingly diverse society and history in terms of gender, race, and ethnicity. But in the 1990s, with more flexible financing structures—frequently a combination of private financing (local and overseas) and monies from the new government institution, the Australian Film Finance Corporation (FFC, established in 1988), which participated in the project after the required pre-sale or distribution deal—a new generation of filmmakers could explore traditionally marginalized areas and make a bid for world markets.

Priscilla is clearly a throwback to the ocker with its familiar drunk and rowdy scenes in bars on the road, as well as scenes done in deliberate bad taste. For example, Adam is far more outlandish and crass than Barry McKenzie, proudly showing off an "ABBA turd" in a bottle to Bernadette while they are on the road. This gesture almost seems intended to one-up the scene in *Barry McKenzie* where Barry graphically throws up on the hair of his unsuspecting psychiatrist. Tick also carries on the tradition of the ocker's phallic-centered humor, that is, telling a tale of his friend "cracking the fat"—enlarging his penis.

Unlike prior ockers, however, *Priscilla* is not a film about male posturing or scoring with women. In fact, soon after the three hit the road, *Priscilla* turns into a full-blown, misogynistic attack on the film's females, which supersedes the sexism and misogyny discussed earlier in this chapter. The film's targets are Ol' Shirl (June Marie Bennett), a bar patron the three meet on the road, and Marion (Sarah Chadwick), Tick's wife, with whom the three rendezvous at their final destination. Further, the film opens up another aspect of ocker chauvinism—racism—in its hostile treatment of Cynthia (Julia Cortez), an oversexed, alcoholic, Filipino stripper. It's worth noting that Asians were the target of derogatory racist comments made by Barry McKenzie when he and Edna stopped over in Hong Kong on the way to Britain. Barry referred to the inhabitants as "honkers" and "tin-eared bastards" and later as "slant-eyed ratbags." On one level, *Barry McKenzie* and *Priscilla* allude to white male alarm over shifting ethnicities in Australia and an increasing Asian presence (though there was a significant Asian population in Australia from the time of the 1850s gold rushes). Both films were made after the end of the white-only Australian immigration policy in the early 1970s, which opened up Australia to non-Europeans, including Australia's Pacific Rim neighbors. Anti-Asian sentiment fueled tensions in urban areas, spawning openly racist and neo-Nazi groups as dramatized, for example, in Geoffrey Wright's *Romper Stomper* (1992).

With respect to the film's attitude toward women, specifically Ol' Shirl and Marion, *Priscilla* disparages them as lesbians, whereas *Don's Party* tolerated the presence of women attracted to each other. This is first of all demonstrated by Bernadette's scorching remarks to Ol' Shirl, who has an unbecoming slovenly and masculine appearance. With her unkempt short hair and her garb of undershirt and trousers, she is coded as butch or lesbian, and in the world of the film her appearance is linked to the unnatural, even the perverse. Further, Ol' Shirl's rough demeanor, as well as her broken English, suggests a low-class white trash, conjuring up a "bulldagger," which carries with it a grotesque and very real threat to masculinity. As if to "unsex" Ol' Shirl, Bernadette quickly bombards her with an openly hostile and vicious outburst, which also implies a violent rape: "Why don't you just light your tampon and blow your box apart, because it's the only bang you are going to get!" Shocked and humiliated, Ol' Shirl hangs her head in shame as the men in the bar burst into peals of laughter.

Unlike Ol' Shirl, Marion does start out positively. She has been a model mother, raising her son on her own while developing a successful career as entertainment director in a large hotel. She has also been a tolerant wife in her open-mindedness about Tick's gay lifestyle and drag performance vocation. But the film quickly demonstrates that Marion is completely fickle and unworthy of her proud motherhood. She not only turns into a "bad" mother but a deceitful wife. First, the film implies that Marion's sexual orientation has distracted her ability to mother, a fact not lost on her son Benji (Mark Holmes), who strongly implies that he felt in competition with Marion's lover and unfairly shunned. Secondly, Marion betrays Tick, causing him to be publicly humiliated in front of his son, as if she were threatened by the presence of Benji's father. She deliberately lies to Tick, telling him that Benji will not be present at Tick's drag performance. (Benji is not aware of Tick's gayness, nor has he seen him in drag.) Yet, Marion brings Benji anyway, much to Tick's embarrassment. His distress is so great that he faints and ruins the show. Finally, Marion further undercuts Tick's attempts to be a good father by ostentatiously and inappropriately trying to pair him up with the hotel busboy, when Tick is clearly not interested in taking on any lovers.

If Ol' Shirl is attacked as an offensive deviant and Marion is belittled and maligned as an improper mother and wife, Cynthia's raunchy and outlandish burlesque act codes her as obscenely sexual. Her main claim to fame is a trick with ping pong balls: she seductively inserts them into her vagina and pitches them from her backside to the bar's frenzied male audience. Poured into a provocative, tight-fitting, black, satin bustier and thong with electric black-and-white, spiraled stockings, Cynthia conjures up the "damned whore," an historical, male-defined, Australian stereotype for women coined during the early days of the country's settlement in the late eighteenth century, when the majority of female convicts were categorized as loose women and objects of sexual gratification whether or not they became prostitutes. By deeming all women damned whores, men could relegate them to an inferior status, yet maintain the power dynamic, reaping the benefits of using them for sexual gratification.

This attitude clearly sums up the ocker viewpoint toward women as discussed earlier in *Alvin Purple*, *Petersen*, and *Don's Party*. Further, like the females in *Alvin Purple* and *Petersen*, Cynthia must be controlled and/or punished for their aberrant sexuality. Indeed, she is roughly dragged off the stage by her husband Bob (Bill Hunter), and painfully held against her will. Significantly, Cynthia's excessive sexuality and lewd behavior are linked to her Asian heritage. Thus, she is a female incarnation of what is perceived as a menace to the purity of white Australian society, not to mention Bob's masculinity, dramatized when she compares the size of Bob's penis to her little finger. Though Cynthia leaves the film in a huff, Bernadette and Adam reinforce her departure by "banishing" her from the film altogether. How do they do this? The life-size, plastic, inflatable sex doll, which they use to signal for help after their bus breaks down in the outback, clearly alludes to Cynthia. The doll disappears into the sky over the outback, and after the film's conclusion and final credits, "Cynthia" lands in an unnamed Asian country, suggesting that this is where Asian women really belong—certainly *not* in Australia.

On the other hand, in a gesture of political correctness, the film treats the group of Aboriginals that Tick, Adam, and Bernadette come across one night quite differently and ostensibly much more cordially. As Emily Rustin has pointed out, two traditionally marginalized groups, homosexuals and Aboriginals, engage in a positive expression of mutual acceptance. One of the Aboriginals, Alan (Alan Dargin), joins the three while the rest clap and dance to Gloria Gaynor's "I Will Survive" (Rustin, 2001, 139). Yet, on the other hand, as Pamela Robertson comments, this sequence features Aboriginals playing "stock stereotypes" rather than complex characters like the drag queens (Robertson, 1997, 280). This is also a case of what David Callahan calls "invisible ethnicity"—attentiveness to an ethnic mix but none to ethnicity as culture (Callahan, 2001, 100). Regardless of the implications of the Aborigine sequence, the film clearly reserves its nastiest or most punitive behavior for Cynthia as a Filipino and for Asians in general.

Bernadette, the male to female transsexual, becomes the film's ideal woman in two significant ways. Consistent with a major dynamic as discussed in prior ocker films, she is clearly a maternal figure to Tick (they have been friends for years) and it is clear throughout the film that Tick enjoys having the stability of a mature, older woman on board, especially with the handling of the unpredictable and immature Adam. In a key sequence, Bernadette courageously and confidently rises to the occasion to rescue Adam, who flirts shamelessly with a group of miners while in drag attire. When they start to beat Adam up, after having discovered his real identity, Bernadette transforms into an awesome phallic (and castrating) woman, coming to Adam's rescue. She decks the avenging miner with a one-two punch and kick to his groin.

Moreover, Bernadette becomes a member of "God's Police." Coined at the beginning of the nineteenth century, this other male-defined stereotype (as opposed to the damned whore) deemed women a civilizing role within family and society. As the young nation grew out from under convict status into social respectability, these "good and virtuous women" (usually wives and mothers, and clearly delineated from the damned whores) were expected to look after the moral interests of the nation under the paternal metaphor. Further, their duties frequently included the policing of other women, a job that Bernadette undertakes with great relish upon setting her sights on Ol' Shirl and Cynthia. It's as if Bernadette has realized her calling, transforming from a brooding widow and lackluster performer to a zealot, as she re-civilizes this "intemperate social environment" (Summers, 1994, 347).

If God's Police functioned in the 1840s amidst the dramatically changing, male-dominated society where women were defined according to the needs of the nation as the foundation of the patriarchal family unit, then Bernadette is the 1990s rendition of God's Police, with an evangelical furor fueled by sexist and racist white anxiety over deviant women—lesbians such as Ol' Shirl and Marion, and oversexed foreigners such as Cynthia—all of whom threaten the traditional status quo. At their final destination in Alice Springs, Bernadette takes Cynthia's place as Bob's very chaste paramour, a role consistent with the puritanical aura associated with God's Police. Bob will stay on with Bernadette at the hotel. Further, Bernadette takes Marion's place as entertainment director at the hotel. Thus, Bernadette stands as the new standard for Australian womanhood—the bastion of reactionary "family values" that privilege the male. There is no room for Asians or lesbians, the film having eliminated biological women in order to create a new customized version of womanhood. The new family unit which carries on the patrilineal line will be Tick and Adam as Benji's parents when they return to Sydney. Though Tick and Adam both sought the temporary guidance of Bernadette rather than a more permanent Oedipal bond with a maternal figure as in prior ocker films, they ultimately achieve their identities separate from her as performers and parents in a reconfigured nuclear family.

Chauvinistic. Hedonistic. Phallocentric. A film revival successfully launched in the early 1970s appropriating a commercially dependable exploitation format. First, a bold and raunchy declaration of difference from the Brits and British culture through the antics of Barry McKenzie. For Petersen, however, despite his quest for Australian comeuppance and independence, he still harbored lingering attractions to the mother country. Secondly, on an internal level, the ocker films launched strong reactions to dramatic changes within Australian society with respect to women, namely their political empowerment post-1960s. In all of the films discussed in this chapter, women became an obsession—desired *and* feared. As objects of desire—voyeuristic, sexual—they were pursued and bedded (*Petersen*, *Don's Party*), though women could turn the tables and actively pursue the anxiety-ridden, not necessarily turned-on men, as in *Stork*, *Alvin Purple*, and *Don's Party*. The downside was that women could be punished and physically attacked, as in *Petersen*, and two decades later, be coded as inappropriately ethnic or deemed hostile and unattractive lesbians, as *Priscilla* demonstrated.

Further, a salient and critical feature in all of the films was a protagonist who chose to be sheltered under the wing of a maternal female in a close bond. Clearly, he was not ready nor willing to mature and grow up with his own identity as a full-fledged adult. For many of the ocker males, a motherly character provided the most fulfillment and security: Aunt Edna for Barry, Anna for Stork, Patricia and wife Susie for Petersen, Tina for Alvin, and Kath for Don. Though a maternal figure could be resentful, Kath vis Don, or monstrous, as Dr. Sort was with Alvin Purple. The connotative "adolescence" of the ocker genre, which other writers have noted (Dermody and Jacka, Morris and Rattigan), could be interpreted as reflective of a young industry—albeit from a white male viewpoint and represented as male—going through growing pleasures, with some growing pains. With respect to *The Adventures of Priscilla, Queen of the Desert*, Tick and Adam did advance to adulthood as fathers to Tick's son, not in need of Bernadette's protection and motherly wisdom anymore. This film's openness to gay men, however, was at the expense of sexism directed at lesbians, as well as sexism and racism directed at an Asian woman. A final word on the Oedipal male: Paul Cox would explore this dynamic in a serious dramatic format in the 1980s with *Man of Flowers* (1983) and *My First Wife* (1984).

But yet, in the latter part of the 1970s and into the 1980s, a new kind of male would appear and evolve, committed to and meeting the challenge of "men's work." First as soldiers on the battlefields of Gallipoli and in South Africa fighting on behalf of Britain in *Gallipoli* and *Breaker Morant* (respectively). Second, in *Mad Max*, wherein a post-apocalyptic warrior pursues and punishes the murderous bikers who killed his wife and son. Max would continue his feats in *Mad Max II*, bravely assisting outback nomads as they protected precious petrol from treacherous predators. Third, Mick Dundee and Jim Craig would emerge as skilled and confident bushmen featured in *"Crocodile" Dundee* and *The Man from Snowy River* (respectively) to tame the wilderness as well as protect and rescue their lady loves. In all of these films the men would survive their rites of passage, achieving heroic adulthood status.

To their credit, the ocker films launched and/or reinforced several careers. Bruce Beresford went on to direct a number of prestigious films, including *The Getting of Wisdom* (1978), *Breaker Morant* (1980, which he also co-wrote), *Puberty Blues* (1983), and *The Fringe Dwellers* (1986). David Williamson scripted esteemed works such as *Gallipoli*, *The Year of Living Dangerously* (1982), and *Pharlap* (1983). With regard to actors, Jack Thompson, who had a minor role in *Wake in Fright*, and who was the protagonist in *Petersen*, played the lead as the seasoned sheep shearer in *Sunday Too Far Away* (1974), and was featured in the male ensemble in *Breaker Morant*. John Hargreaves, the film's namesake in *Don's Party*, was the protagonist in *My First Wife*. Jacki Weaver (Anna in Stork, and Susie, Petersen's wife) and Jeanie Drynan (Kath, *Don's Party*) both enjoyed distinguished careers in television and film in subsequent years.

With the success of the ocker, the industry flourished and diversified with subsequent productions, many set in the past as filmmakers explored the nation's history during early years of the twentieth century, featuring male as well as female protagonists, often with respect to the country's bonds with England (as noted earlier). Included also were a good number of films featuring Aboriginal protagonists such as *Storm Boy* (1976), *Backroads* (1977), and *The Chant of Jimmie Blacksmith* (1978), set amidst contemporary and historical Indigenous–non-Indigenous tensions and conflicts. Films were also set in the 1950s, such as *Newsfront*, which focused on a cameraman in the new age of television journalism, as well as *Sunday Too Far Away*. And situated in the 1930s was *Caddie*, a single mother in the Depression era. Many of these films were made with financial assistance from the new government agency, The Australian Film Commission, as well as newly formed state agencies, such as the South Australian Film Corporation and the New South Wales Film Corporation.

The revival was off and running.

Notes

1. For a history and explanation of the influence of these formats on the ocker, see O'Regan, 1989, 78–80.
2. John Duigan reflects upon the historical underpinnings of the treatment of women in ocker films as well as in Australian cinema. "[S]ex is traditionally treated in Australia … at a bawdy surface level, with talks of male prowess in pubs, so you get the trivialization of sexuality in films like *Alvin Purple* and by television characters like Paul Hogan … [W]e began as a society in which women were at a premium, which perhaps started off the mateship ethos. It meant that men had to deal largely or solely with other men, and to deal with a woman was exceptional, so sexuality gained a heightened or unreal quality which in turn give rise to stories that get encapsulated into bar-room myths and are celebrated in poem, song, and subsequently television and film. I think that pattern is being gradually eroded but I think it is still exerting a significant influence" (qtd. in Mathews, 1984, 221).
3. Elizabeth van Acker also notes other gains during this period, including family allowances for childcare, safe houses for rape and domestic violence victims, access to abortion and contraception, including the birth control pill. (See 1999, 58–60.)

Sources

Barber, Susan (1996–7), "Review of 'The Adventures of Priscilla, Queen of the Desert,'" *Film Quarterly*, 50 (2): 41–5.

Callahan, David (2001), "His Natural Whiteness: Modes of Ethnic Presence and Absence in Some Recent Australian Films," in Ian Craven (ed.), *Australian Cinema in the 1990s*, London: Frank Cass Publishers, 95–114.

Cooper, Ross and Andrew Pike (1981), *Australian Film 1900–1977*, Melbourne: Oxford University Press in association with the Australian Film Institute.

Creed, Barbara (1992), "Mothers and Lovers: Oedipal Transgressions in Recent Australian Cinema," *Metro*, 91: 14–22.

Crofts, Stephen (1996), "New Australian Cinema," in Geoffrey Nowell-Smith (ed.), *The Oxford History of World Cinema*, New York: Oxford University Press, 722–30.

Dermody, Susan and Elizabeth Jacka (1988), *The Screening of Australia: Anatomy of a National Cinema*, Sydney: Currency Press.

Fitzpatrick, Peter (1987), *Williamson*, North Ryde: Methuen.

Mathews, Sue (1984), *35 MM Dreams: Conversations with Five Directors about the Australian Film Revival*, Victoria: Penguin Books.

McFarlane, Brian (2007), "Men Behaving Badly: *Don's Party*," *Metro*, 154.
Morris, Meaghan (1980), "Personal Relationships and Sexuality," in Scott Murray (ed.), *The New Australian Cinema*, Melbourne: Thomas Nelson, 98–108.
O'Regan, Tom (1989), "Cinema Oz: The Ocker Films," in Albert Moran and Tom O'Regan (eds), *The Australian Screen*, Victoria: Penguin Books, 75–98.
Oxley, Harry (1984), *Australian Popular Culture*, Sydney: Oxford University Press.
Rattigan, Neil (1991), *Images of Australia: 100 Films of the New Australian Cinema*, Dallas: Southern Methodist University.
Robertson, Pamela (1997), "Home and Away: Friends of Dorothy on the Road in Oz," in Steven Cohan and Ina Rae Hark (eds), *The Road Movie Book*, New York: Routledge 271–86.
Rustin, Emily (2001), "Romance and Sensation in the 'Glitter' Cycle," in Ian Craven (ed.), *Australian Cinema in the 1990s*, London: Frank Cass Publishers 133–48.
Spence, Nigel and Leah McGirr (2001), "Unhappy Endings: The Heterosexual Dynamic in Australian Film," in Ian Craven (ed.), *Australian Film in the 1990's*, London: Frank Cass Publishers 37–56.
Summers, Anne (1994), *Damned Whores and God's Police*, rev. edn, Sydney: Penguin Books.
Van Acker, Elizabeth (1999), *Different Voices, Gender and Politics in Australia*, South Yarra: Macmillan.

2

Alternate Masculinities of Paul Cox and John Duigan

[Filmmaking] has something to do with using some of your own life, your own deeper thoughts and silences and putting them into film. Within every individual there are so many darker, deeper grounds that are rarely explored that we are conditioned to ignore and neglect. They are what can make us so very rich. Whether they are positive or negative ground, I don't care. To stir those a little is my aim.

Paul Cox[1]

This approach to filmmaking applies not only to the films of Paul Cox but also to those of John Duigan. Both draw from their own lives to inspire and shape their semi-autobiographical films. Through their male protagonists, Cox and Duigan explore alternative masculinities which are opposed to the flamboyant and ribald ockers; the macho, swashbuckling Mick "Crocodile" Dundee; warriors Mad Max and Breaker Morant; as well as the stalwart sons in *Gallipoli*. Cox and Duigan's men are closer to the contemplative and introspective loner, Dr. Edward Trenbow, in *Between Wars* (1974).[2] Like Trenbow, these males are outsiders, isolated and alienated, without the benefit of mateship. Further, they are preoccupied with their own private worlds and personal obsessions, namely the women they desire and love. Through voiceovers, dreams, and/or flashbacks, we gain access to their inner landscapes replete with yearning. (However, *Max*, *Breaker Morant*, *Gallipoli*, and *Dundee* take place primarily on designated "external" male space: the besieged outback, battlefields on behalf of Empire, the bush, respectively.)

This chapter focuses on two films by Cox: *Man of Flowers* (1983) and *My First Wife* (1984), inspired by events from various periods in Cox's life, including the breakdown of his first marriage. Also discussed are two films by Duigan, *The Year My Voice Broke* (1987) and *Flirting* (1991), both based upon his teenage experiences living in a small town and attending boarding school, respectively.

(Duigan emigrated from England with his parents as a teenager.) Rather than appropriating American genres as various filmmakers did in the 1970s and 1980s, for example, (Dr.) George Miller with the *Mad Max* trilogy and (the other) George Miller, *The Man from Snowy River*, Cox and Duigan modeled their films on the works of European filmmakers: for Cox, Ingmar Bergman, Luis Bunuel, and Werner Herzog (who appears as the father in *Man of Flowers*); for Duigan, Francois Truffaut, and Louis Malle.

Paul Cox

We have seen in Chapter 1 dramatizations of an Oedipal scenario which underpin the ocker comedies wherein an adolescent-acting man bonds with a maternal female. In the Oedipal dramas, which structure *The Man of Flowers* and *My First Wife*, protagonists Charles (Norman Kaye) and John (John Hargreaves), respectively, like the ocker male, obsessively focus on a mother or maternal figure. However, these two films clearly do not fit the format, tone, and blatant sexism of the coarse, raucous ocker comedies, nor their commercial aims. These works exude solemn, serious drama, filled with intense and raw emotions, and feature angst-ridden, tormented protagonists in their forties or fifties. However, it must be noted that quirky humor and wit are sprinkled throughout *Man of Flowers*. In contrast, however, lighter moments have vanished in *My First Wife*, as John hits suicidal rock bottom. In both films, to Cox's credit, he includes fathers in various incarnations, a choice which enriches these films. Fathers range from frightful and punitive (*Man of Flowers*), to kind but remote (*My First Wife*), to terminally ill (*My First Wife*). It is noteworthy that fathers are frequently absent in many Australian films; and if they are present, they either become marginal figures or disappear early in the narrative.

The male–female relationships in *Man of Flowers*, Charles and his young friend Lisa (Alyson Best), Lisa and her boyfriend David (Chris Haywood), and *My First Wife*, John and his wife Helen (Wendy Hughes), are consistent with the culturally troubled terrain of misunderstanding and dysfunction between men and women, as Nigel Spence and Leah McGirr have noted about 1980s and 1990s films (Spence and McGirr, 2001, 52–3). Moreover, with respect to Charles and John, there is something deeper going on, that is, a pathology bordering on clinical depression, unusual in the depiction of Australian men, at least in the 1980s time frame. Both men are in fragile states mentally and emotionally, increasingly withdrawn, and unable to cope with family, friends, and the outside world. Cox's earlier film, *Lonely Hearts* (1982), does not feature an Oedipal male. Rather, it dramatizes a *female* Oedipal journey, focusing on a young woman, Patricia (Wendy Hughes), who breaks away from her overbearing father, and finds love and happiness with an older man, Peter, who does not experience the angst of maternal obsession.

Man of Flowers

Whereas Peter in *Lonely Hearts* grows into full-fledged adulthood, able to find love in the wake of the death of his mother, Charles Bremer in *Man of Flowers* (screenplay by Cox and Bob Ellis) desperately longs for his late mother, whose alluring and ghostly presence overwhelms his existence. As played by Norman Kaye, who also played Peter, Charles is several pounds lighter, appearing fragile and gaunt. Charles does not manifest Peter's zest for life as well nor the droll look that he cast upon the world. Charles is reclusive, timid, and sexually repressed like Patricia in *Lonely Hearts*, but he is far more damaged emotionally and psychologically, though he has the poise and veneer of an educated man and connoisseur of art.

In the course of the film, Charles undergoes two intertwined Oedipal crises. In the present, Lisa, a young woman who routinely strips for Charles, seeks his friendship, hoping to be his lover. Lisa's increasingly abusive boyfriend David, a coke-snorting, pretentious, no-talent, "modernist" painter, becomes extremely jealous of their relationship. Fearing for her safety, Lisa turns to Charles for help. This triangle conjures up Charles' childhood past, which is revealed through his flashbacks. We learn of his cruel and punitive father, who stood between him and his beautiful eroticized mother, whom Charles (still) adores. By getting rid of David, Charles ensures Lisa's safety, but more important, he rids his mind and his life of the haunting and fearful memory of his father. He is thus able to advance to a greater degree of emotional stability and maturity.

Charles' mother, introduced via dreamy flashbacks when he is a boy, is warm, open, and loving. In one delirious sequence captured in close shots, she hugs and kisses him—they are both naked—and wraps herself around his body. Because he is stuck in a pre-Oedipal phase, Charles' identity has continued to be closely aligned with his mother. Accordingly, he keeps her spirit alive in his lush, suburban home, a womb-like house featuring long corridors and dark rooms, enhanced by a swimming pool to make his house complete as a protective refuge. However, his strong and lingering bonds to his mother have stunted his emotional growth. He is sexually repressed, and ashamed of his own body. As a safety valve, he keeps all women at a distance. This is demonstrated in the film's stunning beginning as Lisa strips slowly to the soaring soprano from *Lucia Di Lammermoor* by Donizetti, as Charles watches intently.[3] When she is completely nude, Charles suddenly rushes out of his house across the street to the local chapel and vigorously plays the church organ as a form of sexual release.[4]

Cox and Ellis suggest that Charles' self-consciousness originated in his youth when he was dominated by his authoritarian father, who contributed to Charles' psychic scarring. In flashbacks we learn that his father not only imposed himself between Charles and his mother in a classic Oedipal scenario, but he frequently slapped Charles and even dragged him painfully by his ear when he was deemed to be out of line. In one flashback, Charles temporarily succeeds in having his mother all to himself, as he symbolically kills his father by aiming his slingshot at him, smashing the window in front of his father's face. Charles also lusted after his voluptuous aunts, who paraded about in backless and low-cut dresses, events which dramatized his father's hypocrisy. As Margaret Greenwood suggests, Charles' father was probably unfaithful to his more prudish and chaste wife (who of course lavished herself on her son), but selfishly flaunted *his* infidelity by lusting after his wife's sisters in public (Greenwood, 1983, 85). On one level, Charles' guilt about "betraying" his mother with his aunts, as well as his discomfort with own childhood sexual desires, in addition to his primal fear of castration by his father, caused him to repress his feelings about all women, while keeping alive his eroticized mother's image in his fantasies and memories—well after her death—as if to prove *his* fidelity.

The film implies that Charles' way of coping with his mother's eroticized body as well as her absence has been to set up females, namely Lisa, as objects of voyeurism and fetishism. Psychoanalytic theory posits that both of these strategies counter the male's fear of sexual difference as well as the threat of castration; since the mother lacks a penis, the male assumes "she" has been castrated (Haywood, 1996, 394). First, voyeurism (with its ironies of scopophilic pleasure and anxiety over the missing penis) turns the female into a passive object, as the voyeur (the male) safely "contains" her to diminish the threat of castration. As noted earlier, Charles carefully sets up this voyeuristic arrangement when Lisa strips in front of him. He watches from a distance, avoiding any intimate contact, though Lisa desires to be his lover. At one point when he meets her on the street, she breaches his space and affectionately kisses him on the cheek. He pulls away, clearly very uncomfortable, firmly telling her that she shouldn't do that. His behavior also suggests that his powerful reveries about his mother can never be replaced by anything in real life. Moreover, he preserves his voyeurism with Lisa and her new lesbian lover, Jane, going one step further in his imagination. He does this by encouraging them to kiss and touch in front of him while he watches from a distance, "participating," however, by imagining that he is Jane, clearly identifying with her.

Secondly, Charles fetishizes women; that is, he overinvests in and eroticizes their body parts. In her discussion of fetishism, Susan Hayward notes that "[t]he purpose of this over-investment is, ultimately [accomplished by ...] perceiving them as perfection themselves, to make those parts figure as the missing phallus." In the fetishizing process, as with voyeurism, "[t]he female form is contained," but fetishism also transforms "this denial of difference," so that it becomes reassuring rather than dangerous (Hayward, 1996, 395). Or, as Laura Mulvey comments on this dynamic, "[the female] is a perfect product, whose body [is] stylized and fragmented by close-ups" (Mulvey, 1977, 422). As discussed earlier, one way Charles creates fetishes is through his flashbacks of close shots of female breasts (his mother and aunt) and fleshy backs (his other aunt). He also does this in waking life by touching various parts of the life-size, female garden statues he admires, while gazing at them as a voyeur. Moreover, Charles fetishizes flowers in the art he creates. He literally covers the "lack" in a drawing of Lisa (whom he refers to as his "little flower") in his nude drawing class: when he sketches her, he covers the lines and details of her body with large flowers. In fact, his whole house, a virtual shrine of flowers in all their incarnations—freshly cut in vases, rendered in paintings, or woven in the fabric of the comforter and sheets on his bed—is a fetish of his mother's body, hence, the meaning of film's title.

Charles' scopic arrangement is critically disrupted when David—a modern and younger version of his father—encroaches into Charles' neat and ordered life. An imposing and brutish man, David bullies and abuses Lisa verbally and physically, even giving her a black eye. (In a parallel flashback which suggests a similar attack, Charles' father gestures aggressively as if he is going to hit Charles' mother.) David is also menacing toward Charles, and breaks into his home, trashing it, probably looking for money to steal to feed his coke habit. Cox and Ellis have fun sending up and emasculating David, as if to play out Charles' wish fulfillment, while at the same time demystifying David's art, which he deems so vital and ground-breaking. Since Charles' father was fond of pornography, Cox and Ellis suggest by association that David's art—large, ugly canvases of loud colors sloppily thrown together—is similarly depraved. Further, the large bulldog that lives in David's studio (also his living space) with its labored breathing and snorting, waddling around the messy and cluttered studio, suggests that David is functioning only on the level of base animal instincts. He spends his days eating, sleeping, barely conscious, while dependent on frequent hits of cocaine. Much to his own frustration, he cannot even achieve an erection when he is with Lisa because the drug has made him impotent. David's pretentiousness and sexual shortcomings are dramatized à la Jackson Pollock in a sequence where he drip paints, then adds his own touch with a large paint gun, flailing the canvas with a thick, knotted rope. The limp rope and streams of paint suggest autoeroticism: his own bad art is the only thing that turns him on.

In order to save Lisa and get rid of David (or in Charles' words, "dispose of the man who almost crushed my little flower"), Charles kills David by felling him with a deadlier version of the slingshot that was aimed at his father—a barrage of wooden darts as missiles fired by remote from the fence in Charles' yard. This is after Charles cleverly lures David out of his studio with the promise of thousands of dollars for a large canvas of flowers. With its large, garish, blue flowers in a vase, the canvas is a grotesque, cartoon-like parody of French Impressionism. In order to "contain" David for good, Charles enlists the help of the owner of an antique shop to entomb the body. As ghastly as all this sounds, the grislier parts of this denouement are deftly and discreetly handled off screen with great economy and subtle humor. We see David falling after being hit at night, the canvas landing on top of him (ironically "smothered" by his own art that once aroused him), and Charles relieving himself by playing the organ calmly (implying that the death of his "father" functions as a turn-on). This is followed by Charles' visit to the shop and his conversation with the shop owner, whose face beams with excitement as Charles explains his plan. Finally, we see Charles cleaning off the darts in his garden and restoring them to the fence.

The finale to all these events is demonstrated when Charles pays a visit to the public garden where David, embronzed, stands on a slab of concrete, with the ironic title, "The Origin of Art," carefully holding a bouquet of flowers, this "other" man of flowers finally respecting Charles' precious fetish. Charles wryly explains in voice-over, in yet another letter to his mother, that this figure is "a statue to the people. It's nice to know the family name will be remembered." Rather than upright, however, David leans forward, as if he is going to fall over, one final reminder that the joke is on him. Charles is at last free of his father, and has ensured Lisa's safety. Charles is now able to advance to a less distressed and anxious state. Instead of taking Lisa on as his lover, he declares that they will remain friends. Thus, he continues his imaginary relationship with his mother, who is still very much alive in his thoughts.

The final shot of Charles on a grassy hill in front of the ocean suggests a peaceful stasis: he stands in the company of three (unidentified) non-threatening males in comforting proximity to calm, maternal waters.

My First Wife

In *My First Wife* (scenario by Cox, screen adaptation by Cox and Bob Ellis), the male protagonist, John, is married with a daughter. However, as the narrative develops, we learn that John, like Charles Bremer, is still in his pre-Oedipal phase, his identity closely and critically intertwined with a maternal figure. In contrast to Charles Bremer's situation, however, this woman is not John's mother nor a younger woman, nor his mother as a younger woman. She is his wife, Helen (Wendy Hughes), upon whom John is emotionally and psychically dependent. Helen has shouldered much of the parenting with their daughter, Lucy (Lucy Angwin), as John's many responsibilities and jobs as composer, music critic, and lecturer have kept him frequently absent from home. Helen is neglected, bored, and unfulfilled sexually and emotionally. She is also tired of her role as the motherly wife and caretaker. She has taken on a lover, and is having a torrid affair with their friend Tom (David Cameron), who gives her the adult attention and excitement she needs.

When John finds out about the affair, and worse, that Helen intends to leave him and take their daughter with her, he is catapulted into a major life crisis. He is filled with rage and self-pity. Concurrently, he must contend with another family crisis, the imminent death of his father from cancer, and his mother's full-time dependency on John. Unlike Charles, John does not have a contentious relationship with his father; John is actually quite fond of him. The prospect of being severed from one maternal figure and on his own, yet having to rise to the occasion and take care of his own mother, sends John into deep despair, a nervous breakdown, and finally an attempted suicide. Whereas Charles' two Oedipal crises propelled him into action—in one gesture, he rids himself of two threatening fathers—John's problem is not an overbearing and authoritarian father with whom he must compete over his mother. His problem is two mothers—his wife, an imagined mother who rejects him, and his biological mother, who desperately needs and relies on him to be a man—not at all the scenario he desires.

John views his parents' marriage as a model and an ideal, and though his mother was unfaithful to his father in the past, the affair served as a catalyst for his father's passion and love for his mother (as his father tells it), though the intensity of her feelings for him never equaled his. Nevertheless, they stayed together. Because his parents' marriage survived this crisis, John expects Helen to return to him, ready to love him wholly, as if her affair never happened, with the differences between them magically resolved. However, Helen continues her affair with Tom. By the end of the film, John and Helen's future as man and wife is uncertain.

Compared to relative "calm" of the worlds of *gentle men* Peter and Charles, *Wife* is a film bursting with the fireworks of raw emotions, Helen's as well as John's. John becomes highly volatile, and he frequently exhibits aggressive and destructive behavior dangerous to himself and others. John attacks his wife verbally, calls her a liar and a whore in front of her stunned parents, while screaming, "You have killed me." At one point, he even brutally slaps her, and then tries to force himself on her in bed, an act which suggests a rape. Later, he smashes his fist and then his foot through the door of Tom's house. He even kidnaps his own daughter, deliberately keeping their whereabouts a secret.

At the time of this film's release, marital dynamics explored in such a sobering and explosive manner was a relatively new area for Australian cinema[5] as well as for Cox himself. Given that *My First Wife* was based on the breakdown of Cox's marriage, clearly this was an agonizing subject for him. He has commented that the film was a pressure valve for his psyche and nerves, and a way to start the healing process. In light of the personal nature of *Wife*, which could have turned into an attack on Helen as the guilty party (and real-life payback to Cox's first wife), Cox is up-front right away about revealing John's self-righteousness and hypocrisy about his own affairs. Fifteen minutes into the film, after Helen admits to her affair with Tom upon John's intense cross-examination, John soon admits to his adultery, but deems *her* far worse. He declares smugly, "I didn't screw *your* friends!" Significantly, Helen is not an unsympathetic character. She suffers also, and aches for the adult love she and John had. She confesses to her mother, "The loss of love is very real, I miss it."

What has driven John to this point? Intellectually and professionally, he is riding on the crest of a successful career. Yet, as noted earlier, his total immersion in his vocation has removed him from the day-to-day activities of his household, fathering responsibilities, and attention to his wife as an equal partner. Further, like Charles, he is emotionally and psychically stunted, which reinforces John's perception of his close bond to his wife as one-dimensional; love is unconditional. Significantly, throughout the film, John's fantasies and flashbacks reinforce his sense of Helen as a perpetual maternal figure. This is dramatized from the romanticized, such as the scene where Helen helps Lucy play on the swing, to the graphic. In one of John's flashbacks, Helen undergoes an agonizing labor in the hospital, and we see Lucy actually being born.

Moreover, as John becomes more desperate (and as Helen pulls away from him), he fetishizes her, conjuring up fragmented images of her as the sexualized maternal. This is reinforced by shots of her nude torso floating in water, intercut with close shots of her breasts (reminiscent of the way that Charles fetishizes his mother), as well as her abdomen and pubic area. John's compulsion to tighten his pre-Oedipal bond with Helen even extends to his desire to merge himself with her (all the way back to the fetal state). This inclination is dramatized when John tells Helen—while she visits him in the hospital after his attempted suicide—that he dreamed of her womb. He finishes this fantasy once he is home, declaring, "I wanted to disappear inside you, and drown all that agony."

Further, Helen's absence (which could be called Oedipal separation hysteria) leads to John playing the needy boy–man with other designated maternal figures. For example, after railing unhappily at the radio studio where he works, he takes into his confidence one of his female colleagues, Hilary (Anna Maria Monticelli). On the verge of tears, he enlists her sympathy, and she consoles him, taking him into her arms, his head resting on her breasts. Hilary invites him back to her apartment for mad, passionate sex. Later on, John acts like the sullen rejected boy when he shows up at her door unannounced, for she sends him away. John also plays the possessive son going after the father to win back the mother. The scene alluded to earlier where John smashes and kicks through the door of Tom's house gives him access to the primal scene of Helen and Tom together making love. He even threatens to kill Tom in a fit of Oedipal rage.

Finally, as noted earlier, John becomes so desperate that he kidnaps Lucy. This is ostensibly done as payback to Helen, but John treats his daughter like a lover when they "escape" to a motel. As they sleep, John cuddles Lucy from behind, a configuration similar to that of him and Helen after they made love upon his return from hospital. Accordingly, Lucy sees herself as taking Helen's place when she asks her, "Can I marry Daddy if you don't live with him?"

How are John's Oedipal crises resolved? His father's death appears to break the momentum of his Oedipal rage over Helen, and he rises to the occasion as his mother's caretaker to comfort her through her grief, in a reverse of the dependent son role he has played with Helen. He also takes a more active role in fathering Lucy, as shown when he attends her concert and carefully repositions her arm as she plays her cello (rather than ignoring her as he did at the beginning of the film while she practiced her instrument). In the film's closing scene after the funeral, Helen, Lucy, and John walk away from his father's grave in the cemetery, hand in hand, with Lucy in the middle. This configuration suggests renewed bonds within the family. But the reconciliation between John and Helen is likely tentative, given Helen's ongoing liaison with Tom. John *is* brought closer to his estranged love, this scene evoking Charles Bremer's imaginary relationship with his mother alluded to at the end of *Man of Flowers*. However, whereas *Flowers* suggests a reinforced bond, *Wife* implies only a temporary reconnection in a marriage that lost its glow long ago.

John Duigan

Whereas Cox focuses on Oedipal males in crisis, Duigan explores decisive events in the life of an adolescent male in larger social or institutional contexts. *The Year My Voice Broke* and *Flirting*, both written by Duigan, and set in 1962 and 1965, respectively, explore the magic, pleasures, and mysteries, as well as the pain and disappointments of adolescence, all amidst the insularity and cruelty of a community of small town inhabitants (*Voice*), or an authoritarian and repressive boarding school (*Flirting*). Duigan positions Danny Embling (Noah Taylor), the protagonist/narrator in both films (age fourteen and seventeen, respectively), in the context of his loves, friends, family, and the social circles of both environments, specifically exploring his friendships with young women: Freya (*Voice*) and Thandiwe (*Flirting*), who are both richly drawn—to Duigan's credit. Freya and Thandiwe enchant and inspire Danny—he also has strong sexual yearning for each—and they figure prominently in his growth. Duigan balances drama with humor and irony in an acutely sensitive and perceptive rendering of male adolescence, not only in Danny's interactions with these women as well as other characters, but also through Danny's wry and heartfelt voice-over commentary throughout both films. What is remarkable is Danny's determination and resilience as he overcomes oppressive, even damaging, forces that threaten to hold him back. Despite many obstacles, he matures emotionally, psychologically, and intellectually.

The Year My Voice Broke

Duigan establishes *Year* in a rural and isolated community in the Southern Tablelands in New South Wales, where the main obsessions (at least among the men) are drinking, rugby, and razzing others. Danny and Freya (Loene Carmen), who is a few years older than he, have been close companions since childhood. Freya, though loyal to her mate Danny (Noah Taylor), is intimately involved with her boyfriend Trevor (Ben Mendelsohn), an older, charismatic, yet reckless misfit who steals cars for kicks. Though Danny thinks of Trevor as a rival for Freya's attention, Trevor is also Danny's friend and frequent protector at school. For instance, he comes to Danny's aid when a pack of boys give Danny a swirly in the girls' toilet (forcefully sticking his head inside and flushing), quickly and fiercely grabbing the two by the hair and throwing them against the wall outside.

Like Danny, Freya is singled out for ridicule and criticism by her classmates, but she is also teased by the small-minded and heartless men who hang out at the pub. They enjoy taunting her when she becomes pregnant with Trevor's child, their rationale that she must be just like her mother, Sarah, reputedly the town whore, who died at the age of seventeen shortly after Freya was born. (Freya knows nothing about her mother until the end of the film.) Freya is even an outcast within her own family, for her adoptive parents clearly favor their own biological daughter.

To survive and transcend the mean-spirited school and community, Danny and Freya seek refuge in each other, using their vivid imaginations and their belief in the supernatural to create a rich, spiritual life that bonds them and reinforces their friendship, adding an enlightened new dimension to the teenage-centered genre. Throughout the course of the film, their mystical links are dramatized through mental telepathy and their keen perception of the "force field"—the traces left by humans in the material world—a concept taught to them by their adult friend Jonah (Bruce Spence). We are first aware of Danny and Freya's sense of existing on the same wavelength when Danny, in his room, draws the sun, and Freya, at home, draws a star. When they compare pictures later, Danny excitedly links the two creations, reasoning that since the sun is a star, then he and Freya share a special connection. Smiling knowingly, Freya declares thoughtfully, "I can't tell what I pick up telepathically, and what's on my own mind … or your mind."

Danny tries to take telepathy one step further through his humorous attempts to control Freya's behavior. He is frequently in the role of the third wheel with Freya and Trevor, and it is painful for him to see them making out in one of the cars Trevor steals or at the movies when Danny has the consolation date with Freya's younger sister. One night he longingly stares outside Freya's window as she undresses, hoping to get a peek at her naked body. Prefacing his request with an offer, "I promise to give it up on my next birthday," he asks politely, "Please God, help her not to the draw the curtain." When Freya drops the blinds, Danny comments, "I meant the blinds as well." A scene such as this comes across as quite touching as it reveals Danny's earnest innocence as well as his resolute nerve to invoke and bargain with the highest power for assistance.

Later in the film, Danny tries another tactic: hypnosis. Freya's relationship with Trevor has already advanced to sexual intimacy, but he has been sent away to juvenile hall for yet another car theft. Danny intends to take advantage of the situation and make another attempt to reach Freya and divert her passion away from Trevor and onto him. If they have the same thoughts, then why not mutual sexual desire? Like the aforementioned sequence, this scene balances humor with adolescent seriousness and angst. Freya good-naturedly humors Danny and agrees to go along with his scheme. Danny uses a method he has gleaned from one of his "how-to" books in his secret cache in his bedroom. He has Freya lie down on a flat rock in the bush, and goes through the ritual of swinging an object in front of her eyes, softly saying, "You are getting v-e-r-y tired." Once she is "out" (as she continues to indulge him), Danny goes to work, speaking as persuasively as he can: "When you come to, you'll be keen on me, and you'll want to make love to me … desperately." Unable to contain his curiosity any longer, he lifts up her dress to stare at her underpants. At this point, Freya "wakes up" and gives Danny a hard stare. He is completely ashamed and starts stammering, "I wasn't going to do anything, I wasn't … I didn't try to take anything off." Freya smiles and breaks out in good-humored laughter. In a voice-over, Danny comments, "If it would have been anyone else, the whole school would have been laughing at me. One thing about Freya, you could really trust her. You could tell her anything and she'd keep it to herself."

Though Danny's experiment is a failure, his feelings are protected, and most important, Freya does not betray him.

Jonah's theory of the force field inspires Danny and Freya to invoke a different spiritual order. Jonah is the thirtyish railway signalman and author, who lives in self-imposed seclusion in a railroad car away from town. Jonah functions as a prophet of sorts, and from Danny's perspective is certainly more accessible than God. One night Jonah explains the force field to Danny and Freya, that is, the "imprints" that human beings leave in the material world, such as the emotions of happiness, fear, or desire, which "hang in the air like a force field," as Jonah declares. To prove his point (and he is dead serious), Jonah comments, "When you're scared, your brain gives off fear, the fear hangs in the air, and sticks to the wall." He stops talking and suddenly yells loudly—and just as quickly he is silent. Jonah then inquires, "Did you feel it shooting out? That moment's hanging in the air like a *force field*." Wide-eyed, Freya and Danny stare at Jonah, their bodies leaning slightly backward, propelled by the energy in the air.

Later, back in town, Freya and Danny test out their newly acquired knowledge and more acutely tuned senses when they stand on main street in the middle of night. It is serenely quiet as they gaze at the high streetlight with hundreds of moths flurrying around the globe, reflecting the light. Freya softly queries, "Wonder if Mrs. O'Neal's around?" (Mrs. O'Neal is their senior friend who died a few days ago.) Freya continues, "They're all here." Danny replies, "I can feel them too, you know." They look all around them, sensing a force field of human traces, perhaps the soul of a departed and beloved friend. It is a magical moment. Not only are Freya and Danny in tune with each other as soul mates, but they are able to sense and share the intangible.

They have a similar experience at the "ghost house" on the hill, when they decide to spend the night there in order to overcome their deep-seated and long-standing fears of the abandoned dwelling. But this force field is one created by a kindred spirit. As they learned from Jonah, the Amery family lived there, in the 1940s, and a teenage Sarah Amery died in the house a few days after her baby was born. (Danny later figures out that the Amery woman was Freya's mother, a fact that he doesn't tell her until the end of the film.) Trevor comes along, eager to turn at least the first part of the evening into a time to have sex with Freya: Danny, as usual, is the third wheel. The rundown house is dusty, dark, and creepy. Danny lies on the couch on one side of the room, and Freya and Trevor rest on a mattress on the floor. After they all fall asleep, Danny and Freya wake up at exactly the same moment, making eye contact. This scene was preceded by a slow, retreating tracking shot which stopped at the edge of the living room, suggesting they were being observed. With his eyes looking up and around the room, Danny nervously says, "It's here, isn't it," prompting Freya's reply, "Something is." They both bolt from the house, with a sleepy Trevor, confused and half-dressed, running behind them. Standing outside, shivering, Danny declares, "It was there, inside the house. We felt it. It was there, something cold."

This sequence suggests the presence of Freya's mother's spirit (though Danny and Freya don't know it yet), which intrigues, yet scares them, and also further reinforces their strong ties. Duigan even suggests that Freya and Danny may be brother and sister; thus their spiritual bonds are based on blood ties. Danny's investigation into Freya's mother's past (he consults with the men at the pub, as well as his own reticent mother) leads him to his own father, who might have been one of her mother's lovers. To the credit of Danny's father, he is the only one who speaks kindly of Sarah. Like his father, and unlike the majority of the town's males, Danny's genteel sensibility sets him apart from their small-minded sexism.

Ultimately, the close ties between Danny and Freya, as well as her strong force field, draw Danny to her in a lifesaving move when she retreats to a remote part of the bush outside of town—a place she calls Windy Hill, their favorite meeting place.[6] Pregnant with Trevor's child, ostracized by her parents and the town, and deeply distressed, she miscarries. Bleeding profusely, she cries out in pain.[7] Danny, in his room at home, senses her distress and intuits that she is in trouble, and immediately runs to find and help her.

Though critically ill, Freya survives, and with a renewed strength and outlook, she makes the decision to leave town alone to start a new life elsewhere. Though she and Danny will be separated physically, they agree to continue their mental telepathy "on Monday nights," as he notes in a touching farewell scene at the train station. After her departure, Danny returns to Windy Hill to comfort himself, but more important, to capture Freya's spirit and force field, which enriches his own. He wistfully comments, "Part of *us* was still there."

Flirting

In *Flirting*, Danny, now seventeen, explores a thrilling and risky relationship with a young African woman, Thandiwe (Thandiwe Newton), in an even more restrictive, repressive, and cruel environment than the insular town in *The Year*

My Voice Broke. Both Danny and Thandiwe are outsiders at their respective British-modeled, all-white boarding schools, St. Albins for young men[8] and Cirencester for young women. Danny hails from the boondocks and is the designated school "dag"; Thandiwe, from Uganda, is proud and worldly, and is initially looked down upon by her classmates. Her friendship with Danny helps him to mature intellectually and become enlightened politically.

In the three-year interim since *The Year My Voice Broke*, Danny has grown considerably. First, he is more literate, with his favorite authors being Sartre and Camus. Secondly, he is also more confident, for despite a newly acquired stutter, he has developed a thicker skin as well as a poker face to help him weather the taunts and insults hurled at him. Thirdly, he is determined to maintain his individuality, demonstrated on one level by his long and shaggy hairstyle, which contrasts to the regulation shorter, neatly combed cuts of the other young men. Ultimately, Danny bucks the system by meeting Thandiwe secretly, which culminates in their spending the night in a hotel together. Rather than being relegated to "neutral" role of brother (as he was to Freya), Danny actively becomes Thandiwe's lover—if only for a short time.

Though Danny is immediately taken by Thandiwe's beauty and poise when they first meet, their initial mutual attraction also rests on their shared subversive, antiestablishment attitudes, which allude to the antiauthoritarian, 1960s time frame. This is cleverly demonstrated early in the film when they participate in a debate involving both schools on the following topic—"Intellectual pursuits as the highest form of human behavior." With heavy irony, Danny extols rugby as the "highest human endeavor." And Duigan goes to great pains to show later what a brutal and animalistic sport the game is when the St. Albins team plays another school. The carnal violence is a turn-on for cheering audiences. During the debate, when it is her turn to speak, Thandiwe selects the rock and roll song, "Tutti Frutti," co-written by the African American pop singer, Little Richard, deviating unflinchingly from the confines of the debate topic and adding her own cultural spin. She does a stunning and seductive poetic rendition of it, turning the whole debate into a celebration of black female sexuality. Thandiwe brings down the house to the delight of the students, and garners Danny's admiration. Predictably, their uptight teachers are horrified, and one of them accuses a clearly bemused Thandiwe of insolently reducing the occasion "to a gutter level."

For St. Albins as well as Cirencester, people from Africa as well as their politics are way beyond the students' frame of reference; their attitudes and initial racist reactions to Thandiwe show the ethnocentrism and prejudices of the

British-modeled education system as well as Australia's historical geographical isolation, revealing white Australia's "fear of the dark," to use Lola Young's term. The film's 1960s time frame reflects a decade heralding bold nationalistic movements all over Africa, not just Uganda. Significantly, Duigan foregrounds Australia's changing status to a more worldly country by positioning Thandiwe's father, a scholar and political activist, as a guest lecturer in University at Canberra.

As compared to Freya, deemed an outcast and a scapegoat, Thandiwe, though isolated upon her arrival, slowly and remarkably has a liberating and enlightening effect on the students from both schools, especially the young women of Cirencester, who come to accept and respect her. For instance, after Thandiwe arrives, the young women haughtily identify her as an African specimen as she sleeps. One snidely comments, "Anyone got a banana?" However, Thandiwe reworks and slings back their racist taunts while also revealing her classmates' insularity and ignorance of world affairs. While she listens to a television broadcast covering the arrival of the first US troops in Vietnam (where Australia also sent troops as part of its Asian–Pacific commitments), two of the young women, who ignore the broadcast, rudely increase the volume of their rock and roll music. Thandiwe turns it down. Miffed, they turn it back up. On her way out of the room, Thandiwe bumps the table, disrupting the music, commenting sassily, "Oh, I slipped on a banana!"

In a humorous vein, Thandiwe's presence causes male hysteria in the boys' shower. She is determined to see Danny after the notorious debate, but he is denied dance privileges because he refuses to cut his hair. Thandiwe leaves the dance, and boldly climbs up the wall of one of the buildings at the boys' school, appearing outside the window during his class. Startled, one of the boys comments, "There's an Abo in the window," reinforcing his unsophisticated and clumsy uni-grouping of all people with black skin. (Several of the boys also condescendingly refer to Thandiwe as "lubra" lips, lubra a derogatory term for an Aboriginal woman.) When Danny and Thandiwe do meet up, they retreat to his dorm for a chat. To avoid being seen by the large group of boys heading toward the shower, they hide in a stall (fully clothed) within the shower area. When one young man looks under the door, he is so shocked to see Thandiwe standing there that he screams: the rest of the boys flee the shower when they all see the "alien" intruder. Within minutes, rumors fly that Thandiwe was completely nude in the shower, implying the perceived threat of a foreign, black, female body which the boys sexualize. Accordingly, one nervous young man comments, "They can be pretty desperate these black women … Look at

National Geographic!" Significantly, the boy who spotted Danny and Thandiwe in the shower also coughs up the water he was going to spit on them. This convulsive "full body hysteria" in the presence of a woman is consistent with Danny's "nausea," when he and Thandiwe meet outside on the boys' school grounds. He tells his instructor that he is throwing up in the bushes to avoid raising suspicion. Thandiwe's presence, like that of women in the ocker films (the cause of similar cases of body hysteria, as when Stork vomits in the presence of Anna), suggests a strong male fear of females and female sexuality. In this case Thandiwe is a double threat because of her color, though Danny clearly does not share his classmates' uncouth opinions. His awe of and attraction to Thandiwe only intensifies.

Despite his respect for Thandiwe, Danny's perception of Africans and the dark continent can be as primitive as that of his classmates. As he admits in voice-over, his only frame of reference has been old comic books and Tarzan movies where people with black skin were depicted as "cannibals with bones through their noses." For example, during the scene where he looks over an antiquated book about the jungle, we hear a deliberately clichéd soundtrack of jungle sounds—drums, whooping, even Tarzan's wild yodel. Through a series of dissolves we see Tarzan, white hunters, Africans, and wild African animals—crocodiles, hippos, leopards—the implication that Africans are savages too, hardly human. Danny realizes how limited his outlook on the rest of the world has been in the context of his Western education and upbringing. In subsequent talks with Thandiwe, Danny learns about the new age of nationalism throughout Africa. She personalizes it, sadly admitting that her mother was killed during the Mau Mau period in Kenya. Even though Danny is eager to learn about "the dark continent," and listens intently to Thandiwe, he does confess in a subsequent voice-over that he is distracted by the pleasures of her body. Rather than fear of the dark, he is all but overwhelmingly entranced by it. Thus, while Thandiwe talks about history and politics, Danny's eyes wander to her legs. Nonetheless, this sequence is crucial in Danny's education, for the seeds are planted for his political activism: later in the film, he contacts several Australian government officials on Thandiwe's behalf after she disappears in Uganda, acutely afraid that her life is in danger.

Danny undergoes crucial rites of passage into manhood in two subsequent key sequences: one public, the brutal boxing match with his classmate Bourke (Josh Picker); the other private, when he and Thandiwe go to bed together. The boxing match is a culmination of all his pent-up resentment at being taunted and picked on, which now has been mobilized and channeled into an aggressive fury in the name of an old-fashioned, chivalric cause—defending Thandiwe's privacy. The gauntlet was thrown down earlier when Bourke seized and read Thandiwe's letters to Danny out loud, to the delight of the other boys. Danny charged and attacked Bourke, furious with this invasion of his privacy. In this instance, which sets the stage for the boxing bout, Danny pushes Bourke to the floor in order to prevent him from photographing Thandiwe and the other young women—in their underwear—on the other side of the wall that separates the two sexes. Bourke just happens to be the premier boxer in the school, and as for Danny, he probably has never put on a pair of boxing gloves.

The subsequent fight takes on all the pageantry of a world-class sports competition, with the school population noisily rallying behind Bourke, who is buffed and fit, and a good fifteen pounds heavier than the lanky Danny. While his minions watch reverently, Bourke pumps up for the match by repeatedly whacking a punching bag. On the day of the match, it appears that the whole school has emptied out of the classrooms to fill up the gym. With his slight frame, underdog Danny is introduced as the "poofter" and "flea weight," but he energetically and aggressively propels himself from his corner, swinging fast and furious, successfully landing some hard punches onto Bourke's torso. Like his idol, the American boxing champion, Cassius Clay, Danny is light and confident on his feet, jumping spryly. He even appears to identify with Clay, for we see Clay's competitor, Sonny Liston, in a menacing pose facing the camera, and by implication Danny, as the boys chant, "Son-ny Lis-ton, Son-ny Lis-ton." (Clay won the heavyweight boxing championship from Liston in 1964.) However, Danny is no match for "raging bull" Bourke, who overpowers him in a few rounds. He knocks Danny out with a punch that sends Danny flying helplessly to the mat.

Yet despite his defeat, it is clear that the attitude of Danny's classmates has changed from one of mockery to one of quiet respect. They do not leave immediately as instructed by referee upperclassman, Jock, but linger, clearly showing deference for a fallen comrade. Danny even draws admiration from Bourke himself, who defends Danny later at dinner (and compliments his virility) when one of the boys comments, "Embling scored last night with Lubra Lips" (in reference to Danny's first date with Thandiwe). Bourke fires back, "Shut up, you wouldn't know what scoring was."

In comparison to the boxing match—crowded, noisy, raucous, and violent—Danny's night with Thandiwe is quiet, calm, and intimate. The air in their hotel room tingles with anticipation and desire, as Rossini's lyrical and mischievous "Thieving Magpies" plays on the soundtrack. The two shyly drink their champagne, smiling nervously at each other. Later, they huddle in bed, embracing tenderly as Danny gently kisses Thandiwe. Their bed appears suspended in space. They float intimately and pleasurably on their own private planet, if only for a few hours.

Predictably, Danny is expelled from school and sent home, a welcome and more relaxed change from the regimentation of the school, though he is separated from Thandiwe, who has been summoned home to Africa. His rural existence is in stark contrast to the world that Thandiwe has been plunged into—chaos and terrorism in Uganda thousands of miles away where Idi Amin has taken over as military dictator. Tragically, Thandiwe's father, who was critical of the regime, has been assassinated; worse, her stepmother has disappeared. Danny can only imagine the horrors—the riots and killings—that are presented in documentary footage that presumably he has seen from television. He is so intertwined with Thandiwe's world that he imagines her in a car about to be attacked by an armed terrorist.

As he did when he tried to hypnotize Freya, Danny summons up all his telepathic powers and "wills" Thandiwe to be in a "safe haven." But rather than expressing an adolescent yearning, this time Danny proactively immerses himself in a young woman's life-and-death crisis, demonstrating his growing political consciousness that extends beyond Australian shores: he writes to key government officials in Australia asking for their assistance to come to her aid. A younger, less mature Danny from *The Year My Voice Broke* would not have had the confidence to do this. To his immense relief, Danny eventually receives a letter from Thandiwe, and she reassures him that she is away from harm, living in Nairobi. Through her sad and weary voice-over, Thandiwe confesses that she is not the impetuous and carefree young woman that she once was. She has lost both her parents, as well as her home and country. Nevertheless, Danny's fears are eased, and he feels her kindred spirit near. He exclaims, "Suddenly, there were much bigger worlds again and some small place in them for me."

Through their unconventional, unique, and distinctive males, John Duigan and Paul Cox open up new realms of Australian masculinity that go beyond the revival's more well-known men. For Duigan, teenage angst is tempered by pleasures and thrills that ease a teenager's passage into young adulthood; for Cox, life-changing, middle-age Oedipal crises deeply impact and challenge troubled men. Both filmmakers explore characters' complex inner lives—their emotional and psychological landscapes—in the context of insular, working-class towns and boarding schools, on the one hand, and middle-class suburbs and the world of the arts—drama, painting, popular and classical music—on the other. Viewers come to know characters' hearts and minds quite intimately, gaining access to a fuller picture of Australian masculinity.

Notes

1   Rabinowicz, 1985, 85.
2   Trenbow, a psychiatrist on the cutting edge of mental health after the First World War, practices at a turbulent time in Australia's history when the country is fractured over an allegiance to Britain versus an isolationist stance. Despondent over attacks not only on his Freudian principles but also on his belief in protectionist politics, Trenbow becomes increasingly alienated from family and friends.
3   This opera by Donizetti features a woman, Lucia, who is betrothed to Arturo, whom she does not love, in an arranged marriage. However, she is madly in love with Edgardo. Lucia is a woman caught between two males, just as Charles' mother is.
4   The flip side of an adored mother is conjured up by Charles' psychiatrist, drolly played by Bob Ellis. The psychiatrist clearly resents his mother, referring to her as a "bitch." Further, his professional ethics are in question, for he overcharges a very trusting and naïve Charles. All in all, the psychiatrist does very little counseling. The only other male with whom Charles communicates is the delightfully eccentric postman who quits his job, much to Charles' chagrin.
5   Gillian Armstrong's *The Last Days of Chez Nous* (1992) explores familial tensions in the midst of anger, resentment, and pain, but in a more repressed atmosphere.
6   Freya holds a deep respect for nature. As Danny comments in voice-over at the film's beginning, she regards every tree, every rock, etc., as living entities. Indeed, Freya is furious with Danny for hunting rabbits, and makes him promise that he will not do it again. Her bond with Nature conjures up the Dreamtime/Dreamings, the Aboriginal creation myth that living spirits who created all material entities/artifacts are inherent in every aspect of nature: the land, skies, water, animals, etc. All of these elements are "alive" in the sense that they are inhabited by ancient spirits. Freya uses Windy Hill as her retreat where she is at home with the eternal

spirits. Jonah links the Dreamtime/Dreamings to his concept of the force field. In his usual succinct manner, he tells Danny, "The Abos know all about it."

7   In his review of *The Year My Voice Broke*, Raffaele Caputo notes a strong connection with the Demeter/Persephone myth. He notes, "This subplot of an absent mother having some mythical influence on the community through her daughter strongly parallels the myth of Persephone and Demeter in reverse. Instead of the absent daughter influencing the life of the mother and her community, the absent mother impacts the life of her daughter and her community." (See Caputo's review in Murray, 1993, 237.)

8   Duigan notes, "I drew a great deal from my years living in a country town in Victoria, and the two schools in *Flirting* are loosely based on Geelong College and its sister school, Morongo. We staged plays with Morongo, and in fact my initial interest in theater was boosted by the opportunity it gave to meet girls. In those days, schools like Geelong College were arguably even more brutal than the school depicted in the film. Caning was a day-to-day occurrence. There really was a teacher who put chalk on his cane so he could try to repeatedly strike the same mark … As in many schools, there was an on-going, merciless persecution of anybody who was remotely different, either in looks, temperament, disposition or personality—anyone who was an eccentric was a prime target." (See Caputo and Burton, 1999, 18–19.)

Sources

Barber, Susan (2009), "Affairs of the Heart: The Oedipal Films of Paul Cox," *Metro*, 163: 130–4.

Barber, Susan (2011), "Growing Up in the 1960s: The Year My Voice Broke and Flirting," *Australian Screen*, 62: 100–11.

Caputo, Raffaele (1993), "The Year My Voice Broke," in Scott Murray (ed.), *Australian Film 1978–1992: A Survey of Theatrical Features*, Melbourne: Oxford University Press.

Caputo, Raffaele and Geoff Burton, eds (1999), *Second Take: Australian Film-makers Talk*, Sydney: Allen and Unwin.

Cox, Paul (1998), *Reflections, An Autobiographical Journey*, Sydney: Currency Press.

Greenwood, Helen (1983), "*Man of Flowers*," *Cinema Papers*, March–April.

Haywood, Susan (1996), *Key Concepts in Film Studies*, London: Routledge.

Mulvey, Laura (1977), "Visual Pleasure and Narrative Cinema," in Karyn Kay and Gerald Peary (eds), *Women and the Cinema: A Critical Anthology*, New York: E.P. Dutton, 412–28.

Murray, Scott, ed. (1993), *Australian Film 1978-1992: A Survey of Theatrical Features*, Melbourne: Oxford University Press.

Rabinowicz, Les (1985), "Australian Film Industry Profile: Paul Cox," *Metro*, 66: 16.

Spence, Nigel and Leah McGirr (2001), "Unhappy Endings: The Heterosexual Dynamic in Australian Film," in Ian Craven (ed.), *Australian Cinema in the 1990s*, London: Frank Cass Publishers, 37–56.

Young, Lola (1996), *Fear of the Dark: "Race," Gender and Sexuality in the Cinema*, London: Routledge.

3

Historical Women and the Bush

Picnic at Hanging Rock (1975), *The Getting of Wisdom* (1977), and *My Brilliant Career* (1979), all set at the turn of the century, are key films for three reasons. First, with their strong, independently minded, and progressive female characters, these films challenged the male-centered ocker films made in the first part of the decade, while also providing a female counterpart to *Gallipoli* (1981), *Breaker Morant* (1980), and *Between Wars* (1974), which featured historical men. Secondly, these films present and explore the Australian bush as a complex, vibrant "character," which is organic to the narrative and which has strong bonds with the female protagonists. Thirdly, these female protagonists can be considered prototypes for modern young women in films of the 1980s, 1990s, and into the new millennium.

The time frames of these films all allude to Federation (1901), when Australia achieved a greater measure of independence from Britain (in the wake of a strong decade of nationalism in the 1890s), thus providing a context for the female protagonists who seek to break away from repressive social orders: a British-modeled young women's school (*Picnic, Wisdom*) or marriage as the only life choice for a respectable woman (*Career*). Further, with their proactive females, these films resonate in the wake of the women's movement in the 1960s, which gave women more equal footing in Australia's traditionally patriarchal society.

As noted in the introduction, films set in the past, or "period films," were labeled the "AFC genre" by Susan Dermody and Elizabeth Jacka. The AFC, or Australian Film Commission, was the new name for the restructured and expanded former Australian Film Development Corporation (1970–5), and was the principal government funding body from 1975 to 1981, which financed in whole or in part many of the period films. *Picnic* was not funded by the AFC, but was in the spirit of the Commission's newly defined goals. These included "quality" filmmaking (versus the primarily commercial aims of the AFDC) intended for overseas as well as local markets, and exuding international standards: sophistication in narrative, imagery, and sound design. *Picnic* was an extraordinary success abroad as well as at home, giving the AFC, filmmakers, and Australians a sense of pride in their films and the burgeoning industry. Over the next several years, a total of twenty-eight films set in Australia's past were made, including *Wisdom* and *Career*.

However, many of these films were criticized for featuring "bland" characters and encouraging "gentle nostalgia" (Dermody and Jacka, 1988, 33–4). Dermody and Jacka further comment, "The cinematography is dedicated to the glories of Australian light, landform and vegetation, often with clear traces of a romantic, even charm-school, Australian post-impressionism. The approach of the camera is functional rather than expressive" (Dermody and Jacka, 1988, 33–4). Moreover, these films were stuck in an idealized past, as Graeme Turner implies: "The Australia most of these films mythologized was defined by its landscape and by its colonial history rather than the complex contemporary realities of an urban, middle class post-colonial 'multicultural' society" (Turner, 1989, 115). Neil Rattigan, specifically referring to *My Brilliant Career*, alludes to the assumed superficial quality of period films: "teetering dangerously close to being little more than a stunningly beautiful film that gives visual pleasure but not much intellectual substance" (Rattigan, 1991, 221). However, these criticisms overlooked and undervalued vibrant, dynamic, and complex women—Miranda and Sara in *Picnic*, Laura in *Wisdom*, and Sybylla in *Career*. Further, the bush is a far more multidimensional entity than these writers and others have acknowledged.

This chapter seeks to re-evaluate these films using two models, drawing from Liz Ferrier's "Vulnerable Bodies: Creative Disabilities in Contemporary Australia," and Kay Schaffer's *Women and the Bush: Forces of Desire in the Australian Cultural Tradition*. First, Ferrier's model, based on her analysis of 1980s and 1990s films, identifies "an embattled artistic individual, suffering from a disability or difference which isolates him or her socially, [and who] manages to find solace and ultimately social recognition through creative performance and self-expression" (Ferrier, 2001, 58), usually before large audiences (Ferrier, 2001, 60).[1] According to Ferrier, this disability can be physical and/or psychological; further, the individual can also be disadvantaged because he/she is a social outcast. Moreover, "[t]hese characters are stigmatized because of their eccentricity or difference from the norm" (Ferrier, 2001, 67). With these criteria, Ferrier's model facilitates a new and illuminating level of analysis for 1970s female protagonists.

Secondly, Schaffer develops her model through an analysis of literature and historical accounts of exploration and settlement in the larger context of

Australia's patriarchal culture. She argues that the Australian land/landscape or "bush" has traditionally been perceived as the body of a woman, a feminized entity which is essential to the construction of Australian male identity. She argues, "[T]he land as an object virtually always is represented as feminine. It functions as a metaphor for woman—as in father sky to mother earth, colonial master to the plains of promise, native son to the barren bush. ... All of these equations reproduce the 'perfect' couple, masculine activity/feminine passivity" (Schaffer, 1988, 14). *Picnic*, *Wisdom*, and *Career* problematize this ideology, using the bush in highly expressive and dynamic ways in the construction of female identity (though not to the total exclusion of male identity). Using Kay Schaffer's model as a launching point in *Picnic*, I examine the relationship between the featured women and their bush environments in *Wisdom* and *Career*.

This chapter addresses these questions. In what ways does the creative disabilities/vulnerable bodies model give us greater insight into the films' featured female characters? What is the nature of the relationship between female protagonists and the bush? At the end of my analysis of these three films, I include a section on *The Man from Snowy River* (1982) and *"Crocodile" Dundee* (1986), films that restore male mastery of the bush, as if in response to those featuring historical women and the bush. Finally, I conclude by discussing two modern women in *Muriel's Wedding* (1994) and *Sweetie* (1989) with respect to Ferrier's and Schaffer's models.

Picnic at Hanging Rock

Picnic at Hanging Rock (directed by Peter Weir, written by Cliff Green, and based on the novel by Joan Lindsay) opens on Valentine's Day 1900, at Appleyard College, a boarding school for young women who honor the occasion to exchange their love tokens before taking off for a picnic one sunny afternoon at Hanging Rock, a towering and looming presence. While the others nap, read, and observe the pastoral landscape, four of the young women, Miranda (Anne-Louise Lambert), Marion (Jane Vallis), Irma (Karen Robson), and Edith (Christine Schuler), leave their classmates to scale and explore the rock. As the afternoon wanes, all but Edith disappear into one of rock's crevasses. Though Irma is eventually located unconscious on the rock, Miranda and Marion are never found. Throughout the film, Miranda's roommate Sara (Margaret Nelson) keeps a lonely vigil for her beloved.

Sara fits Ferrier's model in intriguing ways. She suffers from a disability *and* difference. Her disability is her frailness, as evidenced by her slender body and pale complexion. Given her sickly appearance, she could be in the throes of an unidentified illness. Sara is timid, reclusive, and shrinks away from social interaction with the other women—except Miranda—suggesting a *social* disability. This can be partly explained by her "difference." She is an orphan, the only one at a boarding school which is populated by young women from privileged families. Sara can also be considered an embattled artist. She writes her own poetry, yet does not have an appreciative audience. We think that she may have a chance to read her verses out loud when Headmistress Mrs. Appleyard (Rachel Roberts) prompts her to recite on the day of the picnic. Appleyard has kept Sara behind for unknown reasons, a decision which reinforces Sara's isolation and difference even more. Sara, holding her head high, states that the work is her own when Appleyard asks for the name of the author. Sara's "passionate ... expression" (Ferrier, 2001, 57) of her Australian creativity fuels Appleyard's contempt and only intensifies when Sara refuses to read any poems by British authors, those which Mrs. Appleyard strongly favors. Appleyard's treatment of Sara creates a bizarre British warden/Australian colonial prisoner dynamic, conjuring up Australia's early days at the end of the eighteenth century as a colony lorded over by British authoritarians.

Sara's naturally withdrawn nature becomes obsessive, reinforcing "the motifs of isolation and incarceration" that Ferrier identifies. Clearly, Mrs. Appleyard recognizes and preys upon Sara's infirmities. Her patronizing and increasingly cruel treatment of Sara increases as the days go by and the missing women have not been found. It is clear that in this oppressive institution lorded over by a matron who enjoys tormenting her, Sara will never have an opportunity to perform for her classmates or receive any recognition for her poetry. Haunted by Miranda's inexplicable disappearance, Sara stops eating and spends her days in bed in her room surrounded by pictures of her. Sara's "performance" is committing suicide, throwing herself out her bedroom window late one night, smashing through the greenhouse glass below to her death. Her whole body appears to be impaled on the branches of the shrubs in the greenhouse, which could be a crude rendition of how she imagines Miranda's fate in the wild. This shocking and self-destructive act suggests that she gives up, "powerless in the face of natural and social forces" (Ferrier, 2001, 64). Her choice, however, differs from that of Miranda, Marion, and Irma, who are entranced by the rock, obsessively climbing and investigating its exteriors and interiors.

How does Sara's tragic death in the greenhouse "bush" compare with Miranda's unknown destiny in the bush, and more specifically, Hanging Rock? For Miranda and the others, the looming monolithic and mysterious rock that soars above the pastoral bush connotes, on one level, a strong masculine presence. Meaghan Morris comments on the rock's "strange and phallic force of nature" (Morris, 1980, 143), a power that hypnotizes and seduces the women, who find it irresistible as they explore its planes and crevices. At one point, Miranda, Marion, and Irma remove their stockings and walk barefoot, suggesting that tactile contact affords them even more pleasure. Miranda and Irma swing and sway as if in an erotic trance, amidst the eerie yet sensual sound of flutes (adapted from Jules Mouquet's "La Flute de Pan").

Yet, on the other hand, the rock connotes a feminine presence. The proximity of the young women to the rock suggests "passive, pliant virgin[s]" (Schaffer, 1988, 62), imbuing it with a different sexual charge, reinforced as the women are observed with strong interest and desire by both Michael (Dominic Guard), the young British man, and Albert (John Jarratt), his Australian steward. They gaze voyeuristically at the women, who become objects of their desire. Albert comments that Miranda's long legs go all the way "up to her bum," prompting Michael to chide him for his crudeness, but also alluding to Michael's probable thoughts. Along the line of the feminine, and with respect to Michael, the rock also implies the maternal, according to Schaffer. In this particular context, she incorporates a psychoanalytic approach in assigning to the rock a pre-Oedipal role, or "maternal omnipotence" (Schaffer, 1988, 56). Thus, the primal, pre-Oedipal mother can "[absorb] its inhabitants, [and assimilate] them into its cavernous, contours" (Schaffer, 1988, 52).

According to Schaffer's analysis of *Picnic*, the film "engages [Michael] and the viewer in a primal scene of seduction between mother and child, outside the constraints of the Father's Law" (Schaffer, 1988, 55–6). She describes how this dynamic is enacted through Michael, who watches the young women approach the rock. After they disappear, he attempts to climb the rock himself in search of Miranda in particular, who has completely enthralled him. Schaffer adds, "For Michael, and through him the audience, the desire for woman [Miranda] merges with a desire for meaning which in turn merges with the desire for a fixed self" (Schaffer, 1988, 55). Schaffer continues, "Man's identity, which might be secured heroically by his possession and control of the land [linked to Miranda] as a primary object of desire ... [is] called into doubt by the threat of the bush as a form of the monstrous feminine" (Schaffer, 1988, 62): the pre-Oedipal rock which absorbs the young women. Thus the film reinforces the double role of the bush as a feminized entity, the presence of the young women who scale the rock, *and* a pre-Oedipal presence. Since the women disappear, "the bush is both no place for a woman" (Schaffer, 1988, 52), as it presents a danger to the young women, and, at the same time, "the place of ... Woman" (Schaffer, 1988, 56)—the embodiment of the maternal. By assimilating the women, "[t]he bush obstructs man's [and Michael's] possession and mastery of the girls, of logical narrative meaning and a coherent self-identity" (Schaffer, 1988, 55). Hence, after his rescue from the rock by Albert, a clearly distracted and distraught Michael spends his days obsessing about Miranda amidst an imagined pastoral bush, conjuring up daydreams of her.

A different interpretation of Michael's quest suggests that, "Oedipus like," as Schaffer notes (Schaffer, 1988, 55), he seeks unity with the maternal himself. His rejection, however—he is found on a ledge by Albert—implies that he does not merge with the rock, suggesting on the cultural level, apart from the psychoanalytic, that the British interloper must remain separate from the bush, which is irresistible and strongly linked to Miranda. The rock and by implication Miranda *resist* him. Britain/Michael cannot define itself/himself in terms of the feminized colony Australia anymore.[2] The rock amidst the wild bush/Australia is too formidable, too dangerous, and too independent.

Along this line, and continuing the cultural context, the film implies that the fearless and courageous Miranda and her classmate Marion, who disappear into the rock, never to be found, escape British control by entering and merging with the rock, thereby "leaping" into the twentieth century, becoming a vital part of a "brave new world" (Roginski, 1979, 24)—Australia in the new millennium. Their merging with the rock is linked to their enlightenment and rebirth. They have found their place in the bush. Notably, before she left to go on the picnic, visionary leader Miranda told Sara that she would be leaving the school, implying that a more important and crucial destiny was elsewhere. She is accompanied by the curious and precocious Marion, who is fascinated right away with the rock's geology, leaving the others below to inspect and take measurements of the rock. These brave, extraordinary women form a vital and vibrant foundation of a new Australia. In this case the rock as the place of women gives them transcendence into a new identity and role. Obviously, Miranda, unlike Sara, is not disabled or vulnerable in any way. When she leads the others in climbing the rock in prior extended sequences, her grace and poise suggest a hypnotic ballet. Her lyrical movements are mirrored in one of the film's final images as she waves, smiling and confident. She/Australia are free of the shackles of imposing, oppressive

British rule (clearly embodied by Mrs. Appleyard). Sadly, her roommate Sara, frail and heartsick, sought her own form of escape, but her merging with the bush—a leap or fall into the greenhouse—extinguished her life. The other death-in-the-bush, that of the imperialistic Mrs. Appleyard, implies that there is no place in the Australian bush for her/her British-modeled institution which faces closure, due to the disappearance of the young women, which fueled the growing reputation of the school as an unsafe institution. Mrs. Appleyard is found dead at the base of the rock, as we learn in voice-over, suggesting that she, like Michael, was cast out.

In *The Getting of Wisdom* and *My Brilliant Career*, the bush, absent an enigmatic and protean rock, will take on an array of different roles for its proactive and self-empowering young women, Laura and Sybylla (respectively).

The Getting of Wisdom

Rather than a solemn drama foregrounding the mystery and power of the bush, which impacts a British-modeled boarding school, contributing to its decline, but more important, heralds a new age for Australia, *Wisdom* (directed by Bruce Beresford, written by Eleanor Witcombe, based on the novel by Henry Handel Richardson), with its strongly satirical edge, focuses on the politics of the upper-crust female society of an elitist boarding school, a Presbyterian Ladies College. The title is pointedly ironic, as little academic learning takes place. *Wisdom* could even be regarded as a parody of the idealized female student population in *Picnic*, where classmates are bonded in love and harmony. By contrast, in *Wisdom*, the atmosphere is frequently mean-spirited and disagreeable. Further, the bush is not an imposing and formidable, androgynous primal "character" embodied in a formidable rock as dramatized in *Picnic*. It is a "civilized," even neutralized, entity surrounding and linked to the oppressive school. Yet the bush functions as an environment ripe for Laura (Susannah Fowle) to appropriate. Rather than being conquered or transformed by the bush, Laura learns to use it to her own creative advantage as she plays out the power of her imagination.

Like Sara, Laura exudes an adolescent awkwardness, immaturity, and stubbornness. However, Laura (age thirteen) has a much stronger constitution than Sara, and is far more assertive, with a tough hide to boot. Whereas Sara is an orphan, Laura has been raised by a loving and decent mother, who has saved every penny to send her to boarding school. Laura is clearly gifted intellectually and artistically, attributes which separate her from many of the rest of the girls, and which initially "disadvantage" her, to use Ferrier's term. She even skips two grades after only being in the school for one term. Yet she must survive in a population that thrives on mediocrity and pettiness, and ruthlessly cuts down the tall poppies. Anyone who is a show-off, as her first roommate Lilith (Kim Deacon) labels Laura, is not behaving like a lady (that is, someone who knows her place in the school hierarchy). Whereas Sara in *Picnic* has only one chance to express herself in the recitation of her own poetry, Laura's passionate "compulsive creative pursuit" (Ferrier, 2001, 60) is embodied in her many "performances" throughout the film—playing the piano, doing literary recitations, and even writing creatively. Fueled by her vivid imagination, she concocts a romance with Reverend Shepherd (John Waters), complete with love letters that she recites in front of her classmates. Laura succeeds in the school on her own terms—which includes cheating on her final exams,[3] and at the end of the film she receives a full musical scholarship to study abroad in Europe.

Laura's first encounter with the magisterial school is a daunting and solemn experience. Upon her arrival, she meets the authoritarian, scowling, and scolding Headmistress Mrs. Gurley (Sheila Helpmann), who makes Mrs. Appleyard downright pleasant by comparison. If Mrs. Gurley's curt reprimands are not enough, Laura shortly faces the gauntlet of a group of snooty girls who instantly prey upon her. However, she demonstrates right away that she can thrive in this caustic atmosphere where the vocation of one's father and material wealth is paramount. Laura has neither; her father is deceased, and she harks from modest surroundings in a remote bush town where her mother makes ends meet as post mistress and seamstress. To add to her oddness and nonconformity, Laura, like Sara, sports girlish pigtails (the rest of the students wear their hair stylishly long or meticulously coiffed), and a garishly bright red, homemade dress, with a large, floppy matching hat, while the rest of the young women wear white or pastel pinafores. When Laura meets the onslaught of her haughty, self-possessed, aristocratic schoolmates, they immediately start making fun of her name. "Rambotham" becomes "Ramsbottom" or "Ramsbum." One uppity young woman demands, "How many servants do *you* have," and another queries, "What's your father," as they look down their noses at her. But right away Laura is on her toes and gives as good as she takes, taking on a girl who demands, "What's your name, what's your father?" with a quick and aggressive retort,

"What's *yours?*" Her nimbleness even prompts one of the girls to say, "Not bad, Tweedledum" (Tweedle is Laura's middle name).

Laura's piano playing in public and private throughout the film is absolutely crucial in the development of her self-confidence and the maturation of her talent. Her inaugural public playing takes place at the home of Reverend Strachey (Barry Humphries), who has requested "cultural offerings" from the group of girls who attend. Laura, deeming this piece a break away from the "dull things they teach us here," enthusiastically plays Thalberg's arrangement of "Home, Sweet, Home," expressing an "exhilarating but undisciplined delight in her powers," as McFarlane has noted (1983, 66).

Laura's favorite piece is Schubert's "Impromptu," which is linked to private and public performances, and which is intertwined with her evolving passion toward an upper-class woman, Evelyn (Hilary Ryan). The "Impromptu" is the piece that they play together at the beginning of the second term. Laura, more sure of herself, serves as a teacher for Evelyn by helping her learn the composition, which Evelyn deems too difficult. By her deft example, Laura shows Evelyn the proper way to approach the music, and it bonds them in a deliriously sensual moment. Evelyn becomes a gentle and supportive maternal figure for Laura, and they later become roommates upon Evelyn's invitation, as well as constant companions. Evelyn eases Laura through some of her fears about growing up, providing her with wisdom in the best sense. For example, Laura listens in on a heated discussion among several of the girls on her floor about the horrors of childbirth as they gorge on sweets stolen from the kitchen, fueling what could be called Laura's sexual and reproductive terror. Clearly distraught, Laura confides later to Evelyn, "I *won't* let men do that to me. I *won't* get married. I *won't* have babies!" Evelyn calmly puts things in perspective, appropriately deeming the girls "little monsters," adding, "Don't you think boys are just as afraid of us?"

However, as Laura becomes more enamored of Evelyn, she (Laura) exhibits downright cruel behavior in her overbearing possessiveness of Evelyn. For example, at the opera, Laura becomes openly jealous of Jim, a friend of Evelyn's and of whom Evelyn is quite fond. On the way home, Laura is resentful and short with Evelyn, accusing her of paying too much attention to Jim. An evening that was to have celebrated their mutual appreciation of music and friendship becomes one marred by Laura's immature spite and reproaches, leading to the eventual rupture of their bond.

It is not long before Evelyn decides to withdraw from the college, not only because of the school's repressive atmosphere but, more important, Laura's increasingly hostile clinginess. As Evelyn declares to Laura, "You are suffocating me." On the day that Evelyn leaves for good and comes to say goodbye, Laura ignores her, compulsively playing the piano, her eyes intently focused on the keys as she shuts out the real world, playing "from her head," and repressing her heart (and hurt feelings) through the music. This alludes to the scene where the two played together earlier. At that time, Evelyn noted, quoting Miss Hicks the music teacher, that she (Evelyn) "played only from the heart," whereas Laura "played only from the head" (suggesting Laura's mental fortitude and intelligence). But this duet scene also implied that Laura was pouring her passion for Evelyn into her beautiful and lyrical playing. Now she can only play solo in her silent misery, using her mental resolve to mask the deep pain that Evelyn's departure causes.

Ferrier notes, "Success, when achieved, is the product of impractical, passionate self-expression, rather than pragmatism" (Ferrier, 2001, 60). Laura's performance on graduation day, when she receives a scholarship to study abroad in Leipzig, Germany, reinforces this notion. Laura plays the "Impromptu" proudly as a tribute to Evelyn, rather than the intended piece to the public as announced—Beethoven's Sonata No. 21 in C Major, clearly a triumph of "heart over head." Coming out, in a way, about Evelyn, Laura reaches a large audience, which includes the graduates and their parents. Since their playing together was private, Laura is the only one who knows the truth behind her piece. Rather than an occasion to celebrate her talents to the whole school by playing another master, this piece is a tribute to her lost love.

On the literary side, with tongue in cheek, Laura's most creative venture is the fabricated affair between Reverend Shepherd and herself. This doesn't just involve her own adolescent yearnings: she wails to her friend Annie, "I do love him, I do, I do … And he must love me." Laura's fantasy also satisfies a devilish need to attract the attention of her classmates, who provide a ready, enthusiastic, and swooning audience for her daydreams. This is another kind of passionate performance which fuels Laura's own emotions as well as theirs. In full view of them, she slips into the Reverend's study, shortly after her arrival at the college, "innocently" requesting help with her Latin; the girls are driven crazy with jealousy. To their surprise, Laura is also invited for a weekend at his house. (The simple truth is that her mother knows Shepherd and in a letter asked him to invite Laura to his home.) For her classmates, this is akin to the beginning of a full-fledged affair. Laura does her best to fuel their fantasies, whipping up a torrid affair when she returns, reading a Shakespearean-like sonnet that he supposedly sent her, and which she wrote. The irony is that Shepherd is hardly the male ideal they all suppose him to be. As Laura discovers on her visit, he is a self-centered prig, as well as an aggressively demanding and impatient husband.

Although much of *Wisdom* takes place within the school, the bush plays a significant role in the film with respect to Laura's growth and mastery of her environment and our understanding of her personality and consciousness. Rather than exuding mystery, danger, and ominousness as in *Picnic at Hanging Rock*, the bush first of all suggests a prison. The "tamed," meticulously landscaped grounds surrounding the school (not at all the open and natural bush in *Picnic*) function as an extension of the formidable building's confining, repressive atmosphere. Thus, after her initiation on her first day by the group of girls described earlier, Laura stands all alone in the green, a small figure in the alienating landscape, adrift and blinking at the immensity of the towering trees and spacious gardens. But just as she learns to live within the rarified school society, she uses the bush to transform this oppressive atmosphere into a backdrop for her fantasies, where her imagination runs wild. At the height of her fantasy about Reverend Shepherd, she selects a shady grove of trees near the school to read the fabricated love poem from him to a group of her classmates, amusing herself and awing them. Sitting on the large stone fence, the trees and shrubs providing an idyllic atmosphere, she "holds court," as the sighing group of young women gaze spellbound, while she reads her impassioned words, turning the setting into a fabular world of yearning, intrigue, and taboo love.

We saw similar powers of imagination and spinning of yarns at the beginning of the film in the bush near her home, a vastly different landscape, one which introduced Laura in the context of her working-class environs. Unlike the lush area with healthy, mature trees surrounding the school, the area where she lives is an expanse of dry and burnt, sand-swept land, populated by a few native trees, including scrub and brush near the modest working-class home that doubles as her mother's post office. But as with the school grounds, the bush can be linked to fantasy, caprice, and wonderment. When we first meet Laura at the film's beginning, she is away from her house, walking among gnarled tangles of dead branches, in the middle of a hot summer day. She is spinning a lushly romantic tale to her younger sister about a prince and princess who meet in a "sylvan glade" in a dark forest. Both are caught up in the fable, where the "prince meets the wondrous fair maiden." Clearly, this is a young woman who can let her imagination run wild, and who can transcend her immediate environment to create a comforting, exciting, and romantic atmosphere. We shall see the ways in which Sybylla Melvyn takes command of her bush environment in *My Brilliant Career*.

My Brilliant Career

In *My Brilliant Career* (directed by Gillian Armstrong, written by Eleanor Witcombe, based on the 1901 novel by Miles Franklin), the bush is not the seductive masculine or engulfing pre-Oedipal maternal as in *Picnic*, nor is it alienating and imprisoning as linked to the oppressive school in *Wisdom*. However, like *Wisdom* and *Picnic*, *Career* characterizes the bush as an inspirational place. Throughout the film, Sybylla (Judy Davis) proactively positions herself within the bush—that is, sitting in a meadow, perched in a tree, or running through a grove of trees. Through these scenes, the filmmakers conjure up Schaffer's myth of the feminized landscape not on the level of the symbolic or the psychoanalytic, but in terms of the bush as the *place of Woman* (Schaffer, 1988, 56) "not in the [patriarchal] ... order as it locates the feminine" (Schaffer, 1988, 56), but in terms of a young woman who proudly and (pro) actively defines and redefines herself. The bush is where Sybylla belongs, and she develops a strong affinity to and rapport with it. The bush becomes a place where Sybylla's identity evolves.

Moreover, and significantly, the bush is not linked to the development of the identities of the film's male principals, Frank Hawdon (Robert Grubb) and Harry Beecham (Sam Neill). In various ways, Sybylla challenges the traditional cultural construct of a feminized landscape linked to patriarchal identity. Thus, Frank and Harry are not the "colonial master[s] over the plains of promise" (Schaffer, 1988, 14). Frank, a visitor from England, like Michael in *Picnic*, is quite out of place in the bush, a greenhorn in every sense of the word. Harry, though the owner of vast estates elsewhere in Australia (in addition to Five Bob, his home), does not work the land; his relationship to it is cosmetic. He functions as a figurehead. The film further suggests that he is not able to manage it or make it profitable; at one point he is even in danger of losing Five Bob.

But first, in what ways does Sybylla fit Ferrier's model? Sybylla is "disadvantaged" and isolated by her tenacious independence as well as her determination to have a career—a *brilliant* career in the world of art, literature, and music, as she announces in voice-over at the film's beginning. She desires to break out of the stifling atmosphere of her working-class home environment where she has two states of existence, as she notes, "work and sleep." Her plan is completely at odds with the intentions of her mother and grandmother, who intend to marry her off, one of the few choices for a respectable woman at the time. As Felicity Collins comments, "Sybylla's gifts or assets are misrecognised by the women of her family as a 'wildness of spirit' which must be tamed" (Collins, 1999, 19). Or as Sybylla's stern grandmother declares, "She needs a man's hand." Rather than institutional restrictions, as seen in *Picnic* and *Wisdom*, Sybylla faces societal constraints. Like Laura, Sybylla is headstrong and stubborn, and does not fit the norm for female propriety; she is tomboyish, verging on the larrikin[4] (Dermody and Jacka, 1988, 33), her small frame accented by her long, full, striking red hair and freckled face. Further, her appearance deviates from her more conventional matronly, brunette, fair-complexioned relatives; she is fully aware of this, and deems herself "ugly."

Like *The Getting of Wisdom*'s Laura, Sybylla expresses herself artistically by playing the piano. But Sybylla also has aspirations to be a writer. As with Laura and her piano skills, Sybylla's writing becomes worthy of a higher (European) standard; at the end of the film, we discover that her autobiographical account of her life is published by Blackwood's of Scotland. *Career* explores three different kinds of performance for Sybylla: piano playing, singing/ dancing, and writing.

At home in Possum Gully Sybylla's playing the piano proudly, passionately, and loudly alludes to her strong personality. Her mother (Julia Blake), irritated with the noise, places her hands over Sybylla's, hushing the sound, misunderstanding as well as repressing her daughter's artistic yearnings. For Mum, home is a place of toil and duty, and is no place for such pursuits. As the eldest in the family, Sybylla is expected to fulfill adult responsibilities, which include chopping wood and milking a cow—man's work "without man's privileges," as Brian McFarlane notes (McFarlane, 1983, 119).

However, Sybylla is rescued in the nick of time with an invitation to visit her grandmother. In this home, Sybylla's playing is appreciated by an attentive audience, including her aunt and uncle, as well as two potential suitors in a far more congenial atmosphere. This kind of audience in a family setting is revisited and reinforced later in the film, where in spare and squalid surroundings, Sybylla plays for the McSwatt family, serving as a governess to pay off the interest on a debt her father has incurred with Mr. McSwatt (an assignment dictated by her grandmother). Despite the enormity of the job, which includes corralling and educating several unruly youngsters, calmer moments do take place, for example, when Sybylla and the McSwatts convene around the piano. With her playing, Sybylla brings this family together, just as she did with her relatives at her grandmother's, creating with her performance a camaraderie and closeness that was missing and not possible in her own home.

But Sybylla is also capable of another kind of performance, folk singing and dancing, which has a completely different function than her piano playing. Not only does she kick up her heels and flirt shamelessly, but she acts subversively to challenge her grandmother's house rules. For example, Sybylla's grandmother hosts a small party inviting Frank and Harry in accordance with her self-appointed duty to find Sybylla a husband. A little giddy and rather flattered that both men find her attractive, Sybylla starts dancing with Frank, singing "Three Drunken Maidens," a raucous song she learned at her father's local pub. She spins him around the room, "falling" on the couch, all but lying on top of Frank, who is flattered and slightly embarrassed. Though all have a grand time, word gets back to her displeased grandmother the next morning, who labels the evening "bacchanalian debauch."

Sybylla's penchant for challenging her grandmother's house rules escalates later at a large party thrown by Harry's Aunt Gussie (Patricia Kennedy) at Five Bob. Her performance is for Harry's eyes this time. The two have had an exciting courtship and are clearly attracted to each other (discussed in detail later). Yet Frank lives up to his reputation as a ladies' man and pairs off with another woman, instantly hurting Sybylla's feelings. When he later seeks her out for a dance, Sybylla, to avenge his slight of her, pulls away in a huff and joins the servants outside. She dances in a deliriously animated way with one of the hands, making a spectacle of herself just as she did with Frank earlier, deliberately rebuffing one of the most eligible and desirable bachelors around. The sequence which follows has been much discussed and criticized.[5] Furious and embarrassed, Harry drags Sybylla, who is smug and defensive, into a nearby room, declaring, "I thought we should get married." Sybylla sarcastically replies, "What a handsome proposal! How could *anyone* say no?" Glowering, Harry grabs her arm, pulls her to him aggressively and menacingly. She quickly hits him across the face with a horse crop. Stunned, he backs off. Almost as quickly, Sybylla winces in shame.

How could Sybylla, in a reversal of earlier scenes, turn Frank down when she openly flirted with him on many occasions prior, and clearly feels deeply for him? At least a partial answer lies in Sybylla's attitudes toward marriage, which she deems as severely limiting to woman's independence and sense of self. Earlier, she said to her grandmother, "I don't want to marry anyone!" She has observed her mother's drudgery for years, even though she knows her mother married for love. She also is fully aware of the in-between state of her Aunt Helen (Wendy Hughes), whose husband left her, essentially leaving her shamed and with no identity. As Helen notes, "neither wife, nor widow nor maiden."

Moreover, this scene dramatizes another way in which women are linked to the land in the larger paternal order: Harry displays a fierce attitude of entitlement with regard to Sybylla, particularly when his "authority" is challenged. By turning Harry down, Sybylla emasculates him. Harry's identity is already in a fragile state as he is on the verge of losing his property at Five Bob. His identity is not only a function of ownership of land, but ownership of Sybylla. His aggressiveness in trying to subdue her by force, as described earlier, suggests his putting a claim on Sybylla, "civilizing" this wild, unruly woman just as he/the Australian male claims authority by controlling and civilizing the land, ideally for him a "passive, pliant virgin" (Schaffer, 1988, 62). This scene adds another dimension to Schaffer's mythology of the bush, picked up later in this section when Sybylla's relationship with the bush is explored further.

Sybylla's final form of self-expression is a more private activity—the writing of her autobiography. This comes as somewhat of a surprise at the film's completion, for we have only seen Sybylla in the actual process of writing in four scenes: in Possum Gully at the beginning and end of the film (where she starts and finishes her book), and twice at Caddagat where she writes alone in her room after she has been living there awhile, and also while sitting in a tree shortly before she must leave Caddagat to go work at McSwatt's. Yet, it is significant that her writing triumphs, because in the aforementioned scenes, her writing is in conflict with or threatened by an outside interference.

For example, at the film's beginning, her writing is interrupted and put on hold by urgent family chores out of doors during the dust storm. Further, at Caddagat, Aunt Helen comes into Sybylla's room when she is writing in order to counsel her about Harry, commenting on his flirtatious reputation with the ladies in Melbourne as well as her sense that Sybylla may be in love with Harry. "Why would he want to marry me?" Sybylla queries, choking up a bit. The point is that this discussion of marriage "interrupts" her writing. In order to end the discussion, and resume her writing, Sybylla picks up the pen, and starts to write again, ignoring Aunt Helen, who leaves the room discreetly. Moreover, when she is up the tree writing, Sybylla is summoned by her grandmother to tell her of her imminent departure to work at McSwatt's—another interruption. (This is after the party where she and Harry have their blow-out.) It is only when Sybylla returns home, sharing a room with a sibling (who does not interrupt), that Sybylla finishes her book. Thus, successful writing has been compatible with (and not eclipsed or postponed by) renewed family responsibilities, which have not interfered with the completion of her book. Earlier, Sybylla inspired the McSwatt children to read by examining the sheets of newspaper and magazines attached to the wall. This activity is linked to her passion for language and evolution as a writer (though we do not actually see Sybylla work on her book at this location). This experience provides a transition to her return home, where she is able to pick up writing again and finish her work. It's as if she needed to do her writing in secret, or alone, in order to protect its sanctity.

Now that Sybylla's artistic endeavors have been discussed, we turn to an examination of the nature of Sybylla's bond with each bush setting. The bush in *Career* is diversified into four locales, each of which impacts Sybylla differently: Possum Gully, the dry, windy, drought-plagued bush which defines the environs of her isolated parents' home; Caddagat, her grandmother's lush estate, which is linked to wealth and class; Five Bob Downs, Harry Beachum's estate; the McSwatts' working-class farm.

In the opening section at Possum Gully, where Sybylla lives with her parents, who are eking out a living on the dry bush, Sybylla is clearly conflicted between her adult duties: helping her bushwife mother and pursuing her writing, which is the cultivation of her intellectual/creative side. This is demonstrated when in the midst of a brewing dust storm, Sybylla is obviously wrapped up in her own private world of words. She ignores her mother's calls for help as the wind blows furiously. This scene implies that the hard physical labor required to live in the bush threatens her artistic side, but as the next three locations will demonstrate, the bush is where she most comes alive.

Once she arrives at her grandmother's estate at Caddagat, Sybylla revels in the dramatic change of scenery, and is clearly delighted to be in a different setting. As compared to her desolate home terrain where little grows, Caddagat boasts acres of lush, green land as far as the eye can see. This shift brings a sense of joy and excitement to Sybylla as she eagerly jumps off the carriage ready for this new world—a more serene place not associated with work. For Sybylla, this bush is a place for solitude and artistic pursuits, such as reading and writing. When she experiences her first rainstorm in over a year one afternoon, she lifts her head and arms skyward, welcoming the cool and refreshing water. This event marks a rebirth into a new and promising existence, which is linked to her intellectual growth.

Sybylla's interactions with Frank and Harry both take place in the bush yet with different results and implications. In both cases she controls the mise en scène and direction of the narrative. When she arrives at her grandmother's and meets Frank, he identifies himself as a jackeroo (an apprentice worker on a sheep or cattle station); yet upper-crust Frank is a man of leisure, like Michael in *Picnic at Hanging Rock*. Frank pretends to be a man of the land, but obviously does not work it. The bush is completely foreign to him. To dramatize his inadequacies and for fun later on, Sybylla leaves him stranded four miles from her grandmother's house. He must walk the whole way home. Frank is in Australia only to find an appropriate, read subservient, Australian wife to take back to England with him.

In Sybylla's eyes, Frank is an interloper, disrupting her self-designated space. Frank's courtship amounts to bringing her a bouquet of flowers while she reads in an idyllic location under a large tree in a meadow next to a pond, already designated as her place for solitude and reflection. Sniffing with self-importance, Frank walks toward her, and in an affected manner presents the flowers to her. She thanks him graciously, cutting her words with sarcasm. When he turns his back, she summarily throws the bouquet into the pond, as if the flowers, indeed the bush, have been tainted by his foreign touch. Rain almost immediately starts pouring down, as if to cleanse away any trace of his presence. Later, Sybylla enjoys using the bush as a way to cut Frank down to size and to (literally) gain the upper hand. When Frank decides to propose to her while the two are sitting on a fence next to a pen of sheep (he has a silly hat on with a veil, that makes him look effeminate), Sybylla, not at all attracted to him, and quite impatient, shrugs off his offer. As he fumbles about, trying to embrace her, she deftly flips him backward helplessly into the pen, deliberately humiliating him.

With respect to Harry, the first time that Sybylla meets him, the bush becomes sexually charged. She is sitting in a branch of a grand tree situated in a lush meadow and is singing, having climbed up there to be by herself. Harry is out riding and, hearing her, comes over to flirt. Neither knows who the other is, and each takes on a different persona. Sybylla pretends to be an Irish servant girl, and Harry a young man on the make without his usual gentlemanly veneer. He all but grabs her down from the tree, quickly embracing her in his arms, insisting on a kiss. Smiling coquettishly, Sybylla begs off and runs away after Harry playfully swats her bottom. Later on, they meet formally at her grandmother's, and each must act properly. After her grandmother leaves the house, Sybylla is so wound up that she shows off for Harry, as discussed earlier, by dancing with Frank, who misunderstands his role in Sybylla's scenario. Significantly, once Harry enters

Sybylla's life, the bush becomes a place of sexual awakening for her. The bush could even be called her playground where she takes charge and actively and playfully courts him.

This is demonstrated when Sybylla later visits Harry, who lives with his Aunt Gussie. Inside his mansion, they behave cordially and stiffly, as they did in the presence of Sybylla's grandmother. Harry's Aunt Gussie is seated on the left, Sybylla is in the middle, and Harry stands on the right. Barely moving, they look like mannequins. Once outside in the open expanse of Harry's estate, Sybylla and Harry play out their mutual sexual attraction with great vigor and excitement. Sybylla breaks the ice by instigating a pillow fight, which takes them out of Harry's house far into the meadows outside where they chase each other through a long row of trees and to the furthest boundaries of the estate. Exhausted after running, they fall back onto the grass, out of breath, but enchanted with each other. It's as if they have just made love, and are basking in the afterglow. Later, Sybylla continues to use the bush to playfully flirt; she mischievously topples over the rowboat when they are out on the lake, after which she encourages Harry to engage in yet another chase, back to the house.

Even after their fight at the dance described earlier (which takes place after she returns to Caddagat from her Five Bob visit), the next morning they convene, embrace, and kiss in the bush. The wildly fun-filled, sexually charged scenes described earlier gear down to the demurely romantic amidst a full-blown, idyllic green landscape enhanced by the sound of water from a nearby stream. This dreamy scene contrasts to a similar pastoral setting used in a comic manner when Frank offered Sybylla the bouquet. This setting would be an ideal place for Sybylla to accept Harry's offer of marriage (she is even wearing a fancy white dress like a bride), but Sybylla gently puts Harry on hold, insisting on a two-year waiting period.

Sybylla's privileged relationship with the bush at Five Bob and Caddagat is abruptly interrupted by her being recalled by her mother and father to the service of their creditors, the McSwatts, where she will be in charge of several unruly children, as noted earlier. The prior idyllic atmospheres are in stark contrast to the family's living quarters: huts on a muddy strip in the bush with livestock living close by, or "the rude, teeming, dirty animalistic lives of the rural working class," as Dermody and Jacka have commented (1988, 136). These are far cruder conditions than even the "genteel poverty" of Sybylla's own family (McFarlane, 1983, 119).

In addition to dramatizing Sybylla's ability to manage at McSwatt's—she shares her artistic skills, as discussed earlier, teaching the children how to read, and plays the piano for the family—this section of the film makes crucial points about the relationship between the land and women in the larger paternal context, expanding the implications of Sybylla's refusal of Harry's offer of marriage. Sybylla's friendship with McSwatt's eldest son Peter (Tony Hughes) is misunderstood by his parents as romantic interest on her part. On the one hand, Sybylla's worthiness for Peter through his parents' eyes would be contingent on her having a dowry, in this case land. Mr. and Mrs. McSwatt choose to let Sybylla go because she has no property to speak of, and is not deemed worthy of their son, who wants to "marry up." On the other hand, Peter's identity as husband as well as his manhood is contingent on land ownership. Sybylla's supposed intentions (through the eyes of his parents) for Peter complicate the McSwatts' lives, as he is already engaged to a woman with property. His future wife, then, functions as part of the patriarchal economic system for land acquisition; once married, she will turn her land over to the ownership of her husband. Both wife and land are possessions to be managed, exactly the situation that Sybylla wished to avoid when she postponed Harry's marriage offer. The difference is that Harry judges *his* worth by the amount of acreage *he* brings to the marriage. At the end of the film, as we will see, Sybylla will again challenge the land/female construct by turning down Harry's second offer of marriage (he has gotten back on his feet, and saved Five Bob), choosing independence over land, in essence refusing Harry's "dowry."

Once Sybylla is released from her obligations to McSwatt's, and is back home on her parent's property, she strides confidently through the bush, content and perfectly comfortable wading into the water to pull out a calf that is stuck in the mud. Compare this to the beginning of the film when she deliberately stayed indoors, ignoring her parents' request for help with the livestock. Perhaps the birth of a calf and the presence of water indicate that the land is more giving than before, easing somewhat her parents' marginal existence. But there are loose narrative ends. What will be her role at home? Will she accept "man's work"? How will she earn her keep? Her mother has a new baby: with a larger family, will Sybylla be sent out to work again to help make ends meet? Though the film does not answer these questions, the filmmakers visually reinforce Sybylla's bonds with the bush, which are linked to this new stage in her life in two final sequences, the first with Harry, and the second where she posts her newly finished book outside her parents' homestead.

In the first sequence, while she helps the calf out of the mud, Harry appears. The two are completely incongruent—Sybylla, sweaty, her hands and clothes muddy; Harry, impeccably dressed in a neatly pressed, tailored suit, their appearance reinforcing different and separate worlds. Though glad to see him—even falling back for a moment into her flirty Irish lilt which she used at Caddagat, querying, "Peeping and prying again, are you?"—her face tightens and registers determination and resolve. This is a more mature woman, certain of her need for autonomy and breathing space. Harry declares, "Aunt Gussie sends her love. She's very keen on my getting married." Sybylla replies, "Yes, Gertie (Sybylla's younger sister) is just right for you. She's everything I'm not." With this deflection, Sybylla starts to run away, with the excuse that she needs to change her muddy clothes. Her movement is picked up in the next long shot as she moves quickly toward the background, suggesting that Harry's presence is an intrusion into her designated bush, making her restless, and eager to remain alone. Further, Harry's raising the question of marriage is incompatible with her need for independence *and* a writing career. She insists, "I've got to do it now. And I've got to do it *alone*."

At the end of the second sequence, two full shots capture Sybylla's figure centered in the shot, her packaged manuscript, soon to reach a larger audience with its publication, tucked safely into the mailbox nearby as she leans on the fence, arms comfortably outstretched. The first shot shows her intent and eager face with a confident stance; the other, behind her, shows Sybylla in silhouette at sunrise, "look[ing] off into the far distance towards another life which only she can envisage" (Collins, 1999, 22). Alone in the bush, a comforting and inspirational environment, with the evidence of her artistic endeavors nearby, Sybylla is a secure and self-assured woman.[6]

Several years after *Picnic*, *Wisdom*, and *Career*, *The Man from Snowy River* and *"Crocodile" Dundee* restore patriarchal mastery over the bush, which is linked to control over the women in the lives of Jim Craig (Tom Burlinson) and Mick Dundee (Paul Hogan), respectively, thus reinforcing the notion that the land (including wildlife) and women are possessions to be recouped and dominated. For Jim and Mick, the bush is their "proving ground for an ethos of dominant masculinity," as Rose Lucas notes in her review of *Snowy River* (Lucas, 1993, 103). In order for the identities of Craig and Dundee to be secure and complete, they need to relegate Jessica Harrison (Sigrid Thornton) and Sue Charlton (Linda Kozlowski), respectively, to dependency-in-the-bush, a situation which conjures up Schaffer's phrase (quoted at the beginning of this chapter, but certainly bearing repeating), "the perfect couple, masculine activity and female passivity" (Schaffer, 1988, 14).[7] In the course of the narratives Jessica and Sue become subservient and docile, deferring to Craig and Dundee. Though these young women are initially introduced as confident and self-reliant, in charge of their own lives, and comfortable on their own in the bush, they both lose their independent status.

The Man from Snowy River

The Man from Snowy River (based on the 1890 ballad by Banjo Paterson, written by Cul Cullen and John Dixon, directed by George Miller) dramatizes a young mountain man's rites of passage into manhood. He proves himself to be an expert horseman, rounding up a herd of wild brumbies, earning the right to live in the mountains and claim his birthright, the land of his late father. Jessica, too, is an experienced horsewoman, having lived around horses all her life on her father's station. When Jim first meets Jessica at the film's beginning, she is not linked directly to the bush but to its wildlife, specifically the spirited, high-strung colt that her father Harrison (Kirk Douglas) has just purchased. Both Jessica and the colt demonstrate fiery temperaments. As the colt bucks and kicks, Jessica pulls the lead rope taut to control the animal; Jim intervenes to assist, and Jessica fights back, resisting his help. Jessica's independent ways are short-lived and are soon challenged by Jim (hired as a hand on Harrison's ranch), who will subdue and "soften" Jessica's wild spirit (just as he manages the brumbies), bringing her under his authority and control.

Jessica comes under Jim's protection and "management" when he heroically rescues her from the mountains. Jessica has already challenged one male domain, that of her father, standing up to him in defense of Jim, whose taming of Harrison's colt was done without his permission.[8] Enraged, Harrison slaps Jessica for her defiance and impertinence, declaring that he will send her away to a boarding school the next day. Overwrought and angry, Jessica runs away on her horse, retreating into the mountain scape. She loses her way in the midst of a fierce rain and wind storm, and her horse is killed by the treacherous conditions. Jessica falls down the face of the mountain, stranded upon a slim ledge on a precipitous cliff. Her helpless and imperiled state suggests that she needs a man's hand in this "man's domain."

Jim heroically rescues her and Jessica looks to him as her guardian in the bush. Moreover, she never ventures out alone again and only when they are together.

Jim even regards her as a possession to be claimed like one of his horses. This "entitlement" is dramatized when Jim returns from the mountains triumphant after his extraordinary and dazzling roundup of not only the wild brumbies, but Harrison's runaway colt as well, after all the other mountain men have given up on such a dangerous mission. As Jim departs to his new homeland in the mountains, he declares to Harrison, "I'll be back for the brood mares" [and then looking directly at Jessica], "and whatever else is mine."

"Crocodile" Dundee

In *"Crocodile" Dundee* (written by Ken Shadie and John Cornell, original story by Paul Hogan, directed by Peter Faiman) the bush/nature is also linked to woman-as-possession. Mick Dundee is a deceptively self-deprecating, yet skilled Australian bushman. When the film begins, he is already Lord and Master of the bush, having proved himself by surviving a "ferocious crocodile attack" and escaping with a battle scar on his leg. (As everyone in Walkabout Creek knows, Dundee is a crocodile poacher.) He uses this lore to draw attention to himself for the wide-eyed American naïf, Sue, the journalist from New York who is interviewing him for a newspaper assignment. Whereas Jim must prove to the mountain men that he has matured into a skilled horseman in order to claim his land birthright, Dundee already holds his own brand of bush title. His next conquest is Sue.

Dundee's bold and flamboyant entrance into the film suggests right away that he sees nature/wildlife/women as entities to be controlled. Dundee bursts through the door of the pub, wrangling with his namesake, a large stuffed crocodile. When he sets eyes upon Sue, to whom he is immediately attracted, he exchanges one "partner" for another, giving the croc over to his manager and mate Wally to hold, while he whisks a pleasantly surprised Sue into his arms for a dance and leads her around the floor. Dundee later exhibits another form of domination with a different animal, which further shows off his special powers in the wild. Out in the bush, Dundee subdues a huge water buffalo that blocks the path of the truck with Sue and Wally. Dundee does not use force, but "mental telepathy." With his wry and intent stare, his head cocked and a thumb and finger pointing mystically at the beast, Dundee calms and seduces the animal into submission. The heaving, even aroused beast collapses on all fours as Dundee strokes his nose. Sue is mesmerized as she watches from the vehicle, appearing to be in as much of an erotic trance as the buffalo, as she too falls under Dundee's spell.

Once the two are alone in the bush, Dundee is perfectly happy to show off his domain, still preserving his façade of the mythical bushman—that is, telling time by the sun, shaving with a huge knife—at one point even commenting, "Me and God, we'd be mates," reinforcing his divine status. Yet Sue upsets the power order when she takes off on her own in the bush after Dundee teases and taunts her with "You? Out here all alone? That's a joke. A city girl like you wouldn't last five minutes. This is a man's country out here." Clearly, Sue poses a serious emasculating challenge to Dundee's control over her and his turf. As in *Snowy River*, the headstrong and foolhardy female must be taught a lesson and heroically rescued from danger, in this case, the deadly jaws of a giant crocodile, which lunges for Sue when she innocently wades in a pool alone. Helpless against the croc, she proves that this bush is also "no place for woman," to requote Schaffer (1988, 52). With lightning quick speed and skill, Dundee quickly and deftly extinguishes the threat, jamming a huge knife into the croc, rescuing the terrified and shaking damsel in distress, while reinforcing his status as master of his dominion.

After this incident, Sue eagerly submits to Dundee's control and never ventures out in the bush alone, just like Jessica. Both women have to be put in their proper places after trying to survive on their own in male territory. Their independence and assertiveness are intolerable to the male order. Male identity is thus reinforced by managing submissive, docile women, as well as horses, water buffaloes, and hungry crocodiles.

Muriel's Wedding and *Sweetie*

Muriel's Wedding (written and directed by P.J. Hogan) and *Sweetie* (written by Jane Campion and Gerard Lee, directed by Campion) present intriguing modern counterparts to the historical women discussed in this chapter. Both films focus on young female misfits who suffer from disabilities and difference, and who harbor a penchant for unusual performances. Both films are clever blends of comedy, satire, and serious drama. (*Sweetie* also delves into the gothic.) There is not enough room to do a complete analysis of both films, but the next section puts them in the context of the historical films discussed in this chapter, with short passages applying Ferrier's model. A further section on *Sweetie* covers the ways in which this film incorporates and appropriates Schaffer's myth of the bush.

Both Muriel (Toni Collette) and Sweetie (Genevieve Lemon) come from dysfunctional families. Ferrier's terms "bad parenting" and "hopeless fathers" (Ferrier, 2001, 58–9) are particularly appropriate for each. Whereas fathers are deceased in *Wisdom*, or absent and marginalized in *Picnic* and *Career* (respectively), *Wedding* and *Sweetie* imply that fathers are a major cause of female disability and vulnerability. Muriel is lorded over by a cruel, abusive father, Bill (Bill Hunter), and is all but ignored by her deeply depressed mother. In addition to being a terrible father, he is also an adulterer and corrupt politician. Sweetie's father Gordon (Jon Darling), on the other hand, is weak, often childish, and continuously dotes on her, treating his daughter as if she were still a little girl. The film also suggests a long-term, incestuous relationship.

Sweetie and Muriel are far more disturbed than prior women discussed in this chapter. Sweetie probably suffers from some form of mental illness; one of the first questions that her sister Kay asks is if Sweetie has taken her meds. Sweetie's reclusive, despondent, and self-absorbed nature is reminiscent of Sarah after Miranda disappears. However, unlike Sara, Sweetie is aggressively antisocial and exhibits aberrant behavior, which includes chewing Kay's china animals in her mouth, barking like a dog, or stripping naked and painting her body black. On the other hand, Muriel frequently retreats into a fantasy world, hiding in her room, listening to ABBA songs while conjuring up wedding daydreams, convinced that marriage is her only way to happiness and success.

Emily Rustin has made some insightful comparisons between Sybylla and Muriel, focusing primarily on the role of marriage in both time frames and settings. "[N]either [woman] adheres to the conventional standards of beauty and desirability" (Rustin, 2001, 137). Further, "both are in some way constrained by society's desire for them to marry. Muriel has internalized these values, while Sybylla is consistently pressured by others to conform to [their] expectations[s]" (Rustin, 2001, 137). Ultimately, both turn down marriage—Sybylla rejects Harry, and Muriel leaves her husband, David, realizing she needs to (and can) live without the security of a man who doesn't love her. Nor does she love him. She teams back up with best friend Rhonda to live together in Sydney. Rustin concludes, "What places *Muriel's Wedding* firmly in the present of the 1990s is that utopia is to be found not through isolated (if brilliant) writing in the outback—happiness through art—but in living the excitement of Sydney with another single woman. [Muriel] has found the support that Sybylla lacked" (Rustin, 2001, 137–8).

With regard to the use of the bush in *Sweetie*, Campion's approach is radically different than any of the historical films discussed earlier. In her insightful article "Restating the Cultural Framework: Kay Schaffer's Women and the Bush and Jane Campion's *Sweetie*," Ellen Strain notes:

> The icon employed by *Sweetie* is not exactly the vast and unknown bush described in *Women and the Bush*, but the tree, an element of Nature, transplanted into the [modern] city landscape of Sydney. The substitution of the tree for the bush in itself suggests the cultural metaphor's loss of relevance in urban times. The battle between man and nature ... no longer pervades Australian life, at least not for the majority of the population. The tree, exemplary of man's triumph over nature, is commonly a benevolent, domesticated form of Nature, drained of the myth generating power of the outback [and bush] (Strain, 1990, 35). [Bush is added here as Schaffer uses the two terms interchangeably in her work.]

As Strain further notes, "Campion must first reattach this fear of Nature to the tree and link it to the female Other in order to evoke the myth" (Strain, 1988, 35).

At the film's beginning, Sweetie's sister Kay (Karen Colston) in her voice-over associates trees with Sweetie (whom she fears and dislikes). "We had a tree with a palace in the branches. It was built for my sister, and it had fairy lights that went on and off in a sequence. She was the princess. It was her tree. She wouldn't let me up it." Trees (with the connotation family tree) also take on ominous overtones in Kay's visions—close shots of roots that grow menacingly into the ground, plants looking monstrous, one even appearing to roar. She comments, "I used to imagine the roots of that tree crawling, crawling right under the house, right under my bed. Maybe that's why trees scare me. It's like they have hidden powers." The baby elder that Kay's boyfriend Louie plants, and which she soon uproots and hides in her house, plays out her fear of family ties. To uproot it and kill it prevents any more families like her own from generating. Strain notes, "Fearing responsibility and the continued growth of family, ... [Kay] stunts the growth of her relationship with Louie. The tree planted in the yard, growing taller and stronger year by year, would have been a symbol of the growth of their relationship and a metaphorical child requiring nourishment and care" (Strain, 1990, 42).

Sweetie's link to trees, as Strain further notes, conjures up the bush as a pre-Oedipal mother, "draw[ing] ... one towards total fusion with itself and recreat[ing] ... a desire for the lost unity between the child and the world before the imposition of the Father's Law and the child's entrance into language and culture" (Strain, 37, quoting Schaffer, 1988, 55). Earlier, Hanging Rock was discussed in the context of the bush as a pre-Oedipal mother. Sweetie, however, already linked to trees, functions as *the* pre-Oedipal maternal for Gordon, her father. Throughout the film he is completely absorbed in her, coddling and indulging her as a great talent, eventually losing his parental authority as well as his identity as an adult male and husband. Thus, when Gordon's wife, Flo, leaves him, Gordon retreats to Sweetie's bed in her childhood room, as if waiting for Sweetie to comfort and nurture him. Like Sara in *Picnic*, Sweetie ultimately self-destructs. They both jump (or fall, in Sweetie's case) to their deaths, in bizarre grand finale performances: Sara in utter despair, Sweetie, having regressed into a childlike state, crashing through her treehouse and plummeting to earth.

Ferrier's and Schaffer's models are flexible enough to accommodate a range and diversity of performers and settings, in films set in the past as well as those set in the present. Unique, talented, iconoclastic yet vulnerable female protagonists, as well as the protean bush in all of its complexities—seductive, dangerous, fatal, yet nurturing and inspirational—can be understood and appreciated in a new light as vital and revealing components of Australian film culture.

Notes

1. Ferrier further identifies this dynamic in the larger context of Australia's anxieties "about the viability of local cultural industries in the context of deregulated international markets" (Ferrier, 2001, 63), which took place in the early 1980s. Thus, Australian films could potentially be "vulnerable bodies" in this new marketplace. Similar concerns were raised within Australia in the mid-1970s about its overseas performance. At this time, few revival films had been screened outside of Australia.
2. Unlike Michael, the bush-wise Albert can master the rock; he successfully scales it twice to rescue Michael and later Irma, bringing them down safely. Unlike Michael, Albert does not need to climb the rock to attempt to possess Miranda. He can enjoy her and other young women voyeuristically at a distance.

3   The question she cheats on is Cromwell's foreign policy, using crib notes pulled from the inside of her sleeve, suggesting a rebellious colonial indifference to knowledge of British history.
4   A larrikin is a rough, rowdy, boisterous young man, but can also be applied to a woman.
5   For example, Pauline Kael notes in her *New Yorker* review, "I think the subject matter is rather bizarre because what we are seeing is Sybylla teasing a man all the way through—a poor girl winning a rich man—then, after all this very sexual teasing, when he finally proposes, she is infuriated and tells us that wasn't what she meant at all … Somehow the audience didn't pay that much attention to the odd feminine logic of it or to the curious phenomenon of a woman who is going off to become a writer not wanting to become involved in human sexual relations, because that doesn't make a lot of sense. She seemed to think that she could only become an artist if she became a hermit, which is generally the last way to do anything." (Quoted by White, 1984, 65, 67.)
6   Tom Ryan comments that *My Brilliant Career* (and other historical films) "have narratives peopled by characters who are governed by forces beyond their control, and who are shown in a position of defeat at the close of the film" (Ryan, 1980, 120). The conclusion of *My Brilliant Career* challenges this assumption. In terms of the evolution of her character and her return home, Sybylla is triumphant: her manuscript is completed, she is perfectly comfortable with the single life she has chosen, and she is surrounded by her beloved bush.
7   Neither of these young women fits Ferrier's vulnerable bodies'/creative disabilities' model with respect to being a social outcast or misfit, or an "embattled artistic individual suffering from a disability or difference" (Ferrier, 2001, 58). Both women are healthy, physically and mentally.
8   Another character in *The Man from Snowy River* dramatizes the male mastery bush-woman link. Spur, the twin brother of Harrison (also played by Kirk Douglas), has been a miner much of his life. The "woman" in his life is not a human, but a mine he has been excavating for years with little success. To Spur, his mine is a seductive female who withholds her treasures from his control and economic pleasure. A "damned old trollop," "harlot," and a "Jezebel" are the names he uses. Spur is no different from Harrison in his attitudes toward the land—his for the taking to reap for its riches. However, unlike his brother, Spur has nothing to show for his efforts but a secluded life in his ramshackle cabin in the mountains. Finally, however, Spur's exploits pay off one day when he takes a two-by-four and wildly smashes the walls, essentially treating his mine like an abused woman; the scaffolding of several tunnels collapses in a series of explosions, revealing a vein of gold. Spur's rampage thus forces this woman to yield her riches.

Sources

Collins, Felicity (1999), "The Films of Gillian Armstrong," *Moving Image*, no. 6.

Dermody, Susan and Elizabeth Jacka (1988), *The Screening of Australia*, Volume II, Sydney: Currency Press.

Ferrier, Liz (2001), "Vulnerable Bodies: Creative Disabilities in Contemporary Australian Film," in Ian Craven (ed.), *Australian Cinema in the 1990s*, London: Frank Cass Publishers, 57–78.

Lucas, Rose (1993), "The Man from Snowy River," in Scott Murray (ed.), *Australian Film, 1978-1992*, Melbourne: Oxford University Press.

McFarlane, Brian (1983), *Words and Images: Australian Novels into Film*, Victoria: Heinemann in association with Cinema Papers.

Morris, Meaghan (1980), "The Personal Relations Film," in Scott Murray (ed.), *The New Australian Cinema*, Melbourne: Thomas Nelson, 133–51.

Rattigan, Neil (1991), *100 Films of the New Australian Cinema*, Texas: Southern Methodist University Press.

Roginski, Ed (1979), "Review of 'Picnic at Hanging Rock,'" *Film Quarterly*, 32 (4): 24–8.

Rustin, Emily (2001), "Romance and Sensation in the 'Glitter' Cycle," in Ian Craven (ed.), *Australian Cinema in the 1990s*, London: Frank Cass Publishers, 133–48.

Ryan, Tom (1980), "Historical Films," in Scott Murray (ed.), *The New Australian Cinema*, Melbourne: Thomas Nelson, 113–31.

Schaffer, Kay (1988), *Women and the Bush: Forces of Desire in the Australian Cultural Tradition*, Melbourne: Cambridge University Press.

Strain, Ellen (1990), "Reinstating the Cultural Framework: Kay Schaffer's Women and the Bush and Jane Campion's *Sweetie*," *The USC Spectator*, 11 (2): 32–43.

Turner, Graeme (1989), "Art Directing History: The Period Film," in Albert Moran and Tom O'Regan (eds), *The Australian Screen*, Melbourne: Penguin Books, 99–117.

White, David (1984), *Australian Movies to the World: The International Success of Australian Films since 1970*, Sydney: Fontana and Cinema Papers.

4

Negligent, Runaway, and Abject Mothers

Fran (1985), *High Tide* (1987), and *Radiance* (1998), all set in the present, break new ground in exploring a dark side of motherhood by featuring flawed mothers who are often deeply ambivalent about their roles. These films focus on difficult and distressed mother–daughter relationships, which are characterized by estrangement, mistrust, misunderstanding, even child endangerment, as well as love, devotion, and commitment—all in a pressure cooker of personal, social, and/or political forces.

In *Fran*, a single mother of three is torn between maternal responsibilities and her own need for a man to fulfill her sexual and emotional needs. This character was based on the many welfare mothers writer/director Glenda Hambly met while researching a documentary for the Western Australian Department of Community Welfare. After the Department decided against proceeding with the project, Hambly, who was captivated by the women she encountered, opted to make her own feature. In *High Tide*, a mother meets her daughter by chance in a working-class, coastal caravan park north of Sydney, having given her over as a baby to the care of her paternal grandmother after the death of her husband. This film originally featured the father as the estranged parent, but director Gillian Armstrong wanted to broach the riskier and relatively unexplored situation of a mother leaving her daughter.[1] She requested that the script be adjusted. *Radiance* focuses on the troubled legacy of a recently deceased Indigenous mother, an object of scorn as well as love by her two estranged daughters and granddaughter, who convene for her funeral in the tropics in Northern Queensland. *Radiance* was based on the 1994 play by Louis Nowra, who wrote the screenplay with input from first-time film director Rachel Perkins. This film had the distinction of being the first mainstream feature directed by an Aboriginal woman with three Aboriginal female leads.

Where do these films fit in with other Australian mother/daughter melodramas? "Bad" mothers, particularly with respect to mother–daughter relationships, are infrequent in Australian cinema, as a significant number of Australian films feature loving and devoted mothers. For example, one group of maternal melodramas features close mother and daughter relationships set in the past, including *Caddie* (1976), *Celia* (1987), *Rabbit Proof Fence* (2002), and *One Night the Moon* (2001); others are set in the present, such as *Soft Fruit* (1999), *Amy* (1997), and *Looking for Alibrandi* (2000). Another category (historical and contemporary) includes films such as *My Brilliant Career* (1979), *The Getting of Wisdom* (1977), and *Muriel's Wedding* (1994), which explore the tensions and conflicts linked to the maturing daughter's need for independence from her mother's protection as she undergoes her rites of passage into womanhood. Though the films in this third group have different narratives, the mothers in each essentially want their daughters to grow into responsible and mature young women. The films discussed in this chapter fall outside the usual cinematic norm of devotion, commitment, and sacrifice common in a culture that has traditionally viewed mothers as the stable center of the family and keeper of the home.

These films are unusual because they broach the unthinkable—what if a mother abandons her daughter(s) and/or relinquishes her title and role as a stable, nurturing figure well before her daughter is an adult? *Fran* and *Radiance* also venture into taboo areas such as child molestation and rape (including a cover-up of the rape), and even attempted matricide. Yet, the mothers in these films are not entirely unsympathetic. They live in the "perfect storms" of the consequences of their own choices within situations and events often outside their control.

Several common themes emerge in *Fran, High Tide*, and *Radiance*. First, mothers are part of incomplete or ruptured families without a committed husband (or father figure): he is deceased or chooses to live away from the family. Mothers are thus faced with double duty as parent. When mothers take on lovers, they can be predatory or intrusive, "trespassing" into domestic space, threatening the mother and/or daughter and/or the mother–daughter bond. Secondly, because a mother is unable to, or chooses not to take care of her daughter(s), a surrogate parent steps in and takes responsibility as caretaker (temporarily or permanently), facilitating and/or complicating the child-rearing process and the biological mother/daughter bond. Thirdly, for a variety of reasons, mothers live on the margins of a community, town, or housing development, and are regarded as outcasts. Nevertheless, the setting where each lives and/or works becomes an organic part of the narrative. Fourth, the mother's house/living space takes on a variety of connotations, ranging from safe to claustrophobic to dangerous; this house can be a place of closeness, familial warmth, and togetherness, or a center of contention and estrangement. Finally, the mother can be associated with death, be regarded as dead, actually be dead, have a brush with death, be self-destructive or suicidal; however, she can be resurrected in a number of ways, or a theme of maternal resurrection can underlie the evolution of the film.

This chapter addresses the following issues: What is the nature of the mother–daughter relationship? What are the personal, social, and political factors that impinge on a mother's willingness or ability to raise and nurture her daughter(s)? How do the settings—the suburbs, ocean side in the winter, and the tropics, including the mother's house—contribute to the film's narrative and dramatic tone?

Fran

Fran is situated in a sun-baked suburb in Perth, which Anna Dzenis specifies as a "drab, uninspiring suburbia of housing commission estates ... bland backyards, parched streets dotted with souped-up cars" (Dzenis, 1993, 170). A single mother living with her three children, Fran (Noni Hazlehurst) leads a delusional life, rationalizing, "my kids come first," then acts on self-satisfying personal whims—primarily her obsessive pursuit of male company. She becomes increasingly alienated from her children through her own irresponsibility and bad decisions. Subsequently, Fran robs her eldest daughter, eleven-year-old Lisa (Narelle Simpson), of her childhood by setting her up as a victim of sexual abuse. Lisa, her nine-year-old brother Tommy (Travis Ward), and six-year-old sister Cynthia (Rosie Logie) ultimately become wards of the court, taken away from their mother. How could this happen to a woman who says she loves her children?

One of the central dynamics of the film is set up right away as it opens: the reversal of mother–daughter roles. Fran is the flirty adolescent in tight pants and stiletto heels, parading down the street, a "bubbly cheerful, coquettish young girl" (Byrnes, 1986, 62), spied by an unidentified man who is cruising the streets on the prowl for women. As Fran walks into a phone booth, he eases his body in closely behind her. Fran playfully pushes him away. Her self-centeredness and immaturity is in contrast to Lisa's grown-up behavior and role as "keeper of the house." Back at home, Lisa makes dinner for her brother and sister in the kitchen, covering for her mother, whom she is eager to please. With her high forehead and deep, sad eyes, and an "old-before-her-time-look" (Byrnes, 1986, 62), Lisa rarely smiles, suggesting a wary façade of fragile confidence; she has been the caretaker for quite some time.

Lisa's role as mother extends to the protection of her brother and sister. For example, later that night when Cynthia's estranged father Ray (Danny Adcock) comes unannounced to the house, he is furious Fran is not there. (She has walked to the local pub to buy some liquor.) He sits in the living room, brooding in the dark until Fran returns, turning argumentative and abusive. As their conversation escalates into a high-pitched argument, the three children huddle together in Fran's bed, shaking and crying. Putting her arms around them, Lisa comforts Tommy and Cynthia. In the other room, Ray hits Fran in the face and punches her in the stomach. This ugly incident spills over into the children's lives the next morning, as Cynthia and Tommy, mimicking Fran and Ray, settle their dispute over breakfast by smacking and shoving each other.

The suburban setting is particularly apt for Fran's living space. Catherine Simpson in "Suburban Subversions: Women's Negotiation of Suburban Space in Australian Cinema" discusses late 1980s and 1990s films which feature female suburban dwellers. These films challenge prior representations of this setting as a "cultural and spiritual desert." According to Simpson, female protagonists "negotiate feelings of alienation in the suburban sphere by [1] rendering subtle transformations within it, or [2] escaping from the physical space itself" (Simpson, 1998, 24). These processes can be creative and/or destructive. In her suburban space, Fran is adrift and unfocused: clearly bored, restless, and insecure in her role as mother and homemaker. Though she attempts to busy herself while her children are at school by vacuuming and taking out the trash, she ends up wandering aimlessly from one cluttered room to another. For Fran, this house *is* a prison. She sits in the center of her kitchen, fidgeting uncomfortably, "compressed" between a bulky refrigerator on the left side of the shot, and a cabinet and table on the right. To beat the tedium, and temporarily break out of her constricted surroundings, she stands up, opens the refrigerator, and pulls out a bottle of beer, commencing an afternoon of drinking until she passes out in the living room. When Cynthia comes home from school, all excited and eager to share her day with Fran, Fran is grouchy and hostile, growling, "Get off of me … You're so bloody stupid," pulling away and stomping out of the room. As a "creative" solution to this claustrophobic domestic environment which makes her miserable, Fran chooses not only to transform her surroundings dramatically rather than subtly, but also to escape her home more than once, setting up harmful and damaging consequences for her family as well as herself.

Fran's first change, which satisfies her compulsion for male company, is to encourage Jeff (Alan Fletcher), who works in the local pub, to move into her house after they meet and have a three-day fling. In a perverse way, she tries to create an "ideal" nuclear family. With this drastic shift, Fran disrupts her children's lives, transforming their home to an unsafe place. Jeff, the son of an abusive father himself, starts to treat Tommy the same way he was raised. Tommy is already disturbed, as he wets his bed and does not play well with the neighborhood children. With Tommy, Jeff is aggressively authoritarian, barking orders from Fran's bed, where he spends much of his time as a glorified boy toy. When Marge (Annie Byron), Fran's neighbor, tells an unbelieving Fran that Jeff has hit Tommy, Fran's solution is to tell Jeff to stop, and assume that he will without any attempt talk to Tommy or monitor when Jeff and Tommy are together.

Fran's alteration of her domestic environment most profoundly impacts Lisa, who is soon preyed upon and molested by Jeff. Their relationship starts off congenially enough when Jeff, alone with Lisa, admires the puzzle she is working on, and they lightheartedly exchange jokes.[2] We think that perhaps Jeff is earnestly trying to get along with one of Fran's children. Yet, as his friendly voice becomes more seductive, he moves closer to Lisa; the safe space between them disappears. Jeff drops down on the floor next to Lisa, wrapping his arms around her as he nuzzles her hair. "Don't the boys do that at school?" he "innocently" asks. Stuck in his embrace, her eyes showing fear, Lisa noticeably stiffens. Jeff's arms encircle her body like a lover, and his hands start to rub her abdomen. In an unctuous voice, he comments, "You've got a hard little tummy. It will get soft when you grow up." Lisa cautiously gets up and leaves under the guise of making herself a drink in the kitchen, politely offering to pour one for Jeff, putting as much distance as she can between them. Lisa is the new prisoner of the house, only able to serve and please, too innocent to make any necessary changes to protect herself. As Jeff's treatment of Tommy and Lisa demonstrates, Fran has been blatantly self-serving in the worst way with respect to the changes she makes to her domestic status, "liberating" herself and putting her children in harm's way.

As compared to Jeff, Mike (Steve Jodrell), a committed social worker, is the only decent man in Fran's life. Mike helped Fran several years ago, and she now seeks him out for a consultation about welfare relief. Mike had intervened when

Lisa was three so Fran could keep Lisa out of permanent foster care. (The film isn't clear what happened to Fran at that time. We learn later that she needed to be hospitalized, suggesting a nervous breakdown or suicide attempt.) When Fran first comes into Mike's office, she immediately compliments him, referring to him as "my favorite social worker," adding with warm gratitude, "I would have lost Lisa for good if it wasn't for you." The irony is that she has already lost Lisa now that Jeff has violated her (at this point, Fran does not know the truth about Jeff). Mike is a caring and thoroughly professional man. Sympathetic to Fran amidst her current financial problems, he offers Fran temporary stability in the form of an emergency relief check to tide her over. However, Fran declines, revealing her deep distrust of a system that she fears will step in and perhaps discover her inadequacies and bad decisions. Sidestepping her own failings, she declares, "I don't want them telling me how to live."

Fran trusts men such as Mike to a point, but this kind of man is completely foreign to her. She is much more comfortable with a male such as Jeff, who is another in a chain of abusive and freeloading losers (such as her first husband, Ray). Fran alludes to her upbringing around menacing and molesting men when she lived with her alcoholic mother, commenting, "I had lots of uncles." Judging from the way Fran met Jeff, when she boldly came on to him, Fran's sense of control over her life is contingent on using her sexuality as a way to keep men close. This mode of operation was alluded to at the film's beginning by an elderly man from Fran's neighborhood, who sharply scolded her, calling Fran "a little slut" and a "bloody nympho." More than once Fran seduces Jeff into submission when he threatens to leave her. In turn, Jeff also has his own form of control as we have seen, using his friendly boyfriend façade as a way to ingratiate himself to Lisa and take advantage of her.

Fran's second change in her life is to leave her house. Jeff accepts a job up north—perhaps a lame attempt to break away from Fran, who is increasingly possessive and needy. She insists on going with him, bringing along her children, uprooting them from their neighborhood. However, she decides to leave them with her foster sister in order to have a holiday with Jeff. Once again, Lisa must cover for Fran and assume the role of mother to Tommy and Cynthia. "Don't worry, Mom, I'll look after them," she cheerfully declares to Fran. But a few days turns into four weeks, and Fran's absence initiates the foster care system: Lisa, Tommy, and Cynthia officially become wards of the state and are placed in holding houses. These events take place behind the scenes; all we see is Fran's holiday in montage, similar to a travelogue, accompanied by upbeat and lively country western music. She frolics on the beach and hikes in the bush with Jeff in a style deliberately opposed to the film's dominant social realist mode—long takes with characters framed in unglamorous, suburban welfare housing settings. Fran's vacation suggests a high-flying fantasy, which is in stark contrast to the structured and sobering world she will face when she is summoned back home by the welfare officers to answer to foster care authorities.

Fran's leaving her home, albeit with her children, is a critical turning point in the film. She successfully escapes from the tedium of her environment, but her happiness and relief is only temporary, and clearly proves to be a crushing and alienating process for her children. By seeking out her foster sister as (yet another) maternal caretaker, Fran inadvertently takes the first step in relinquishing and institutionalizing her children. She also regresses emotionally, becoming even more demanding of and dependent on Lisa.

Initially, Lisa must bear the brunt of Fran's indignation and denial about Jeff as a sexual predator. Unlike Tommy and Cynthia, and because of Jeff's molestation, Lisa falls under special protection. When Fran first sees Lisa in her new foster cottage, Fran behaves like an angry teenager who has lost her boyfriend, blaming Lisa, and treating *her* like the perpetrator. "Lisa, what in the hell have you told these [foster care] people? … You said you liked him [Jeff]!" Looking ashamed, Lisa casts her eyes downward and falls silent. Later, in a quieter frame of mind, Fran inquires, "Jeff *didn't* do anything, did he? They (foster care officials) are lying, aren't they?" Lisa dutifully gives Fran the answer she wishes to hear: "No, Mum." In another key scene, with Fran weeping and shaking, Lisa keeps a stiff upper lip and veneer of calm, updating Fran on the foster home where she, Tommy, and Cynthia live, mitigating the effect on them, as she comforts her mother. In one sentence she reveals the devastation of Fran's absence to her two youngest. She softly comments, "Cynthia and Tom cried all the time … but they got over it."

Yet Lisa is not enough. Fran needs yet another maternal figure—her friend Marge, a single mother of two small children. Marge is everything Fran is not: a-stay-at-home, model mother, responsible and devoted to her son and daughter, choosing not to date at all. There are no male partners in her life. Initially Marge is sympathetic to Fran, serving as a mother confessor. For example, when Marge first hears that Fran's children have been relocated into the foster care system, she listens with compassion. However, as Marge learns more about the circumstances, she wises up, becoming impatient and brutally honest, asking Fran, "When are you going to grow up?" She scolds Fran harshly for setting Lisa up to be sexually abused, exclaiming, "You'd put your kids' lives at risk for some bloke!"

Ironically, Fran's home becomes the same imprisoning environment she resented and escaped from earlier. This time, however, the house is eerily empty and silent without her daughters and son. She is utterly alone. Yet her every activity is linked to her children. Fran sits on the stoop as the dutiful mother waiting for her children to come from school. She also lies down in Tommy's bed. She later works on a puzzle just as Lisa did. None of these activities satisfies her. Full of rage, Fran breaks apart the puzzle with her fist and hurls an ashtray into her bureau mirror. The last we see of Fran is her lying in bed silently crying. We wonder if she is on her way to another nervous breakdown or suicide attempt.

The film ends in the foster cottage as the children prepare to leave, and we learn that they will be split up in different foster homes. As she has done in the past, Lisa earnestly nurtures her siblings, fussing over Tommy, brushing Cynthia's hair, and gently encouraging them like a mother sending her children off to school. In the film's haunting final shot, Lisa is alone. We see her take on an unexpected new persona as she turns to the mirror: she stares at her reflection, slowly and carefully brushing her hair in a gesture similar to that of Fran before she went off to the pub at the beginning of the film. Lisa's look is a mixture of girlish self-fascination and coy, newly discovered adolescent sensuality, a formidable change from the innocent eleven-year-old we met at the film's beginning. She is on the brink of following in her mother's footsteps.

Paul Byrnes has called *Fran* an Australian tragedy. Given Jeff's molesting of Lisa, as well as Fran's carelessness and subsequent denial of any wrongdoing, Lisa emerges as the most tragic character. Nonetheless, as we have seen, Lisa does not exhibit the rage toward her mother that another violated woman, Cressy, will forcefully demonstrate in *Radiance*. The film leaves us wondering whether Fran will be able to resurrect herself this time as she did when Lisa was a toddler, and fully commit herself to motherhood for all three of her children. As she noted earlier, in a rare moment of self-awareness: "I'm a rotten mother ... I've got to change."

High Tide

High Tide (written by Laura Jones) explores the friendship and growing attachment between a mother, Lilli (Judy Davis), and her daughter, Ally (Claudia Karvan), who meet by coincidence in a caravan park where they both live. Lilli left Ally in the care of her paternal grandmother Bet (Jan Adele), when she was an infant, after her husband John died in a surfing accident, a traumatic event which still haunts her. Since then, she has been a drifter, her most recent job performing as a backup singer for an Elvis impersonator. Lilli's sudden firing by the group's manager results in her unplanned stay in the park after the group's most recent performance. Her new relationship with Ally is problematized by Lilli's skittishness about any family ties, as well as her testy relationship with Bet, who is openly vindictive toward Lilli and protective of Ally, now thirteen.

High Tide breaks new ground in several ways. Barbara Creed has argued that *High Tide* is a significant alternative to the usual female Oedipal journey, the Freudian view that the daughter rejects the mother and directs her love toward the father. In *High Tide*, however, Ally develops a strong bond with Lilli. Rather than being held up as a "figure of abjection" (Creed, 1992, 22), the mother is held up as a figure of love for the daughter.[3] As dramatized in the film, the mother–daughter bond is not replaced by the one that the daughter develops with a male (a father figure, or a love interest). *High Tide* extends this subversive dynamic even further, for Ally breaks away from her surrogate mother/grandmother to be with her biological mother. *High Tide* is also feminist melodrama in the best sense,[4] as it resists female stereotypes. Lilli is not demonized (Crofts, 1991, 18), Bet is not a monster (Kael, 1988, 84), nor is Ally sentimentalized as a "victim of parental absence" (Crofts, 1991, 18). Moreover, in a film where the men are secondary characters, *High Tide* is not "concerned with a patriarchal order's stymieing of female desire" (Crofts, 1991, 18), a frequent theme in melodrama. Finally, the narrative defiantly takes place outside the home, the usual female cinematic space.

As opposed to the hot, dry suburbs in *Fran*, a site of distress and familial rupture, the coastal environment during winter in *High Tide* is a crucial setting for the development of the attachment between mother and daughter. Lilli and Ally are both attracted to the ocean, which functions as a primal maternal site where they realize their blood ties. The filmmakers set up this dynamic right away at the film's beginning, when Lilli and Ally are introduced and linked through sea motifs and settings, one artificial, the other natural. Lilli appears in mermaid garb, a blonde wig and green-sequined, form-fitting gown, performing on stage against a backdrop of shimmering blue streamers. This sequence is followed by Ally in a rock pool, lying on her back in a wetsuit, suggesting, as Lucy Fischer notes, "an intimation of fetal life in the amniotic … sea" (Fischer, 1996, 221). Moreover, the caravan location where they both stay is aptly named "Mermaid Park." In addition, the first time the two appear in same shot together (before they first meet) is in the context of the ocean setting, both surrounded by and touching the seawater. As Crofts notes, "Lilli [is] ... in the shallows, while her daughter surfs the deep—as if to point doubly to the child in the woman: both Ally unborn in Lilli, and also Lilli's childishness, her own past acting on her present" (Crofts, 1991, 20).

When Lilli and Ally first encounter each other in the shower—a deft continuation of the water–mother–daughter motif—Lilli is drunk, propped against the wall under the sink, and Ally has just come out of the shower stall. Ally isn't frightened of Lilli, and Lilli heartily hails Ally right away, affectionately calling her "fish-feet." As Steve Warrick notes, "we can believe that, from the first, each sees some of herself in the other without either knowing their true relationship" (Warrick, 1989, 24). Ally and her boyfriend help Lilli up on her feet as she staggers about, unable to keep her balance. They guide her to her trailer, each holding one of Lilli's hands. As if out of instinct, Lilli, who is loose and jolly, takes Ally's hand and studies it, noting that she has a long life line in her palm. Their second meeting takes place the next morning, when they happen to meet outside the caravan Laundromat. Ally is eager to have Lilli continue her palm reading; they chat and carry on like old friends, even speaking in Italian when they start to compare their travels. Lilli's fascination with Ally's hands and feet suggests the loving care a mother bestows upon a child's body. However, the jovial mood ends abruptly when Bet enters the Laundromat, breaking the spell. Seeing Lilli and immediately scowling, Bet quickly beckons Ally to come with her. Lilli's wide-eyed look is a mixture of shock and longing as she casts a burning and haunting stare at her newly found daughter. From that point on, Lilli "can't take her eyes off Ally," as Pauline Kael notes (Kael, 1988, 84).

How does the growing bond between Lilli and Ally function in the larger context of the film's other couples or familial configurations? Bet's boyfriend, Col (John Clayton), functions as an unofficial father for Ally. Like Bet, he insists on restricting Ally's activities. She is on the brink of adolescence, and wants to spend more time with teens her age. During several occasions, she begs Bet to let her go to the disco, rather than tag along with Bet on her performance nights. Increasingly, Bet realizes that she needs to allow Ally more freedom, while Col, ever the authoritarian, often puts his foot down. This is demonstrated on one of the nights that Bet prepares for her performance. Ally declares that she doesn't want to go, and scolded harshly by Col. Defiant, she stubbornly pulls away to join her friends at the disco. As if drawn to wherever Lilli is, she later drifts over to the club where Lilly does a strip routine.[5] Col, like Bet, is threatened by Lilli's presence. To him, Lilli is an interloper, an irritating complication to his relationship with Bet and Ally. The more Ally becomes enamored with Lilli, the more authoritarian and hostile Col is toward Ally.

In addition to her loose nuclear family with Bet and Col, Ally has a boyfriend her own age of whom she is quite fond. Ally is just several years shy of the age of Lilli when she married and gave birth, and the innocent relationship between Ally and her boyfriend suggests a younger version of Lilli and John. After they surf together, we see them kissing affectionately. Ally is a well-adjusted and emotionally stable young woman, a testament to Bet's skill and love in raising her. Clearly, she and Bet have a loving and warm camaraderie.

For her own part, Bet is clearly torn between her own insecurities about raising a teenager, her desire to perform, as well as her own love life. Warrick comments, "[Bet is] … an emblem of those working mothers who've sacrificed their dreams—in Bet's case, her own dreams of becoming a nightclub singer—to take care of their children" (Warrick, 1989, 24). This ambivalence is dramatized when Bet has a one-night stand with an oh-so-charming country Western singer, whom she meets on talent night. When she brings him to her trailer, she treats Ally like a little girl, quickly tucking her in with a stuffed bear, reassuring her, "Here's Teddy to keep you company." However, Bet's holding on to Ally also implies that Ally is Bet's only tie to her lost son in a lingering mother–son attachment. The moment Lilli comes into the caravan park, Bet explodes with long simmering, maternal resentment toward Lilli. "You screwed up my boy's life!" she angrily exclaims, as if John abandoned Bet to be with Lilli.

Finally, Mick (Colin Friels), the young man whom Lilli meets at the chook raffle (in the club where she initially performs as a backup singer), is attracted to Lilli right away. When she hands him the chooks (chickens) she won as a gift, he boldly plants a kiss on her cheek. Lilli is drawn to Mick's decency and easy charm, and they become lovers, though he is clearly more enamored of her. Their weekend away gives Lilli the opportunity to open up, and in the car she speaks wistfully of her late husband. Later in the motel room she goes even further, declaring that Ally is her estranged daughter. (At this point, Ally doesn't know the truth about Lilli.) Mick, however, who is a single parent, is already planning a new life with Lilli, using their time away to essentially propose to her. He speaks of leaving the area permanently with Lilli and his young daughter, starting a business together, even having a child "of our own." With Ally preoccupying her thoughts, and far away from Mick's dreams, Lilli all but ignores him as he tenderly embraces her on the bed, keeping her as close as possible. Lilli tunes him out, just as she did earlier when she and Mick had coffee in the local café, preferring to gaze at Ally working the pinball machine with her friends. Wary of setting of any commitments to Mick and future familial configurations, Lilli abruptly (though not angrily) leaves in the middle of their weekend together. As Crofts notes, Lilli's perspective of family as "entrapment" is also implied by her subjective point-of-view shot of the rear window of the car as she and Mick pulled away for their holiday: Mick's daughter, mother, and aunt are visible through the "bars of the rear window's sungrille" (Crofts, 1991, 19).

Earlier, it was noted that the ocean is linked to new life and the reinforcement of mother–daughter bonds.[6] But as the place where John perished,[7] the ocean is also linked to death. At one point, Lilli tells Ally that she wanted to die after John was killed. Her porcelain white face and long, billowing, black coat that she wears as she walks along the shoreline in various scenes gives her a specter-like presence. In the scene right after Mick has revealed to Ally that Lilli is her mother (a few days after their weekend together), Ally, distraught and confused, runs up to Lilli and asks, "Are you my mother?" Lilli, her face showing alarm, then composure, in a controlled voice, utters, "No." Ally then shouts, "My mother's dead," then turns and runs away. This is a chilling scene. From Ally's viewpoint, she may think that Mick and Lilli are playing tricks on her. Whom should she believe? Has Bet, who has always told her that Lilli was dead, deceived her?

Along this line, Bet would prefer that Lilli were dead, and even threatens to kill Lilli in a fit of rage if she continues to hang around Ally. Bet is not a murderer, but the strong language, not the act itself, is clearly intended to scare Lilli away. Even Ally is linked to death. After Ally's intensely emotional and distraught conversation with Lilli in her car parked on a cliff overlooking the surf (which comes just after Ally confronts Lilli on the beach, and is discussed later), where Lilli tries to explain why she left Ally when she was an infant, we next see Ally lying face down in a rock pool in her wet suit, as if she is (or wishes she were?) dead. However, given that Lilli put Ally out of her mind when she gave her away as an infant to Bet, and that Ally thinks her mother has been dead all these years, the growing attraction dramatized between a mother and daughter amidst an ocean setting suggests that each has been resurrected for the other. So the sea takes on another connotation: rebirth.

Which is why the scene in Lilli's car is so crucial. By giving Ally away, Lilli gave her life, even though Ally cannot yet fathom why Lilli left her. They sit in the front seat of Lilli's car: Lilli, her face puffy and swollen from crying; Ally, sobbing, and alternately looking at Lilli quizzically and then turning her face away in pain. Ally declares, "I love you! Do you love me? ... Did you ever try to find me? You loved me before he died?" Lilli explains: "After John died, I didn't want anything, nothing. I got used to that. I gave you away. It wasn't your fault. I wanted to die. I was so angry. I felt useless. I didn't choose to stop loving you. It just happened. I'd have hurt you. I'm sorry, I'M SORRY!" With this climactic scene, Lilli finally understands her daughter's love for her as well as Ally's deep feelings of abandonment. Lilli's own passionate and instinctive maternal love has been reawakened. From this point on, she is able to openly return Ally's love.

Ally gives Lilli purpose in her rambling life, and Lilli gives Ally the roots she so desperately needs. When Lilli and Ally take off on the road together at the film's end, it makes emotional, dramatic, and visual sense that these two belong together. Lilli musters up the courage to ask her beloved to go with her; Ally chooses the high road with her rediscovered mother over the tedium and restrictive security with her grandmother, whom she deeply loves and leaves with a tearful farewell. However, the film *does* romanticize Ally's choice to trust and be with Lilli. As Lilli told her in the car when Ally pronounced without reservation that she loved her, Lilli, in an almost cautionary tone stated, "You don't know me." We are still not certain if Lilli is up to the task of motherhood.

In the final scene, when they stop for a bite to eat, Lilli sits in her car, staring forward, hands clinging to the steering wheel for several minutes while Ally patiently waits for her in the restaurant on the road. Lilli could leave at any second and abandon Ally again. But no, she chooses to stay and embrace her daughter. She enters the restaurant, and playfully covers Ally's eyes, before sitting down at the table, smiling lovingly at her, and holding her hands. Lucy Fischer has commented that this is a tentative decision on Lilli's part, adding "the film leaves us in limbo, without the moral or narrative assurance that the family circle has been permanently restored" (Fischer, 1996, 224). We are relieved that mother and daughter, so intricately bound, are together, but can Lilli stay the course she has chosen?

We shall see in *Radiance* another maternal drama enacted against a coastal setting where mother and daughter are reunited but under very different circumstances.

Radiance

Radiance, like *High Tide*, is the story of a reunion between a mother and daughter long separated, and, like *Fran*, features an abused mother who puts her daughter in sexual danger. *Radiance* differs, however, from *High Tide* and

Fran in that the mother, Mary, has just died as the film begins, so we never know her directly, only through the perspectives of her adult daughters and granddaughter. The film's focus is on the reconvening of the two sisters: the eldest Mae (Trisha Morton-Thomas), and Cressy (Rachael Maza) with Nona (Deborah Mailman), Mary's granddaughter, for the funeral after many years apart. This occasion forces them to face Mary's dysfunctional and chaotic life that severely and negatively impacted the lives of Mae and Cressy. Unlike *High Tide* and *Fran*, where the daughters love their mothers, these daughters have no desire to celebrate or draw closer to their mother or her memory. Further, there are actually two mothers featured in *Radiance*. In addition to Mary, the second daughter, Cressy, is the biological mother of Nona, the third "sister." This information has been kept from Nona, as Mary raised Nona as her own.

Significantly, with its focus on four Indigenous women, *Radiance* adds another dimension to the mother–daughter drama: racial politics and Australia's internal colonial legacy with respect to Indigenous Australians. Mae, Cressy, and Nona lived at least the early part of their lives in the shadow of colonizer paternalism. Mary was a kept woman: her non-Indigenous lover Harry owned the house where she lived and died, and where Mary and her daughters lived in relative isolation within a white community. Further, the eldest daughter Mae, and Cressy, both mixed-race, were victims of assimilation, a practice which started in the 1930s, wherein mixed-race children were taken from their families by government officials to live in white foster homes. Mae and Cressy were forcibly removed from Mary's house when they were in their early teens. (The subject of the "Stolen Generations," as these groups were coined, is discussed in more detail in Chapter 5.)

Marguerite Nolan points out that an acute tension exists in *Radiance* between the specific—colonial politics—and the universal—a psychoanalytically informed melodrama (Nolan, 2004, 175). Even though the racial politics (and in particular any mention of the term "Stolen Generations") are not explicitly stated, they are intertwined with and infuse the lives of this family. However, rather than the institutional patriarchy serving as the focus of the blame for Mae's and Cressy's kidnapping, Mary is set up as the one at fault. Thus *Radiance* ups the ante for rage against the mother, an emotion barely present in *Fran* and *High Tide*.

First of all, *Radiance* positions Mary as a negligent mother. Cressy in particular is intensely bitter about her forceful removal, angrily declaring to Nona, "She [Mary] didn't fight for me!" Ceridwen Spark comments, "Confirming rather than challenging the notion that Aboriginal women willingly gave away their children and suffered little emotion as a consequence, the film renders the notion of stolen-ness spurious, and simultaneously perpetuates a racist construction of Aboriginal women as unfeeling, bad mothers" (Spark, 2001, 46). Secondly, Mary brought one of her lovers into her house, who then beat up and raped Cressy when she was twelve years old (a fate worse than that bestowed upon Lisa by Jeff in *Fran*, though his molestation of her is nonetheless horrific). Worse, when Cressy told Mary what had happened, Mary denied the rape. As we discover, this lover was one of many. Mary is thus characterized as a loose woman whose sexual appetite and lapse in judgment in protecting her daughter led to the assault, an event which has continued to traumatize Cressy.

Finally, with respect to Mae, Mary was abusive toward her when Mae cared for Mary in the interim before her death. Adding to Mae's distress was Mary's adamant refusal to tell Mae about her Indigenous heritage, and withhold information about Mary's mother and father, who once lived across the bay on Nora Island, where she (Mary) was born. Mae's lingering hostility toward Mary is demonstrated at the beginning of the film when she stands outside the house, roughly tossing Mary's clothes into the metal barrel where they burn, as if to forcefully eradicate any memory of her. For Cressy and Mae, then, Mary is a "witch mother" (Spark, 2001, 4) or, as Nolan argues, an "abject mother" (Nolan, 2004, 175). Moreover, Mary's curse on their lives is so intense that Cressy and Mae "attack" her house at the end of the film and burn it down.

Fueling the hostility of both sisters is Nona, who shows up pregnant and unmarried, and an uncomfortable reminder of the worst excesses of their mother's behavior which rubbed off on her granddaughter. To their disgust, Nona proudly declares, "Mum and I were sluts; we fucked." Moreover, Nona's unconditional love for Mary is incomprehensible to Mae and Cressy. Nona's ongoing fondness for Mary led to her plans to return from the rodeo circuit and live with Mary and raise her child, essentially replaying her own idyllic early years.

Yet, even given *Radiance*'s "relentlessly harsh portrayal" of Mary's bad motherhood (Nolan, 2004, 185), the filmmakers nevertheless intend to recoup the maternal, primarily through the growing bond between Cressy and Nona. This relationship is contrasted to the "failed" mother/daughter bond between Mary and Mae. Mae initially attempted to be a "good mother" to an ailing Mary, and expected love in return to make up for their years of estrangement. Unlike Cressy, who wanted nothing to do with Mary, Mae yearned for her mother's approval in the hope of having a stronger sense of (her)self as an Indigenous woman. In the discussion which follows in the rest of this analysis, both of these relationships are explored with respect to the following: (1) the dynamics of the attachment that develops between Nona and Cressy, given their long separation, very dissimilar lifestyles, and radically different relationships with Mary in their formative years; (2) the evolution of Cressy's maternal identity; (3) Mary's legacy as an unfit mother, and its impact on Mae and Cressy.

Seeing her grown daughter for the first time in years, Cressy views Nona with affection, fascination, and even amusement. Like Lilli with Ally, she can't take her eyes away from her. And similar to Ally and Lilli, Nona is instinctively drawn to Cressy. Trying to impress Cressy, an accomplished and internationally successful opera star, Nona shows off by doing what she thinks Cressy would most appreciate—sing. With Cressy watching patiently, Nona pulls out Mary's CD of "Madama Butterfly" with a glamorous picture of Cressy on the front. Nona enthusiastically tells Cressy that she saw her perform as Butterfly on television, and that she bought her red silk robe in honor of Cressy. Nona playfully reenacts Butterfly's suicide scene, gesturing and lip synching as she pays homage to Cressy's beautiful voice. Cressy is warmly amused and smiles tenderly, the irony of course that Cressy, like Butterfly, had to give up her child. The links between Madama Butterfly and Mary's family are discussed in detail later.

As with *High Tide*, the ocean coastline setting (the tropics in Northern Queensland)[8] plays a role as the primal site of reconnection between an estranged mother and daughter from two different life paths: Cressy, a diva, sophisticated and worldly; Nona, a scrubber, crude and unruly. As they walk along the sand near Mary's house, they loosen up and joke (whereas the house environs thus far have only made Cressy anxious and uncomfortable, Nona petulant and sassy). Their growing bond is reinforced even more when Nona shows off her own vocal skills with a country Western song. However, when Cressy does not turn around right away and compliment her, Nona becomes impatient and pointedly declares, "You're ashamed of the way I look." Cressy stops walking, turns, looks Nona directly in the eye, and declares with great passion, "I could *never* be ashamed of you!"

This beach environment reinforces their bonding in another way as they walk further. Nona finds a large sea turtle on the sand, and excitedly hails Cressy. They are thrilled with their discovery and marvel at this magnificent creature. They carefully circle around it, with Nona lifting the turtle and transporting it back to the house. She links the turtle right away to Mary, declaring that they can make turtle curry in her honor, a dish "just like Mum used to make." Nona's mindset reinforces her strong bond with her "false" mother, the truth of which will figure prominently later in the film. As the huge turtle wriggles on the table, the problem arises, how shall Nona prepare it? Mae sees the opportunity for some fun, and joins the two, eagerly offering a solution. She selects and hands a large kitchen knife to Nona to slit the animal's throat, smiling devilishly, adding a mock gothic edge. Nona gingerly takes the knife, not knowing where to start, walking around the table, looking for the right place to position the knife. The turtle suddenly nods its head; Nona is startled, jumps back, and drops the knife. The turtle is spared. They all crack up. Mary's "gift from the sea" has provided much-needed relief for the three.[9]

The growing bond between Cressy and Nona is in contrast to the enmity in the past between Mary and Mae, when Mae returned to care for Mary, each taking on the role of the monstrous mother as Mary's health declined. Mary's house, already a site of sexual assault, took on another connotation of domestic violence wherein both women became fierce adversaries. Mary's declining health and dementia created a difficult situation for Mae, whose move back home was an attempt to revive and hopefully nourish the mother–daughter bond. Since Mae had to step in as caretaker (she was trained as a nurse), the roles were reversed. Her dream of a mother who would demonstrate her love and devotion turned into a nightmare. At first, Mary abused Mae verbally, screaming at her "hour after hour, day after day until she went hoarse," as Mae notes in her long, tearful confessional to Cressy and Nona. Mae, upset and frustrated, retaliated with counter-abuse, at one point tying Mary up "like an animal." Soon, Mae became so exasperated and angry that one day she lashed out and attacked Mary, grabbing her by the neck and almost choking her to death. As appalling as her potential matricide sounds, Mae comes across as sympathetic as she relates these details. Though she is embarrassed over her past behavior, Mae is still full of rage as she declares, "I just wanted ... [Mary] to say, 'I love you, Mae.'" Though Nolan argues that Mae's scream at the end of her confessional exorcises the mother's ghost, Mae (like Cressy) needs a more radical event to completely rid herself of Mary's ghost, so she is able to let go of the past and begin her path toward peace of mind.

Even more painful for Mae was Mary's refusal to enlighten her about their Indigenous heritage, and address Mae's question: why Mary, her mother, and father were thrown off Nora Island, which is in full view across the water from Mary's house. This fueled Mae's growing sense of alienation and isolation. Her identity had already been crippled as a result of her removal during assimilation and forced living at a foster home. Mary's refusal to enlighten Mae about her own lineage implies that she tried to pass her own lack of self-worth on to Mae, thus failing to provide her with an identity, the "classic flaw of the Freudian mother" (Nolan, 2004, 180). By her own life actions, Mary repressed her Indigenous heritage, and lived in a state of cultural amnesia, often under the power of non-Indigenous men.

If Mae's identity is missing, Nona has been living with a false identity, that is, she has assumed that Mary was her mother, and a "black prince" (Nona's term) was her father. Nona's attraction to her father is a full-blown, erotic fantasy, for she never knew him. She boasts to Mae and Cressy about her vision of thrilling sex with him, complete with "the best orgasm I have ever had." Thus, whereas Cressy and Mae associate Mary's house with sexual violence and maternal irresponsibility, Nona associates Mary's "pleasure house" with the excitement of lowdown sex with any man who came into the house, fueling her incestuous fantasy about her father.

Earlier in this chapter in the discussion on *High Tide*, it was noted that the usual female Oedipal journey features the daughter's rejection of her mother and directing of her love toward her father, a dynamic which *High Tide* challenges. Though Nona follows this female Oedipal journey, she reverses the order, that is, she fixates on her father, and *then* rejects her biological mother in a rage during the house burning sequence, when Cressy declares to Nona the truth of her conception. This is a key scene (described in more detail below), kicked off with the painful destruction of Nona's illusion about her familial lineage, and followed by an act of fiery exorcism by Mae and Cressy to rid them of the burden of their mother. For Cressy in particular, she is finally freed from the haunting memories of the vicious rape by Nona's father. Shifting from the friendly, accommodating sister to the outraged mother, Cressy resolutely declares to Nona that her father was not a prince but "a filthy pig smelling of petrol," adding, "You were born from dirt! Your father was dirt!"[10] It's no wonder that Nona, stunned, runs away, clinging to Mary's ashes in a can, the only actual "proof" she has at the moment.

As Mary's house burns,[11] the Madame Butterfly connection becomes particularly crucial, adding visual, acoustic, and thematic richness. Already coded as Cressy's signature opera, Butterfly's final aria wafts through the air as the house is engulfed in flames. Puccini's cross-cultural tragedy is briefly summarized here as the story has several links to *Radiance*. A young, fifteen-year-old Japanese geisha, whose name is Cio-Cio-San, is nicknamed Butterfly by an American naval lieutenant, Pinkerton, stationed in Japan, who fancies her. Pinkerton arranges to marry Butterfly through a broker. Shortly after the marriage, Pinkerton leaves for three years, during which time Butterfly gives birth to a son. When Pinkerton returns to Japan to claim his son, he brings his American wife with him. Butterfly, devastated and shamed, turns over her son, and then kills herself hari-kari style with her dagger.

Both Mary and Cressy are variations of Madame Butterfly. Mary had two children with non-Indigenous males as fathers, and under the imposed assimilation rules, she was forced to give them up, just as Butterfly had to give up her son to her American husband. However, rather than a single suicidal act, Mary gradually self-destructed, collapsing on her own despair with the loss not only of her two daughters, but also of her lover Harry, whom she had hoped would marry her (hence the unworn wedding dress hanging in her closet for years). Harry stayed with his non-Indigenous wife, just as Pinkerton remarried within his own race and nationality.

In the case of Cressy, she had to give her child up, not, however, to the father, but to her mother. But neither Butterfly nor Cressy had any choice about the compromising situations that favored the male, who regarded each as a sexual possession: an arranged marriage with an American husband for Butterfly, and a violent act by an Indigenous man imposed on Cressy. The destiny of their children was out of their hands. Unlike Butterfly, however, whose actions are suicidal, Cressy's burning down the house is an act of vengeance, and is not self-destructive. Whereas Butterfly's actions are directed inward, Cressy's are directed outward. Torching the house incinerates the horrible memories and destroys the physical space where the abominable act took place. This deed is clearly a recuperative move. It also exorcises Mary's ghost, a haunting presence for Cressy since she stepped foot in the house. With Butterfly's deliriously heart-wrenching aria playing (before she commits hari-kari) during the house burning sequence, this scene is "a triumphant reversal," as Nolan notes: the aria by which the mother kills herself is the same aria by which the child now kills the mother (Nolan, 2004, 181). Cressy wipes the slate clean, further exorcising the burden of the character of Butterfly. Further, she and Mae (who also participates in setting the fire) are free of the specter of colonial paternalism, whereas Mary could never be, as she desperately depended upon Harry for her identity.[12]

However, in the process of driving away her demons, Cressy appears to go into a suicidal trance, as if hypnotized by the flames around her. She seems to forget herself, eyes wide and glazed over with the thrill of this liberating ritual. She lingers in the collapsing structure, oblivious to the immediate danger. We think she will burn up with the house, and inadvertently sacrifice herself as Butterfly did as a tonic for her shame and despair. Suddenly, Mae runs in and pulls Cressy safely outside. This is a significant move for Mae, who up until this point has been sullen and withdrawn, subject to outbursts, as discussed earlier. Reaching out to Cressy is a crucial step in Mae's growth, for she begins to leave the past behind, and accept her sister in a loving and clearly protective way. Mae thus initiates a reconstitution of a family ruptured and tainted by the mother. Burning down their mother's house, a fiercely aggressive, yet ultimately rejuvenating act bonds them. Cressy and Mae are invigorated and ready to start afresh.

Though *Radiance* began with an almost unbearable anguish of the legacy of an Aboriginal mother who did not protect her daughters, and who was an unhealthy role model, Mae and Cressy have boldly empowered themselves. The next morning we see them in the front seat of Mae's Falcon, incognito with wigs and sunglasses, suggesting their new identities: adult sisters in charge of their lives. They are both upbeat and smiling. But what about Nona, who fled the burning house the night before, her arms clutching the can which contained the ashes of her grandmother? She is still closely bonded to Mary, and has carefully spread her ashes on Nora Island, restoring Mary's spiritual link to her island birthplace. Wary of Cressy as her mother, Nona is wordless as she gets into the car. Eying Cressy rather defensively—yet not contemptuously—she suddenly exclaims, "[t]here's no fuckin' way I'm calling you Mum," as if to say, "I am not ready for this maternal arrangement—yet."[13]

Mother and daughter, newly reacquainted, traveling on the road together, also mark the end of *High Tide*. In *Radiance*, however, Nona is certainly not in the mental and emotional state that Ally is: eager, trusting, and confident, clearly secure in the company of her beloved mother Lilli. However, despite Nona's petulant attitude and soft refusal to acknowledge Cressy, she does at least *choose* to stay in the car with her. As with *High Tide*, there is no narrative assurance that either new family will remain together. Yet, in both films, there is palpable excitement and anticipation on the part of mothers and daughters (and sisters in the case of *Radiance*) embarking on the high road together. These scenarios are radically different from the conclusion of *Fran*. She is alone in her house, which is unbearably quiet. Her face registers sadness and distress, sorely missing the company of her daughters and son.

Fran, *High Tide*, and *Radiance* are bold and unflinching films set in present day that explore the difficulties and challenges facing young, single mothers who are on their own without the assistance and companionship of a responsible loving father or father-figure. These sensitively written and insightful female-centered works break new ground with respect to class, race, and socioeconomic status. The cycles of birth, death, and rebirth are enhanced by the ocean-side settings in *High Tide* and *Radiance*, the tropical setting for the latter film also conjuring up usurped Indigenous land rights and the Stolen Generations. In *Fran*, on the other hand, community housing on the fringes of desolate suburbs is an apt setting for a broken family with fragile ties. These three films explore the delicate subject of troubled motherhood through flawed, yet nonetheless sympathetic women. Negligence, desertion, and abjectivity are balanced with a newfound self-awareness as well as a spirit of forgiveness (for self and others) and/or reconciliation.

Released in the 1980s, *Fran* and *High Tide* benefited from the 10BA scheme (1981–8), the funding option which encouraged private financing to complement reduced government support. *Radiance* was financed in part by the new federal government agency, the Film Financing Corporation (1988), along with additional private funding. The success of these films with audiences as well as acclaim at film festivals, in both cases locally and internationally, helped to pave the way for more female-centered films, many focusing on motherhood, for example, *Sweetie* (1989) and *Muriel's Wedding* (1994), both discussed at the end of Chapter 3, and *Rabbit Proof Fence* (2002), discussed in detail in Chapter 5.

Notes

1   Armstrong has explained the gender shift in Lilli's character. After reviewing two drafts of the script which featured a male protagonist, she felt that something was not right. "And I suggested to Laura that maybe we should make the main character a woman. Once we thought about it, we realized it would make for a tougher, more original film. We had all seen stories about the lonely, alienated 1980s man who is touched by a relationship with a child … And we thought it would be great to create a modern woman who was a drifter, because the behavior of a mother who deserts her child is still not condoned by society. It's much more accepted that a man will walk out on his child." (See Forsberg, 1988.)

2   Cate Shortland's *Somersault* (2004) can be compared to *Fran*, though *Somersault's* focus is on the teenager, Heidi, rather than the mother. Heidi could be Lisa a few years older, back living with Fran, and if Fran were to take on a new lover. Like Lisa, Heidi is neglected, and there is no father in the single-parent family. Heidi, however, is more sexually adventurous and seductive than Lisa. She comes on to her mother's live-in boyfriend, who cannot resist her advances. Heidi's mother finds them together and is furious. Heidi runs away, and is on her own for several weeks in search of companionship and love. Mother and daughter are tentatively reconciled at the end.

3   With regard to mothers and daughters, Creed also examines *Shame* (Steve Jodrell, 1988) and *A Woman's Tale* (Paul Cox, 1991). (See Creed, 1992, 20–2.)

4   Stephen Crofts has commented that *High Tide* is a deft blend of three genres: social realism, art film, and melodrama. As dramatized in *High Tide*, Crofts defines social realism as attention to gritty, working-class Australian life and culture in the coastal environment, while he notes that the art film is associated with stylishness (innovative and adventurous camerawork), psychologization of its characters, and narrative irresolution. (See Crofts, 1991, 18, 20.)

5   This is Lilli's only way to make fast cash to pay for her car so she can leave the park as soon as possible, at Bet's insistence.

6   Bet has little organic connection to the ocean, as if she wishes to barricade herself from the setting of John's death. She doesn't go near it, and threatens to take Ally away from it in her hurry to whisk Ally away from Lilli. The closest she comes to the ocean is through her job at the fish-processing plant where she wears a long, plastic apron and gloves which, however, serve to insulate her from anything linked the sea.

7   The ocean is also Lilli's and Ally's connection to the husband/lost father—to be close to it offers a comfortable proximity to his memory.

8   Perkins wanted a fresh new location, rather than the outback or bush, the usual settings for dramas featuring Aboriginal characters.

9   Mae has been wary and judgmental of Nona ever since she arrived, even taking on the role of an outraged mother who is disgusted with her "daughter" behaving badly—for example, Nona's tasteless outfit that she wears to Mary's funeral—cowboy boots and hat, and a revealing short black dress.

10 Ceridwen Spark argues that "Cressy's reference to the smell of petrol … inflects with racist constructions of Aboriginal men as petrol-sniffers and pigs." This supports her argument that the film constructs Black maleness, rather than whiteness, as Aboriginal women's primary problem (Spark, 2001, 43).

11 As Catherine Simpson argues, the mother's house can be interpreted as a microcosm of the nation: living a degraded borderline existence under the thumb

of the colonizer hierarchy. Burning down Harry's house functions as "a symbolic overthrowing of the power relations manifested in this home [as well as] …an attempt to undermine the … colonial hegemony manifested both symbolically and literally in the house" (Simpson, 1999, 29, 30).

12 The dynamic of an Aboriginal female dependent upon non-Indigenous males for her happiness and identity is consistent with films such as *Walkabout* and *The Chant of Jimmie Blacksmith*, with the genders switched, wherein the identity of Aboriginal males is contingent upon acceptance by non-Indigenous society and, in particular, non-Indigenous females.

13 The film ends more positively than the play, wherein each woman goes her separate way.

Sources

Byrnes, Paul (1986), "Fear and Loathing in WA: Fran," *Cinema Papers*, 55: 62.

Creed, Barbara (1992), "Mothers and Lovers: Oedipal Transgressions in Recent Australian Cinema," *Metro*, 91: 14–22.

Crofts, Stephen (1991), "Genre, Style and Address in High Tide," *Metro*, 87: 17–20.

Dzenis, Anna (1993), "Review of Fran," in Scott Murray (ed.), *Australian Film, 1978–1992: A Survey of Theatrical Features*, Melbourne: Oxford University Press.

Fischer, Lucy (1996), *Cinematernity: Film, Motherhood, Genre*, Princeton, NJ: Princeton University Press.

Forsberg, Myra (1988), "Partnership Swells 'High Tide,'" *New York Times*, March 6. High Tide file, Academy Library, Beverly Hills, California.

Kael, Pauline (1988), "Review of High Tide," *The New Yorker*, February 22: 84–5.

Nolan, Marguerite (2004), "Exorcising History: Radiance and the Abject Aboriginal Mother," *New Cinemas: Journal of Contemporary Film*, 2 (3): 175–87.

Simpson, Catherine (1998), "Suburban Subversions: Women's Negotiations of Suburban Space in Australian Cinema," *Metro*, 118: 24–32.

Simpson, Catherine (1999), "Notes on the Significance of the Home and the Past in Radiance," *Metro*, 120: 28–31.

Spark, Ceridwen (2001), "Gender and Radiance," *Hecate*, 27 (2): 38–49.

Warrick, Steve (1989), "Review of High Tide," *Film Quarterly*, 42 (3): 21–6.

5

The Indigenous Road Film

A rich array of ground-breaking films featuring Indigenous Australians have reworked and put new spins on the conventions of the road picture, illuminating and exploring Aboriginal culture and history in gripping and insightful ways. Some films are set in the past, while others take place in contemporary times. Even the titles allude to the primacy of the road journey—*Walkabout* (1971), *Backroads* (1977), *Wrong Side of the Road* (1981), and *The Tracker* and *Rabbit Proof Fence* (both 2002). This chapter examines these films, in addition to another road film, *The Chant of Jimmie Blacksmith* (1978), in detail, all of which cover a range of journeys: quests for manhood, searches for home and family (established or new), escapes from the law, adventures on the high road, political activism through performance, and hunts for fugitives. Regardless of the initial reasons for the journey, each trek turns into a life-changing experience for protagonists amidst frequent life or death situations, where survival (physical, mental, and/or spiritual) is uncertain or impossible. Significantly, in all but two films, the protagonists are children, adolescents, or just entering adulthood. These narratives dramatize the ways in which colonizer oppression and dispossession invade and rupture the formative years of innocent and vulnerable members of Indigenous families and communities. The films explored in this chapter exude filmmakers' acute sensitivity to Indigenous Peoples, their history, society, and culture, thus broaching and investigating a variety of hot and timely issues: reconciliation, frontier violence, rural racism, land rights (in light of the Mabo decision), the Stolen Generations, and the history wars. Beyond the areas outlined above, what makes these Indigenous road films unique?

Given the critical role of the land in Indigenous history and culture, road journeys take on special significance. First, the land has a deeply spiritual meaning. According to the Dreamtime/Dreamings, the Aboriginal creation myth, the land is inhabited by ancient spirits which created the land and all its natural features. Traveling on the land implies a sacred communion and primal connection, a dynamic that directly or indirectly underpins at least three of the films discussed in this chapter. Secondly, in light of historical dispossession—Indigenous land usurped and claimed by invading British colonizers at the end of the eighteenth century—as well as ongoing tensions, conflicts, and clashes over land rights, the themes of trespassing and racial boundaries are inherent or dramatized in all of the journeys.

Thirdly, four of the six journeys are on foot, where great distances on rough (unpaved) terrain are covered, underscoring the physical difficulties protagonists face, whether the journeys are self-directed or coerced. Thus, protagonists can be confronted with a variety of taxing elements, including bitter cold, blistering heat, driving rain, and/or blinding dust storms, as well as hazardous terrain in the mountains, outback, or bush, any or all of which threaten their well-being and survival. Often, however, the road and its environs become a proving ground. Without the benefit of mechanized transportation, and especially in the case of fugitives or those who are lost, this absence curtails their ability to cover long distances in order to return home or successfully escape. In the two films where cars are used on the trip—for a getaway and fun as well as a practical mode of transportation—the security of the car is temporary. Safety can be violated, the car stolen, or subject to invasive searches. Along this line, cars in Indigenous road films play a different and less demonstrative role than in non-Indigenous films. For example, in the Australian Gothic films *The Cars That Ate Paris* (1974) and the four *Mad Max* films, *Mad Max* (1979), *Mad Max II* (1981), *Mad Max Beyond Thunderdome* (1985), and *Mad Max Fury Road* (2015), all discussed in detail in Chapter 6, Australia's obsessive car culture is boldly dramatized. High-powered mechanical vehicles and excessive speeds become linked to male identity. In Indigenous road pictures, the car is not so firmly bonded to male identity.[1]

Walkabout merges two journeys: two British children lost in the outback meet a young Aboriginal man on his walkabout; he befriends and cares for them. *Blacksmith* (based on an actual historical, turn-of-the-century Indigenous man) features a youth of mixed-race, who embarks on a journey to enter white society. Though *Walkabout* and *Blacksmith* have been the subject of much analysis, the attraction and interaction between young Aboriginal men and non-Indigenous women, who represent powerful symbols of Black oppression, have not been examined thoroughly. Further, Roeg's depiction of the Dreamtime/Dreamings, as well as his innovative camerawork, sound design, and editing, has not been explored fully. *Backroads* is a cross-racial, male buddy film, featuring two Indigenous men and one non-Indigenous man who take off joyriding on rural roads in a stolen car. *Wrong Side of the Road* is not only a touchstone film for Aboriginal performance by young men playing popular music on the road, but also examines the personal journeys of two of the band members toward maturity.

The Tracker, set in 1922 during the frontier period when mass murders of Aboriginal Peoples were common, focuses on a wily Indigenous tracker, who reluctantly leads three non-Indigenous policemen into the bush to capture an Aboriginal fugitive accused of murdering a non-Indigenous woman. *Rabbit Proof Fence* is set approximately a decade later, when assimilation of mixed-race children was instituted. This film features three girls kidnapped from their mother, and who courageously escape a settlement house to walk over a thousand miles back home. Significantly, with its female protagonists and matriarchal family, *Rabbit Proof Fence* challenges the traditions of the male-dominated road picture.[2]

Throughout this chapter, I use the terms Indigenous, Indigenous Australian, Indigenous Australians, Indigenous Australian Peoples, Indigenous Peoples, Aboriginal person, Aboriginal Peoples, Australia's First Peoples, Australia's First Nations Peoples, in the larger framework of Aboriginal and Torres Strait Islander Peoples, depending upon the context, to refer to a person/persons of Indigenous descent, "… [those] who identif[y] as such and who…[are] recognized by the Aboriginal community to be so," adapting Karen Jennings' definition (Jennings, 1993, 8). Further, I use the term mixed-race to describe children/descendants of Indigenous/non-Indigenous parentage. Finally, my analyses do not intend to diminish or understate the presence of many different tribes/communities of Indigenous Australians throughout the Australian continent and the Torres Strait Islands, each with unique cultures, histories, and languages.

Before moving on to the analyses of the individual films, it is necessary to briefly summarize Indigenous politicization in the post–Second World War period as a context for subsequent cinematic representations. Historically, Indigenous Peoples had never been allowed to vote, nor had they ever been included in the census. The historical British invasion and colonization of Australia that began with the first landing in 1788 desecrated sacred Indigenous land and systematically destroyed the lives within Aboriginal communities. As Philip Hanson has commented, waves of subsequent immigrants provided source material for "trauma narratives" (Hanson, 2017, 1), accounts of persecution, loss, and displacement impacting generations of Australia's First Nations Peoples, who had lived on the continent for at least 60,000 years. After the Second World War,

Indigenous activists from a variety of Aboriginal organizations accelerated their lobbying for civil rights. As Christine Jennett notes:

> The 1960s was a watershed in Aboriginal affairs, with increasing challenges being posed to the old paternalistic racial order that had been dominated by pastoral, church and government interests. The churches were rethinking their attitudes to matters of social justice; Australian governments were forced to respond to a whole range of new pressure groups demanding increased socio-economic equality and participation by citizens in decisions about the physical and social landscape created by business and government.
>
> (Jennett, 2001, 121)

This more enlightened and tolerant climate amidst Indigenous activism paid off. In 1962 the Electoral Act was amended; all Aboriginal and Torres Strait Islander adults—Australia's First Nations Peoples—were granted the right to vote in federal elections, with state voting privileges established a few years later. Moreover, in 1967 Australia's constitution was amended to confer citizenship status to Indigenous Peoples; they now had the legal status to be counted as citizens in their country. Both these events fueled the Land Rights Movement. Though the impetus of the Land Rights Movement focused on the recovery of land taken away from Indigenous Peoples, land rights was not just about land, as Nicolas Peterson points out. He argues, "It is, importantly, about the restoration of some of the political autonomy and self-determination that existed prior to European colonization" (Peterson, 2000, 623). In other words, land rights encompasses the "range of rights and levels of independence" that go with land ownership in the larger context of resisting the yoke of white paternalism (Peterson, 2000, 623).

Several years after the referendum, the Whitlam Labor administration (1972–5) provided strong government support for Indigenous Australians, which included legislating federal funding to improve Aboriginal housing, education, welfare, health, employment, and legal aid. Further, upon the establishment of a federal Department of Aboriginal Affairs (DAA) with Indigenous representatives in key leadership appointments, "Whitlam ... [created] a policy of self-determination enabl ... [ing] the creation of self-managing community organizations which handled health, legal aid, land and welfare services" (Haebich, 2000, 572–3). Significantly, in 1975 the landmark Racial Discrimination Act was passed by Parliament, which outlawed discrimination on the grounds of race, color, and national or ethnic origin. Shortly thereafter, the Aboriginal Land Rights Act of 1976 resulted in the return of over 40 percent of the Northern Territory to

Aboriginal Peoples, putting into place, as Peterson notes, "structures and access to financial resources that have given Indigenous Peoples in this territory considerable autonomy" (Peterson, 2000, 623).

The reforms described above, amidst the increasing visibility of Indigenous leaders in Australian politics and society, provided a strong incentive and framework for revival filmmakers to feature a range of Indigenous characters in their films with compassion and an informed open-mindedness to Aboriginal culture and history.[3] It is within this enlightened atmosphere that filmmakers, non-Indigenous and Indigenous, created the films discussed in this chapter.

Walkabout

Walkabout, directed by Nicolas Roeg, written by Edward Bond[4] (both British), and based on the book by Australian author James Vance Marshall, was not officially part of the Australian Film Revival, as it was American financed. But with its debut at Cannes, *Walkabout* focused the attention of world audiences upon an unfamiliar country through the perspective of a young Indigenous man from the sensibility of "European outsider[s] Roeg [and Bond] who perhaps needed a dark continent for mythological investment," as Dermody and Jacka have noted (1988, 82).

Walkabout is an interactive, ultimately tragic journey of growth, friendship, and mutual attraction between agents of two cultures. It is a parable of reconciliation between Indigenous and non-Indigenous Peoples long before this word was in public circulation. Though the young Aboriginal man (David Gulpilil), approximately sixteen, has a wondrous trek across the outback with a non-Indigenous girl (Jenny Agutter), fourteen, and her brother (Luc Roeg), age six, whose lives he saves, their increasing proximity to urban civilization taints his walkabout and leads to his death. A self-destructive, sexually repressed, and oppressive white Australian society has a profoundly emasculating and crippling impact on this Indigenous man in body and spirit.

Balancing lyrical poetic and realist styles, Roeg dramatizes the journey through his bold, innovative, and dazzling camerawork (he also served as cinematographer), sound design, and editing—techniques often overlooked in other analyses. Roeg fine-tunes his stylistic innovations throughout the film to capture the allure, mysteries, and dangers of the Australian desert, as well as the complexities of Indigenous culture, including the

Dreamtime/Dreamings—Indigenous creation mythology. Roeg's attention to the perspective of the young Indigenous man, along with David Gulpilil's intelligence and vigor, creates a more proactive, dynamic, and complex character than other writers have acknowledged. The complexities of this young man—his sensibility, thoughts, and feelings—are brought to life by Gulpilil, who brings sensitivity and vitality through a nuanced rendering of his character. Thus, he *drives* the narrative, and is not merely a "solitary, silent figure ... who ... [moves] through magnificent landscapes ... [completing] the picture of the primordial Australian scene" (Jennings, 1993, 20, quoting Moore and Muecke). Further, he transcends the stereotype of the noble savage who is "vague and mysterious" (Hickling-Hudson, 1990, 265). With acute sensitivity, Roeg explores the modern-day impact of eighteenth-century British invasion, desecration, and dispossession of sacred Indigenous land, including the destruction of the lives and culture of Indigenous Peoples in the context of historical colonization of Australia that began with the first landing.

It is useful at this point to define walkabout and its connection to the Dreamtime/Dreamings.[5] First, Roeg challenges the meaning of the European-created word "walkabout," a crude and blatantly racist distortion of the role and purpose of an Indigenous ritual spiritual journey. As James Cowan argues, the word "walkabout" was fabricated to patronize and disdain Aboriginal Peoples. He writes:

> During the 19th century, European settlers coined ... [the] phrase ... [walkabout which] to this day implies a moral condemnation of the Aboriginal work ethic and a desultory incomprehension of Aboriginal religious life. If an Aboriginal stockman chose to go walkabout—that is, make a Dream Journey—his employer would inevitably conclude that the man wished to avoid work. Thus, an attitude of suspicion was born which pervades any dialogue between white and black Australians even today.
>
> (Cowan, 1989, 43)

Cowan, Australian born, studied Indigenous culture for ten years, living with their communities in the Kimberly Region and the Northern Territory. He also lived in Balgo Hills, a remote Indigenous community in the Tanami Desert, dedicating himself to improving their lives. For Aboriginal Peoples, as Cowan notes, a walkabout or Dream Journey can take place on two levels. It can be a social activity involving the participation of family members, or a "more personal activity embarked upon alone ... [so] that the individual might experience a closer understanding of his sacred nature" (Cowan, 1989, 45). For either purpose, and as dramatized in the film, a walkabout facilitates contact with ancient spirits through nature by way of activities such as hunting, singing, dancing, and painting. Cowan adds: "[Indigenous individuals'] encounter with ... 'country' as they roam across it is an encounter with a spiritual genesis, both personal and collective" (Cowan, 1989, 49), and is closely tied in to the Dreamtime/Dreamings, the Aboriginal creation myth. In this context, nature has a deeply spiritual significance.

Secondly, the Dreamtime/Dreamings is a belief common to all Aboriginal tribes that the ancient spirits, who possessed superhuman powers, rose up through the earth, lived on and reformed the land, creating all of its natural features—that is, waterholes, rivers, mountains, and gorges. At the end of their journeys they disappeared back into the earth. Some merged themselves with the land into rocks and deserts; others changed into animals such as birds, fish, even trees, stars, or transient entities such as wind or rainfall (Primrose, 1982, 179-80). The Dreamtime/Dreamings or "sacred time" implies that the land is alive in the sense that it is inhabited by ancient spirits: "an expanded consciousness," as Munya Andrews comments (Andrews, 2019, 6), as well as an "essence that is in the permanence of the land," as Ian Primrose remarks (Primrose, 1982, 180). This worldview is consistent with one of the ways in which Indigenous Peoples perceive time, which Bob Hodge and Vijay Mishra identify as "secular," [wherein] "present and past merge into one" (Hodge and Mishra, 1991, 101). Thus, throughout *Walkabout*, Roeg and Bond suggest not only the presence of ancient spirits inherent in wildlife and environment who watch over the children, but also the existence of a deeply spiritual link between the young Indigenous man on his walkabout and the Dreamtime/Dreamings. Both of these dynamics are dramatized through image and sound design.

The Dreamtime/Dreamings is evoked during the girl and boy's first full day in the outback as they scale the rocky terrain after having run away from their father (John Meillon), who suddenly and inexplicably started to shoot at them during their picnic in the outback. As they advance further into the outback, Roeg's cinematography captures the beauty of the land: the rich blue of the sky, the vibrant greens of the trees and brush, in contrast to the reddish-brown shale which the two scale. A large bird soars majestically through the sky in an extreme long shot. Captured in a low angle shot, the children stand on the edge of a huge cliff: a reverse zoom miniaturizes them. This shot dissolves to a pan of a rocky landscape, and we relocate the children in another extreme long shot on another precipice. We are then brought closer to them by a forward zoom. This sequence suggests that the land and bird spirits are watching the girl and the boy. A short time later, the soundtrack reinforces the presence of the Dreamtime/Dreamings spirits after the girl convinces her brother to take his mind off his fatigue; he can play with his airplane while she practices singing. Several dissolving shots of sand dunes are followed by a shot of the moon, which dissolves to a bright sun. We hear the sighs of breathing or whispering, as if these images are alive with the collective consciousness of the land and the universe. This combination of visuals and sound create the sense of a powerful spiritual presence, and that larger forces are at play.

When the young Indigenous man enters the film, the visuals are dramatically altered, as if the film is responding organically and instinctively to his presence. He takes control of the narrative, dictating a new vocabulary in imagery and sound. This happens when the children have been alone for several days at the mercy of the relentless sun with diminishing water and food. They face certain death. Though the outback initially exuded a lyrical splendor and majesty via Roeg's long takes, which revealed huge expanses of desert and sky with radiant sunrises and sunsets, amidst a range of wildlife, including a scorpion, lizards, and various species of birds, the imagery of death is now everywhere. This motif began with the father's abrupt suicide by gunshot and his igniting his car, but is further suggested by the dried-up water hole, a vulture hovering above the children, and one lizard swallowing another. However, the young Indigenous man gives an impetus and new perspective to the narrative, which could have ended with the deaths of the girl and her brother. Further, he literally brings them life by quickly finding water in a deep basin beneath the sand.

When the children first see the young Indigenous man, his graceful and skilled movements suggest a lyrical dance: he runs and leaps, throwing his spear at lizards with great precision and poise. The hunting sequence that follows reinforces his power over the image and narrative. It opens with a shot of a bird in flight, a snake winding on the ground, and several kangaroos in motion. The grainy film captures the texture of the animals, enhancing the beauty of their form. As he runs after a kangaroo, the quivering movements of the hand-held camera make us feel as if we are following and running with the young Indigenous man. We feel immersed in a dazzling choreography between hunter and hunted. This is a vibrant land controlled by and in tune with a magical presence, a young man on his sacred journey of survival and maturity while he communes with and is watched over by ancient spirits—voices heard on the soundtrack in the sequence earlier, when the girl and boy had all but given up hope for survival with no water in sight.

Once the young Indigenous man has made his stunning entry, the film shifts to a delicate balance between his spiritual odyssey[6] and the sharing of his walkabout with the boy and the girl. The boy, not yet indoctrinated by Western culture, is more open to the company of his new male companion, his culture, and way of life on the outback. When the boy first saw the young Indigenous man on the sand dune, he remarked, "Dad!" Subsequently, the three function as a loose family, the girl having already taken a maternal role. As a result of his interaction with the young Indigenous man, the boy experiences his own walkabout full of revelation, enlightenment, and growth: the journey is fabulous adventure for him. Further, his new friend has a powerful effect on the boy's imaginary powers. For example, as they trek across the outback, the boy has a vision of a band of camels and riders. He also hunts with the young Indigenous man, who becomes a trusted mentor, who paints dazzling designs on the boy's back, arms, and chest. The boy is thrilled, exclaiming, "I think he [the young Indigenous man] is going to take us to the moon," then qualifies his statement in more extravagant terms, "I think he is going to take us to Mars!"

The girl reacts quite differently. Several years older than her brother, and engrained with a highly ethnocentric perspective, she is more reserved and wary. Her immediate reaction to the unfamiliar stranger when they first approached him was one of condescension and an imperative: "Water, drink, you must understand that," unlike her wildly enthusiastic brother, who accepted the young Indigenous man as a comrade right away, and communicated successfully with sign language. The girl also blurted out, "We're English," instantly setting up an imposing European arrogance and self-righteousness of the invasive colonizing culture. Yet, when she observes the invigorating effect the young Indigenous man has on her brother, which includes his protective care of him—for example, he puts animal blood on her brother's sunburnt back—she eagerly joins them in an afternoon of play in a huge eucalyptus tree.

As a sign of girl's sexual awakening, she stares at the young Indigenous man's back, buttocks, and thighs, responding with awe and pleasure as she walks behind him. The evening after the three play together, he talks to her gently in the darkness as she carefully touches the brush burns on the insides of her legs. His viewpoint of and sexual attraction to her was suggested earlier by shots of the long limbs of the tree intercut with shots of her legs as she climbed the tree. Now they regard each other in close shots with more than a hint of desire as we hear their breathing on the soundtrack, creating a feeling of intimacy and sensuality. This is a powerfully sublime moment of understated, yet poignant understanding between the two.

Their mutual attraction and perspectives are examined in the larger context of an enlightening cross-cultural comparison later in the film as Roeg juxtaposes a satirical sequence of several British and Italian meteorologists on the salt flats (a good distance away from the three), with lyrical scenes of the young Indigenous man hunting while the girl swims in a lagoon. Specifically, Roeg contrasts cultural attitudes toward nudity and nakedness. In the meteorologist sequence, the behavior of the males and female reinforces the Western perspective toward the nude, yet also makes fun of it. The woman who works with several male meteorologists holds a privileged position among them. She ignores them as she does her work at a table where two other men work, while the rest play cards at a table nearby. The woman is a nude for these male spectators. John Berger has distinguished between "nudity" and "nakedness" in *Ways of Seeing*. To be naked is simply to be without clothes (Berger, 1972, 53). The Aboriginal women seen in an earlier sequence, sitting in the father's charred Volkswagen, are naked, comfortable in a state of being without clothes. On the other hand, to be nude, a phenomenon in artistic representation in Western civilization, according to Berger, implies that the image of a female body is specifically on display for a male spectator (Berger, 1972, 54). She is the source of his visual pleasure, and is also an object of desire. When the girl, her brother and the young Indigenous man played in the eucalyptus tree, the girl was highly self-conscious of her exposed legs and thighs, implying her internalization of the Western concept of nude—she was aware that she was being observed by a male spectator, in this case the young Indigenous man.

Unlike the girl, who modestly covered her legs, the woman, aware of the gaze of the meteorologists, provocatively displays her thighs by crossing her legs, and by opening her blouse so her breasts are visible. She eagerly plays up her image as an object of desire by giving the men the privilege of the look. This notion is reinforced by the playboy style nudes on the playing cards who sit seductively. Simultaneously, the men's behavior toward the woman makes them look silly. As they stare at any slight movement that the woman makes, their voracious, even grotesque looks are captured in freeze frames. One man's teeth appear distorted and huge as he looks through a magnifying glass, transforming him into a predator. Moreover, the men play useless power games: one cuts the line of the weather balloon so that another, who tries to seduce the woman, must run after it.

The men's boredom with work on the outback and resulting eroticized play are contrasted to the young Indigenous man's integrated delight with hunting in nature while visualizing the girl swimming in the raw. Unlike the non-Indigenous men, he is not a spectator obsessed with a look at a woman as a passive object. Instead, his vision assigns the girl a role that is as active as his own. While the young Indigenous man hunts and the girl swims, the lyrical music on the soundtrack reinforces his contentment with this harmonious activity of play and work. The girl's naked body twirls and ripples in the water like a silverfish. As he spears his catch, preparing fish and lizard for cooking, we have the impression that his attraction to her is an extension of his love and respect for nature, so that killing his prey is part of a life cycle, and the girl's swimming in the pool is a symbolic representation of rebirth from death. Both the young Indigenous man and the girl are equally central in their own scenes. Beverle Houston and Marsha Kinder add, "[His] … totemistic identification of the girl does not reduce her to an object but expresses his animistic sense that her female spirit is powerful and lives in things [i.e., the fish that he spears] that look like her" (Houston and Kinder, 1980, 445).

However, despite her attraction to the young Indigenous man, the girl is unable to bridge racial boundaries and accept him as a sexual partner. Subsequently, she soon assumes a position of power and control over him, and even begins to treat him like a slave. This change in attitude was first suggested in the swimming/hunting sequence described above. Roeg's intercutting between the two activities suggests that the girl thinks of the young Indigenous man as she swims, yet relegates him to a hunter and preparer of food for her and her brother. This is a very different attitude than her gaze suggested earlier, when she admired his body from behind while following him, or regarded him with obvious affection after the afternoon of play in the eucalyptus tree. The girl's new attitude is demonstrated in a subsequent key sequence where they cross a stream; she rides on the Aboriginal's back across the water.[7] This stream represents a dividing line between the outback wilderness and civilization. The radio the boy carries plays the song "Los Angeles," indicating the proximity of non-Indigenous civilization, which is signaled visually by the meteorologists nearby whose balloons the three subsequently find. Soon thereafter, the young Indigenous man discovers a paved road which he shows to the boy, who relays this information to his sister. At this point, as Brian Adams and Graham Shirley note, the desert for the girl becomes "an alien environment to be traversed as quickly as possible" (Adams and Shirley, 1983, 246). Her walkabout comes to an end, and she reverts to her obsession to return to her home. Subsequently, the young Indigenous man loses control of the narrative, his walkabout, and his special bond with the Dreamtime/Dreamings.

His fate, death by suicide, was foreshadowed earlier during the boy's telling of a story to his sister as the three walked through a grove of eucalyptus trees. This inset narrative, which features a boy and his mother, functions as a metaphor for the girl's changing attitude and increasing coldness toward their Indigenous companion, despite his growing attraction to her. Her brother begins his tale, "He lived with his mother in the house on the top of the hill. She'd never spoken to him. He'd never heard her say a word. He thought she was dumb and she was blind too … He saw her sitting in the window and she was talking. And when he got inside, she wouldn't say a word." The girl's brother then goes through the steps that the boy takes to attract his mother's attention, using a ladder to climb and reach the window where he sees her, also attempting to hear her, "with her blind eyes staring straight at him … her mouth opening and shutting." Like the boy in the story, the young Indigenous man tries to reach out and understand the girl; like the mother, the girl chooses to be deaf to his attempts, refusing to understand him, speaking "silently to herself." The girl's brother continues, "[H]e knocked the ladder down, so he was stuck." Clearly, the young Indigenous man is "stuck" in an impossible situation, his inability to reach the girl, compounded by her reticence and increasing indifference to him. Her brother adds, "He couldn't jump down … So he just sat there … He couldn't climb down." He then abruptly concludes his story with a sudden turn of events. "He slipped off the windowsill, fell down and broke his neck." As if trying to give his story a happy ending (and perhaps change the course of events in their evolving journey), the brother says of the mother, "She began to be worried." His sister corrects him, "No, she didn't say anything," clearly pointing to her own apathy and insensitivity. Throughout this sequence, Roeg superimposes rolling pages with words, suggesting the dominance of a Western perspective, as well as the girl's willful actions from this point on in the film.

The girl soon assumes another power position in the abandoned house where they stay for the night. Once inside, the girl's first glance of the room, shot through a wide angle distorting lens, exaggerates its size and the importance she places upon it. Roeg dramatizes her empowerment in a high-angle shot where her shadow replaces that of the young Indigenous man in the center of the house as she takes control of the structure, thus displacing him and casting him out. In a few minutes, she sends him for water like a servant, and insists that he say the

English word for water. This is an abrupt change for the young Indigenous man, for thus far he has spoken in his own tribal dialect.

Their closeness to civilization is further signaled by the white hunters nearby who shoot game only for sport with high-powered rifles, leaving carcasses to rot, or carting them away as trophies. As the hunters speed away in their truck, they narrowly miss the young Indigenous man, who jumps out of the way at the last minute. This scene conjures up *The Cars That Ate Paris* (1974), *Mad Max* (1979), and *Mad Max II* (1981), in which motor vehicles function as killing machines. Accordingly, in *Walkabout*, the hunters relegate the outback to a staging ground for their destructive pleasure. The young Indigenous man sadly watches from a distance as his sacred means of survival is taken away and destroyed. White encroachment is also reinforced acoustically: the soundtrack is devoid of the Dreamtime/Dreamings spirits heard prior, their voices silenced by the sounds of shotguns and the truck engine. As compared to the hunting sequence described earlier that the young Indigenous man orchestrated and dominated, this sequence has none of the grace, kinetic energy, or symbiosis with nature. Beautiful choreography is replaced by the graphic imagery of the slaughter. Stills of fleeing kangaroos, buffalo, and birds suggest that they are frozen in fear, their terror intensified by the explosion of shotgun blasts. Nearby, a water buffalo collapses on the ground in slow motion more than once, as if the slaying plays over in the young Indigenous man's mind, reinforcing his distress.

His subsequent suicide is not just a function of the girl's sexual rejection of him during his dazzling and heartfelt courtship dance. The young Indigenous man's will and his means to live have been crushed by the destructive presence of the hunters who slaughter his game, who disrupt his walkabout, and rupture his symbiotic and sacred relationship with the Dreamtime/Dreaming—denying his rights of passage into manhood. The asphalt road that the young Indigenous man found earlier and eagerly pointed out to the boy signals another sign of colonizer trespassing; it slices through the outback as if slashed with a knife. Though the young Indigenous man experienced a wondrous trek filled with pleasures and friendship across the outback with the girl and her brother, whose lives he saved, their increasing closeness to their civilization has tainted his walkabout and led to his death.

Back in her home society at the film's end as a married woman, she drifts into a safely distanced, fantasized reconstruction of her walkabout where she, the young Indigenous man, and her brother frolic naked in an outback pond as pre-adolescent innocents. It is easier for her to relegate their companion to a non-sexual, non-adult status, keeping him as an eternal boy while she has the luxury of womanhood in her real world. On the soundtrack we hear John Barry's "lush and haunting" score (O'Shaughnessy, 2004, 85), which wafts through the film's final images of the three together. Michael O'Shaughnessy continues, "[These lingering] … soundtrack referents are specifically Western and English, and while all three children are remembered in the lost paradise, it is only the Western children who survive" (O'Shaughnessy, 2004, 86). Gone are the sounds of Indigenous instruments—the didgeridoo and clapsticks—which accompanied and enriched the Aboriginal's courtship dance for the girl. The Dreamtime/Dreamings spirits have been silenced.

In *The Chant of Jimmie Blacksmith*, we shall see a similar non-Indigenous female/Indigenous male dynamic where women function as powerful agents of a controlling society, managing Aboriginal manhood and identity.

The Chant of Jimmie Blacksmith

Like the young Aboriginal man in *Walkabout*, Jimmie Blacksmith[8] (Tommy Lewis), in a film written by Fred Schepisi based on the book by Thomas Keneally, and directed by Schepisi, aspires to manhood by crossing racial boundaries through sexual liaisons and marriage with a non-Indigenous woman, Gilda (Angela Punch-McGregor), who lives with a large family of farmers who are descendants of colonizing farmers. In Jimmie's case, however, he sees marriage as the road to legitimacy in non-Indigenous society, which comprises the first part of his journey. The second part is his frantic escape from the community of farmers after going on a bloody killing spree, murdering the wife and daughters as well as the governess of his boss, and evading capture for several months until wounded, jailed, and hanged. *Jimmie Blacksmith* takes place during the latter years of the "frontier stage" (1788 to early 1930s), a time when any Aboriginal resistance "was crushed brutally and outside due legal process" (Hodge and Mishra, 1990, 38).

More specifically, this film is set during Federation (1901), when the six states of Australia unified under the British Commonwealth, increasing interstate cooperation and diminished competition. Though Australia gained more autonomy from Britain, the Queen of England—Victoria at that time—was still Australia's sovereign head. The status of Indigenous communities remained the same: dispossessed since the end of the eighteenth century, and without citizenship status. Or, as Constable Farrell crudely declares in the film, Indigenous Australian Peoples would continue to "have the same rights ... none."

The role of non-Indigenous society in *Jimmie Blacksmith* is expanded and more complex than in *Walkabout*. Jimmie's associations with its women (and also Aboriginal women, discussed later in this section) contribute to his fluctuating empowerment and disempowerment in his self-delusional journey to manhood and presumed acceptance into the non-Indigenous community. Though Palmer and Gillard argue that the positioning of Aboriginality is central to the formation of white Australian identity (Palmer and Gillard, 2001, 128), the inverse is also true: Indigenous Peoples are dependent upon "their superiors" for the construction of *their* identity. This is the case for Jimmie wherein non-Indigenous women play a key role as the arbiters of power, as we saw in *Walkabout*.

In the film there are two kinds of non-Indigenous females: Jimmie's underclass wife, Gilda (Angela Punch-McGregor), the promiscuous, dim-witted domestic at Boss Newby's; and the kept, landed gentry women, Mrs. Newby (Ruth Cracknell), her two daughters, as well as their governess, Miss Graf (Elizabeth Alexander), all of whom barely tolerate Jimmie. Jimmie naively believes that a non-Indigenous wife assures his acceptance into this community. An Aboriginal man raised on a mission, he was under the tutelage of Minister Neville (Jack Thompson), who essentially "[gave] his life to destroying the blacks," as Pauline Kael notes (1985, 208), by insisting that Jimmie, whose mother was Indigenous and father non-Indigenous, integrate into non-Indigenous society, so that his race would be extinguished. (In *Rabbit Proof Fence*, another Mr. Neville, "Chief Protector of Aboriginals," will practice official assimilation by overseeing the kidnapping of mixed-race Aboriginal children from their mothers to be placed in foster homes.)

However, when Gilda gives birth to a white baby (who may or may not be Jimmie's), the jeering laughter and snide looks of Newby and his sons foreground the folly of Jimmie's marriage. He has no rights as father, this child physical evidence of his deepening estrangement from the community he craves. The taunts of the Newby family add insult to injury. Jimmie's various jobs for local farmers—ironically, he often pounded fence posts into former Aboriginal land—resulted in their consistently cheating him on his wages. When Jimmie asked for his pay, they would kick him off their property, berating or hitting him. Thus, each part of his search for work reinforced his shame and growing rage. How could he be a man, that is, start a family, be a husband and father without money or land to work? Later, however, when he is on the run after the murders,

Jimmie recoups "his" land, having "declared war." He transforms the bush from a thicket prison to his own domain, enjoying mastery as a mighty bush warrior, hiding and avoiding capture successfully for several months.

Jimmie's interaction with the uppity Newby women and Miss Graf in particular is even more daunting than with the non-Indigenous male contingent. As Dermody and Jacka have pointed out, white women are "more powerful signs of black oppression than the white males who oppress them both" (Dermody and Jacka, 1988, 118). Miss Graf takes advantage of her privileged position in the family, frequently teasing Jimmie and flaunting herself as the unobtainable and untouchable female, dramatizing her power in the racial–sexual hierarchy. An educated woman who will marry a wealthy landowner, she is an even more potent symbol than Mrs. Newby. Graf mocks Jimmie's mixed-race family, cuddling his infant son, putting her face next to his, presenting a "superior" and "ideal" model family, white skin next to white skin.

Jimmie's subsequent sudden, violent, and bloody attack singles out Graf, Mrs. Newby, and her daughters: he and his Uncle Tabidgi (Steve Dodd) hack them to death with hatchets. This assault has several implications: brutal demonstrations of empowerment and violent symbolic rapes, in addition to retaliation for Jimmie's emasculation at the hands of an oppressive community. These acts also suggest a reverse genocide, its ferocity functioning as payback for one hundred-plus years of Aboriginal destruction. Accordingly, in his novel, Keneally graphically refers to the women's bodies as "hacked out wombs" (Keneally, 1972, 86). Further, Jimmie escalates his ferocious rampage, returning to all of the farmers who denied him fair wages for payback. For example, in one scene he seeks out and shoots the wife of boss Healey (Tim Robertson) and infant daughter point-blank, effectively taking away the non-Indigenous man's "most prized possessions—their robust, well-fed women, their pink-and-white children" (Kael, 1985, 207). Yet, it is ultimately a non-Indigenous and chaste female, who restores the colonizer dominance and its assumption of God-like power: a nun reports Jimmie to the police after finding him unconscious (wounded by a member of the posse) in one of the rooms of a remote nunnery in the bush when he is at large.

In comparison to the non-Indigenous female characters, Indigenous women are minor characters (only one is given a name), but they are critical in the racial/sexual order. First of all, they are used by farmers and their hands who visit Aboriginal camps for quick sex. The husbands of the Indigenous women cooperate for fear of retaliation or trouble with the police. Clearly, Indigenous females dramatize the irony which resonates throughout Australia's invasive and violent colonizing history. The colonizers disdain the "barbaric and parasitical other" (Palmer and Gillard, 2001, 128), distancing Aboriginal women (and men) through containment (camps) or extermination. Yet, ironically, sexual possession of Indigenous women by non-Indigenous males is regarded as a form of entitlement. Even Jimmie himself illustrates this dynamic. When he visits the Indigenous camps, he plays the dominant male, calling one Aboriginal woman a Black bitch, engaging in rough and forceful sex that implies a rape. He also assumes the airs of a presumptive high and mighty Indigenous man, chastising the woman with a vengeance for letting the farmers have their way with her and other "gins" (a condescending term for Aboriginal women).

The positioning of this scene at this point in the narrative is crucial in two ways. First, earlier that day, Jimmie was stiffed by Healey, who refused to pay him for his work. Significantly, Healey threatened to "cut off [Jimmie's] ... bloody black balls" if he "messed up the fence post job"; Jimmie thus uses the Aboriginal woman to re-empower and re-masculate himself. Secondly, in the camps near Jimmie and the woman, an Aboriginal man, Harry Edwards (Jack Charles), stabs a young non-Indigenous man who threatened Edwards' wife Sally and then attacked her. This murder starts a chain of events wherein Edwards is hunted down by the sadistic Constable Farrell (with Jimmie assisting). Edwards is jailed and "commits suicide" that night. Farrell uses Edwards as his "Black bitch" (just as Jimmie uses the Aboriginal woman—though Farrell is far more brutal), torturing and probably sodomizing Edwards before hanging him with his belt. This enactment of aggressive sexual domination over Indigenous victims was alluded to earlier when Farrell paid Jimmie for his work, leering at him, patting and fondling his cheek, suggesting a perverse foreplay for the events later with respect to Harry.

On the run from the police after the murders, Jimmie sets up his own hierarchy when he captures a hostage, the sickly, wheezy, and effeminate non-Indigenous schoolteacher, McCready (Peter Carroll), turning him into his bitch–slave, reversing the power order, and playing the boss man. Jimmie orders McCready to do the "domestic" chores—collect firewood and cook—while he scolds and bullies him. In a reverse of Newby's accusation of Jimmie turning his (Newby's) land into a Blacks' camp, Jimmie accuses McCready of turning the bush into a "filthy whites' camp."

Jimmie has fun with McCready, finally having his own captive to kick around for an extended time, and upending the colonizer/colonized dynamic. As Lance Pettitt comments, "According to colonial logic, the colonized can never match its master since the colonized is deemed to possess no worthwhile Indigenous culture ... and comes to be personified by a raft of negative characteristics ... stupid, irrational, dirty, disordered, feminine and infantile" (Pettitt, 2000, 11). These attitudes are embodied in Jimmie's litany of insults directed at McCready. Correspondingly, as Pettitt further argues, "[T]he coloniser tries to monopolize all the opposite positive attributes such as being peace-loving, sober, intelligent, logical, pure, ordered, manly, and adult" (Pettitt, 2004, 11). Ironically, Jimmie embodied most of these traits in the first part of his journey; thus, the film contends that Jimmie's interaction with non-Indigenous society has tainted and corrupted him, fueling his aggression, underscoring the film's strong separatist position.

By the end of his journey and at large for several months, Jimmie, like the young Indigenous man in *Walkabout*, is emasculated before he dies but in a more violent way. The young Indigenous man was ignored and thus spurned by the girl during his courtship dance, subsequently hanging himself. Jimmie is shot through his jaw by a posse as he swims across the river, shattering several teeth. His face is grossly disfigured. This attack suggests a grotesque distortion of Aboriginal initiation rites of manhood when a tooth is knocked out by a tribal elder. Rather than becoming a man, Jimmie is now infantilized, for when he is found hiding in a bush convent by the nun, he is sleeping on the bed in a fetal position. Emaciated and weak, he is as helpless as a baby, unable to talk or ambulate as he is captured and carried to jail by the police. Mort (Freddie Reynolds), Jimmie's half brother, is also emasculated in yet another way. He accompanies Jimmie for several days during his escape before they part their ways, and is shot in the eye by the posse after they shoot him in the back. Mort's "blindness" alludes to a symbolic castration. Like Jimmie, Mort is cut down in the prime of his youth.

A young Aboriginal man denied adulthood is a dynamic that develops in *Backroads*, but this film is initially more focused upon transcending racial barriers than in charting hostilities between Indigenous and non-Indigenous individuals. The road has a new purpose, and is linked to fun and adventure in a freewheeling episodic narrative, that, however, turns tragic.

Backroads

Backroads (written by John Emery and directed by Phillip Noyce, and featuring Gary Foley, a well-known Indigenous activist, who plays the character of Gary) explores the easygoing camaraderie and mateship that develops between two

Indigenous men, Gary and his Uncle Joe (Zac Martin), and a non-Indigenous drifter, Jack (Bill Hunter). The three take off joyriding in a stolen car, a '62 Pontiac Parisienne, ideal for cruising at high speeds along the wide open road. Though Gary and Jack are eager to escape their aimless and unemployed lives, the trip also gives Gary the chance to visit his young son, if only for a short while. Joe joins on a whim, jumping in at the last minute after an afternoon of singing and drinking with his friends and relatives. *Backroads* is set in a critical time frame: in the wake of the Indigenous civil rights movement and a more enlightened non-Indigenous populace, amidst, however, lingering rural racism.

Shot in a naturalistic documentary style, which captures the bush in long, leisurely, and picturesque takes, *Backroads* is the first film in this chapter to incorporate a car in the journey. Speaking of the role of the car in road pictures, Meaghan Morris comments, "[C]ars promise a rabid freedom [with] a manic subjectivity: they offer danger and safety, violence and protection, sociability and privacy, liberation and confinement, power and imprisonment, mobility and stasis" (Morris, 1989, 124). *Backroads* incorporates many of these dynamics with freewheeling unpredictability as the Pontiac careens across the broad expanses of the Australian landscape from the western deserts of New South Wales all the way to the ocean. For much of the film, this car is a catalyst for and emblematic of a range of exciting and pleasurable possibilities, rather than linked to the destruction of the environment or a sign of non-Indigenous encroachment, as discussed earlier in *Walkabout*.

The first part of the journey is full of exhilarating delights: speeding, getting drunk on jug wine, and shoplifting. As the men settle in to long hours on the road, Uncle Joe is perfectly happy in the back seat relaxing and singing. In front, Jack and Gary, hailing from completely different backgrounds, banter back and forth as they get to know each other. Redneck, "know-it-all" Jack has lived on the periphery of Aboriginal life; he reveals his ignorance of their culture and his knee-jerk racism as the wine loosens his tongue. The more urbane Gary was raised on a reserve, yet lived for a time in a non-Indigenous community, as he was once married to a non-Indigenous woman, and probably encountered men such as Jack. Nevertheless, they get along remarkably well, mostly due to Gary's easygoing nature. He is no wimp, however, and is proud and assertive in his defense of his people.

Right away, Jack spouts off, denigrating Indigenous Peoples, referring to them as lazy layabouts. "What a dump!" he exclaims, when they drive by an Indigenous reserve.[9] However, as Marcia Langton points out, this reserve shows happy people, inebriated, yes, but possessing ... "a radical sense of humour ... [as they] sing in the laconic Aboriginal country and western style" (Langton,

1993, 42). They are enjoying themselves, thus deviating from the squalor and despair of the Aboriginal camps dramatized in *Jimmie Blacksmith*, and immune to Jack's condescension. As the subject turns to women, Jack continues his harangue, contemptuously referring to Aboriginal women as "whores," "winos," and "'fuckin' gins." With his swaggering machismo, Jack casually relates a horrific story where he and a group of his mates gang-raped an Indigenous woman Jack knew and liked, foisting the blame on her because she did not tell him that she was attracted to him soon enough for his liking. Jack's crude invectives soon extend to a new target, European immigrants later in the trip, when they pick up a French hitchhiker, Jean-Claude (Terry Camilleri), prompting Jack to gleefully unreel a new litany of slurs, ranging from "Froggy" and "Wog" to "Dago."

Jack's racism and sexism evoke the ocker, the popular male persona and genre from the first half of the 1970s. Jack is an angrier version of Barry McKenzie, for example, whose racism singled out Asians in particular, callously referring to them as "slant-eyed rat bags." As argued in Chapter 2, the ocker comedies touted male chauvinism, their targets Australian women as well as Asians as the end of the white Australian Policy led to stepped-up immigration to Australia from Asia as well as other countries, and the women's movement challenged the white patriarchal status quo.

In Jack's case, the feared Other extends from Indigenous Australians (excluding Joe and Gary) to all post–Second World War immigrants. His racism is directed at anyone *not like him*, the essence of the ocker perspective. Jack's hostility toward Jean-Claude in particular is fueled when another hitchhiker, Anna, joins them and finds Jean-Claude much more attractive than Jack, and starts to make out with him, bruising Jack's ego and rousing his misogyny. Soon Jack is aiming the end of a 12-gauge hunting rifle menacingly at them both; shortly thereafter, he abruptly orders Jean-Claude out of the car.

For his part, Gary is not about to give Jack the last word on Indigenous Peoples in particular, even as he attempts to enlighten him. For example, he gives Jack a short history lesson, explaining that members of Aboriginal communities were involuntarily placed on reserves by government officials far away from non-Indigenous communities; they certainly had little choice in the matter. Further, Gary forcefully and succinctly explains the consequences of assimilation on Indigenous Peoples, concluding, "We all get wiped out in the end." Moreover, Gary's conversations with Jean-Claude show another side to Gary—his inherent decency and tolerance. After Jack kicks Jean-Claude out of the car, Gary behaves in a warm and hospitable manner, which contrasts to

Jack's hostility and condescension. "You enjoy my country, brother," he exclaims with enthusiasm and cultural pride (a gesture which is reminiscent of the spirit of the young Indigenous man's openness to the children in *Walkabout*). Gary also shows his streetwise instincts when he wisely instructs the Frenchman, "Let them *think* they've got the upper hand," in order to get along with bristly ockers like Jack.

For Gary, the trip also involves a personal mission, as he takes time out along the way to visit his son who is staying with relatives. (We do not know where his ex-wife is; we only see her in a family picture which Gary tears up at the film's beginning, alluding to their estrangement.) Gary playfully wrestles with his son on his bed, and is clearly glad to see him. This scene between father and son is touching and represents a quiet interlude away from the "adult" road picture. However, their time together abruptly ends when Jack bursts into the room, loudly and forcefully telling Gary that they have to hit the road. Though it appears that Gary may stay, he soon leaves, attracted to the excitement of a responsibility-free road trip which supersedes family ties.

But Gary, Jack, and Joe can only go so far, for the trip loses its sense of fun and serendipity when realities pile up: a gun-toting, racist owner at a road stop refuses to serve them; their money runs out; the car needs gas; hitchhiker Anna takes off with the car. Further, Jack's ire and sexual frustration get the best of him. When they arrive at the beach, he fires his rifle aimlessly and irresponsibly into the air, while Joe and Gary horse around with another rifle, pretending to fight. This quick-draw attitude and the thrill of gunplay foreshadows not only the low-key Joe's sudden, shocking, and unexpected shooting of the Mercedes owner when he returns to his car (which Gary and Jack steal), but also Gary's arming himself and firing at the local police, who surround the fugitives very quickly.

The police do not ambush Gary, but offer him a chance to give himself up. Scared and cornered, Gary continues to fire at them, and after several rounds, he is shot dead. We last see Jack and Joe as they are placed in police custody. The film's "residual racial violence" which Dermody and Jacka refer to is certainly inherent in the film's settings, that is, the country small town where the store owner kicks them out, or the overly eager policeman who is delighted when he hits Gary. But Emery and Noyce make it clear that the police sergeant in charge wishes to avoid harming Gary. This officer—firm but humane—is at the other end of the spectrum from the redneck racists seen in *The Chant of Jimmie Blacksmith*, *Wrong Side of the Road*, and *The Tracker*, thus giving the film a more balanced perspective. Further, the film dramatizes how quickly otherwise decent Indigenous men, such as Joe and Gary, turn to aggression and violence in fear and self-defense when threatened by non-Indigenous law-enforcement.

Still, the narrative does take an odd turn with respect to Gary, who has proven to be a conciliator and pacifist. He is the last one we would expect to turn aggressor. To arm himself and shoot at the police is inconsistent with his non-confrontational and non-violent stance. The original conclusion in the script took place in Sydney, where Gary and Jack are entangled in a huge traffic jam (thus reinforcing the ironies of a fast-paced, rural road film ending abruptly in a claustrophobic urban environment where the car is gridlocked—quickly losing its "rabid freedom," to re-quote Morris). This conclusion also included a scene where Gary abandons the car and disappears into the city. Yet Foley insisted on a different finale: a tragic ending where the police hunt Gary down. This change represents a decision more consistent with Foley's attitude about ongoing racism at the time than in the attitude of his character—that a "Black fella had to die," as Foley noted, in the wake of the crimes the three had committed. However, Foley has recently commented that he now prefers the original ending—one more consistent with his character.

With sensitivity and panache, *Backroads* takes to the high road, giving its travelers a reprieve from the daily tedium of unemployment and casual crime. A stolen car initially leads to an exciting trip for three itinerant men, which encourages quick mateship that crosses racial boundaries. Yet the excursion turns dangerous and deadly, especially when the lines of non-Indigenous law are crossed and the stakes are raised with the allure of powerful flashy guns and yet another fancy car leading to abrupt and tragic turns in the narrative.

In *Wrong Side of the Road*, the road will provide a very different milieu and purpose.

Wrong Side of the Road

Wrong Side of the Road (directed by Ned Lander, co-written by Lander and producer Graeme Isaac) is a forty-eight-hour odyssey featuring two real-life Indigenous bands—No Fixed Address, playing reggae, and Us Mob, playing hard rock—as they perform across South Australia. The film also charts the personal journeys of two band members. Les (Leslie Graham), a guitarist for No Fixed Address, initiates a search for his biological mother, having been taken away as a baby under the practice of assimilation. *Wrong Side* thus raises the issue of the Stolen Generations before it was in public circulation, and long before *Rabbit Proof Fence*. Ron (Ronnie Ansell), a guitarist for Us Mob, takes a proactive and aggressive stance with the surly, non-Indigenous men he encounters throughout his journey, showing and reinforcing his Indigenous pride.

Significantly, *Wrong Side* was the first feature to showcase an entirely Indigenous cast in major roles, with non-Indigenous actors playing subsidiary parts (i.e., policemen, a social worker, and a pub owner). The film grew out of the lives of the band members, as well as their families and friends, enhanced by additional dialogue coming from the performers during writing and rehearsal—much as Gary Foley helped to shape the narrative as well as his own performance in *Backroads*. *Wrong Side*'s documentary style—grainy footage, hand-held cameras, episodic narrative, and naturalistic acting—is reminiscent of *Backroads*. The effect is a touching, compelling, and comfortable intimacy on the road and during the performances.

Several concerts by the two bands are featured in the film, enhancing the journeys of its protagonists, which foreground one of the main purposes of their music—political activism, and which reverberates into contemporary times and into the new millennium. For example, as Us Mob performs their lively introductory number, "Black Man's Rights," on stage, the Aboriginal Land Rights Movement flag stands behind them "with the rock at Uluru[10] as the central motif, overpainted by the figure of a man with a click stick in either hand … [both hands] … raised in the Third World posture of political liberation" (Maksay, 1981, 503). Uluru's inclusion in the film is critical with respect to Indigenous Peoples in the larger historical context of dispossession and reconciliation. A few years later, in 1985, this rock (a popular tourist site) was formally returned to Aboriginal and Torres Strait Islander Peoples when the Commonwealth government granted Australia's First Peoples inalienable freehold title to the Uluru–Kata Tjuta Land Trust on condition that the park would be leased to the Australian National Parks and Wildlife Service for ninety-nine years. Moreover, in validation of Uluru's crucial and ongoing significance to Indigenous Peoples, most recently in May 2017, the "Uluru Statement from the Heart" presented during the First Nations National Constitutional Convention called for structural government reforms, including constitutional changes to establish a "First Nations Voice" to be enshrined in the Constitution so that "Aboriginal and Torres Strait Islander peoples would be formally consulted on legislation and policy affecting their communities" (McKay, 2017). The Statement's momentum grew and thrived, culminating four years later, in May 2021, when the Uluru Statement was awarded the Sydney Peace Prize.

When *Wrong Side* reaches its conclusion during the film's grand finale, when No Fixed Address exuberantly performs "We Have Survived the White Man's Way" to a large Indigenous audience, young and old, this song speaks of solidarity and self-respect within the community. This song took on a life its own outside the context of the film, and served as a rally point and anthem of the Land Rights Movement during the 1980s, which culminated with the Mabo decision eleven years later, a High Court decision that recognized Native Title (discussed later in this chapter).

Behind their public performances, Les and Ron pursue two very different quests with regard to living with "the white man's way." Les is easygoing but persistent, tirelessly devoting his time off stage to look for official records of his birth mother.[11] He encounters a frustrating maze of tight-lipped and somber bureaucrats, who are determined to tell him as little as possible. Though they patronize him, Les does not lose his cool, but perseveres with many courteous but pointed questions. Les' relationship with his non-Indigenous foster father is cordial at best, and is certainly not warm and loving; they barely seem to know each other. This is demonstrated when Les (who lives with his fellow band members elsewhere) stops by to see his adopted father (Derek Scott). As he puts a plate of food in front of Les, he repeatedly scolds him, treating Les like a bad child, patronizing him, muttering, "Your [foster] mother won't be happy" (that Les will not be home for future meals). After a few minutes, Les pushes away his plate, his food barely touched, politely excuses himself, and leaves the kitchen. In another room, he secretly and very carefully opens his father's desk, and finds his birth certificate—his ulterior motive for his visit—which gives him his biological mother's name—Kelly. Later, his bandmate Vonnie (Veronika Rankine) gives him a contact for the Kelly family. As the film ends, Les, reinvigorated from playing before a large appreciative audience, and full of renewed hope and faith, embarks on another kind of road journey apart from performance, as he gets into the car with a man who knows his biological mother's family and who has offered to help Les find her.

Ron at first appears to be similar in temperament to the low-key Les, exuding diplomacy and keeping his cool, for example, at the film's beginning, when the police invade the dance hall where his band performs. "Let's get back to the music," Ron cautions the agitated crowd, as the police disrupt the concert and harass the spectators. Yet Ron has a low flash point, as demonstrated in subsequent situations. Whereas mild-mannered Les avoids conflict, the more militant Ron aggressively stands up to it, as if following the dictates of one of his songs, "Fight for your Life." For Ron, being a man is to be in defiance of authorities. This is first demonstrated when he and his bandmates show up at the pub where they are to perform. Instead of a welcome, they are met with scorn and hostility by the racist pub owner who concocts a story that he already hired a band for the same night. He cancels Us Mob on the spot, and orders them off the premises. Ron angrily confronts the owner, loudly and forcefully challenging him on his obvious prejudice. Moreover, Ron is also capable of physical violence when provoked. In a flashback, he knocks down his condescending and cheating boss, who had sold him a lemon for a car (for which Ron paid six months' wages). Finally, when the band is on the road and they are stopped by the police, who blatantly harass them by ordering them to take out all of their equipment, Ron again takes the lead and challenges the police. One testy policeman taunts him, calling him a Sambo. Ron punches him, is quickly arrested, and must be bailed out by his Aunty Veronica (Veronica Brodie).

Although Aunty Veronica is not part of the band tours, she experiences her own journey—similar to that of Ron—mustering up the strength and confidence to speak up to non-Indigenous officials, having suffered humiliation in silence and fear under paternalism for many years. Veronica (whose character is based on the actual experiences of the woman who plays her) provides first-person insight into racial injustices endured by Aboriginal women in the 1950s and 1960s, thus expanding the film's viewpoint beyond that of the younger generation through the perspectives of young male characters. Veronica married an Aboriginal man whose father was non-Indigenous; subsequently, her children were classified according to their skin color by government officials. As Veronica wryly notes, they were "graded like fowl's eggs."

Veronica also raises the issue of "exemption," as Catherine Peake comments, "conjur[ing] up a whole world of reference for every Indigenous individual over thirty years of age" (Peake, 1981, 1), dramatically revealing how authorities' classification by skin color impacted Veronica's early married years. As with assimilation, exemption was another way to disrupt and demoralize Aboriginal families. Isaac and Lander elaborate:

> [Veronica] … carried a [government-issued] Dog Ticket—an exemption card which, despite the evidence of the photograph, stated that she was a white person since she had married a man whose father was white. The ticket allowed her to visit hotels, to vote and to assert her status as an Australian citizen. The catch was that she was no longer allowed to associate with her Aboriginal mother, father and sister, or she would be charged with consorting. Prior to 1966, when the act in … [South Australia] was changed, Veronica was forced to stand up in Parliament and demand permission to return to her reserve and her father's funeral. She was allowed to return for 48 hours.
>
> (Peake, 1981, 1)

Subsequently, Veronica demonstrates in a critical scene that she is a tougher woman now: she will not stand silently and be pushed around as she was in the past. She has become a strong and proactive anchoring presence in her local Indigenous community, bringing wisdom and experience to share with other women and men. As feisty as Ron, she takes on an aggressive and rude truant officer who comes to her house to check up on her son's frequent absences from school. Articulate and pugnacious, Veronica stands squarely in her doorway, giving the officer a concise history from her son's viewpoint, declaring that the non-Indigenous children at the school taunted her son, calling him "nigger." In no uncertain terms, Veronica summarily orders the officer off the property.

At the film's conclusion, Veronica joins her Aboriginal relatives and friends as a member of an appreciative and spirited audience when the two bands play at Point Pearce. Unlike the earlier concert, there are no police present to harass and them and thwart their fun and celebration. Ron plays confidently, pouring his enthusiasm and pride into his music, suggesting his resilience and vigor in spite of obstacles he has encountered from non-Indigenous people. The music resonates throughout the hall as Aboriginal audience members, young and old, dance joyfully and with pride.[12]

Before analyzing *The Tracker* and *Rabbit Proof Fence*, both made in the wake of a "strong reflective interest in … [Australian] national history as many Australians endeavoured to come to terms with the darker aspects of our past," as Anna Haebich has commented (Haebich, 2000, 568), it is necessary to briefly update the political climate. As noted earlier, Aboriginal activism, a more enlightened populace, and reforms expedited by supportive government administrations improved living conditions and facilitated self-governance for Indigenous Peoples in the 1960s and 1970s. In the 1980s and 1990s, they achieved gains but also encountered setbacks. The key issues continued to be land rights—climaxed by the stunning Mabo decision in 1992—and self-determination (which included self-management and self-sufficiency), in addition to reconciliation, amidst, however, an undertow of conservatism which gained momentum in the early 1980s, challenging key improvements for Indigenous Peoples.

The Labor administrations of Bob Hawke (1983–91) and Paul Keating (1991–6) were sensitive and responsive to Indigenous activists. Further, like Whitlam, Hawke and Keating actively encouraged Aboriginal participation in political decisions impacting their communities. Both their administrations were instrumental in laying the groundwork for the Aboriginal and Torres Strait Islander Commission (ATSIC), established in 1990 (which replaced the Department of Aboriginal affairs). As Sylvia Lawson noted, ATSIC represented "Aboriginals' strongest voice in the [federal] government, [and was] made up of elected officials with the power to distribute federal funds through a vast network of smaller Indigenous Peoples' organizations across the continent in the areas of welfare, education and health" (Lawson, 2004, A23).

Two years later, in 1992, the Land Rights Movement was given a huge impetus when the High Court handed down the Mabo Decision which recognized Native Title, thus giving official recognition to Indigenous ownership of the land, and challenging two hundred years of colonizer entitlement. The doctrine of "terra nullius"—an empty land, that is, a land without owners, which also included a disavowal of the dispossession and its attendant brutal colonial violence—had been the governing principle of the colonizing culture prevailing since the end of the eighteenth century, when the first convict ships arrived from Britain. A year after the Mabo decision, the Keating administration instituted "The Native Title Act" (1993) in order to bring recognition of native title into land and resource management, and also to set up processes for settling native claims through mediation rather than through litigation.

In 1991, shortly before the Mabo decision, Parliament passed the Council for Aboriginal Reconciliation Act. With a tenure of ten years, the Council (a cross-cultural and cross-party body) set forth three specific goals under the larger philosophical framework of Indigenous and non-Indigenous Peoples working together to establish a better future for all Australians. The Council's objectives were the following: healing the wounds of the past; addressing the disadvantages facing and impacting Aboriginal and Torres Strait Islander Peoples; and promoting an appreciation and respect for the cultures and achievements of these two groups.

The Council held its first convention in 1997 in Melbourne where "Bringing Them Home: The National Inquiry into the Stolen Generations," conducted in 1996 by Australia's Human Rights and Equal Opportunity Commission, was made public. With testimony from over five hundred witnesses, the commission ultimately concluded that a minimum of 10 percent and as many as 30 percent of primarily mixed-race Aboriginal children during the time frame—early 1900s through the 1970s—were forcibly removed from their families. The 1,800 delegates unanimously asked the nation as a whole to apologize for assimilation. Subsequently, the Governor General, Sir William Deane, apologized, as did a number of state and territory premiers and other public figures in church and community organizations.

By the time of the Reconciliation convention, the new Coalition (Liberal–National) Howard government (1996–2007) was already in place, ushering in an era of conservatism, which was fueled by the rise of Pauline Hanson's reactionary One Nation Party. As Christine Jennett notes, One Nation "explicitly attacked pluralistic policies for Indigenous Australians" (Jennett, 2001, 126), and put the blame on former Labor administrations for giving non-Indigenous Peoples preferential treatment. Jeffrey Archer points out that Hanson conjured up "… an intensely nostalgic recreation of an historical golden age of triumph for ordinary, unpretentious, hardworking, white Australians … The powerful symbols of Aboriginal Reconciliation and Land Rights … [were] seen as particularly dangerous threats to this white Australian heartland" (Archer as quoted by Ian Anderson, 2000, 437). The Howard government proved to be responsive to contingencies that supported Hanson and One Nation (including pastoralists and those in resource industries). In 1998, it passed the Native Title Amendment Act, critically watering down the 1993 legislation. Essentially, the process to claim native title would be more difficult and cumbersome, with the rights of negotiation for specific land claims severely diminished for Indigenous communities. For instance, this act contained loopholes that favored pastoral and mining leases issued *after* the Mabo decision. Moreover, in contrast to the 1993 Act, the 1998 bill was drawn up without consultation with Indigenous leaders.

Further, the Howard government not only shelved the recommendations of the Reconciliation Council, which included recognition of Indigenous rights through a constitutional amendment and a treaty, but also discredited the findings and conclusions of "Bringing Them Home." Unlike the aforementioned government and public officials, Howard declined to offer a formal apology on behalf of the government to Indigenous Peoples for the Stolen Generations, his rationale that such an apology could imply that contemporary generations were responsible and accountable for the policies of earlier generations, the prospect of large monetary compensation claims notwithstanding. However, the Howard government promoted "practical reconciliation," with a provision of $54 million over a four-year period to address family separation and its consequences. These monies would go toward [1] "indexing and copying archival records, [2] providing 'Link-Up' services to help Indigenous Peoples trace family members and effect reunions, [3] expanding mental health services, and [4] running an oral history project to record the stories of separation" (Bongiorno, 2019). In addition, and for the record, in August 1999, the Howard government "formally expressed its 'deep and sincere regret' for past injustices and continuing hurt and trauma suffered by Indigenous Australians" (Wright and MacDonald, 1999).

Though the public proclamation of "Bringing Them Home" induced national shame and collective remorse (Collins and Davis, 2004, 135), it received ongoing criticism by conservative politicians and community leaders for its reliance on "fallible memory" (Haebich, 2000, 570). Further faultfinding included accusations of the report's denigration of Australia's national identity (read non-Indigenous identity) "by promoting a 'black armband' rendition of Australia's past, ... an excessive emphasis in recent historical writing on past wrongs ... [inflicted upon Indigenous Peoples], creating an unduly negative account" (Macintyre and Clark, 2003, 3).

The subsequent highly publicized "History Wars," which actually originated in the early 1980s but intensified in the mid-1990s in the wake of the public circulation of "Bringing Them Home," refer to the bitter and very public debates between conservative factions and revisionist historians over the addressing of past abuses of Indigenous Peoples in the wake of the events outlined above. Whereas conservative groups played down, dismissed, and frequently denied accounts of frontier murders and assimilation, historians such as Henry Reynolds, Lyndall Ryan, and Lloyd Robson argued the critical importance of bringing "factual recovery" (Macintyre and Clark, 2003, 158) of Indigenous persecution into public awareness. Macintyre and Clark note, "Talking about the past ... [is] the whole basis of reconciliation. Talking about the injuries of the past, listening to the victims, acknowledging what had happened, offering contrition and receiving its acceptance ... [is] how such injuries ... [are] to be healed" (Macintyre and Clark, 2003, 158).

The Tracker and *Rabbit Proof Fence* were the first feature films to delve into and dramatize past Indigenous traumas, events clearly resonating into the present: early-twentieth-century frontier massacres and the impact of assimilation on Indigenous families with mixed-race children (respectively). As Collins and Davis note, both films "backtrack," not only to focus on unreconciled issues, but also to imbue contemporary audiences with an "historical consciousness" (Collins and Davis, 2004, 173). Accordingly, Keating declared in his 1992 Redfern Speech, "[T]he starting point ... begins ... with the act of recognition, recognition that it was we who did the dispossessing. We took the traditional lands and smashed the traditional way of life. We brought the disasters. The alcohol. We committed the murders. We took the children from their mothers. We practiced discrimination and exclusion" (Keating, 1992).

The Tracker

Before discussing *The Tracker* (written and directed by Rolf de Heer), I would like to briefly compare and contrast this film with *Walkabout*. Both films feature David Gulpilil in complex and rich roles which balance human and mythic qualities. *Walkabout* is set in the present in the midst of heightened public recognition of Indigenous civil rights and lingering racism; *The Tracker* takes place in 1922 during the Frontier stage (1788–early 1930s),[13] when colonizer hostility toward Indigenous Peoples was full blown; their communities were under siege by a self-righteously brutal and ruthless white power order.[14]

In *Walkabout*, as discussed earlier in this chapter, the young Aboriginal man willingly guides a lost sister and brother whose lives he saved across the outback in a lyrical journey of growth and friendship that ultimately turns tragic. He enters the film as a magical figure, yet becomes more human and vulnerable as the journey evolves. In *The Tracker*, a middle-aged Tracker is forced by a fiercely volatile and violence prone racist police officer, the Fanatic (Gary Sweet), to lead a search for an Aboriginal fugitive accused of killing a white woman. Unlike the young Aboriginal man in *Walkabout*, who loses control of his walkabout, the Tracker gradually takes control of the trek and the narrative, empowering himself through an intense psychological and physical struggle with the Fanatic, even committing the "unthinkable crime of enslaving [him]" (Collins and Davis, 2004, 15). Though the Tracker starts the journey as a lowly slave and is shackled for much of the trip, he achieves mythic status at the film's conclusion as he rides off into the horizon on horseback like a Western hero, having eliminated the violent and murderous outlaw. Significantly, both *Walkabout* and *The Tracker* feature stunning climaxes of unexpected hangings: the young Indigenous man commits suicide; the Tracker hangs the Fanatic. Moreover, a spirit of reconciliation is implicit in each film: a young male (the boy in *Walkabout*, the Follower [Damon Gameau], a junior police officer in *The Tracker*) is enlightened and transformed by an amicable and mutually beneficial interaction with the respective Indigenous man whose survival skills and expertise each admires (though at first, the Follower is quite wary of the Tracker).

Though *The Tracker* is realist drama,[15] it also frequently plays as a satire, with Gulpilil deftly putting a comic spin on his role (which is a more expanded and complex version of his solemn and primarily silent tracker role as Moodoo in *Rabbit Proof Fence*). He is an astute observer, a wry commentator, a mocker, and a trickster. Gulpilil gives a deft, confident, controlled, and graceful performance full of poise, even down to his elegant walk, often with a heavy chain around his neck, tethered to the Fanatic's arm.

As Belinda Smaill notes, the Tracker is an "indispensable source of labor [to the authorities] … [enjoying] … few of the privileges of his [non-Indigenous] fellow travelers, he is also frequently mistreated by them" (Smaill, 2002, 32). Thus, the Tracker must walk while they have horses; he is subsequently whipped, slapped, knocked down, and also threatened with a cocked pistol. Further, he must witness two violent and bloody attacks by the Fanatic on groups of peaceful Indigenous People.

One component of the Tracker's strategy in controlling the search is consistent with that of historical Indigenous tribes. As John Scheckter has commented, upon encountering non-Indigenous individuals, Aboriginal men would often withhold or manipulate information as a form of "cultural reticence." Scheckter elaborates, "[A]side from the obvious thrill of pleasing an audience or playing a joke, such limitations would keep secret the locations of hunting grounds and water sources vital to a tribe's survival" (Scheckter, 1999, 125). Clearly, the Tracker's cultural reticence protects the Fugitive, keeping the party at least half a day's travel behind to the point where the search becomes secondary to the psychological interplay (and physical confrontations) between the Fanatic and the Tracker. Given the pathological state of the Fanatic, the Tracker could be killed by him at any time; thus, he must walk a fine line between servitude and assertiveness, "playing" the explosive Fanatic very carefully.

The Tracker's initial tactics include a variety of inflections of "boss," ranging from the obedient to the sarcastic. First of all, he can be serious and respectful. When the four approach the first group of Indigenous individuals in the bush, the Tracker comments, "They're peaceful, boss" (this in the hope that the Fanatic will pass them by, unharmed). Or he can turn sardonic; as the Fugitive continues to elude them, the Tracker deadpans, "Dumb Black fella sure slippery, boss."

In addition, the Tracker's politically correct yet ironic statements put the quest in the larger perspective of the Indigenous/non-Indigenous hegemony. He is no fool. After the first slaughter of several men and women, the Tracker mutters to the Follower (probably masking his own distress), "No such thing as an innocent Black. The only innocent Black is a dead Black." And then to the Fanatic, "We better keep after the *other* savage, boss." Further, when the Fanatic threatens the Tracker with hanging for disobeying one of his orders, repeatedly whipping him, and shooting at his feet, the Tracker declares with a straight face and sarcastic tone, "Poor Black fella' been born for that noose." The Fanatic, in spite of himself, is so taken back by the Tracker's clever assessment of the proceedings, that he joins the Tracker in a prolonged hearty laugh.

However, as the trip progresses, no amount of wit and humor can counter or mitigate the atrocities committed by the Fanatic. One of de Heer's most powerful visual features is his incorporation of paintings by artist Peter Coad, who was present during part of the shoot, and who made sketches during the filming, coloring them in on location and back in his studio. These paintings are intercut with live footage throughout the film to present the climax of many of the film's most violent scenes, particularly the cruel acts inflicted upon Indigenous communities. A horrific sequence takes place early on which dramatizes the Fanatic's monstrous tendencies and actions. The party comes upon a group of innocent Aboriginal men and women. The Fanatic tortures and kills them, then orders their bodies strung up in trees. When the scene begins, the Fanatic and his assistant, the Follower, line the men and women up, put them in chains, slap them, pull their hair, and scream at them a few inches away from their faces. The Fanatic yanks on the tongue of an elder Aboriginal man, and pressing his cocked pistol downward into the tongue. At the moment the Fanatic fires his gun, de Heer cuts to the painting that shows all the Indigenous men and women lined up (as if in a long shot). Blood gushes from the man's tongue, as well as the breast of one of the women who has also been shot. Their eyes—rendered larger than life—are wide in terror, their arms thrown back with the impact of the bullets. The background is awash in ochre—its reddish-orange hue reinforcing this bloody act. On the soundtrack we hear the victims screaming and groaning as they are hit by the barrage of gunshots. This painting or "still" halts the narrative flow, forcing the spectator to examine the larger canvas, graphically and historically. Further, this painting is reminiscent of Aboriginal rock paintings, functioning as an indelible rendering of history and a permanent record of these crimes perpetrated by the police against Indigenous Peoples. The gruesome totality of the event lingers for the several second duration of the painting-shot. When de Heer cuts back to the aftermath of the slaughter, the Aboriginals are lying on the ground, dead, in pools of blood. On the soundtrack we hear Archie Roach whisper, "They're my people," suggesting the Tracker's thoughts and thinly masked devastation as he kneels on the ground for support, his head bowed.

Though this massacre functions as an immediate catharsis for the Fanatic (but not for the Follower, who sobs uncontrollably, his face in his hands), the Tracker's "inability" (read reluctance) to find the Fugitive makes the Fanatic even more impatient. He becomes increasingly unpredictable and bloodthirsty. For example, the Fanatic is foolhardy enough to insist on continuing the search even when the pack horse with all the food and half the ammunition is speared by an Indigenous man hiding in the hills; the animal plummets to its death in a deep unreachable ravine. Later, the Fanatic lashes out at the Tracker, who temporarily leaves camp one night to hunt for bush tucker (food). When the Tracker returns with rabbit for dinner, the enraged Fanatic summarily knocks the Tracker down and shackles him by putting a heavy clamp around his neck with a chain for a tether. Unbelievably, the Fanatic soon kills one of his own, sadistically attacking the critically wounded Veteran (Grant Page), the third policeman in the party, late one night by jamming a red hot stick from the campfire deep into the open wound, muffling his screams with the palm of his hand—an act the Tracker observes.

Realizing the Fanatic's volatility, the Tracker executes a series of moves to undermine the trek, or stop it completely. Rather than using cultural reticence, however, he becomes more proactive, still demonstrating, however, his playful sense of humor and trickster persona. First, he plays with the Follower's naiveté. Even though the Follower was clearly shocked by the actions of the Fanatic during the massacre (and forced to participate), he is still wary of the Tracker and continues to align himself with his boss. Unlike the boy in *Walkabout*, who trusted the young Indigenous man right away (as discussed earlier, they became constant companions, hunting, painting, and exploring together), the Follower deliberately keeps his distance from the Tracker, secretly admiring, however, his savvy and nerve. Yet, partly due to his indoctrination within the police force (he is a young man in his twenties, whereas the boy was only six), and frustration with the apparent futility of the search, he tries to one-up the Tracker, questioning his tracking methods and even the Tracker's worth on the journey. This is demonstrated when the Follower openly challenges the Tracker, who "reads" the landscape, pointing out the tracks of the Fugitive. Irritated, the Follower complains to the Fanatic, "Anyone can see he's not really tracking … just following his nose, hoping for the best." In a rare moment of calm reflection, the Fanatic lets the scenario play itself out, enjoying the humiliation of the Follower, who cautiously gets off his horse, beckoned by the Tracker, who chuckles silently.

In the middle of a large expanse of crushed white rocks, the Tracker, smiling, motions to the Follower to kneel down and study a tiny indentation in the soil where a rock has been disturbed and moved. He exclaims, "There, that stone, boss, belongs there, been kicked away two hours ago." The Follower, confounded, comments, "There's *millions* of stones," as he looks at the large field of tiny white rocks ahead of him, as if to wonder how one microscopic shift can be discerned. But he realizes that the Tracker has him, because of the precision of evidence presented. "Is that all you need?" he queries innocently, and then softly apologizes for being so critical. The Tracker smiles, either out of relief—he has been convincing enough to satiate the Follower—or delight—he has put one over on him. Later on, with the stakes higher, the Tracker will again prey on the Follower's gullibility in a clever scenario designed to have the Follower think he and the Fanatic were all attacked by a party of avenging Indigenous men.

Secondly, the Tracker even puts one over on the Fanatic, using tongue-in-cheek "cultural mystery" to confound him. As they approach a clearing, the Tracker spies the Fugitive (Noel Wilton) about 100 meters ahead in the brush. To distract the Fanatic, who could easily see the Fugitive, the Tracker stops and turns, his body blocking that of the Fugitive in the background. The Tracker starts a giddy dance and chants, his body rolling from side to side, arms flailing, as he kicks up his legs, his face in a silly grin. He remarks, "That sacred country there, boss, no good at night." The Fanatic stares at the Tracker and sighs, even though the Follower urges the Fanatic to keep moving until nightfall. The Fanatic shakes his head, wary of going forward, commenting (with respect to the Tracker), "He's useless, no point in trying when the spirits get into him."

And then, out of the blue, the Tracker attempts to kill the Fanatic. It's as if the Tracker's aforementioned "crazy behavior" was designed to throw the Fanatic off balance and give him a sense of false complacency so that when the Tracker tries to drown the Fanatic, it comes as a complete surprise. The scene begins when the three are climbing the rim of rocks which jut out several hundred feet above a deep pool of water. The Tracker walks in front of the Fanatic, who is on horseback, and eyes the pool below. He suddenly jumps, slipping and sliding down the face of the rocks, dragging the Fanatic off his horse by the chain that connects them. They both plunge into the water below with a loud splash, struggling underwater and wrestling for control. The Fanatic surfaces from the water several times, as the Tracker jumps on him, continuing to dunk him. Heaving and coughing, and gasping for air, they both finally emerge from the water, grabbing the rocks at the edge of the pool. Furious, the Fanatic moves menacingly toward the Tracker. However, without missing a beat, the Tracker surprises and completely disarms the Fanatic, "innocently" explaining his behavior, when he comments, "Can't swim, boss!" adding a subversive comic snap to this event.

By now, the Fanatic is not only jumpy and paranoid after his near-death, but doubly vengeful as well. To make things worse, his horse has just been hit by an Aboriginal spear and runs away. Thus when the Fanatic spies a group of Aboriginal men, women, and children around a campfire a few hundred feet ahead in the brush later, he fires point-blank without hesitation. This time the intercut painting renders four victims in close-up rather than in long shot. In the center of the painting is an elder whose beard is white with fright, his right shoulder bloodied; to his right (our left) is a child with a gunshot wound in the head. The child's hand is clutched by his mother on the left portion of the screen as if she is frantically trying to pull him away. Their eyes bulge with terror, their mouths wide open in silent screams as we hear several blasts of the shotgun. When we return to the aftermath of the attack, it is the Follower who explodes, outraged with this second massacre, and resolutely unable to sit passively by anymore. "They were innocent women and children!" he screams at the smug Fanatic, as he boldly disarms and shackles him. This event precipitates a drastic shift in their quest. Now that the Fanatic has been disempowered, we wonder, will the Follower continue with the search for the Fugitive given his disgust with the whole search anyway? How will he treat the Tracker? What will the Tracker do now that he is free from the Fanatic's control?

As the new boss man, the Follower is tested right away that night when it appears that the Tracker is planning to poison them both. Like the pool sequence, this scene mixes a very real threat of death (to the Fanatic, as well as to the Follower) with casual humor, reinforcing the Tracker's ingenuity. At this point, he deftly takes charge of the narrative as well as full control of the journey, imbuing it with a strong moral imperative. Off by himself, he prepares a mysterious mixture of leaves, berries, saliva, and an insect, which is crushed together. Sitting around the campfire, the three start to eat the rabbit that the Tracker caught and prepared. In chains under a tree, the Fanatic attempts a power play in order to intimidate the Follower and disrupt any sense of camaraderie between him and the Tracker. He taunts the Follower, stating that the Tracker has poisoned the rabbit, and challenges the Follower to exchange portions with the Tracker. On the other side of the campfire, the Follower stops in the middle of chewing, his face frozen in horror; he immediately spits into his hat, and stares at the Tracker, mouth open. The Tracker calmly and confidently gets up, and exchanges his rabbit with the Fanatic. Without hesitating, he eats the Fanatic's portion, bursting into laughter, and, yes, remains very much alive.

The Follower sleeps all too well through the night from the Tracker's "potion," while the Tracker enacts his plan to bring the Fanatic to justice. In subsequent sequences, de Heer compares two crimes, and the nature of justice in each, with the Tracker serving a vital role as a judge for both.

The sequence where the Tracker hangs the Fanatic is stunning in its daring and economy. In the background, the Fanatic, in chains, sits against a tree facing forward, reeling off a litany of angry, self-righteous accusations implying his assumed privilege of a colonizing culture, ranging from evoking the highest power—"We could not serve God any better than improving these poor degraded creatures"—to the self-delusional, "I taught him (his former Tracker) the white way. He's a happy man."

Standing tall and solemn, the Tracker steps back, giving the Fanatic about as much time to offer his plea as the Fanatic did before he fired upon the second group of Aboriginal men, women, and children—a few seconds. The Tracker declares: "You are charged with the murder of innocent people. How do you plead? ... [silence] ... On behalf of my people and all people I'm your judge and jury. I find you guilty as charged. By your actions you have forfeited the right to live among your fellow humans. I sentence you to hang by the neck until dead."

The Tracker hoists the Fanatic up and hangs him, his limp body dangling in silhouette against the rising sun. The dazzling color scheme approximates the Aboriginal flag, which uses the colors black, red, and yellow. The shot of the horizon is equally split with black filling the top (emblematic of Indigenous Peoples), red on the bottom (for the earth and the Indigenous spiritual bond to the land, as well as the bloodshed caused by the settler culture), and the yellow globe in the middle (for the sun as giver of life). This shot is a powerful image of Aboriginal payback: a dead white racist in silhouette against a modern rallying sign for Indigenous Peoples. On the soundtrack we hear Archie Roach singing, "You have taken my country, exterminated by your hand. I can never return until there's contrition." The song suggests not only the Tracker's thoughts, but also a collective Indigenous scolding of the former Howard Administration over its reluctance to give an official apology for the historical persecution of Indigenous Peoples.

The Fanatic's hanging conjures up the hanging scene at the end of *Walkabout*, when the young Aboriginal man takes his own life out of despair. Despite their very different contexts, these two scenes are linked not only by the discovery of the bodies by non-Indigenous males, but by the subsequent shifts in their respective journeys. On the one hand, the boy in *Walkabout*, saddened by the loss of his friend and mentor, stares incredulously at the body of the young Indigenous man. His death marks the end of the boy's special walkabout and friendship, and his imminent return to a comparatively diminished, non-Indigenous existence with his sister. On the other hand, in *The Tracker*, though the Follower is shocked when he sees the Fanatic's body, his immediate thoughts are clearly not about mourning, but for his own safety—he could be the next to be hanged by the Tracker. Frantic, he quickly jumps to his feet, pointing his rifle all around him at his imagined attackers. Yet, the hanging of his boss marks the beginning of a less contentious, more cordial, and trusting relationship with the Tracker, who insists that they continue the pursuit of the Fugitive. As the Follower's new mentor, the Tracker offers protection within and direction into "his" country just as the young Aboriginal man in *Walkabout* offered safe passage for the boy and his sister in the outback. Like the boy, the Follower is an innocent on the brink of enlightenment and growth as he and the Tracker are escorted by the tribal elders, who have taken custody of the Fugitive, so obsessively pursued by the Fanatic.

The Follower observes intently as the Tracker consults with the Fugitive, and a tribe of Indigenous elders. The Tracker then solemnly picks up and heaves a long spear into the thigh of the Fugitive (who has admitted his crime to the elders and the Tracker). The Tracker explains to the dumbfounded Follower, who is shocked by this quick and aggressive act, that the Fugitive (who did not kill a non-Indigenous woman) not only raped an Indigenous woman, but that she was the "wrong skin for him"—that is, he violated strict tribal kinship laws, in addition to committing a serious assault. The hurled spear, a painful and debilitating means of tribal justice, also implies a greater punishment—judgment of the Fugitive by spiritual forces. The Fugitive could suffer even more, or die, due to his own shame. Significantly, rather than perpetrating cultural mystery as the Tracker did at the beginning of the trek, he now shares cultural knowledge with the Follower. Collins and Davis comment, "The Tracker is now recognized as the one who is 'at home,' welcoming the Follower to … [his] country" (Collins and Davis, 2004, 16), where the Follower is indeed a welcome guest.

The friendship between the Tracker and the Follower is in the spirit of reconciliation—the warming of relations between Indigenous and non-Indigenous Peoples as well as the active cultivation of respect by non-Indigenous communities for Aboriginal communities and their culture. The Tracker and the Follower began their road trip foreign to each other. Both were forced to acquiesce to the Fanatic; yet, each was driven to self-empowerment by the Fanatic's monstrous crimes.

When the Tracker jumps on the back of a horse and rides off into the wilderness at the film's end, he takes on mythical proportions: a Western-styled hero who, at least temporarily, has tamed and civilized the land with his own code of ethics—clearly rightfully so. This romanticized view can be understood as the wide-eyed perspective of the Follower, in whose eyes the Tracker has grown in stature; not only is he an adept tracker, but a judge, go-between, mediator, teacher, dispenser of punishment, and executioner. No wonder the Tracker appears larger than life as he rides away, leaving the Follower with the confidence and skills to find his way back, clearly with a more enlightened perspective.

We shall now turn to a different trek which takes place a decade later as the era of assimilation was ushered in: three young Indigenous female fugitives embark upon a dangerous and life-threatening cross-country escape.

Rabbit Proof Fence

Rabbit Proof Fence, directed by Phillip Noyce and written by Christine Olsen, was based on the 1996 biographical book *Follow the Rabbit Proof Fence* by Doris Pilkington-Garimara,[16] who served as script and cultural consultant. The film takes place at the beginning of the "Institutional Phase" in the early 1930s, when the nationwide process of government endorsed and managed assimilation began. As Bob Hodge and Vijay Mishra (1991) note, the frontier ethos that condoned colonizer violence against Aboriginal Peoples (as depicted in *The Chant of Jimmie Blacksmith* and *The Tracker*) became an official embarrassment—hence, the commencement of a new strategy to contend with the "Aboriginal problem." Mixed-race or "pale children" throughout Australia were kidnapped from their families and forcefully incarcerated in "settlement houses." Settlement houses represented a form of institutionalized slavery and were essentially work prisons for children and teenagers, who were eventually farmed out as indentured servants for non-Indigenous Australians.

Hodge and Mishra add, "'Assimilation' sounds like a recognition of an Aboriginal contribution to the dominant society but what it aimed at was the total transformation of Aborigine to White, preserving the principle of purity by dividing Aborigines into two categories of black and white Aborigines, with nothing in between" (Hodge and Mishra, 1991, 51). Mixed-race children—the unwanted "third race"—would integrate into non-Indigenous society through assimilation, and Aboriginal bloodlines would gradually disappear through successive generations. "Full blood" Indigenous individuals, families, and communities on the other hand, would continue to be pushed by the settler culture with official government support to isolated remote areas, far away from non-Indigenous communities. Assimilation amounted to genetic cleansing in the larger historical context of what many historians have termed Indigenous genocide. Though this practice was phased out by the early 1970s, it has infiltrated Indigenous life to present day. As Noyce notes, many contemporary families remain scarred in some way by the policy of assimilation.

One of the ironies of assimilation is that colonizers had historically preyed on Indigenous women, forcefully initiating and perpetuating the "problem" of mixed-race children in Indigenous communities. Indigenous women could be the victims of rape, or under duress, would consent to sex as a form of cooperation with male predators (as we have seen in *Jimmie Blacksmith*). As Pilkington notes in her book, during the actual construction of the rabbit proof fence, many itinerant non-Indigenous workers fathered children, and then moved on,[17] leaving behind Indigenous mothers and their mixed-race children to fend for themselves.

Rabbit Proof Fence is the first mainstream Australian feature to focus on the tragedy and national blight of the Stolen Generations. This film examines the actual kidnapping in 1931 of Pilkington-Garimara's mother, Molly Craig, fourteen (Everlyn Sampi), as well as her cousin Gracie, eleven (Laura Monaghan), and sister Daisy, eight (Tianna Sansbury), all of whom escaped from the Moore River Native Settlement Home after their abduction. They walked over 1,000 miles back home to Jigalong in nine weeks (sometimes covering as many as 20 miles per day). Gracie did not complete the trip as she was captured by police along the way. The girls consistently eluded the police and Aboriginal trackers, using the north–south rabbit proof fence as a guide. This barrier had originally been constructed by colonizing settlers in Western Australia to keep out the rabbits so crops wouldn't be decimated, the irony that rabbits were non-native animals, and represented another form of colonizer imposition on Indigenous land. At the end of the film, to our surprise, we learn that Molly made this trip again as an adult nine years later, after she had been forcefully returned to the settlement. This time she took her infant daughter, Annabelle, having to leave toddler Doris behind; Doris did not see her mother again for twenty-one years. The book and the film are a testament to Molly's fortitude and perseverance: she could have died or been recaptured—the fates of many others who ran away from the homes.

The key agent in the assimilation process is the paternalistic and self-righteous A. O. Neville (an actual historical figure). Neville (Kenneth Branagh) oversees the Moore River Settlement House where his staff, the matrons, the police, and the trackers keep the children interned. With his heavily ironic title, "Chief Protector of Aboriginals" for Western Australia, Neville perceives mixed-race children as a pathology. This is demonstrated during his slideshow to a group of non-Indigenous, middle-class women, where he comments that three crosses with whites (representing three generations) will stamp out the black color—the result, no trace of "native origin," and a purified white Australia.[18] The actual Neville once asked, "Are we going to have a population of 1 m. Blacks in the Commonwealth or are we going to merge them into our white community and eventually forget that there were any Aborigines in Australia?" (Simmons, 2003, 47). Along this line, "effacing the Black" appears to be precisely what the matron does to Molly the morning after she arrives at Moore River. The matron roughly and vigorously scrubs Molly in a makeshift shower with a wire bristle brush as if her color is supposed to disappear down the drain.

One of Neville's favorite songs is Stephen Foster's "Way Down upon the Swanee River." Neville's affection for this song suggests his attempt to identify with Foster, whose song was intended as a sympathetic tribute to enslaved Black people in pre-Civil War days in America. Neville's attraction to this song alludes to colonizers' self-deceit. For public purposes this paternal boss man holds Indigenous Peoples dear, matching his pretentiously ridiculous "best of everything our culture has to offer" credo for the Moore River children. Clearly, the aims of Neville are similar to those of (the fictional) Minister Neville in *The Chant of Jimmie Blacksmith*. A. O.'s plan recalls the "friendly" advice the Minister (and his wife) gave to Jimmie: "Marry a white woman, so your children will be one quarter caste, grandchildren one-eighth, scarcely black at all."

With his blondish hair and piercing blue eyes, Neville suggests an Aryan ideal, and given the film's early 1930s setting, his ideology draws an eerie and appropriate parallel with Hitler's Fascist agenda in Germany in the 1930s to create the Master Race by first eradicating Jews. As Gary Simmons comments, "Some historians and cultural theorists argue that the slaughter of up to 20,000 Indigenous Australians in the nineteenth and twentieth centuries bears a strong resemblance to the extermination to Jews at the hands of the Nazis" (Simmons, 2003, 46). Further, as Lola Young notes, in *Fear of the Dark*, eugenics, or the selective breeding that Neville endorses for the "health" of the white colonizers, was one of the founding ideologies of Nazism (Young, 1996, 50). Along this line, the train that carries the three girls to Moore River Station conjures up the trains used by Nazis used to transport Jewish prisoners to concentration camps. And as Pilkington-Garimara notes in her book, Molly deems Moore River a concentration camp.

In addition to overseeing the settlement house and orchestrating the tracking of Molly, Gracie, Daisy (and other runaways), Neville also regiments the marital (read sexual) behavior of adolescent and adult Indigenous women in the larger context of assimilation. His position gives him the power to determine whether a mixed-race woman can marry a mixed-race man. Accordingly, he notes with alarm that Daisy "has been promised to a full blood." The day after Molly, Gracie, Daisy, and others arrive, Neville gets right to work, inspecting and selecting the "fair ones"—those with the lighter skin. (He does this with the girls as well as the boys, who all reside at Moore River together.) As Pilkington-Garimara points out, mixed-race children were regarded by non-Indigenous officials as smarter than Indigenous Peoples (Pilkington-Garimara, 2002, 40), hence the need for tighter control and "training," that is, immediate isolation and a fast track to be domestics and laborers.

Neville's inspection of Molly, who is on the brink of puberty, holds a special fascination for him, and his scrutiny of her has strong sexual overtones. He carefully looks at her head, neck, and back, touching her skin as if she is some sort of trophy. This examination functions as a powerful and empowering turn-on for a sexually repressed and color-obsessed policeman. But these scenes also suggest the perverse coercive means that self-designated officials use to be near to that which they fear most. The wide angle close shots of Neville's distorted puffy face from Molly's frightened perspective not only allude to his authoritarian role, but also mock him and his bloated self-importance. Accordingly, several girls in the settlement house make fun of Neville and his pseudo-Christian humanist values, calling him "Mr. Devil." Even Maude, Molly's mother, makes fun of Neville to a government official, giggling, "If he [Neville] wants ... [a child of mixed-race], he can make his own!"

Yet the sexual menace of a non-Indigenous station owner is frighteningly real and imminent when Molly, Gracie, and Daisy are on the road and rest at a cabin where the owner makes nightly visits for non-consensual sex with the domestic, Mavis (Deborah Mailman), who could be a grown-up version of Molly facing the same awful destiny. This is dramatically demonstrated when he comes through the door to Mavis's quarters in the middle of the night (where she is keeping the girls hidden until daybreak). His undressing is presented from Molly's viewpoint. In a shot reverse shot construction, she watches him warily from behind the covers, with close shots focusing on his midriff and groin area, as his hands undo his belt, unzip, and remove his pants. Her eyes, wide in fear, imply that she knows exactly what his intentions are. Yet, he is the one who is jolted when he finds the three girls and Mavis under the covers. Even though this scene is creepy and foreboding, it is slightly humorous as the farmer jumps back: "fear of the dark" means finding not one Black female but four! This farmer is a cruder version of Neville, directly acting on his sexual desires as a form of entitlement, just as Neville interprets his self-imposed role as "chief protector" to manage the sex lives and families of Aboriginal women.

However, not all non-Indigenous on the girls' journey are predators: for example, a nomad they encounter redirects Molly to the right portion of the fence to follow to Jigalong. And with regard to Aboriginal men, even though some work for the local police (and help to recapture Gracie), others are sympathetic to the three girls. Two men share their kangaroo catch and give Molly much-needed matches, while admonishing the girls about the dangers of being alone in the bush. But the most unlikely ally turns out to be Moodoo (David Gulpilil), the chief Aboriginal tracker working for Neville. Significantly, over the course of his following the girls, Moodoo takes on a paternal presence, which balances the girls' strong maternal ties to Maude and their grandmother Frinda. These two parental poles provide a vigilance in strong defiance of Neville's pernicious and pervasive police network as well as an unofficial "family" that counters the coerced foster family at Moore River.

At first, Moodoo is introduced to the girls as an awesome and fearful man whom the girls associate with brutal capture. They initially see him at Moore River tall and solemn on top of his horse in his striking blue police uniform, as he returns a runaway girl about Gracie's age on a rope tether. Molly, Gracie, and

Daisy observe the "bad girl" and her very public punishment, which could be their own—a flogging, shorn hair, and solitary confinement. Molly knows that Moodoo will be the most formidable of trackers once she, Daisy, and Gracie are on the run. However, even though Moodoo is hot on their trail from the beginning of their escape, she and the others deftly elude him—at one point even hiding in some brush literally right under his horse as he rides by.

As the search intensifies, Moodoo is summoned at various points along the fence, while the girls further distance themselves from Moore River and venture closer to Jigalong. Though Moodoo doesn't actually see them, he is never very far away. And even though Molly utilizes her bush skills, for example, sweeping their tracks with a large broom as they leave the station mentioned earlier, or walking with thick socks so as not to leave imprints on the sand, the girls still leave signs, however small, which the seasoned Moodoo is able to follow. Yet he develops a respect and admiration for them, and very subtly starts to take his time in his pursuit, clearly more interested in keeping a distance than closing in on them. In a key scene, Moodoo scrutinizes the ground, then lifts his head and smiles, knowing they are out there, and not far away. He comments to his supervisor, "She pretty clever that girl," the implication that he has decided not to pursue them any further. This is confirmed in the subsequent scene at Neville's headquarters in Perth, when the chief of police declares to Neville that Moodoo has "lost them."

Clearly, Moodoo practices the same passive behavior as the Tracker does in *The Tracker*, as discussed earlier, going through the motions of tracking with no intention of apprehending the fugitives. Once Moodoo "gives up," the search is severely hampered. Without his expertise and stamina, the police are unable to withstand and navigate the rough terrain and heat. Alone, they prove to be ridiculously inept on the outback. The greenhorn lead officer, after a three-week vigil next to a section of the fence where the girls are supposedly heading, just walks away from his post, muttering that the search is a waste of time. The cruel tragedy, however, is that Moodoo suffers under the force of assimilation himself, for Neville uses Moodoo's daughter as a hostage in the settlement house, knowing that Moodoo doesn't dare take off on his own and abandon her. Though Moodoo prefers to return to the station where he was a hand, Neville, always in need of an expert tracker, insists he stay on. This arrangement works as a form of blackmail to keep him on the job. On the rare occasion that Moodoo is allowed to see his daughter (Tracy Monaghan)—his deep-set, sad eyes sadly gaze at her—he dare not show any emotion lest Neville send her away for "further training" as a domestic to suffer the same fate as Mavis. But by allowing Molly, Gracie, and Daisy to continue their trek, it's as if Moodoo watches over them as surrogate daughters, which implies a secret wish fulfillment for his own daughter's safe escape, were she to bolt.

Balancing Moodoo's indirect guardianship is Maude's (Ningali Lawford) and grandmother Frinda's (Myarn Lawford) strong maternal bond with the girls, even though the two parties are hundreds of miles apart. The introductory scenes of the film established a close-knit, cozy, and loving family as the women and the girls hunted together in the bush, with scenes shot in warm colors, an "oasis-like" imagery, as Collins and Davis have noted (Collins and Davis, 2004, 141). However, this community was violently ruptured during the horrific kidnapping of Molly, Gracie, and Daisy in spite of Maude's and Frinda's desperate attempts to rescue the girls. The policeman (Jason Clarke), who had eyed the girls for a long time, abruptly drove up to their camp in his police vehicle, leaped out, ran after, and grabbed the terrified girls one by one, first roughly pushing Daisy and Gracie into the car. When Frinda grabbed a spear, the policeman spun around, screaming at her, aggressively asserting his authority as he jabbed his finger into the document signed by Neville giving him authorization to take the girls. Molly fought the hardest, kicking and screaming as the policeman wrenched her away from Maude.

The girls' loving natural family contrasts to the forced family at the Moore River Settlement, where stern matrons in their starched uniforms bark orders day and night to the multitudes of Indigenous children, ranging from infants in cribs to teenagers, who live in a dormitory-style arrangement with beds crammed into the stark tin structures, a pail in the corner functioning as a bathroom facility. The morning after her arrival, Daisy stares dumbfounded and sickened at the bowl of inedible food before her. An angry and bullying Aboriginal steward (Trevor Jamieson), who woke them up earlier by rattling his nightstick against the metallic wall of the structure, behaves like an abusive father who threatens to "hold your nose and force [breakfast] down your throat." When Daisy speaks in her tribal dialect, he barks, "None of that jabba here!"

While the girls are at large, Maude's only way of knowing of the status of her daughters and niece is via word from the locals in Jigalong. When she first hears about the girls' escape, she smiles confidently. Later, when they are well into their escape, the rabbit proof fence is transformed into a lifeline that reinforces mother–daughter spiritual ties. After the girls have been helped by another maternal figure—a sympathetic station wife (Edwina Bishop), who gives them food and coats, and points Molly in the direction of the fence—the girls rest, with Molly gently touching the fence. This scene is intercut with a shot of Maude placing her hand on top of the fence wire as if the two parties are communicating telepathically. Her face radiant, Maude is assured that the girls are still alive, just as the girls are able to feel and be comforted by Maude's presence.

During the last days of Molly's and Daisy's trek across the salt flats, where heat waves shimmer in the air over the sun-bleached terrain (the flats are the final obstacle between them and home), the mise en scène further reinforces the mother–daughter bond when the Dreamtime/Dreamings' spirit bird appears in the sky right above the girls. They collapse on the sand, dizzy with fatigue, their faces burnt and peeling, appearing to be dead. Within a few seconds, the spirit bird hovers overhead. Hearing its call, Molly slowly opens her eyes and smiles. This is the wondrous creature whom Molly and Maude observed together at the beginning of the film before they were separated. At the time, Maude reassured Molly that it would always look after her. When the bird reappears in the desert, it's as if the bird was sent by Maude to protect and inspire Molly and Daisy forward on the last leg of their journey.[19]

This time, Maude and Frinda establish a safe terrain for the girls as they await their arrival, aggressively challenging the policeman who initially stole their children. Maude brandishes a long sharp spear as she advances menacingly toward him, fearlessly holding her ground. Surprised by Maude's sudden boldness, the jittery policeman quickly retreats and flees into the brush. With the power dynamic reversed (in contrast to the abduction of the children earlier), Molly and Daisy run freely into the arms of Maude and Frinda, seemingly airborne with relief and jubilation.

As a testament to their longevity, the real-life Molly and Daisy are featured in documentary footage walking in Jigalong in the film's epilogue; Molly is in her early eighties; Daisy, late seventies. The women stand tall and proud. Molly's voice and stance are strong and resolute as she declares, "Daisy and me, we're here living in our country Jigalong. *I'm* never going back to *that* place [Moore River]."

Molly's journey and successful return home fulfill her quest to rejoin and reintegrate into her own community where her future life choices as an adult, including marriage to a man from her own community, are on her own terms. Her extraordinary courage, pluck, and stamina position her as a new breed of Indigenous heroine, who stubbornly defies the law of the colonizers and refuses to be a pawn in their law of racial politics.[20] Molly has matured into a strong and persistent leader, who refuses imprisonment and the termination of her Aboriginal way of life.[21]

Collins and Davis note the enormous significance of *Rabbit Proof Fence* as a post-Mabo film which conjures up the recurrent "lost child" motif in the Australian cultural tradition: "the European settler's vulnerability in a hostile and indifferent landscape ... reinforcing long-standing settler anxieties about belonging" (Collins and Davis, 2004, 141). Applying this motif to an Indigenous child, they continue:

> *Rabbit Proof Fence* invokes the lost child films of the past while at the same time bringing something new to the genre. Unlike the tragic ending of *Walkabout*, where the Aboriginal boy rescues the girl and the boy only to take his own life in despair, *Rabbit Proof Fence* offers a powerful image of Aboriginal survival of colonial violence and subjugation. In doing so, it inverts two centuries of the representation of Aboriginal Peoples as a doomed or dying race, a group of people who have no place in modernity. More specifically, it reorients the peculiar sense of loss and belatedness associated with the lost child narrative away from settler anxieties of belonging to the post-*Mabo* issues of how the nation can best face up to the shame of the Stolen Generations.
>
> (Collins and Davis, 2004, 143)

Though there is not room for a detailed analysis, three notable new millennium films directed and/or written by Indigenous filmmakers represent works infused with and informed by their own lives and experiences in the larger context and impact of generations of dispossession and colonizer oppression. (As noted earlier, many of the characters in *Wrong Side of the Road* shaped their performances from their personal lives.) Each film explores different versions of a journey: a lost non-Indigenous child and the Aboriginal tracker who searches for her in *One Night the Moon* (2001, written by Rachel Perkins and John Romeril, directed by Perkins—her second feature after *Radiance*, 1998); itinerant teenagers who undertake distinctive and daring treks in *Beneath Clouds* (2002, written and directed by Ivan Sen) and in *Samson and Delilah* (2009, written and directed by Warwick Thornton, who also shot the film). These films benefited from increased financial assistance and support for Indigenous filmmakers from television channels, SBS and the ABC, as well as the Film Finance Corporation, Screen Australia, in addition to state funding and private financing.

One Night the Moon is composed of several treks, with the main characters frequently expressing their feelings and states of mind through song. Long shots of the barren bush and soaring ominous cliffs, set against a pure blue-black sky and a glowing moon, create awe-inspiring and mysterious settings. (Much of the film takes place at night.) Deviating from other Indigenous road films, the film's focus is on the search for Emily (Memphis Kelly), who, intrigued by the full moon, wanders away from her remote home in the bush one night and disappears (unlike the girl and the boy in *Walkabout* whose outback picnic turned into a last-minute escape from their father's gunfire attack). A search party is organized with a seasoned and earnest Indigenous tracker (Kelton Pell), who is selected by the police to lead the group, but who is abruptly rejected by the girl's openly hostile and racist father (Paul Kelly), who declares, "No Blacks on my land!" The father's sense of entitlement is challenged later in scenes where the tracker sings, "This land owns me," reaffirming the sacred bond Indigenous Peoples have with the land. Like the tracker in *The Tracker*, this man is proud and determined. Scenes featuring him are intercut with those of the father singing, "This land is mine," as he insists upon his ownership over stolen land. Predictably, the inexperienced police, the father, and his neighbors fail to find the girl, wasting precious time. However, a bond develops between the determined tracker and the girl's grieving mother (Kaarin Fairfax) to go on their own quest. In a powerful scene as they work their way through the bush, they sing a beautiful, harmonious duet entitled "Unfinished Business," which alludes not only to the missing child and their aching hearts, but also to the blatant historical inequalities foisted upon Indigenous Peoples. The mother deliberately crosses the line to befriend the tracker, realizing that the shortsightedness of her husband has not only offended the tracker, but hampered and delayed the search. Though the tracker is successful in finding the girl, she is lifeless, having fallen from a precipice. The father, devastated with shame and sorrow upon hearing the news, takes his own life with his shotgun.

Beneath Clouds and *Samson and Delilah*, both set in the present, feature adolescent travelers who are alienated from their families and/or communities and who develop tentative friendships when they take to the road together. Both films are shot in a neorealist mode in natural settings: vivid landscapes under a sunlit sky; dry and perilous deserts, with many of the characters played by first-time actors and actresses. In each film the road offers the possibility for companionship, comfort, and healing, but it is also fraught with dangers, such as racist non-Indigenous police on the prowl and merciless kidnappers. In the former, Lena (Dannielle Hall), a young mixed-race woman (yet a fair-skinned Aboriginal woman, as Sen has noted, with her blonde hair and blue eyes), runs away from an abusive mother and stepfather, and meets up with Vaughn (Damian Pitt), a young Aboriginal man who has escaped from work prison detail, having been incarcerated for auto theft. Both long for their lost parents, the girl her idealized Irish father, the boy his estranged and dying mother, who abandoned him and his sister when they were children. Though Vaughn is on the run from the police, he is determined to return to the home where his mother has lived and hopefully reconnect with her. At first, Lena and Vaughn are defensive and contentious with each other, using the road to keep a safe distance, one following the other several feet away. Yet, as they walk and converse, the distance—physical and psychological—between them narrows as they reveal their desire and need for companionship. A mutual trust develops, suggesting they see each other as soul mates. Given Lena's appearance, Vaughn assumes that she is non-Indigenous, and uses their time together to call her attention to landmarks in territory he knows (and perhaps grew up in), "educating" her about the haunting perils of historical colonizer transgression on Indigenous land. At one point, he identifies a towering cliff, explaining that in the recent past, a group of Indigenous men and women were forced by a band of angry, racist non-Indigenous men to fall to their deaths below. As their journey progresses, Vaughn and Lena are faced with situations where one quickly comes to the aid of the other without hesitation. For example, Vaughn saves Lena from a violent kidnapping when two non-Indigenous male bullies in a car grab her off the road, attempting to yank her inside the car. Later on, during Vaughn's confrontation with a hostile and racist non-Indigenous policeman outside his squad car, Lena picks up a baton to distract the officer, thus giving Vaughn the few seconds he needs to fight back against the unprovoked assault. He knocks the policeman to the ground. Lena also takes on a parental role, gently chiding Vaughn at least once, advising him to give himself up and serve the rest of his sentence. As a result of their trek together, Lena and Vaughn find much solace in each other's company before they finally go their separate ways, though their destinations are unknown: she steps on a train, and he returns to the road, perhaps continuing with his escape, or taking Lena's advice to turn himself in to resume his sentence.

In *Samson and Delilah*, Thornton includes frequent interactions with Indigenous groups or individuals (family, acquaintances, community members), thus presenting revealing perspectives of Indigenous life. Speaking of the settings in *Samson and Delilah*, Liz McNiven comments, "The lack of infrastructure, services and resources in this small community in central Australia sets the scene for ill health, unemployment and poor housing … the empty refrigerator, the wheelchair, the ever-ringing but never answered payphone, the broken-down cars and the abandoned church symbolize various dimensions of the community's ... depressed state" (McNiven, 2009). Moreover, Thornton doesn't shy away from the hostility Delilah (Marissa Gibson) and Samson (Rowan McNamara) suffer from their own: elders and family in their living spaces. First of all, we are initially introduced to Delilah as the sole caretaker for her beloved, ailing grandmother (Mitjili Napanangka Gibson), who is teaching her the art of dot painting on canvas. However, when her Nana dies suddenly, Delilah is viciously attacked and shunned by the female elders who accuse her of neglect—clearly not the case. Secondly, Samson, who lives nearby, is not welcome to participate in his brother's band or to hang out with the members, though he likes to listen to music and dance. Out of frustration one afternoon, he smashes a guitar and is subsequently beaten up by a band member. Addicted to petrol sniffing, Samson spends many of his days alone and isolated, lost in a vapor fog. He watches Delilah, often playfully throwing pebbles to attract her attention as she walks by. However, once Samson and Delilah begin their trek together—she willingly obliges when he takes her to safety away from the abusive women, and he wisely decides to leave his abode after more altercations with hostile band members—each seems to instinctively understand the mood and needs of the other without speaking a word. Thus, Delilah comforts Samson, taking his hand in hers; he rests his head on her shoulder. Moreover, they huddle together at night in their temporary resting place under a bridge. When the film takes a more violent turn—Delilah is badly beaten up by a carload of non-Indigenous men and she staggers back, her face black and blue and swollen—Samson shelters her, making sure that she stays close to him. (Her appearance is a rude awakening for him, for right before she was kidnapped, he was walking in front of her, high on petrol, fully unaware when she was abducted.) As she recovers from her injuries, Delilah takes charge of assisting Samson through an uneven recovery, transporting him to "her country" away from hostile neighborhoods when Samson almost does himself in by inhaling too much petrol. Unlike *Beneath Clouds*, however, Samson and Delilah stay with each other, and there is a sense of hope that they will survive together on their own. Delilah heals, clearly stronger and more confident, demonstrating not only her evolving maternal instincts with Samson—reminiscent of the role that Lena frequently exhibited with Vaughn—but also her bush skills. She wisely parks the borrowed truck away from their dwelling to keep Samson away from the vapors. She also helps him clean up and detox with a bath in a trough. Even though her leg is in a cast (from a sudden accidental and unexplained hit by a car captured in a brief shot), she is able to ambulate, nimbly balancing her body and moving adroitly with the aid of a crutch. Armed with a rifle like an intrepid hunter, she returns with a freshly killed kangaroo for their meal, preparing a fire for cooking. She even has time to work on a beautiful dot painting with vivid colors, just like the ones her grandmother created, lovingly keeping her Nana's spirit alive in "their country." In the film's final scenes, Delilah and Samson are setting up their "safe house" in a deserted out-station dwelling, surrounded by the security of open land and no intruders. They are at home in their personal domain, which is very different from their original environs. When we last see them, each regards the other with a gaze of deep and tender affection.

Samson and Delilah was released approximately one year after the February 2008 Apology by newly elected Labor Prime Minister Kevin Rudd (2007–10, June 2013–September 2013) to Aboriginal and Torres Strait Islander Peoples that took place at Parliament House. His carefully chosen words specifically addressed the abuses inflicted upon Indigenous Peoples during the era of the Stolen Generations and were also contextualized within the historical destructive impact of generations of colonizer dispossession. His speech was the government's first official act with the new Labor parliament and passionately embodied the spirit of reconciliation that had evolved during the past decades. Rudd began his speech, "[w]e apologize for the laws and policies of successive parliaments and governments that have inflicted profound grief, suffering and loss on these our fellow Australians," then continuing, "[t]o the mothers and the fathers, the brothers and the sisters, for the breaking up of families and communities, we say sorry" (Brett, 2001, 71).[22] Rudd's words echoed and reinforced those of Prime Minister Keating in his 1992 speech quoted earlier, both addresses vigorously underscoring the fallout of violent and pervasive colonization upon Indigenous generations so powerfully dramatized in a myriad of ways in the films discussed in this chapter: innocent and vulnerable young people in *Samson and Delilah*, *Beneath Clouds*, *Rabbit Proof Fence*, *Wrong Side of the Road*, *The Chant of Jimmie Blacksmith*, and *Walkabout*; the young father in *Backroads*; the seasoned Trackers in *One Night the Moon* and *The Tracker*; and last but not least, the young women in *The Chant of Jimmie Blacksmith*, as well as a mother and grandmother in *Rabbit Proof Fence*.

This chapter has examined diverse and challenging journeys which give a strong and passionate voice to Indigenous Peoples, past and present. The popular road film format—as adapted by a range of filmmakers who demonstrate sensitivity to and respect for Aboriginal history and culture—opens up key eras in Indigenous history: the Frontier and Assimilation periods, the Stolen Generations, the formative years of civil and land rights movements, steps toward reconciliation. Further, selected films feature a crucial dynamic entity for Indigenous Peoples—the land. It is the sacred place of eternal ancient spirits, a source of nourishment, livelihood, and beauty, a tragic site of conflict—a place where Aboriginal and Torres Strait Islander Peoples belong, a "site for … [the] reclamation of national space," as Fiona Probyn-Rapsey has stated (2006, 97). To travel on the road, then, is to "Indigenise" it (Probyn-Rapsey, 2006, 99) regardless of the reason: restoring a primal (Ab)original bond, reclaiming land—sometimes forcefully—convening with family, friends, and new acquaintances, demonstrating survival skills, even boldly, proudly, and amicably bridging racial boundaries. Each trek turns into an empowering and transformative experience.

Notes

1. Australian cinema features a broad array of road films. Films such as *Midnite Spares* (1983), *Dead End Drive-In* (1986), and *Metal Skin* (1994), as Adrian Martin notes, capitalize (like *The Cars That Ate Paris* and the *Mad Max* trilogy) on Australia's car and motor bike culture. The road picture can also coexist with at least one another genre. Ocker films such as *The Adventures of Barry McKenzie, Barry Rides Again*, and *The Adventures of Priscilla, Queen of the Desert* are also road pictures. "*Crocodile" Dundee* is a romance/adventure on the road in Australia and New York. Romance and crime merge in *Kiss or Kill* and *Heaven's Burning* (both 1997). For a survey of selected road films, which include those made in Australia as well as others, see Martin's "On the Road," *Cinema Papers*, February–March 2001, 14–17.
2. *Manganinnie* (1979) and *Backlash* (1987) are road films featuring female Aboriginal protagonists. *Manganinnie* takes place in the 1830s during the "black drives" in Tasmania to eradicate Indigenous Peoples. The film focuses on the friendship that develops between the only survivor of a massacred tribe, Manganinnie, and a young non-Indigenous girl, Joanna. *Backlash* is set in the present and features two non-Indigenous police, a young man and young woman, who arrest and escort a young Indigenous woman who allegedly killed her white boss.
3. Prior to the 1970s, Indigenous Peoples were primarily the subjects of ethnographic films and documentaries. If they were included in features, which was rare, negative stereotypes predominated. For example, in Charles Chauvel's *Uncivilised* (1936),

Aboriginal individuals were stock characters, and at least one character was played by a non-Indigenous actor. However, in 1955, Chauvel made *Jedda*, which develops into a road picture, and which was intended to be more sympathetic to Indigenous Peoples. This film has been embraced and condemned. (See Crilly, 2001, 36–44; Hodge and Mishra, 1991, 64–8; Jennings, 1993, 33–7.)

4 Bond's initial "screenplay" was fourteen pages of handwritten notes. His next draft was sixty-three pages with "no scenic detail, only dialogue," as Louis Nowra notes, thus giving Roeg latitude to explore his vision in every sense of the word as cinematographer and director (Nowra, 2003, 15).

5 Another less common term is the Dreaming.

6 The title card at the beginning of the film reads, "In Australia, when an Aborigine man–child reaches 16, he is sent out into the land. For months he must live from it. Sleep on it. Eat of its fruit and flesh. Stay alive. Even if it means killing his fellow creatures. The Aborigines call it the WALKABOUT. This is the story of a 'WALKABOUT.'" In the commentary by Roeg on the DVD (released 1998), clearly exasperated, he noted that 20th Century Fox added this information, implying that it was not in the script. This title card clearly simplifies the journey into one of survival, ignoring the larger context of the spiritual component of the Dreamtime/Dreamings.

7 When *Walkabout* was rereleased theatrically in 1998, a sequence originally cut from the 1971 release was added back in. This sequence comes after the three cross the river (and is also included in the DVD). In this sequence, the young Indigenous man passes by a young non-Indigenous woman who tries to speak to him; he answers her in his tribal dialect and joins the girl and her brother in the background. The woman joins her elder male companion, who is also non-Indigenous, and who is working with a large group of Aboriginal children. He supervises them while barking orders as they make cheap-looking souvenirs, such as kangaroo statuettes and statues of Aboriginal elders dipped in white paint. This exploitation of Indigenous Peoples (and their culture) can be compared to the girl's treatment of the young Indigenous man like a slave later in the film, which begins when she rides his back as they cross the river. This reinserted sequence, presented in a social realist mode, is very different from the idyllic mood and narrative which privileges the young Indigenous man, the girl, and her brother.

8 Fred Schepisi had always wanted to make a "great Australian film." When he read *The Chant of Jimmie Blacksmith*, he saw his chance to dramatize brutal, turn-of-the-century Indigenous/non-Indigenous conflicts. With its seething white racism, cycles of violence and bloodshed, not to mention the shocking transformation of an apparently peaceful young Aboriginal man into a mass murderer, *Jimmie Blacksmith* was too confrontational for (primarily non-Indigenous) audiences, as

Schepisi himself has subsequently commented. Though it was the first Australian film in the revival to ever be selected for competition at Cannes, where it was well received, *Jimmie Blacksmith* was not popular within Australia. Nevertheless, Schepisi resolutely put frontier racism into mainstream cinema; *Jimmie Blacksmith*'s rigorous realist style and bold vision subsequently served as a model for other directors, including Rolf de Heer for *The Tracker*, James Ricketson for *Blackfellas* (1993), Nick Parsons for *Dead Heart* (1996), and Paul Goldman for *Australian Rules* (2002).

9   For the scenes in the reserves, Noyce asked permission from the elders in the Bourke Reserve and Brewarina for filming privileges. These scenes are shot with a sensitivity to community life.

10 Located in the center of Australia near Alice Springs, Uluru (formerly called Ayers Rock), a huge and magnificent geographical phenomenon, has historically been an Aboriginal sacred site and a sanctuary for Aboriginal tribes.

11 According to Isaac, "Les was playing out the story of the band's roadie who had been taken from his family as a baby, and was in the often painful process of trying to find them. It would have been too confronting for [the roadie] to tell his own story in the film, but we felt it was sufficiently important for someone else to tell it instead" (December 31, 2003 letter to the author from Graeme Isaac).

12 Isaac comments, "Us Mob and No Fixed Address were two of the first Aboriginal bands in Australia to be writing original songs in a contemporary idiom about their own lives, pre-dating Indigenous bands such as the 'Warampi' and, 'Yothu Yindi.' *Wrong Side* presented a view into a world unknown to most white Australians, and was regarded by the contemporary Aboriginal community as a truly Aboriginal film and ... a validation of their experience" (Isaac, 2003, 2), or as Almos Macksay has noted, "what it's like to be young and black in Australia" (Maksay, 1981, 503). Over two and a half decades later, *Wrong Side* is still shown on television, and continues to be run in film programs with a new generation of Aboriginal filmmakers, including Ivan Sen and Rachel Perkins. Within the Indigenous artistic community, *Wrong Side* was a stimulus to the Indigenous music scene and to the promotion of contemporary Aboriginal music. There are now Aboriginal bands all over the country, on the national stage as well as in small country towns. Lander adds, "What the music had to offer was the chance to make a really positive statement about urban Aboriginal culture, [and] about the close-knit relations between its people and their daily struggles. Music is an extremely powerful way of speeding people through their prejudices" (Peake, 1981, 2).

13 *The Tracker* was not based on a particular incident, but upon an original idea inspired by research done by de Heer, who read the early 1920s diary of police officer Captain Willshire (upon whom the Fanatic is based). According to de Heer,

Willshire killed between 2,000 and 4,000 Aboriginal individuals during his career (Phone interview with Rolf de Heer, July 15, 2003).

14 Aboriginal communities were also victims of European-introduced disease, poor health, and inadequate food supplies. By the early 1920s, the Aboriginal population, estimated to have been 300,000–500,000 in 1788, had been reduced to approximately 60,000–75,000. Aboriginal food sources were either destroyed by white settler farming, or made inaccessible when tribes were forced to move.

15 *The Tracker* was shot in the Flinders Range in the Arkaroola Wilderness Sanctuary in South Australia. de Heer used a 2.35 aspect ratio, as Fred Schepisi did in *The Chant of Jimmie Blacksmith* in his presentation of the lush wet bush landscape. de Heer's long takes dramatize the broad expanse of the hot, dry, and harsh rocky terrain where temperatures well over 100 degrees are common.

16 There are significant differences, however, between the book and the film. In the book, the girls' most formidable foes are the elements, for example, rain and cold. In the film, the human predators are more dangerous. Moreover, frequent passages in the book read like an adventure story, a tone that the film eschews in favor of presenting a harrowing trek. This passage serves as an example: "The morning was pleasant, everything was quiet and peaceful. The sun was shining through the clouds and the raindrops on the leaves and spiders' webs sparkled like diamonds. Below them was an open grassland of lush green pastures that would soon become a field of bright yellow dandelions. By their manner, one could have thought that the girls were taking a leisurely stroll in the bush. They appeared very relaxed as they walked along together" (Pilkington, 2002, 95).

Further, the book goes into great detail about the wonders and glory of nature, often taking on the tone and characteristics of the Dreamtime/Dreamings with its frequent reverential references to the environment and wildlife that Molly, Gracie, and Daisy see and admire. These sections conjure up the vibrant images of *Walkabout*. For example, well into their journey, Pilkington-Garimara writes, "One late afternoon, the girls were enjoying the mild winter day, with the sun shining on their backs. It was the kind of day when you felt happy to be alive. The absconders gleaned all the positive energy from the environment, from everything that lived and breathed around them" (Pilkington, 2002, 107).

17 According to Pilkington-Garimara, Molly learned her bush survival skills from her non-Indigenous father, who was a fence inspector, as well as her Aboriginal stepfather, who had been a desert nomad.

18 Felicity Collins and Therese Davis comment that this scene contributes nothing to the plot (Collins and Davis, 2004, 139). I would argue that this scene provides very strong evidence of Neville's assimilation philosophy, which shapes his treatment of the children at Moore River. When he examines Molly and the others, he evaluates them not as human beings, but clinically, as if they were specimens.

19 Christine Olsen gives another interpretation for the spirit bird, which is based on her experiences with the residents of Jigalong where she stayed as she researched her screenplay: "Jigalong people believe that at night their spirits can leave their bodies and fly out over the land and return with a new song" (Letter from Christine Olsen to the author, October 28, 2003). Along this line, the film suggests that the spirit of Molly's mother inhabits the bird that watches over and inspires Molly when she falls exhausted in the desert.

20 Molly also exudes mythical status. As Stephen Holden notes, this "radiant folk heroine … is [p]rofoundly intuitive, indomitably courageous, and endowed with superhuman resilience, she is the stuff of legend" (Holden, 2002, B8).

21 Though presented in a realist style like *The Chant of Jimmie Blacksmith* and *The Tracker*, amidst an often harsh and unforgiving terrain, like the arid bush in *The Tracker*, *Rabbit Proof Fence* does not feature the level or intensity of violence or frequency of death that these two other films have. With its Mature rating for Australian audiences (translating to PG-13 for American viewers), *Fence* was clearly intended for the broadest audiences possible, so that young people Molly's age, and even those the ages of Gracie and Daisy, within and outside of Australia could see and learn from the film.

22 As Judith Brett notes, on the day prior to Rudd's speech, "local Indigenous people had conducted a Welcome to Country ceremony for members of the new parliament. When Rudd delivered his Apology, the galleries of the House of Representatives were filled with Indigenous people; many more gathered outside [the] Old Parliament House at the site of Aboriginal Tent Embassy. First erected in 1972 to accompany demands for recognition of Aboriginal land rights and for self-determination, it is a long-standing symbol of Aboriginal dispossession and continuing oppression" (Holmes and Ward, 2011, 71–2).

Sources

Adams, Brian and Graham Shirley (1983), *Australian Cinema: The First Eighty Years*, Sydney: Currency Press.

Anderson, Ian (2000), "Aboriginalities," in Sylvia Kleinert and Margo Neale (eds), *The Oxford Companion to Aboriginal Art and Culture*, South Melbourne: Oxford University Press, 427–53.

Andrews, Munya (2019), *Journey into Dreamtime*, Victoria: Ultimate World Publishing.

Barber, Susan (2020), "Walkabout: A Timeless Cross-Cultural Journey," *Quarterly Review of Film and Video*, 37 (7). https://www.tandfonline.com/.

Berger, John (1972), *Ways of Seeing*, London: BBC and Penguin Books.

Bongiorno, Frank (2019), "Inside Story: Bringing Them Home," January 1. https://insidestory.org.au/bringing-them-home/ (accessed March 7, 2022).

Brett, Judith (2011), "Apologizing to the Stolen Generations," in Katie Holmes and Stuart Ward (eds), *Exhuming Passions: The Pressure of the Past in Ireland and Australia*, Dublin: Irish Academic Press, 71–90.

Byrnes, Paul (2002), "Review of *The Tracker*," *Sydney Morning Herald*, August 8, Vertigo Films Press Kit.

Collins, Felicity and Therese Davis (2004), *Australian Cinema after Mabo*, Cambridge, England: Cambridge University Press.

Cowan, James (1989), *The Mysteries of the Dream-time: The Spiritual Life of Australian Aborigines*, Bridport, Great Britain: Prism Press.

Crilly, Shane (2001), "Reading Aboriginalities in Australian Cinema," *Australian Screen Education*, 26/27 (Winter): 36–44.

Dermody, Susan and Elizabeth Jacka (1988), *The Screening of Australia: Anatomy of a National Cinema*, Volume II, Sydney: Currency Press.

Gibson, Ross (1994), "Formative Landscapes," in Scott Murray (ed.), *Australian Cinema*, St. Leonard: Allen and Unwin, in association with the Australian Film Commission, 45–59.

Gleeson, Veronica (2002), "Tracking David," *Inside Film*, August.

Haebich, Anna (2000), *Broken Circles: Fragmenting Indigenous Families 1800–2000*, North Freemantle: Freemantle Arts Centre Press.

Hanson, Philip (2017), "The Aboriginal Trauma Narrative and Roeg's Walkabout," *Studies in Australasian Cinema*, 11 (1): 1.

Hickling-Hudson, Anne (1990), "White Construction of Black Identity in Australian Films about Aborigines," *Literature/Film Quarterly*, 18 (4): 265.

Hodge, Bob and Vijay Mishra (1991), *Dark Side of the Dream: Australian Literature and the Postcolonial Mind*, North Sydney: Allen and Unwin.

Holden, Stephen (2002), "Review of Rabbit Proof Fence," *The New York Times*, Arts Section, November 29: B8.

Holmes, Katie and Stuart Ward (2011), *Exhuming Passions: The Pressure of the Past in Ireland and Australia*, Dublin: Irish Academic Press.

Houston, Beverle and Marsha Kinder (1980), *Self and Cinema*, Pleasantville, New York: Redgrave Publishing.

Isaac, Graeme (2003), Letter written to the author, December 31.

Jennings, Karen (1993), *Sites of Difference: Cinematic Representations of Aboriginality and Gender*, Melbourne: AFI.

Jennett, Christine (2001), "The Movement for Indigenous Peoples' Rights: Land Rights and Self-determination," in James Jupp (ed.), *The Australian People: An Encyclopedia of the Nation, Its People and Their Origins*, Cambridge, England: Cambridge University Press, 123–7.

Kael, Pauline (1985), "A Dreamlike Requiem Mass for a Nation's Lost Honour," in Albert Moran and Tom O'Regan (eds), *An Australian Film Reader*, Sydney: Currency Press, 204–10.

Keating, Paul (1992), Redfern Speech, "Australian Launch of the International Year for the World's Indigenous People," December 10. http://apology.west.net.au/redfern.html (accessed January 23, 2005).
Keneally, Thomas (1972), *The Chant of Jimmie Blacksmith*, Victoria: Penguin Books.
Langton, Marcia (1993), "*Well, I Heard It on the Radio and I Saw It on the Television ...,*" 4th printing, Woolloomooloo: Australian Film Commission.
Lawson, Sylvia (2004), "Regressive Politics in Australia," *The New York Times*, June 14: A23.
McKay, Daniel (2017), "Uluru Statement: A Quick Guide," Parliament of Australia Website, June 19. https://www.aph.gov.au/About_Parliament/Parliamentary_Departments/Parliamentary_Library/pubs/rp/rp1617/Quick_Guides/UluruStatement (accessed March 4, 2022).
McIntyre, Stuart and Anna Clark (2003), *The History Wars*, Carlton: Melbourne University Press.
McNiven, Liz (2015), "Curator's Notes: Samson and Delilah," Australian Screen NFSA Website. https://aso.gov.au/titles/features/samson-and-delilah/notes (accessed February 14, 2022).
Maksay, Almos (1981), "Review of Wrong Side of the Road," *Cinema Papers*, November/December.
Morris, Meaghan (1989), "Fate and the Family Sedan," *East–West Film Journal*, 4 (1): 124.
Nowra, Louis (2003), *Australian Screen Classics: Walkabout*, Sydney: Currency Press and Screen Sound.
O'Shaughnessy, Michael (2004), "Walkabout's Music: European Nostalgia in the Australian Outback," *Metro*, 140: 82–6.
Palmer, Dave and Garry Gillard (2001), "Aborigines, Ambivalence, and Australian Film," *Metro*, 134: 128.
Peake, Catherine (1981), "Facts of Life in Black Urban Australia," *The National Times*, November 15–21, *Wrong Side of the Road* press kit, Ronin Films, Distributor.
Peterson, Nicolas (2000), *The Oxford Companion to Aboriginal Art and Culture*, ed. Sylvia Kleinert and Margo Neale, Melbourne: Oxford University Press.
Pettitt, Lance (2000), *Screening Ireland: Film and Television Representation*, Manchester, England: Manchester University Press.
Pike, Andrew and Ross Cooper (1998), *Australian Film: 1900–1977*, South Melbourne: Oxford University Press.
Pilkington, Doris (Nugi Garimara) (2002), *Rabbit Proof Fence*, New York: Miramax Books/Hyperion.
Primrose, Ian (1982), "Dreamtime, the Popular Idea," *Dreamworks*, Spring.
Probyn-Robsey, Fiona (2006), "Bitumen Films in Postcolonial Australia," *Journal of Australian Studies*, 88 (8): 97–109.
Rowley, C. D. (1972), *The Destruction of Aboriginal Society*, Harmondsworth, Middlesex, UK: Pelican Books.

Scheckter, John (1999), *The Australian Novel, 1830–1980: A Thematic Introduction*, New York: Peter Lang Publishing.

Simmons, Gary (2003), "The Other Side of Rabbit Proof Fence," *Australian Screen Education*, 31: 47.

Smaill, Belinda (2002), "The Tracker," *Metro*, (134): 30–3.

"The 'Ten Point Plan' and the 1998 Native Title Act Amendments" ANTAR (Australians for Native Title and Reconciliation). www.antar.org.au (accessed July 5, 2004).

Wright, Tony and Janine MacDonald (1999), "Howard Sends His Regrets," *The Age*, August 27. https://www.theage.com.au/national/from-the-archives-1999-howard-sends-his-regrets-20210820-p58kms.html (accessed March 6, 2022).

Young, Lola (1996), *Fear of the Dark: "Race," Gender and Sexuality in the Cinema*, London: Routledge.

6

Australian Gothic

Australian Gothic taps into and flaunts the dark side of the Australian psyche as filmmakers unleash their imaginations in wildly creative ways with great daring, gusto, and flair. An array of vivid terms and phrases have been used to describe the iconography, traits, and "essence" of gothic films: "the perverse, the grotesque, the malevolent" (Dermody and Jacka, 1988, 51); "the ... uncertainty and desperation of the human experience" (Turcotte, 1998); "disturbed, unstable characters" (Thomas, 2007) [who can be] "deliberately pathological" (Dermody and Jacka, 1988, 51); "the unfathomable menace of ... location" (Thomas and Gillard quoting Jonathan Raynor, 2003, 40). Society in disarray. Civilization crumbling and collapsing. A morbid fascination with the monstrous, anarchy, and death.

Fertile ground, certainly, for the horror genre, but gothic—a hybrid—can also incorporate and deftly balance varied genres such as melodrama, science fiction, the road picture, the Western, in addition to the horror film, demonstrating the versatility of gothic as a protean "supergenre." Often Australian Gothic is peppered with black humor and/or features a satirical edge in order to leaven otherwise bleak visions. One initial influence on Australian Gothic was an outburst of adventurous spirit from the "underground of experimental filmmaking," as Dermody and Jacka note (Dermody and Jacka, 1988, 51). Gothic was also fueled by the easing of censorship in the early 1970s with the "R" classification, particularly in the areas of sexuality and violence, which can be linked.

Seven prominent, cutting-edge gothic films that eagerly delve into the areas outlined above, selected from three decades, are discussed in this chapter: *Shirley Thompson Versus the Aliens* (Jim Sharman, 1972), *The Night the Prowler* (Sharman, 1978), *The Cars That Ate Paris* (Peter Weir, 1974), *Mad Max* (George Miller, 1979), *Mad Max II* (aka *Road Warrior*, Miller, 1981), *Mad Max Beyond Thunderdome* (1985, co-directed by Miller and George Ogilvie), and *Mad Max: Fury Road* (Miller, 2015). Before exploring the ways in which these filmmakers fashioned novel and unique visions of Australia, we need to locate the origins of

Australian Gothic within the country's history and culture. What were the larger forces at play prior to and during the 1970s (and later on) that generated such bold and unusual films? What did the gothic mode reveal about Australia that other formats and modes did not?

Events from two critical time frames in Australian history unique to the country can be linked to the shaping of the gothic: (1) the post–Second World War period; (2) Australia's founding in 1788 as a convict colony. First—focus on the more recent period two and a half decades before the film revival began. After the end of the Second World War in 1945, Australia shifted into a new economic and political role in the Pacific as a political and defense ally of superpower United States. There was exhilaration as well as anxiety—a huge sense of relief at the end of a world war, the dawn of a new partnership, hope for the future, increasing affluence, and a growing economy. Internally, Australia was undergoing profound changes amidst social/political upheavals which challenged the country's white patriarchal society, including women's and Aboriginal civil rights movements.

Filmmakers working within and contributing to the evolution of the gothic mode reacted to and interpreted these events and changes in different and inspired ways, turning a wry and critical eye on contemporary Australia with a sense of playfulness, subversiveness, even outrageousness. They pushed their visions into the realm of the fantastic, with narrative surprises and shocks, often with an overlay of the nightmarish. (Gothic clearly deviated from social realist, poetic realist, and raunchy comedic modes used in other films discussed in earlier chapters.) Unlike British Gothic (literary and filmic), Australian Gothic in film is rarely situated in the supernatural, for example, the "living dead"— ghosts in haunted houses or castles with lurking vampires—to terrorize dwellers and curious visitors (usually frightened young women). Absent also are religious mysticism and the demonic.

Shirley Thompson Versus the Aliens uses the backdrop of the chill of the atomic age as well as the excitement of a new space age to explore mental illness and instability as well as familial dysfunction lurking beneath the thin veneer of Australian social complacency. *The Night the Prowler* focuses on the rise of "provincial" (Turcotte, 1998, 7), middle-class families fractured and turned monstrous by prosperity and materialism in burgeoning upscale suburbs. With an overlay of melodrama, both films enter the subjective realms of female protagonists, exploring dark wells of fear, desire, and/or repressed/violent sexuality. *The Cars That Ate Paris* dramatizes moral disintegration in an inbred, isolated, and carnivorous community (read Australia itself). The inhabitants are hooked on violence and cars, the latter a well-known Australian obsession. *Mad Max* examines a civilization in decay, bursting into full-blown anarchy. The subsequent three *Max* sequels are all contextualized in the aftermath of a nuclear holocaust with factions battling each other over scarce resources and territory. Speaking of *Fury Road*, one writer quipped, "No one enjoys the end of the world like George Miller" (Mathieson, 2015), a description which could apply to at least *Mad Max II* and *Thunderdome*. (In an ominous foreshadowing, *Mad Max* is set "a few years into the future," these words subtitled against an extreme long shot of the blown-out, barren, and bleak outback hinterlands at the film's beginning.)

The evolution of Gothic through the 1970s and into the 1980s (at least as demonstrated through selected films in this chapter) and into the new millennium dramatizes a progressively more violent and despairing vision as civilization regresses and collapses. The threat of the apocalypse—the unthinkable—in *Shirley Thompson* becomes the aftermath of the event itself in the three *Max* sequels. The nexus of society and civilization, the nuclear family, which began as dysfunctional (*Shirley Thompson*, *The Night the Prowler*), nonexistent, or artificially constructed (*Cars*), is destroyed (*Mad Max*) and absent (*Mad Max II*, *Beyond Thunderdome*, *Fury Road*), though there is hope of the formation of new, peaceful, if tentative communities at the end of the latter three *Max* films. Obviously, Australia did not disintegrate socially or economically in the post-war period forward, but the country certainly felt the weight of world events. These included the East–West Cold War, along with fears of a nuclear attack by Russia on the United States and its Pacific allies. Australia also sent troops to Vietnam (1962–72) to honor its defense commitments to the United States, a decision which created ruptures within Australia. Moreover, Middle East sectarian conflicts and turmoil in oil-rich countries sent ripples globally. Clearly filmmakers mined these situations to energize their films.

The second time frame, Australia's founding as a convict colony under British jurisdiction,[1] initiated a wave of gothic literature from the late 1700s into early 1800s. (Convict transportation took place through the middle of the nineteenth century, with the last prisoner ship disembarking in 1868.) Writers such as Marcus Clark, Barbara Baynton, and Henry Lawson described the harsh conditions for convicts in their fiction, detailing alienation and anguish in a strange, foreboding environment in the newly minted penal settlements on the other side of the world. Gerry Turcotte notes, "From its inception, the Gothic ... dealt with fears and themes which are endemic in the colonial experience: isolation, entrapment, fear of pursuit and fear of the unknown" (Turcotte, 1998). The Australian convict legacy, or "stain," is deeply embedded in the national culture and psyche and has its origins in the Imperial/colonial hegemony: British sovereign/superior; Australian inmate/inferior. "Crims" (some deported for petty crimes, others for more serious ones) developed a resentment, even hatred toward their "masters." Significantly, this power structure launched the staunch, antiauthoritarian Australian creed which has resonated through history, literature, and in many films, *and* which is boldly and imaginatively dramatized in the *Max* films in particular (even though these futuristic films do not feature historical convicts). In *Mad Max*, the vengeful biker outlaws attack and challenge the police; in *Max II*, besieged nomads are "imprisoned" by a band of vicious marauders (some former coppers); in *Thunderdome*, Bartertown's underworld serfs dream of overturning the elite establishment ruling class; in *Fury Road* a band of female sex slaves challenge a Fascist-style ruler and his cohorts.

Through these power struggles, the underdogs, the subordinates, fight for their lives, territory, family, and mates. History resonates into the future where the post-nuclear setting on the outback—desolate and inhospitable—stands in for the historic outposts. In all but three cases, with *Mad Max* the exception, we root for the beleaguered and the imprisoned. Moreover, the landscape functions as a battlefield staging ground for primal, deadly clashes. Both sides can be vengeful (and historical convicts were known to stage uprisings and attack their masters), especially in *Mad Max*. The sheer spectacle, the "sensationalist" presentation—another gothic term—and emphasis on confrontations and chases (detailed later in individual discussions of the films), "hyperrealized," as Tom O'Regan notes (1996, 232), and cut with send-up humor, as well as a flaunting of a fascination with morbidity and violence *lands* (pun intended) these films squarely in the gothic arena. In all of the *Max* films, as well as in *The Cars That Ate Paris*, filmmakers cleverly and imaginatively appropriate the Australian bush and outback, incorporating the iconography and themes from the Western and the road picture in particular, exploring the binaries wilderness/civilization, savages/heroes, servitude/freedom. Further, twentieth-century technology (twenty-first in the case of *Fury Road*), with a dazzling range of motorcycles, cars, and trucks in all sizes and shapes, become weapons of destruction, reinforcing the "horror of the road" (Gelder, 2012, 8), adding another component to these gothic renderings.

The three directors whose films are examined in this chapter kicked off their feature film careers with Australian Gothic (and also wrote or co-wrote their films). Jim Sharman did cutting-edge work in *Shirley Thompson* and *The Night the Prowler*, setting the trend in Australian Gothic by combining various genres in intelligent, clever, and dazzling ways.[2] Unlike *Cars* and the *Mad Max* trilogy, Sharman's films feature strong and plucky women. (*Mad Max: Fury Road* is a notable exception with its valiant and intrepid heroine, Imperator Furiosa.) Both Shirley and Felicity Bannister (*The Night the Prowler*), though eccentric and disturbed, ride on the crest of the concurrent women's movement (though they are not self-consciously aware of it). Shirley and Felicity must, however, continue to bear the brunt of society's limitations, deficiencies, and undertones of sexism. As for Sharman's males, they are either sexually repressed or asexual, as well as equivocal about their new domesticated status in post-war, middle-class suburbia. The males in *Cars* as well as the warriors in the *Mad Max* films, on the other hand, insist on a world which privileges them; women are frequently marginalized and/or victimized. For *Mad Max* in particular, women become the primary objects of male rage. Further, the majority of men in *Cars* and the *Mad Max* films act out savagely and aggressively in amoral and fierce settings where violent aggression, death, and destruction are the norm.

After their debut features, Peter Weir and George Miller became major figures in the film revival. Weir followed *Cars* with two extraordinarily successful films. *Picnic at Hanging Rock* (1975) is a seductive blend of mysticism with gothic undertones. As discussed in Chapter 3, the mysterious and perilous rock is linked to the disappearance of young women and their teacher. *Gallipoli* (1981) explores Australia's rites of passage into nationhood by fighting in Europe on behalf of Britain during the First World War. Miller achieved international clout and commercial success with all three *Max* films. Most recently, and three decades after the release of *Thunderdome*, he co-wrote and directed *Fury Road*, one of the big global hits of 2015. Notably, with the triumph of the initial *Mad Max*, Miller established Kennedy Miller Productions in Sydney, which represented a new Australian infrastructure for the production of culturally specific Australian films and television programs as well as more internationally oriented productions.

Both Weir and Miller show the influence of the seminal gothic film, *Wake in Fright* (1971), an odyssey into the territorial and psychological Australian "heart of darkness" (Dermody and Jacka, 1988, 80): the hot, dry outback as well as the disturbed psyche of an ostensibly stable, young male teacher, who descends into primal, self-destructive urges, fueled by alcohol and the company of his all-too-friendly and domineering ocker cohorts in the remote hinterlands. As in *Cars* and the *Max* films, *Wake* shows the unleashing of the barbaric side of Australian masculinity.

Australian Gothic was at first associated with low budgets, but as the decades evolved, costs increased dramatically. *Shirley Thompson* cost Australian $17,000 and was financed with Sharman's own money. (All quoted production costs and profits in this chapter are in Australian dollars unless otherwise specified.) *Cars* received partial funding from the Australian Film Development Corporation, with the film's budget between $220,000 and $269,000. Notably, the AFDC was eager to support riskier, less formulaic, and commercial projects after kicking off the revival with the successful ockers. Sharman's *Prowler* was much more expensive, with $417,000 provided by the state funding agency, The New South Wales Film Corporation. Miller and his partner Byron Kennedy did not finance *Mad Max* via government bodies, either the Australian Film Commission, or state corporations, realizing early on that their commercial goals were inconsistent with the federal government rationale for film support—"quality" projects with serious-minded examinations of Australian history and culture. They went the private investment route, and their success with *Mad Max* (which found eager audiences locally and abroad) helped to pave the way for the tax write-off period under 10BA in the early 1980s, which encouraged private funding outside of government bodies. The increased scope and grander scale of *Mad Max II* and *Beyond Thunderdome* pushed their budgets way beyond the norm for the time. *Mad Max II* cost between $3.5 and 4 million, ten times the budget for *Mad Max* (approximately $380,000); *Beyond Thunderdome* hit a new high, costing between $12 and 13.5 million; *Fury Road* soared to between $150 and 185 million (partly due to an array of special effects, digital enhancement, and stunt work with primary live-action filming taking place in Africa). With respect to *Fury Road*, Miller received Producer and Location offsets from Screen Australia Production Screen Incentives.

Australian Gothic is frequently undervalued and misunderstood; yet, it stands as a rich, highly imaginative, and adventurous genre. Seven of the films introduced earlier are analyzed in detail in the following pages, with close attention paid to each filmmaker's strikingly original vision of Australia. A shorter section follows on a recent female-centered gothic release, *The Dressmaker* (Jocelyn Moorhouse, 2015).

Shirley Thompson Versus the Aliens

Shirley Thompson Versus the Aliens is a wry criticism of post-war complacency, foregrounding in Sharman's own words, "Australian ignorance in the face of any idea that might disturb the status quo" (Stratton, 1980, 160). Sharman and co-writer Helmut Bakaitus cleverly balance the horror film, melodrama, and science fiction, deftly shifting in tone from the comical to dead serious to the genuinely scary, while intercutting black and white with color. *Shirley Thompson* has a stunning and disquieting beginning in a foreboding asylum where Shirley (Jane Harders) is a patient, shot in garish, overexposed black and white. Through her flashbacks we learn that ten years ago in 1956, she was visited by aliens who selected her as an agent to publicize the inevitable destruction of Australia (as well as the rest of the world). Ultimately, Shirley experienced a mental and emotional breakdown, for despite her best efforts, no one, including family, friends, the larger community, and by implication Australia, took her warnings seriously.

Through the asylum and Shirley's home, Sharman/Bakaitus present and compare two kinds of madhouses. On the one hand, Shirley is isolated and imprisoned in a terrifying place where her body is punctured with huge needles by callous matronly nurses, who are made even more horrific through a distorting wide angle lens. Further, Shirley is relentlessly interrogated by an earnestly paternal but nonetheless creepy psychologist. She is also at the mercy of a hideously bandaged and clearly disturbed over-sexed male inmate, who not only gropes her, but continually and delusionally speaks of their "unborn child."

On the other hand, at home (via flashbacks) Shirley is badgered by her nagging and insular mother (Marion Johns), who is driving Shirley as well as her father and sister crazy. The home environment—a place where familial tensions overflow amidst the stifling banalities of suburban life—is presented via melodramatic scenes infused with dark comedy and tongue-in-cheek horror. As Robin Wood has commented, the family is the true milieu of horror in the horror film ([1986] 2003, 77); in this case, Shirley's monstrous mother is simultaneously frightening, pathetic, and comical. Like a permanent fixture in the kitchen, Mrs. Thompson is trapped in her mundane life of chopping up food as well as her current obsession: the garbage workers' strike. Her meddling in Shirley's life has resulted in her posting of Shirley's engagement in the local paper without Shirley even knowing it! No wonder Shirley has another far more satisfying life as queen of the biker gang (scenes which are intercut with her domestic life), which is "an obvious and necessary answer to her home life," as Dermody and Jacka have commented (Dermody and Jacka, 1988, 83).

The rest of the family includes Mrs. Thompson's other daughter, who is similarly brow-beaten and almost catatonic, as well as Mrs. Thompson's beleaguered husband (John Llewellyn), who can barely walk across the kitchen floor without his wife stopping him in his tracks with a barrage of criticism. As Mrs. Thompson loudly proclaims to her daughters, Mr. Thompson has done his own share of bad boy acting-out, such as getting drunk and exposing himself in public to urinate. At one point, Mr. Thompson, perhaps on the verge of spousal abuse, retaliates against his wife and the din of her complaints by suddenly hurling her beloved whirring mix master—an acoustic barometer for rising emotions and familial tensions—out the window to its "death" below. This act reveals Mr. Thompson's destructive rage against a modern convenience which hasn't made *his* life any easier, underscoring his miserable domestic treadmill.

Yet Shirley's parents manage to hang together as they stubbornly cling to the security of the status quo when Shirley urgently tries to warn them of the aliens' message of total annihilation. "It's the old Fascist routine," her father flippantly and defensively declares, when she draws his attention to her broadcast on the radio. He smugly adds, "So they're here, so what?!" By falling back on empty political rhetoric (which perhaps masks his own fears of the unknown), Shirley's father foreshadows the horror of community and national indifference to the aliens' warning, a dynamic which is subsequently played out on a larger scale at the Melbourne Olympics in a devilishly funny and outrageous, yet ultimately chilling sequence.

A come-alive wax figure of the Duke of Edinburgh (Ron Haddrick), a walking and talking medium for the aliens (earnestly picked out by Shirley herself at a museum for maximum visibility), speaks to the huge Olympics' crowd of "certain destruction of Australia and the world," after introducing himself as a "creature from outer space." Gleefully impervious, the crowd ignores the message, cheering and waving. This key sequence foregrounds the dynamics of the open versus closed community that Bruce Kawin discusses as a merging/diverging point for the science fiction and horror genres. The selection of Shirley by the aliens suggests that her family and the community (and Australia) can be enlightened by her and them; thus, the aliens' presence expands community boundaries, as Kawin has remarked about the science fiction genre. He argues:

Science Fiction is open to the potential value of the inhuman ....The opened community can be curious about and learn from the outsiders, while the closed community [characteristic of horror] talks only among itself. Horror emphasizes the dread of knowing, the danger of curiosity, while science fiction emphasizes the danger and irresponsibility of the closed mind.

(Kawin, 2012, 371)

Ignoring the aliens' message, Australia remains unreceptive to the possibility of enlightenment and salvation, shrugging off certain destruction. The horror is not only the apocalypse itself, but Australia's imperviousness to its own destruction. As the enlightened one, and confined to the asylum, Shirley must live with the monstrous indifference of her community and the tragedy of a woefully serious missed opportunity. It's no wonder that she goes mad in the asylum at the end of the film.

The Night the Prowler

The Night the Prowler, based on Patrick White's novella, and co-written by White and Sharman, continues Sharman's disillusionment with Australia as dramatized in *Shirley Thompson*. Here he focuses on the materialistic and self-centered Bannister family, which reflects White's stinging indictment of the middle class. *Prowler* is a skillful balance of melodrama and horror, linking family and wealth with sexual repression and violent pleasures.

As in *Shirley Thompson Versus the Aliens*, Sharman uses melodrama to explore and critique a dysfunctional family. *Night* opens with the Bannister family in crisis. Felicity Bannister (Kerry Walker) has allegedly been attacked and raped by an intruder who broke into the house. This event has ruptured the family's veneer of respectability and normalcy. Rather than pulling themselves together to share compassion and mutual support, they regress and fragment. Mrs. Bannister (Ruth Cracknell) runs down the stairs and throws up, while her timid husband, unable to face the aftermath of the crime, retreats to another part of the house to hide. Felicity, paralyzed with shame, sits silently at the dining room table.

Sullen, with dark, deep-set eyes, and an eerie inward stare, Felicity is stuck on the edge of puberty, apparently reluctant to enter womanhood. Self-consciously overweight, she frequently wanders about the house in a flimsy nightgown, which makes her look like an overgrown child. Alienated and alienating, she has no friends, rarely goes out, and escapes into pulp novels such as *Peyton Place*. Felicity's mother is another version of the self-absorbed Mrs. Thompson. However, rather than taking out her frustrations on her family as Mrs. Thompson does, Mrs. Bannister willfully remains impervious to the needs of her family. For example, she flits about from one dust-less, gleaming room to another, obsessively and narcissistically checking her reflection in a large mirror. Her repetitive acts suggest a compelling need to project a normal household, particularly after the rape, regardless of the family's estrangement, its emotional repression, and Felicity's fragile mental and physical state. Further, Mrs. Bannister treats Felicity as a material extension of her fussy, little world—a possession to show off to her bridge party friends. As Rod Bishop and Fiona Mackie have noted, Felicity's "parents want a delicate girl whom they can wrap up like a chocolate box and present, intact, to a worthy husband with appropriate status. And status means money—to the parents, the neighbors, to everyone" (Bishop and Mackie, 1980, 157).

With respect to the horror, *Prowler* presents a very different kind of monster from the comic Mrs. Thompson. Robin Wood has commented that the monster, a protean and vital component of horror, is "seen as a profoundly ambiguous figure which challenges social norms and so reveals society's repressive monstrosity" (quoted by Mark Jancovich, 1996, 1). At first, monstrous is the last word that could be used to describe Felicity, for ostensibly she is a sympathetic victim, having endured a brutal attack in her home where she already felt alienated.

Yet, she makes a stunning switch in her behavior and appearance when she becomes a night prowler herself, suiting up in black leather, vampire-like and predatorial, going on a rampage in her neighborhood, thereby revealing the dark desires of her secret life. Instead of feasting on victims, however, Felicity vandalizes nearby homes, playing out her hostility toward her parents and their middle-class lifestyle. In one particularly vicious attack, she rampages through a nearby house, slashing paintings and smashing furniture. This scene also plays out her repressed sexual feelings toward her father (John Frawley) in an unexpected manner. In the aftermath of the assault, Felicity seductively sits at a desk in the study and imagines her father's smiling portrait in front of her. Earlier in a flashback, we saw that as a child Felicity fancied her father. She crawled up on his lap and bit him, playing the bad girl desperate for his attention. He rebuffed her then, just as he ignored her after the rape. It's as if Felicity needs to imagine her father approving of her inappropriate aggressive actions in order to feel close to him.

This sequence is intercut with a flashback revealing what really happened on the night of Felicity's attack: *she* was not raped but used the break-in of the intruder (Terry Camilleri) as an opportunity to turn her aggression against *him*, shaming him into having sex with her. Laughably, the intruder is a puny and helpless man about half Felicity's size, who turns out to be impotent. Sharman's juxtaposing these two attacks, one against property, the other upon a male, suggests a displaced and disturbed sexuality. Felicity associates sexual pleasure with material destruction as well as dominance and coercion over a male far weaker than she. With reference to her initial "rape," she used this incident to masquerade as the shamed and deflowered virgin, as if to punish herself for her own act of guilty pleasure, thus enforcing her dual roles of victim and predator.[3]

The bizarre final sequence of the film adds an additional narrative twist, where Felicity, on another night prowl, finds an emaciated, dying old man (Harry Neilson) in a rundown shack. On the one hand, he represents a different level of horror—that of a forgotten and neglected member of the older generation lingering on the fringes and out of sight of the middle class, a view consistent with White's critique of this component of Australian society. On the other, the man's emaciated body and his references to his "prostate that went" allude to the film's undertones of impotence and emasculation—allusions to Felicity's father. Nevertheless, the old man's helplessness and despair touches Felicity. She has an epiphany, breaks down and cries, and then resurrects herself with renewed purpose and direction. Unlike Shirley Thompson, who succumbs to madness, Felicity—facing death, the old man's as well as her own mortality—decides to embrace life as the day breaks.

Interestingly, the film's final image of Felicity, leather-clad, facing the camera with her penetrating stare, is much like that of the battle-weary Max at the end of *Mad Max II*. Both are victims who turn into survivors, acquiring (re-acquiring in the case of Max) compassion for others. Just as Max's intersection with the nomads restores his humanity, so does Felicity's confrontation with a dying man instill in her a renewed vigor for life.

The Cars That Ate Paris

Situated in an isolated bush town, Peter Weir's *The Cars That Ate Paris* (screenplay by Weir, Keith Gow, and Piers Davies) is far away from Jim Sharman's suburbs in *Shirley Thompson Versus the Aliens* and *The Night the Prowler*. The insularity in these prior films has turned to xenophobia and brutal, deadly aggression against outsiders in *Cars*. The small (fictional) town of Paris, located somewhere in Australia's bushland, has a monstrous secret: unsuspecting drivers are hoodwinked into horrific auto smashups just outside of town where they meet grisly and violent deaths. Those who survive become prisoners, in some cases functioning as guinea pigs in lab experiments under the hand of a twisted doctor. Moreover, the car wreckage is either chopped up for parts and used as barter, supporting the town's economy, or recycled into souped-up vehicles which are driven aggressively and ruthlessly by the town's listless young men, who prowl the dusty roads in search of adventure.

The idea for *Cars* came from Weir's own experiences in Europe when he was driving through France wandering through "very strange little villages" (Stratton, 1980, 38), hence his choice of Paris in his title. He then read about a murder in England which caused him to think, "If you are going to kill someone you kill them [sic] in a motorcar accident, not with a shotgun" (Stratton, 1980, 38). This dynamic is playfully exploited metaphorically in *Cars* through the conflicts between the young men and the establishment town "elders." With his devilish imagination, Weir incorporates elements of the road picture, the horror film, and even the Western, creating an outlandish scenario: a savage community where all roads nightmarishly end, its citizens thriving on perverse economic pleasures. As Dermody and Jacka have commented, "Paris is certainly ... not the preserve of innocence and virtue we have come to expect from the long running split between city and bush in ... Australian culture" (Dermody and Jacka, 1988, 95).

By focusing on baser human instincts, including savagery, greed, and lust for destruction, rampant in this festering frontier outpost, Weir conjures up the horror film, which expresses "the struggle for recognition of all our civilization represses or oppresses," as Wood has commented (Wood, 1986, 81). This is territory Weir had examined earlier in *Homesdale* (1971), which he wrote and directed, wherein a group of guests unleash their violent and erotic fantasies on each other during their stay on an isolated island. With respect to the monstrous, *Cars* conjures up new human incarnations which differ from those in *Shirley Thompson* and *Prowler*. The character of Charlie (Bruce Spence), a car-wreck victim himself, duly "reconstituted" by the mad sadistic Dr. Midvale (Kevin Miles), who performs his human experiments at the town's hospital, is the embodiment of the town's barbarity and cannibalistic economy. With a predilection for hanging around garages, Charlie is introduced in one scene swinging several gleaming jaguar icons from car hoods above his gaping mouth, as if trying to devour them and become that which he craves. (The transformation of men into machines is reinforced later in the film, when several cars driven by the town's equally rapacious youths anthropomorphize into growling machines.) Moreover, Charlie has become a member of the pack that sets traps for drivers who come too close to the town's boundaries, targeted for certain death in a crash, or sent to Dr. Midvale, as Charlie was for "treatment." Almost seven feet tall, with a long face, a mouthful of huge menacing teeth, and dead liquid eyes, Charlie is a modern Nosferatu, and a different kind of vampire than Felicity from *Prowler*, who invades and trashes homes in a sexual fury.

The suave yet demented Dr. Midvale is another resident monster. This "Dr. Frankenstein" uses them for unspeakable experiments. At one point, the latest accident victim is dragged kicking and screaming into the operating room. The doctor's surgical tool of choice is a whining drill pointed at the victim's head. The morbid casualness of Weir's dark humor (and the town's blasé attitude toward the victims) is exemplified by one of the hospital attendants, Darryl (Chris Haywood), who flippantly speaks of the "patients" in condescendingly non-human terms: "full veggies, half veggies, or quarter veggies." For the local pioneer dance, Midvale's patients, in various stages of mental and physical deterioration, create a peculiar and garish procession with ridiculous makeshift costumes. They are covered in sheets and head bandages, one with a cartoon-like face drawn on the dressing, others with biscuit and cereal boxes functioning as masks. The mayor (John Meillon) and the populace keep up their airs, pretending that nothing is out of the ordinary. The strangeness of the patients' costumes is "balanced" by the townspeople's equally out-of-place, turn-of-the-century garb: women in long dresses and bonnets, the men in tailored black suits and top hats.

The self-righteous mayor is a more subtle monster. He has the veneer of propriety and civility with a strict law-and-order agenda, but his tacit approval of the town's economy gives his henchmen license to lure motorists off the road, then close the roads so no one can get in or out. The mayor presents himself as a family man with a wife and two daughters; yet, this nuclear unit has been artificially created, as the two girls were kidnapped from another deliberate wreck. The telling gash on the face of one (who appears to be brain-damaged) adds an eerie aura to dinner one evening, when the long red scar on the temple under her hair is accidentally exposed. Whereas *Shirley Thompson* and *Prowler* feature monstrous biological mothers who are alternately scary and comical, as well as domineering and self-serving, this self-designated father puts a chill into the word "family" as a perverse head of the household. In comparison to Charlie, the mayor has an even more voracious appetite for car violence and killing. He shows his true colors when the town's rebellious young men start attacking the town, using their cars to ram into his house one night, with town hall the target the following evening. The mayor turns into a bloodthirsty ghoul, cheering on his lackey and adopted "son" Arthur (Tony Camilleri), the town's latest prey from an ambushed car, to kill Daryl, the leader of the rebels. The mayor's actions are so horrific that he becomes alarmingly funny as he encourages Arthur to repeatedly smash into Daryl's car and crush him into a bloody pulp. Arthur is duly transformed from a timid victim plagued by guilt over his brother's "accidental" death outside of town (so much so that he has been unable to drive), into an eager, bloodthirsty predator himself, his confidence in his driving skills reborn, as if the killer instinct of the town has rubbed off on him.

Consistent with the horror genre, sexuality is distorted or channeled into violent pleasures. The mayor, who is completely asexual with his wife, is clearly turned on by the bloody killing of Daryl; Dr. Midvale's vicious attacks on his patients with his phallic drill to torture and maim play out his craving of sexual thrills. The town's young men, whose raging hormones would normally be directed at the opposite sex, displace their sexual aggression onto their cars, which they flaunt and drive recklessly, via speed and stunt derbies on the town's main street. Clearly, as Christopher Sharrett has pointed out, Weir graphically plays out the phallic power of Australia's car culture (Sharrett, 1985, 84), a dynamic that George Miller would enthusiastically capitalize on in the *Mad Max* series.

The horror elements in *Cars* are enhanced by allusions to the road picture and the Western. Dermody has aptly commented that *Cars* is "a freakishly arrested road film" (Dermody, 1980, 82). Cohan and Hark add, "Paris is literally the end of the road, [representing] the fury and suffering at the extremities of 'civilized' life" (Cohan and Hark, 1997, 1). Yet, unlike a good number of road pictures, the road is not liberating, nor does it lead to a newfound identity. Instead of travelers voluntarily escaping from an oppressive society to adventure and freedom, they are ensnared by a barely civilized, alien community that causes them to die violently, holds them prisoner, or tortures them in ghastly experiments. For innocent outsiders, the road translates to extreme danger, maiming, mutilation, and death. Weir makes this point graphically in the opening sequence with two sets of drivers, a young man and woman, as well as Arthur and his brother, both of whom are deliberately tricked into blind traps, meeting grisly deaths in car wrecks engineered by Paris's henchmen. Only Arthur survives. Traumatized mentally and emotionally disabled, as noted earlier (and under the seductive sway of the mayor), he is confined to the environs of the town under the mayor's watchful eye.

The ultimate showdown on Main Street between the young men and the mayor conjures up the Western: the youth with their ten-gallon hats, kerchiefs, and prairie coats; their "horses" parked nearby, amidst the wail of a harmonica wafting through the air. Instead of the confrontation at high noon ending in a shoot-out, the mayor burns one of the cars to cinders, taking charge of his town, re-establishing law and order, inciting, however, the young men's revenge on the town. However, rather than using horses and guns to invade and attack the town, the young outlaws use their cars as weapons, which prowl and lurch down Main Street.

Ironically, the hero of the town turns out to be Arthur, originally designated as the "parking sheriff" by the mayor. Arthur is a complete reversal of the classical Western hero—hardly courageous, highly unskilled, and pathologically shy. However, during the attack on the town, he rises to the occasion, as described earlier, ridding the town of ringleader outlaw Daryl, his (Arthur's) car a substitute for a six-shooter. Arthur is able to escape from Paris, heading for new horizons, commencing on a new road journey, having broken free of the mayor's rule and the town's spell. Yet he leaves the town not in a better state, as in the classical Western. Though Paris is free of the official outlaws, the town has not become more civilized, the usual resolution of classical Westerns. It has completely disintegrated as people flee in all directions with their belongings. And typical of the modern road picture, Arthur's car is the only promise of self in a culture of mechanical reproduction, as Timothy Corrigan has argued (quoted in Cohan and Hark, 1997, 2), a dynamic that would be further explored by George Miller in *Mad Max*.

Mad Max

Mad Max (story by George Miller and Byron Kennedy, screenplay by James McCausland and George Miller, directed by Miller) is a fitting film to culminate a decade of social and political angst in the larger global context, as discussed earlier. The apocalypse is upon Australia, as the aliens in *Shirley Thompson* predicted. Further, as the sequel *Mad Max II*, three years later, makes perfectly clear, Australia has indeed been caught in a nuclear crossfire between the United States and Russia. The suburbs in *The Night the Prowler* and bush towns in *The Cars That Ate Paris* have deteriorated into vast stretches of wasteland under the perpetually gray and cloudy skies of nuclear winter. The landscape is dotted by ghost towns and isolated pockets of human life. The one remaining family unit—Max's family—faces certain peril.

If *The Cars That Ate Paris* charts a civilization in decline—a monstrous and bloodthirsty town feeding and thriving on car wrecks as well as the ravaging of human life—then *Mad Max* plays out full-blown anarchy and the beginning of the end of civilization. It's as if the younger generation in *Cars* has regressed into two battling factions: a sadistic pack of killers on wheels—a gang of bikers or "scoot jockeys"—and a band of equally savage and volatile cops, "the bronze." The remnants of the police force are as brutally violent and destructive as the predatory bikers who roam the barren land. They battle it out on the open road via high-speed chases with cars and motorcycles as weapons. As the film commences, one of the gang members, Nightrider, has killed a cop. He is subsequently pursued by Max Rockatansky (Mel Gibson), and the chase ends in a fiery crash with Nightrider's death. Toecutter (Hugh Keays-Byrne), the leader of the gang, vows a deadly revenge on Max and his partner Goose (Steve Bisley) as well as Max's family.

In *Mad Max*, there is a salient escalation of male fury and road rage, which reflects an aggressive, pumped-up, macho ethic. First of all, the filmmakers appear to have run with Weir's original conceptualization for *Cars*, which was "very much of that post-Vietnam period." Weir continues, "I never took it as far as I wanted to, the feeling of a country in some sort of economic chaos. There were to be troops in the countryside, anarchy in the air, odd radio reports of massive road accidents" (Mathews, 1985, 92). This predicament is the unstated milieu for *Max*—a country in crisis, ruptured and in turmoil. Miller/Kennedy/McCausland streamline the home divisions into opposing male factions at war, revving them up, using the outback as battlefield. Men are all pumped up for war, taking out their wrath on each other as well as the small population of civilians.

Secondly, *Mad Max* suggests an apprehensive white male sensibility. In the 1970s, the white male was no longer a privileged sector of Australian society, due to a variety of forces. First, the White Australia Policy was abolished in the early 1970s. This practice had severely limited non-European immigration since the end of the Second World War. Once it was gone, stepped-up immigration from Asian countries in the Pacific Rim (as well as other countries) was initiated, dramatically altering Australia's primarily Anglo-European population. Moreover, in the wake of Indigenous and women's rights movements, the Labor Administration of Prime Minister Gough Whitlam instituted a variety of social and political reforms for Aboriginals and women. These included an increase in federal funding for Aboriginal welfare, the Racial Discrimination Act, as well as equal rights and anti-sex discrimination legislation. The country's increasing ethnic diversity, as well as the empowerment of Indigenous people and women, posed deep threats to white males. *Max* captures metaphorically this sense of endangered white masculinity as its males flaunt aggression and confrontation that intensifies into frenzied brutality and destruction.

We saw this macho fierceness throughout *The Cars That Ate Paris*. In *Max*, the filmmakers do not target Aboriginals or Asians. Subsequent films in the 1990s such as *The Adventures of Priscilla, Queen of the Desert* (1994) and *Romper Stomper* (1992) directly dramatize the perceived Asian "menace": a Filipino woman in the outback (as discussed in Chapter 1) and Vietnamese immigrants who have settled in Melbourne (respectively). Significantly, however, women bear the brunt of white male rage in *Max* through a variety of different ways to be discussed later. This sexism and misogyny escalates that of the ockers and ocker genre, which responded to the increasing empowerment of women with crude posturing and libidinal machismo.

To play out white male anxiety and identity crisis, the filmmakers appropriate the road picture, wherein "the road protagonist readily identifies with the means of mechanized transportation, the automobile or motorcycle," as Timothy Corrigan notes (as quoted by Cohan and Hark, 1997, 2). And as noted earlier with respect to *The Cars That Ate Paris*, "the car becomes the only promise of self in a culture of mechanical reproduction" (Corrigan, 1991, 146) amidst "the destabilization of male subjectivity and [the destabilization of] masculine empowerment" (Corrigan as quoted by Cohan and Hark, 1997, 2). Therefore, the high speeds, the chases, and the road rage in *Mad Max* are attempts to recoup and stabilize white male subjectivity, so males can resurrect themselves as one turbocharged unit on the road, simultaneously reinforcing the phallic power of Australia's car culture, as dramatized in *The Cars That Ate Paris*.

By setting *Mad Max* on outback roads and spiking this film with high-velocity chases and crashes, the filmmakers capitalize, as Weir did, on the Australian car fetish. Miller notes, "In Australia we have a car culture the way that Americans have a gun culture … violence by car … There are great networks of empty roads … and there's no way of policing the speed limit. We have a disproportionately high road toll and so we seem to use the car as a means of recreation and of violence" (Van Hise, 1983, 33). Or as Tom O'Regan has wryly and aptly put it, "Australians *dream* of cars coming over hills on the wrong side of the road" (O'Regan, 1996, 105; emphasis mine). It should be noted that before becoming a filmmaker, Miller, who holds a medical degree, was an emergency road doctor who would tend to victims of car wrecks in remote areas. He thus experienced first hand the bloody violence and death that hot cars and high speeds cause. His admittedly morbid fascination with Australian autocide fuels his desire to give viewers the sensation of being in car crashes—a dynamic which could apply to all of the *Max* films. Miller's passion blends well with Byron Kennedy's love of machines and speed, which infuse the action sequences featuring cars and motorcycles with vitality and bravado. For example, *Max*'s opening sequence brandishes Australia's aggressive car culture while playing out the merging of man and machine as one entity, destructive to himself and others. Nightrider (Vince Gill) is so wound up by high velocities (and drugs?) as he careens down the road that he is simultaneously funny and horrifying. He laughs and screams, "I am a fuel-injected suicide machine!" Nightrider is pursued at breakneck speed by two high-strung, bloodthirsty cops in a patrol car, who are also turned on by the thrill of speed. During the chase, they become so distracted, all but ignoring innocent civilians along the road, that they smash into a van parked on the side. One of the policemen is graphically impaled through the throat by a splintered steering wheel.

One of Miller's most immediate models for *Mad Max* was Roger Corman's *The Wild Angels* (1966), a road picture featuring Corman's typically lean, hard-driving narrative exploiting action and violence. *Angels* features a group of counterculture Southern California bikers, who are harassed and preyed upon by heavily armed police. Consistent with the road picture, they seek the freedom and safety of the roads—in this case the open highways on the outskirts of Los Angeles. In *Max*, the bleak outback hinterlands replace the picturesque, sunny Southern California landscape. The scoot jockeys use the roads as a lethal weapon to retaliate against the cops. They are the oppressors who attack, torture, and kill. This is a reversal of the situation in *Angels*, wherein the cops were the initial aggressors.

Though the main dynamic of *Mad Max* is the bikers/cops conflict, including a sadistic attack upon Max's partner Goose, whom they brutally set afire, much of the bikers' hostility and contemptuous behavior is directed at women. Their bikes function as killing machines—most dramatically and horrifically demonstrated when the bikers chase and run over Max's wife Jessie (Joanne Samuel) and son Sprog (Brendan Heath) toward the end of the film as they run for their lives. They are left to die. Toecutter's gang also terrorizes, beats up, and rapes a young woman on the road. The film dramatizes her terror from her point of view as the gang attacks the car with axes and huge mallets, while she is trapped inside. When Max and Goose find her with a rope around her neck, her clothes shredded, she is in shock, shaking and sobbing. Although her boyfriend was also attacked, he was able to run away, apparently unharmed, when Max and Goose approached the car, suggesting that the gang's worst behavior was directed at this helpless female.

Consistent with its misogyny, the film even suggests that Jessie is a bad mother. When she and Max go on holiday in the bush, she leaves her son and indulges herself in a swim and sunbath. In her absence, Sprog is kidnapped by the bikers, who also subsequently stalk and severely frighten Jessie in the bush. Discovering that her son is gone, she tearfully begs the gang to give Sprog back. Toecutter teases and belittles her, sarcastically and condescendingly referring to her as "little mother." In another scene, the female mannequin which the gang fondles and gropes at the seaside for their amusement is emblematic of the film's attitudes toward women—sexual objects to be ravaged and snuffed out. One of the gang members shoots off part of the mannequin's face with a shotgun, mutilating her. This gesture resonates in a later scene when Toecutter threatens Jessie with disfiguration—"You may lose your pretty face."

The gang's viciousness toward Max's wife and the young woman operates on another level, male fear of castration, as Tom O'Regan has argued. "*Max* inscribe[s] … upon the male bodies on screen an almost hysterical anxiety … a hand missing here, a limb there, a leg in plaster" (O'Regan, 1996, 104). This deep fear of the loss of male potency is implied in a scene when the gang members are off their bikes, emasculated without their vehicles. Toecutter walks toward Jessie, ready to grab and rape her. She kicks him in the groin, disabling him (at least temporarily), thus underscoring how vulnerable he is without his machine. However, Toecutter is soon back on his motorcycle; he and his gang are fully re-empowered, and they use their bikes as weapons to mow over Jessie and her son. Disempowerment and emasculation also apply to Max, who, without the safety of his car, is at *his* most vulnerable. When the bikers go after him, he is on the road alone, having stepped out of his car. He is completely helpless and at their mercy. They doubly "castrate" him, first shooting him in the thigh: Max falls to the ground, writhing on the ground in pain. They then run over his arm, crushing it.

In addition to the road picture, *Mad Max*'s filmmakers appropriate the Western. Miller has commented, "People were saying that the traditional Western was dead, but I said no, it wasn't. It was really being retold as the cop picture, and the car chases had replaced the gunfight" (Mathews, 1985, 237). The "post-industrial scrap heap of civilization" (Sharrett, 1985, 85) that Max patrols is reminiscent of the desert wilderness. However, instead of growing and expanding, civilization has regressed and eroded to one outpost, the peaceful bush enclave where Max and his family live, arguably the only component of civilization left. The filmmakers go to great lengths to personalize civilization so that its loss is ultimately all the more devastating for Max. Publicly, "civilization" is represented rather cynically by the "Halls of Justice," the entrance to the shabby police headquarters with its crooked, rusted sign. As discussed earlier, the bronze make up their own rules of the road as endorsed by their Chief, Fifi, who declares, "As long as the paperwork is clean, you men can do what you want."

Clearly, Max conjures up the classical Westerner. He is reminiscent of the hero who has links to both wilderness and civilization—at least initially, Max can balance both worlds. As a loving family man away from the mean streets, he exhibits devotion to his wife and toddler son, their home the last locale escaping encroachment by the bikers. Yet, skilled and "streetwise," he also relishes his job as a member of the elite, interceptor police force, which cruises and patrols the outback roads. Max is attracted to the thrill of high speeds and the chase, just as the Westerner is attracted to the freedom and danger of the open wilderness which tests him, and where he frequently and voluntarily ends up to roam in search of other communities in need of his help. Also consistent with the Western hero, Max adheres to a strong moral code, killing only to protect and ensure the safety of civilians, as he did when he took out the homicidal Nightrider at the film's beginning.

But whereas the Westerner's job was to be the agent of expanding civilization, Max ultimately becomes the agent of brutal revenge and total anarchy, regressing from a hero with scruples to one emulating the savagery of the bikers. Once his mate Goose and his family are gone, he sadistically kills all the remaining members of the gang, including Toecutter, whom he entraps in a gruesome and spectacular head-on crash with a semi-truck. Max's pièce de resistance is reserved for Johnny Boy (Tim Burns), whose leg he handcuffs to a soon-to-explode car, taunting him with some sardonic advice: Johnny can save himself *if* he quickly saws off his foot. As Max casually walks away, the car explodes, killing Johnny in a huge fireball.

Christopher Sharrett has compared Max to the hell-bent psychopath Ethan Edwards from *The Searchers* (1956). Indeed, John Ford's revisionist Western de-myths the a priori honorable and noble classical Western hero. Edwards loses most of his family, and avenges their deaths in a bloodthirsty pursuit of the Comanches. But even Edwards ceases his obsessive killing spree, safely returning his niece home, after choosing not to take her life, thus restoring his bonds with civilization—albeit temporarily—before he departs into the wilderness alone. Max, on the other hand, who loses all his family, foregoes all traces of civilized behavior, becoming "amoral, self-serving and unapologetic," as Delia Falconer has noted (Falconer, 1997, 258). By the end of his killing spree, he is hardly equipped with the mental and emotional stability to assist another community in need. The irony, is, of course, that there are no visible communities in the outback!

It is worth noting that during an earlier scene when Max is on holiday with his family in the bush, away from the outback where he has proven to be invulnerable, he loses his special hero status. Out of his element, he is unable to protect his wife, son, or even himself, miscalculating the pervasiveness and cunning of the bikers who encroach upon the bush. At this point in the narrative, Miller uses the road picture to challenge the conventions of the Western, especially with respect to a mechanized vehicle functioning as the crucial component of male identity. The motorcycle supersedes and defeats the gun, a central icon of a Westerner's identity (and Max's defensive weapon). Max lets his guard down, falsely perceiving this bush to be as safe as the environs of his home or outback turf. Though he arms himself with a shotgun, it proves to be a useless relic in this environment where high-speed, mechanized vehicles reign. By driving the lumbering family station wagon, which is frequently disabled (a flat tire, a malfunctioning fan belt), and nowhere near the power of the motorcycles, Max compromises his masculinity. He is vulnerable and unfit for the inevitable showdown with the bikers. On foot, he is always several paces behind the lightning quick bikers who elude him, kidnap his son, terrorize his wife, and run them down. May (Sheila Florance), Jessie's aging bush relative, who joins Jessie in their futile defense against the bikers, suggests an inept Max as she slowly drags her crippled and metal-braced legs, unable to shoot straight.

Without his interceptor police car, which is linked to strength and potency, Max is stripped of his protective bronze identity. Once his family is out of his life (his son dead, his wife on life support in the hospital), he is only able to re-empower himself by "re-arming" with his Interceptor, using speed and metal as a killing machine, thus assuming the savage behavior of the bikers. In the film's final shot, Max is presented as the ultimate road machine, compulsively driving, his hands gripping the wheel, his dead eyes mechanically focused only on the road ahead. He has lost the thrill of the chase that he confidently demonstrated at the film's beginning. Max's humanity has been stripped. He is a hollow man.

The response to *Mad Max* within and outside of Australia was, in a word, extraordinary. In Australia, *Mad Max* soon became the most commercially successful film until *Gallipoli* in 1981. Overseas, it also achieved vast appeal, ultimately grossing over US$100 million, firmly establishing Kennedy and Miller as two of Australia's favorite sons, who cracked the international market as well as creating a film that appealed to enthusiastic Australian audiences. As Delia Falconer aptly put it, Kennedy and Miller [became] "fast drivers in the new economic landscape" (Falconer, 1997, 259). Significantly, *Mad Max* added a commercial component to gothic, shifting the venue for this genre away from art houses, film festivals, and limited distribution (the theatrical sites for *Shirley Thompson Versus the Aliens*, *The Night the Prowler*, and *The Cars That Ate Paris*). Further, *Mad Max* opened up Australian Gothic. Instead of experimental and low budget, this film was grander in scale and expense, one more global in scope and appeal. A cinema of small, closed, and primarily female spaces (at least with *Shirley Thompson* and *Prowler*) in the larger context of insular and repressive suburban societies hit the open road as males used blacktop and high speeds to forcefully forge their identities.

The success of *Mad Max* shifted the perception of Australian cinema within the country, initiating serious talk of a film industry, that is, an organized and evolving system of film funding with production houses and companies supported primarily by private financing versus the one-by-one green-lighting by federal and state government agencies. As Falconer argues, "*Mad Max* was actually used in the 1980s as an exemplary success story for re-gearing government film policy in terms of exports to global markets" (Falconer, 1997, 259). Thus *Mad Max* helped to propel forward and reinforce the rationale for Australian films financed by the private sector through tax write-offs, which came to be known as 10BA, the second phase of the Australian Renaissance (1981–8). 10BA was the means by which Kennedy/Miller financed *Mad Max II* and *Mad Max Beyond Thunderdome*, as the AFC downsized to developmental monies, primarily script development, still investing in films, but fewer projects. Miller and Kennedy had raised the money for *Mad Max* themselves from private investors, rationalizing that their commercial goals—they perceived Max as an exploitation film—were incompatible with AFC guidelines. As Falconer points out, half of *Mad Max*'s budget came from local distributor Roadshow, when the industry financing norm could be as much as 50 percent government funding (Falconer, 1997, 258).

Yet, despite the success of *Mad Max*, and the bestowing of several prestigious Australian Film Institute awards for its technical achievements, including musical score, sound design, and editing, as well as a special jury prize to Kennedy and Miller, the film was faulted for compromising and co-opting its Australianness as well as Australian originality through its deliberate use of Hollywood models. Further, its dark and deliberately violent vision was deemed "an assault on an industry (and a critical audience) trained to value 'serious' and 'original' [Australian] work" (Falconer, 1997, 259). Producer Phillip Adams spoke of *Mad Max* as "[t]he dangerous pornography of death … a special favourite of rapists, sadists … [and] child murderers" (Stratton, 1980, 242). On the other hand, *Mad Max* was admired by critic/historian David Stratton, who lauded Max as "an astonishing film debut" (Stratton, 1980, 243), and critic John Lapsley, who designated Max as a "first class horror movie" (Stratton, 1980, 243). The success of *Mad Max* and its subsequent commercial and critical response broached a sensitive area: a cinema reborn almost a decade earlier on the premise of proud nationalism, seeking to tout its own culture and define its own genres by breaking away from a tradition of American and Hollywood cultural hegemony. Was Max turning back the clock, or was it visionary filmmaking?

A useful approach to address and analyze the "hybrid" nature of *Mad Max* and its sequels (and as a prelude to introducing *Mad Max II*), in order to transcend value judgments about the appropriateness or integrity of adopting outside models, is the application of the cultural transfer theories of semiotician Yuri Lotman. Lotman perceives cultures as interactive, coexisting as sending and receiving entities in a "semiosphere"—a "synchronic semiotic space which fills the borders of culture, without which separate semiotic systems cannot function or come into being" (Lotman, 1990, 3). As Tom O'Regan comments, "[Lotman takes us] beyond the simple import/export, unoriginal/original dichotomies and related notions of cultural imperialism which are usually used to distinguish receiving and sending cultures" such as Australia and the United States, respectively, and Lotman takes "into account the mutuality of a situation in which cultural imports are connected to local cultural production and its export, while unoriginality and derivation is connected to the very possibility of originality" (O'Regan, 1996, 213). This is a key point because Lotman recognizes and argues that a receiving culture is capable of and can actively create unique original works which can be stimulated by transmitting cultures. Further, he encourages us to see the interplay between cultures, or in O'Regan's words, the ways in which cultures "negotiate with" and influence one another. Given the influence of *Max* worldwide and subsequent spin-offs—many of them American—this point is particularly relevant.

As discussed in the Introduction, Australian film and television screens were dominated by Hollywood in the post–Second World War years with "unequal flow and transfer" (O'Regan, 1996, 217). With respect to movie theaters, American films populated the majority of Australian theaters as far back as the late 1910s. This situation reinforced cultural cringe—a sense of inferiority and an inherent devaluing of Australian culture. Whereas a group of filmmakers in the early 1970s proudly presented authentic Australian genres such as the ocker, thus bucking the "crouch," Miller, Kennedy, and McCausland eagerly appropriated American models. Yet they just as enthusiastically foregrounded and dramatized Australian elements, including landscape, locally inflected characters, and Australian idioms, transforming and also transcending American genres in their creation of a novel Australian work. In other words, *Mad Max* "rema[de] ... and reposition[ed] ... the imported culture on native terms" (O'Regan, 1996, 213). I will briefly summarize Lotman's five stages. From the point of view of the "receiving side," the process of reception falls into the following stages:

> [Stage] 1 "The texts coming in from the outside ... [and] hold a high position in the scale of values ... [They] are considered to be true, beautiful, of divine origin ... Already existing texts in 'one's own' language, and that language itself, are correspondingly valued lowly, being classed as untrue 'coarse,' 'uncultured.'

> [Stage] 2 The 'imported' texts and the 'home' culture restructure each other ... Translations, imitations and adaptations multiply. In this second stage, however, there is a predominant tendency to restore the links with the past, to look for 'roots.'

> [Stage] 3 The culture which first relayed these [imported] texts falls out of favor and the national characteristics of the texts will be stressed.

> [Stage] 4 The imported texts are entirely dissolved in the receiving culture; the culture itself changes to a state of activity and begins rapidly to produce new texts; these new texts are based on cultural codes, which in the distant past were stimulated by invasions from outside, but which now have been wholly transformed through the many asymmetrical transformations into a new and original structural model.

> [Stage] 5 The receiving culture, which now becomes the general centre of the semiosphere, changes into a transmitting culture and issues forth a flood of texts directed to other, peripheral areas of the semiosphere."

> (Lotman, 1990, 146–7)

Mad Max fits into phases 2 and 3. Miller adapts and reworks two American models, giving them an Australian spin. First, *Mad Max* appropriates the Roger Corman exploitation film model from American culture, specifically *The Wild Angels* (1966), renovating and customizing the road picture, adding an alluringly nihilistic, morbid spin to the fun-seeking, sex, drugs, rock "n" roll-loving motorcycle gang members, who seem innocent in comparison to the monstrous scoot jockeys. Rather than the motorcycle being an object of pride, status, and beauty set against the picturesque highways of Southern California, the high-powered bikes in *Mad Max* are killing machines. The anarchistic scoot jockeys are sneering sadistic predators turned on by high speeds, torture, and murder. They are a vicious and terrifying vision of white male Australia, whereas *The Wild Angels* focuses on the victimization of the bikers in the Vietnam era through a heavily armed and militant police force.

With respect to the Western genre, *Mad Max*'s filmmakers resurrect, modernize, and "translate," to use Lotman's word, this waning genre (climaxed by the Mel Brooks' parody *Blazing Saddles*, 1974). The Western was often transformed into the Vietnam War film and science fiction films by a number of American filmmakers in the 1970s and 1980s, where the new frontiers were foreign fields and outer space. In *Max*, modern-day "lawmen" take on outlaws in a post-apocalyptic wilderness, as detailed earlier. This Western—filmed in the unique radiating light of the Southern Hemisphere where the outback stretches to infinity—features recognizably local characters (the bronze, scoot jockeys), all of whom exhibit a good dose of Australian anti-authoritarianism. The scoot jockeys defy the law; even the police dismiss and/or ignore their own codes of lawful behavior. Max, a deft blend of a classical and revisionist Western hero, is the ultimate anti-authoritarian: he boldly and blatantly ignores all codes of civility and becomes an agent of anarchy, killing all of the bikers (guilty or not) in a carefully planned series of murderous paybacks. Max himself represents a striking and appealing new vision of Australian masculinity on screen (judging from the box office within and outside of Australia), honed in the post-industrial futuristic outback. He is tough, savvy, cool, and self-reliant, committing as much brutality as the predators, relishing his revenge.

Max's enormous popularity within Australia suggests that he filled a void in Australian culture, "embod[ying] the fantasies and aspirations of the [Australian] public," as Sharrett has noted (Sharrett, 1985, 83). Max is an arresting contemporary Australian action hero, who exudes the vigor, courage, and guerrilla fighting instincts of historical warrior heroes Peter Handcock and Harry Morant (both from *Breaker Morant*), for instance. Like them, Max takes the law into his own hands, killing, as they do, many times over to exact revenge for the loss of loved ones and mates. Yet he refuses to be a victim and is not the colonial scapegoat, deferring to and sacrificed for a higher British Imperial power. Max is a survivor on his own terms. (Mel Gibson would embody another survivor, Frank Dunne, a cocky and callow youth, in *Gallipoli* two years later: another set of colonials—not including Frank—are sacrificed for yet another British cause.) However, by the end of the film, Max is completely alone, his family and fellow bronze gone, with only the companionship of his killing machine, his high-performance Interceptor. As a renegade cop, Max has an uncertain future. He has defeated the enemy and conquered the wasteland, but at what price? Roger Lukhurst, author of *Gothic: An Illustrated History*, captures the state and aura of *Max*'s setting: "defined by its negation of everything civilized: unknown, inhuman, unruly, untamed, uncultivated. It is the place of the savage other, populated by unimaginable beasts" (Lukhurst, 2021, 117). What will be Max's fate? What is his destiny?

Mad Max II

Mad Max II (directed by Miller and written by Miller, Terry Hayes, and Brian Hannant) stands out as an "original structural model," conforming to and illustrating Lotman's Stage 4. Not only does this film proudly foreground Australian culture, it also confidently demonstrates Australian audaciousness (its vision of an anarchic world amidst a deft blend of adventure and suspense sprinkled with comedy), ingenuity (in particular, the craft and choreography of vehicle chases and stunts), and imagination (its range of colorful, often flamboyant characters) in the creation of a new "text" and an enormously influential prototype, the post-apocalyptic "crash and burn genre" (a term coined by David Chute). "Dissolved" in this new text, to use Lotman's terminology, are two primary outside models: (1) Joseph Campbell's monomyth from *The Hero with a Thousand Faces*, a multicultural anthology of hero mythologies from history and literature; (2) the American Western, specifically *Shane* (George Stevens, 1953), as well as Akira Kurosawa's *Yojimbo* (1961), clearly influenced by *Shane*. Moreover, this film brings a new flair and complexity to the road picture: *Max II* is a series of crucial journeys across the wasteland outback, what Miller has called the "extreme outback." Searches, escapes, and pursuits culminate in a dazzling and transcendent grand finale chase. The film also dramatizes Max's internal odyssey: his growth from an antisocial loner into a bona fide "road warrior," who bravely and heroically puts his life on the line for a community in desperate need.

Max II picks up Max (Mel Gibson) several years after the end of *Mad Max*, as he wanders the post-apocalyptic desert in search of petrol, driving his trusty, nitro-boosted Interceptor. He is chased by scavengers and predators on motorcycles, who crave his fuel as well as the thrill of the chase. As depicted by the documentary-style and actual newsreel footage which serves as the film's introduction, Australia has been caught in a worst-case scenario—the fallout from a nuclear exchange between the "great warrior nations" (as stated by the narrator who introduces the film) United States and Russia over an oil crisis in the Middle East. Instead of a police force, bikers, and a few isolated, sparsely populated settlements from *Mad Max*, there are two factions of survivors: a group of settlers, owners, and defenders of the last remaining petrol refinery; and a gang of aggressive, bloodthirsty marauders, who continuously attack the primitive settlement in order to steal the precious resource. As Miller has commented, he was inspired, rather gleefully, by the actual gas shortages within Australia in the early 1980s that had created long lines and short tempers.

If *Mad Max* demonstrated the flaunting of homicidal male aggression to reinforce (white) Australian male identity, then *Max II* presents a brazen and newfound macho confidence by the post-apocalyptic predators. The earlier masculinity crisis is over. The new plight focuses on stealing and securing a rare commodity, a situation tied into larger world economics, rather than an "in-house" threatened Anglo-European Australian identity. For maximum ferocity and intimidation, many of the predators proudly display their pumped-up, muscular bodies, a look that achieves a new male aesthetic. Colorful and flamboyant, they sport multicultural garb, influenced by American Indian, British punk, as well as "gay S & M, B-grade Nazi movies, and heavy metal" (Falconer, 1997, 269). How and why did this new look come about, when the street attire in *Mad Max* was primarily 1970s-style denim and leather? After the release of *Mad Max*, Miller and producer Byron Kennedy visited a variety of different countries worldwide to better understand the appeal of their film. As Miller noted, in Italy, there would be talk of spaghetti Westerns; in Scandinavia, Viking folklore; in Japan, samurai warriors. He adds, "We had tapped into a universal hero almost by accident." The appearance of the *Max II* predators deliberately and cleverly reflects the filmmakers' savvy commercial bid for continuing international appeal, inadvertently kicked off by *Mad Max*. Hence the warriors look like all-purpose global athletes, blending different cultures and mythologies. For example, the buffed Commander, Lord Humungus (played by Swedish body builder Kjell Nilsson), is dressed in a pair of black leather trunks with a cod piece, wristbands, a body harness, and collar to expose his powerful arm, chest, and leg muscles. He looks like a mod Viking, and as Adrian Martin commented, he (and others) also appears to be primed for World Wrestling competition (Martin, 2003, 49). Instead of a helmet, Humungus wears a hockey-style metal mask, giving him an aura of menacing mystery. Consistent with the Viking look, some of Humungus' soldiers wear makeshift helmets with horns. Humungus' first officer, Wez (Vernon Wells), looks like a punk Indian, with white war paint on his face, his hair in a bright red Mohawk, feathers encircling his neck, a crossbow as a weapon. A loincloth exposes his bare and brawny thighs and buttocks. Like Wez, various other members of the gang display Mohawks, some silver, some black; all are dressed in various combinations of leather. Their appearance links them to Indians in classical Westerns. They circle and fire at the settlers' compound fortress like a tribe of Indians on wheels, but "whereas those Indians were the victims of encroaching white civilization desperately defending their native land and resources, these 'Indians' are true savages, pillaging and killing for gas and fun" (Jewell, 1983, 7).

How do the vehicles in *Max II* differ from those in *Mad Max*, which were such a bold extension and reinforcement of male identity? Recall the gas-guzzling cars, some with V8 engines, as well as the heavy-duty motorcycles. In *Max II*, given the scarcity of fuel, just about all vehicles are lightweight and are designed for maximum mileage. Both predators and settlers use low-riding (*Easy Rider*-style) motorcycles with extended front wheels. Also used by both are a range of dune buggies. Each chassis rides a few feet above the ground for least air resistance. In particular, Humungus' custom-made "utility" model dune buggy is composed of a steel frame with no body or cab. It is larger than the others to accommodate his V8 engine with nitro-boosting capability for quick bursts of speed for full-throttle chases.

Humungus' dune buggy also features a clever "extra." Attached to the front bumper is a special, several-foot-tall, vertical platform to which two wounded prisoners are tied, bleeding and screaming. (Historically, the Vikings tied prisoners and corpses to carts to frighten their enemies.) With his hordes of men scattered on the area in front of the compound, Humungus confronts the settlers and demands petrol, threatening a full-scale attack on the refinery. When one of the lashed prisoners screams, "Give them nothing," Wez, impatient and feisty, runs over and head-butts him, knocking him out.

Despite its bleak, post-apocalyptic crisis and conditions, however, *Max II* exudes a lighter, even comedic tone in several scenes, in contrast to the consistently somber, frightening milieu and events of *Mad Max*. In the aforementioned scene, for example, the gravity of Humungus' death threats is leavened by Australian-style, send-up humor. The driver of Humungus' vehicle proves to be not as bright or as skilled as Humungus and Wez. He grabs the center of attention by introducing Humungus as the "Ayatollah of rock 'n' rolla"—adding a sardonic and hip spin to the Middle East-inspired oil crisis, which led to the East–West nuclear exchange. The driver (Max Phipps) is covered in a silly-looking fur and leather outfit, topped by the skin of a dead rodent, its head perched ridiculously above the man's forehead. He attempts to be chic with his 1960s-style sunglasses and leather pants exposing his bare buttocks as he struts across the ground. He also attempts to show off by running and catching the razor sharp metal boomerang flung by the feral child (a young boy adopted by and living with the settlers). As the driver reaches for the spinning boomerang, it severs the fingers on one of his hands: his fingertips go flying into the air like confetti. The predators all burst into laughter, making a joke of the situation. As Garry Maddox noted about *Mad Max: Fury Road*, an insight which could apply equally to *Max II*, "just because it's a wasteland doesn't mean people lose their sense of humor" (Maddox, 2015). Given the castration anxiety that fueled the male identity crisis in *Mad Max*, this scene shows that emasculation can now be a subject for laughter.

Even Max shows glimpses of a sense of humor, though still exhibiting the qualities from the first film that made him so memorable: fearless, vigilant, coolly confident, quick on his feet, and focused. As the narrator (the adult feral child who speaks in voice-over at the beginning and end of the film) comments during the film's prologue, he (Max) has "learned to live again." The hollow dead stare that Max had at the end of *Mad Max* is now replaced by a more relaxed, mirthful look. Though he has become a hardened laconic loner with a "rough larrikin cheekiness," as Adrian Martin has noted (Martin, 2003, 4), who shuns any company beyond his blue heeler cattle dog, he enjoys sparring with the Gyro Captain (Bruce Spence), a scavenger who flies a one-man, modified helicopter, or "gyrocopter" (and who later joins the settlers). Max finds Gyro essentially harmless and easy to control, and puts him on a leash like a pet. At one point, fully aware of the rivalry that will develop between his dog and Gyro, Max deliberately and mischievously throws a nearly empty can of Australian-manufactured Bonza dog food close to his dog, which snarls protectively when Gyro tries to encroach upon his meal.

How do the aforementioned imported texts, *Yojimbo/Shane*, and Campbell's monomyth blend together as the filmmakers "customize" them, to use O'Regan's term, to Australian culture, in order to create a uniquely Australian work? Though other writers have noted Campbell's monomyth and *Shane* as sources for *Max II*, no one has detailed the ways in which the filmmakers blend these imported texts to fashion an original Australian vision. For their narrative structure and character inspiration, the filmmakers incorporate the second part of Campbell's monomyth adjusted to Australian specificity.

> Beyond the threshold, then, the hero (a personage of exceptional gifts) journeys through a world of unfamiliar yet strangely intimate forces, some of which severely threaten him (tests) and some of which give magical aid (helpers). When he arrives at the nadir of the mythological round, he undergoes a supreme ordeal and gains his reward.
>
> (Campbell, 1972, 245)

The strangely intimate forces are the settlers and the predators, both of whom have links to Max. Like the nomads-turned-settlers, Max is a former family man and member of a community, but also an ex-policeman, perhaps similar to some of the predators. One of the magical aids is the feral child (Emil Minty), an expert scout with the ability to fling a razor-sharp boomerang with deadly accuracy, as noted earlier. As Dermody and Jacka have pointed out, with his mane of tangled hair and animal skins, the feral child implies "latter-day, white Aboriginality" (Dermody and Jacka, 1988, 177). (Though race is not an issue in the film, the nomads have clearly adopted this "pale skin" boy with open arms.) The other aid is the aforementioned savvy wasteland survivor Gyro, a towering seven feet tall and a mechanical wizard with his gyrocopter that he uses for transportation. Though he and Max begin as adversaries, and the wary Max is less than cordial, Gyro valiantly comes to Max's rescue after Max is driven off the road by Wez and almost killed in the crash and explosion. After Wez leaves—thinking Max is dead—Gyro transports Max safely to the settlement. Their relationship grows into an unlikely (and unspoken) mateship during the film's grand finale chase. Gyro provides Max with expert air defense, throwing much-needed fire bombs on predators' vehicles to protect Max as he drives the tanker.

With respect to the classic Western *Shane*, which features a wondering loner with a mysterious past who fights with his fists and packs a six-shooter, which he uses with precision skill, the film's namesake empowers a community of farmers to stand up to a ruthless cattle baron and his henchmen. Though Miller has not specially referred to *Shane*, he did view *Yojimbo*, which focuses on a rōnin, an out-of-work samurai warrior, in the post-feudal period in Japan in the mid-1800s. The rōnin (whose official name is "Sanjuro," but who is referred to as "Yojimbo," a word which translates to "bodyguard") intervenes in a vendetta between rice and sake merchants. Max is closer to Toshiro Mifune's cynical, ill-tempered, antisocial warrior than he is to the noble and well-mannered Alan Ladd's Shane, who aligns himself immediately with the besieged farmers (though the patriarch who owns the cattle empire tries to hire Shane to work for him). Like Shane, however, Max mobilizes the settlers against the marauders, regaining his humanity in the process. Max has a magical effect on them, just as Shane does with the farmers, and also upon Joe Starrett. The bickering among the farmers ceases and they bond together in a new spirit of confidence and cooperation. And just as Starrett's son Joey befriends Shane, who becomes his idol, so does the feral child eagerly align himself with Max.

What are Max's exceptional gifts? Like Shane with his trusty gun, and Yojimbo with his sword, Max is deadly accurate with his sawed-off shotgun. This skill is fearlessly and unflinchingly demonstrated during the film's final chase, as Max confidently fends off predators leaping onto the tanker, threatening to enter the cab, one from the top, the other from the driver's side. With one hand on the steering wheel, and one on the precisely aimed gun, Max coolly fires one shot through the ceiling and one shot through the side window, easily taking out each man. Problem solved.

Max's second gift is his driving expertise perfected from his job as a highway policeman in his reliable and powerful V8 Interceptor in *Mad Max*. Recall his calm control at high speeds, when he chased after the cop killer Nightrider, and also his road rage judiciously executed as he violently and with precision avenged the attack on his wife and son by setting up collisions that killed the majority of the bikers. Max's road skills are splendidly demonstrated in the film's final chase as the driver of the tanker of petrol. Essentially Max re-masculates himself via the phallic transporter—merely one day after his near-death at the hands of Wez, who caused the crash that separated Max from his Interceptor. Max's role as driver of the tanker implies that man and machine (re-)merge to bolster and reaffirm Max's identity. Notably, Max's "mission" is not linked to sadistic murder or revenge, as it was in *Mad Max*. Though he volunteers in part to save face, his cause is a righteous one, and demonstrates his redemption from his "killer" status dramatized in the final scenes of *Mad Max*. He escapes from the predators, preserving precious fuel, and helping the settler community re-situate in a secure new place far away from danger. (He thinks the tanker contains petrol, but as we discover at the end of the chase, the nomads have devised a secret plan to transport the fuel in other vehicles, far away from the tanker. This ploy is discussed later.) Max proves his "road skills" right away to the nomad leader, Pappagallo (Michael Preston) and the others, even before the predators start their charge on the tanker. As an eye-catching warmup, he aggressively plows into a group of predators revving up their vehicles, which immediately burst into flames.

Taking on this prodigious and dangerous mission is also linked to Max's shedding of self-serving ways. Early on in the film, Max offered his help only to obtain petrol for his own needs so he could move on, maintaining his solitary existence. Thus he rises to the critical occasion, and risks his life for the future of the community. This mission is truly Max's greatest challenge, to pave the way for the establishment of a new, post-apocalyptic civilization, safe from invaders. The successful driving of the tanker is truly his "supreme ordeal," to re-quote Campbell, similar to Shane's self-appointed job of taking on the cattle baron, his hired hands, and the formidable gunslinger in the film's final shoot-out. For his role, Yojimbo has even greater odds, as both warring sides ultimately seek to do him in. With his powerful sword, he defeats, single-handedly, nearly the whole village population of corrupt businessmen, thugs, and criminals.

Now we come to the film's grand finale: a delirious, twelve-minute, white-knuckle chase sequence that soars with rich mise en scène, bold camerawork, and crisp dynamic editing, which includes vigorous cross-cutting, montage, and striking shot-reverse-shot constructs. Several simultaneously running cameras were used to film this sequence, most from moving vehicles, often clocking in at 105-plus kph. This predator–settler pursuit exudes enormous kinetic energy and extraordinary stunts: flying, spinning, and leaping bodies, as well as mid-air assaults with gravity-defying jumps between speeding vehicles. The chase, or more appropriately, the "mad dash," is captured from various vantage points, giving viewers the exhilarating sense of being in several places at once. From high above, aerial camerawork opens up a bird's-eye view of the road winding through the vast outback, "sliced" by the long, lean tanker, a flurry of settlers flanking it, and an army of predators closing in from behind and on both sides. The rush of vehicles appears as an almost liquid stream of high-velocity movement. Intercut with these scenes are a variety of road-level long, medium long, and close shots capturing the action and characters' reactions, immersing spectators in the drama. Viewers can almost feel the heat of the friction of the tires on the bitumen. As Ross Gibson aptly comments, "the filmmakers build a *hot rod* of a film" (Gibson, 1992, 160; emphasis mine). This sequence is ramped up with a full orchestral score of brass, strings, and percussion as visuals and sound design merge to create a virtual tour de force, and, as Stuart Cunningham has argued, this climax boldly demonstrates—and clinches—Miller's complete mastery of the road picture genre (quoted by O'Regan, 1996, 220).

Further, this part of the chase triumphantly merges key elements of the Shane myth and Campbell's monomyth. The wide open desolate roads of Broken Hill evoke Campbell's "mythological round," a battlescape where the forces of good and evil clash and a bona fide road warrior hero emerges. Max drives with expert skill in spite of a serious visual impairment—he has sight in only one eye; the other is swollen shut after his near-death crash the day earlier—while the tanker is threatened with a full-scale siege. The predators have superior weapons. These include a variety of maces, grappling hooks, and crossbows, as well as stronger and more powerful vehicles, in addition to the formidable Wez, who, as we have seen, is clever, cunning, and wildly aggressive. How will Max manage a situation where the odds are not in his favor?

When this particular part of the chase begins, at first it appears that the settlers and Max might just succeed in escaping the clutches of the predators. An exuberant, airborne Gyro knocks a predator's car off-course with a well-placed firebomb. The car ricochets off the tanker, rolls, and crashes. Several incapacitated cars careen off the road; one is pulverized under the wheels of the tanker, as if it were made of plastic and the rider a rag doll. However, the predators gain ground on the tanker in their lightweight vehicles, some with superchargers on their bonnets. One predator fires a dart gun, exploding two of the tanker's tires. It swerves, yet Max holds it steady. However, Humungus has already "released" Wez, who was held back by a heavy chain harness, as his master waited for the perfect moment to unleash his "dog of war." Once the chains are cut, Wez (perched in front of Humungus' dune buggy) leaps onto the tanker, shown in a full-figure low-angle shot which stretches out his height, making him look far taller and more massive, adding a bold verticality to the fast-moving horizontal line of the tanker. Wez heads for the cab, running across the top of the speeding tanker, grinning with glee and anticipation.

From inside the cab, Max swings the feral child from the outside where he hangs on, positioning him safely in the passenger seat. The feral child has attached himself to Max ever since Max gave him a present of a hurdy gurdy toy when he came into the nomad camp. The grateful child has, in turn, rekindled

Max's paternal instincts. The feral child has looked up to Max, imitating his walk, proudly helping him stand and walk after his crash, and now, refuses to ride in any other vehicle but the tanker cab with Max. The child is clearly headstrong like Max, but eagerly follows his orders. Thus, Max takes on the challenge of not only driving the tanker, but also serving as a protector of and mentor to the feral child. The cab has a temporary security of safety, and is a retreat from the high-speed dangers outside. However, the tide turns. Gyro is shot down by a flamethrower, and crashes to the ground in a whoosh of flame, no longer serving as the much-needed aerial aid to Max and the nomads. The situation worsens. Pappagallo, a highly skilled driver himself in his dune buggy, is a victim of a whirling mace thrown into his back. Mortally wounded, he veers off the road as his vehicle flips and is engulfed in flames.

Now the cab is in jeopardy as Miller cuts to just outside. A predator, covered in black leather with metal studs, his face hidden behind a hockey mask, which reinforces his menacing and formidable appearance, sneaks up behind the cab, reaches around, and digs his steel glove with sharpened points into Max's left shoulder. From inside the cab we see Max (facing the camera) yanked back, writhing in agony, his shoulder and chest held in a vice grip. From above, Wez, standing triumphantly on the top of the cab (again in a low-angle shot to emphasize his mighty stature), swings a huge grappling hook, smashing the windows and the ceiling of the cab. Max strives to hold the wheel with his right hand as the tanker again swerves unsteadily. However, in the midst of his last swing, Wez loses his balance and somersaults forward, apparently landing on the road in front of the tanker, ostensibly crushed underneath.

Max uses this moment of reprieve to beckon to the feral child, half inside the cab, half out, who has been frantically attacking and biting the predator who assailed Max. Max orders the feral child to retrieve the remaining bullets, which have rolled to the front of the bonnet and are lodged in a crevice in front of a large iron plate, which serves as a second bumper. Turning gravely serious and focused, the feral child begins to crawl on his hands and knees across the bonnet, facing the camera (mounted on the front of the hood). His eyes wide, he is a little shaky and clearly frightened, but determined. Suddenly the soundtrack is silent—the brass and strings are hushed. There is no sound of metal or tire friction, only a whistling wind and a steady heartbeat of the feral child. These crucial moments feel suspended in time and intensify the suspense. Will the feral child be able to gather the bullets and give them to Max? Will he prove himself worthy to his "father?" When the feral child is able to keep his balance on the car bonnet, he reaches out. Suddenly, from out of the blue, in a reverse close shot, Wez's war-painted face bursts onto the screen, contorted into a battle cry. He is very much alive, having secretly hidden out of sight, behind the bumper, lying in wait for the right moment to strike. In a subsequent reverse shot, the face of the petrified child, his mouth wide open in terror screaming, is followed by one of a snarling Wez, who tightly grips the arm of the shrieking feral child, who is now trying to free himself from Wez's vice-like grip.

We are outside on the road in the next shot, as Miller cuts to Humungus speeding down the road in his high-powered, turbo-charged dune buggy. Earlier, the tanker changed direction, as Max turned it around to throw off the predators. Thus, instead of pursuing the tanker now, Humungus is now heading straight toward it. He punches his vehicle with a nitro boost, propelling it forward, accelerating his speed toward the oncoming tanker, in a clear last-ditch effort to stop it. We wonder if this is a suicidal move to retrieve the precious fuel once and for all. We recall O'Regan's wry words, "Australians *dream* of cars coming over hills on the wrong side of the road." The last we see of Humungus and the tanker is when the two collide, as Humungus' vehicle smashes full force into the cab. Crushed in between the tanker and the dune buggy is Wez, whom we glimpse in a brief close shot, his face contorted, mouth open in a scream, his eyes all but popping out of their sockets. A wide long shot reveals the immense fiery explosion as metal parts, tires, and dirt fly everywhere high into the air. Thrown off balance, the tanker veers off the road, and collapses, like a huge felled dinosaur in a huge cloud of dust. We wonder if anyone, man or child, could survive an impact of a crash as massive as this.

A series of slow dissolving tracking shots—there is no sound—brings us closer to the twisted wreck. There is no sign of life. However, we soon see slight movement, as Max, lying on his back, the unconscious feral child resting on his chest, slowly moves his arm and pulls himself out of the heap of crushed metal. He stands up, dazed, a little shaky and limping, but stays on his feet, gently holding the child in his arm, gingerly moving away from the wreckage, as he carries him to safety.

The two-lane road in the outback has become Max's proving ground against the predators. He has succeeded in protecting the petrol, and is a full-fledged Road Warrior. Consistent with the monomyth formula, he has survived his "supreme ordeal," while the opposition's leaders have been blown to bits. The few predators that remain stare at the smoking wreckage and humbly drive away. Also critical in Max's rite of passage is his internal journey, which represents another kind of "reward": the restoration of his paternal skills, the awakening of his humanity, and the re-establishment of his community instincts. Clearly, he is in a more stable "social state" (Corrigan, 1991, 144). As Corrigan further notes, this optimistic outcome is not a common trait of the post-war (the Second World War) road picture. Nor would this denouement be expected in the wake of an even more horrendous event: a nuclear explosion and the lawless fallout afterward. The ending of *Max II* turns the tide for this version of Australian Gothic into a guardedly optimistic perspective, unlike the nihilistic, violent, and murderous conclusions in *Mad Max* and *The Cars That Ate Paris*, where chaos, anarchy, and madness reign. (The conclusion of *Shirley Thompson* is equally pessimistic with pending destruction for Australia.) Miller implies that there is hope after all. In the film's final scene, this "hero with heart" is presented in a full shot, exhausted, hunched to one side, wounded, yet triumphant, and fondly remembered by the adult feral child in voice-over. He has learned from Max's courage and guidance, and speaks from the rank of head of the Great Northern Tribe.

As in the classical Western, Max ensures the safety of the new civilization, thereby fulfilling the role of the Western hero. Like Shane, Max acted to protect the community. However, unlike *Shane*, where the community had strong emotional ties to the hero, and regarded him as a friend, Max is used by and becomes the unwitting pawn of the settlers, who have set him up as a decoy: what pours out of the tanker is red sand, not gas, as Max discovers after the crash. As noted earlier, the petrol has been secretly deposited in the vehicles taking another route. Max's half smile suggests an Australian hero "on to himself," as Dermody and Jacka have commented (Dermody and Jacka, 1988, 176). Max can laugh at the ruse, again showing his lighter side, which has not been extinguished by his ordeal. His job done, Max reverts to his loner status, as do Shane and Yojimbo.

When released in Australia, *Max II* exceeded the success of *Mad Max*, with box office receipts totaling $10.8 million. It also won many Australian Film Institute Awards, including editing, sound, art direction, costume design, with Miller also winning for best director. In the United States (where *Max II* was renamed *The Road Warrior*), even amidst heavy summer competition from *E.T.* and *Rocky III*, *Max II* held its own, garnering another US$23.6 million. *Max II* was equally popular in Europe as well as an instant hit in Japan.

It bears repeating that *Mad Max II* stands as an original, highly innovative work and a new structural model, consistent with Lotman's Stage 4. It inspired a variety of spinoffs including *The New Barbarians* (aka *Warriors of the Wasteland*,

1983, Italy), *Wheels of Fire* (aka *Desert Warriors*, 1985, United States), *Steel Dawn*, and *Robo Cop* (1987, United States). James Cameron has praised *Max II* as a strong influence on *The Terminator* (1984), which he wrote and directed. Adrian Martin notes other films: the "delirious, supernatural or sci-fi fantasy-thrillers of Tsui Hark from Hong Kong," as well as the films of French filmmaker Luc Besson and those of Mexican filmmaker Guillermo del Toro (Martin, 2003, 1). In *Lethal Weapon* (1987, United States, the success of which led to three sequels), *Max*'s Mel Gibson as Detective Briggs does a manic reworking of Max with some new flourishes—psychopathic, self-destructive, suicidal, and a loose cannon. Briggs is more Australian than he is American (though Gibson speaks an American dialect) with his self-deprecating humor, antiauthoritarian attitude, and irreverence. In the 1990s, Kevin Costner conjured up *Mad Max* and *Max II* in two apocalyptic dramas: *Waterworld* (1995) and *The Postman* (1997). Most recently, the *Fast and Furious* series (originating in 2001), which features wildly spectacular vehicular chase sequences on the ground (and in the air), also shows the influence of *Mad Max* and *Max II*.

Flush with the proceeds from *Max II*, Miller and Kennedy bought an old movie house in King's Cross, Sydney, for the headquarters of Kennedy Miller Productions. With in-house contracted writers and directors, Kennedy Miller Productions was modeled on the classical Hollywood studio system. This enterprise produced not only internationally targeted productions such as *Dead Calm* (1989), *Babe* (1995), and *Happy Feet* (2006), but also high-quality television miniseries drawn from Australian history and intended for Australian audiences, such as *The Dismissal* (1983) and *Vietnam* (1987). Kennedy Miller Productions (renamed Kennedy Miller Mitchell in 2009) has also produced culturally specific films such as John Duigan's *The Year My Voice Broke* (1987) and *Flirting* (1990). The success of *Mad Max* and *Max II*, as well as other KM projects, did not turn Australia into a full-scale "transmitting culture" (in reference to Lotman's Stage 5, where the "receiving culture becomes the general centre of the semiosphere"). Hollywood, with its financial resources, corporate ownership by national and international media companies and worldwide distribution channels, holds that position. To its credit, however, Kennedy Miller Mitchell continues to be a thriving and profitable Australian media production company. The line of *Max* successors, including the third, *Mad Max Beyond Thunderdome*, and fourth, *Mad Max: Fury Road*, as well as two planned sequels (*Mad Max: Furiosa*, in pre-production, and *Mad Max: The Wasteland*), is certainly an Australian success story. Ironically, after the release of *Max II*, Miller did not have immediate plans for another *Max* film, but he and Doug Mitchell almost spontaneously began discussing the continuing saga of Max. Soon, a third film was being planned and written.

Mad Max Beyond Thunderdome

Whereas *Mad Max* and *Mad Max II* appropriate a variety of outside generic models and cross-cultural elements to create bold, original Australian films, *Mad Max Beyond Thunderdome*, directed by George Miller and George Ogilvie, screenplay by Miller and Terry Hayes, shows an almost overwhelming American influence, demonstrated in particular during part II of the film, which compromises the salient Australian features from *Mad Max* and *Max II*. Though part I of *Thunderdome* kicks off with the "flavor, accent and social text" of the prior *Max* films (O'Regan, 1996, 218), the second part of the film marks a shift (back) to Lotman's stage 2, where Hollywood furnishes the structure, values, and mythology.

In Part I, we pick up a significantly older and grizzled Max (Mel Gibson), who wanders into another primitive, post-apocalyptic society. (Fifteen years have gone by since the end of *Max II*.) Despite his worn-out appearance, Max retains his agility, strength, and resourcefulness. Still the mercenary, he is hired by the ruler of Bartertown, Auntie Entity, a refreshingly tough, competent, and intelligent woman (played by the formidable American musical performer/songwriter Tina Turner) to kill the giant, Blaster (Paul Larsson), guard and protector of the rebellious dwarf, Master (Angelo Rossitto), who holds the secret formula for the city's new energy source in the absence of oil—methane (made from pig excrement). Max's restored paternal instincts, a carryover from *Max II*, prevent him from killing the childlike Blaster, and he is banished to the desert, which commences part II, "Crack in the Earth."

Part II of *Thunderdome* is reminiscent of 1970s and 1980s adventure films by George Lucas and Steven Spielberg, and in particular, *Indiana Jones and the Temple of Doom* (1984, which Lucas produced and Spielberg directed). In *Indiana Jones*, the children have been kidnapped by a diabolical cult of Himalayan bandits, whereas in *Thunderdome*, a cache of children hides out in the desert. In each film the children are rescued by a hero (Jones and Max, respectively) with special powers. Both Jones and Max grow into father figures for the children. Further, both Jones and Max play out the children's mythology, appearing seemingly out of nowhere to perform wondrous deeds, each character shedding his rather self-centered persona in the process. Moreover, both men are sky-gods; Jones a pilot, and Max (as the children see him) their legendary hero, Captain Walker, who brought them to safety from the destroyed city of Sydney. (He promised to return, but did not.) Max soon embodies the image and legacy of Captain Walker, a transformation which invigorates him, giving Max a renewed sense of purpose. Thus his parental instincts, seared away in *Mad Max* and rekindled in *Max II*, are fully restored in *Thunderdome*. Finally, both Jones and Max ensure the children's safety, bringing them "home." Jones returns the kidnapped youngsters back to their mountain village, and Max arranges to fly his charges back to Sydney (by way of Bartertown) with the promise of a restart of a new civilization.

By featuring child and teenage protagonists, the filmmakers follow the Spielberg strategy of expanding the appeal of the *Max* trilogy to younger viewers, as Spielberg did with *E.T.* and *Poltergeist*, for example (both 1982, Spielberg directed the former, and co-wrote and co-produced the latter). In contrast to *Mad Max* and *Max II*, *Thunderdome* is closer to wholesome family fare, its violence far less graphic, its visuals less gruesome (this is not a criticism). *Thunderdome* is even cartoon-like and playful. For example, the Bartertown contests suggest a subdued and collapsed version of the primal battles and ripping masculinity in *Mad Max* and *Max II*. Max's swinging aerial match with Blaster within the Thunderdome structure itself in part I of the film is more amusing than spellbinding, unlike the riveting and arresting violent life and death confrontations and chases in *Mad Max* and *Max II*, which are more in keeping with the gothic components of these films. Further, this "spectator sport" for the pleasure of Bartertown's populace foregrounds the film's self-conscious entertainment mode.

Significantly, many sequences in *Thunderdome* seem a parody of *Max II*. Given the rash of *Max* spinoffs worldwide in the wake of *Mad Max* and *Max II*, it's as if *Thunderdome* marks the end of one cycle of this post-apocalyptic genre, suggesting that the filmmakers designed *Thunderdome* as a comedic pause before embarking upon the continuation of the *Max* saga. In other words, once the filmmakers successfully created and established a breakthrough genre, they felt comfortable sending it up in a playful Australian fashion. Accordingly, Delia Falconer has noted the "strangely jokey quality" of *Thunderdome* (Falconer, 1997, 264). This dynamic is dramatized in the character of Ironbar, the queen's henchman (blithely played by rock performer Angry Anderson), who becomes

Max's nemesis. Ironbar is short and paunchy—and does not even come close to the formidable predators from *Max II*. He is also dimwitted and slow; Max easily disarms him in the queen's quarters. The female doll face perched on the post that hovers above Iron Bar's head is soft, round, and feminine, unlike the craggy-faced, macho predators or snarling scoot jockeys from *Max*. This decorative touch comes across as a joke about Ironbar's masculinity. Further, he frequently has a quizzical, even bemused look on his face, which suggests that even *he* does not take himself too seriously. Though the predators in *Max II* were able to laugh at themselves—that is, the finger slicing scene, or the introduction of Humungus as the "Ayatollah of Rock and Rolla"—they could quickly snap into aggressive, frightful, and deadly action, which gave *Max II* its jolts of visual and dramatic power.

The climactic chase of *Thunderdome* where Auntie, Ironbar, and their cohorts go after Max and the children is more comical than breathtaking. Ironbar looks like a clown trying to manage serious acrobatics as he hangs—of course—from an iron bar attached to a fast-moving vehicle, narrowly missing metal landmarks. Pigkiller (Robert Grubb), the gaunt slave newly released from Bartertown's underworld methane factory, takes on the persona of Max when he drives the huge truck, evoking Max's legendary drive in *Max II*. Any excitement and sense of adventure during this sequence is undercut by Pigkiller's obvious lack of skill and finesse. When he is shot in the leg by an arrow right through the truck's metal door, which welds him to the metal, Max comes to his aid to remove the shaft, declaring, "Now, I am going to count to three." On the count of "one," Max yanks the door out, and Pigkiller all but faints. This sequence adds to the cartoon-like, parodic quality of *Thunderdome*. Perhaps Miller and Hayes meant it to be a light-hearted homage, but at times *Thunderdome* comes across as a weak second-string effort that sorely lacks the exhilaration and sense of awe that is engendered in *Max II*.

Nevertheless, *Thunderdome* performed well in key markets. In Australia, with a box office of $4.3 million, it ranked number five in the all-time top grossing Australian films (at the time). Significantly, *Thunderdome* became the first Australian film to take advantage of ancillary rights with lucrative television and cable sales. Abroad, *Thunderdome* continued its successful release. In the United States and Canada, it grossed US$36.2 million even amidst heavy competition from *Back to the Future, Rambo: First Blood Part II*, and the rerelease of *E.T.* As with *Max II, Thunderdome* was very popular in Europe and Japan.

Through the trilogy, Miller, Kennedy, and Hayes launched a powerful and profitable mythology that transmitted worldwide to eager receiving cultures, to use Lotman's terminology, serving as a model for an array of road warriors and apocalyptic visions all the way into the first fifteen years of the new millennium that climaxed with the release of the fourth Max film, *Mad Max: Fury Road*. The *Mad Max* trilogy emerged as an Australian success story from the late 1970s into the 1980s, and along with *"Crocodile" Dundee*, firmly positioned Australia on the international map, fueling "cultural strut." Miller, the late Byron Kennedy (killed in an 1983 helicopter accident scouting locations for *Beyond Thunderdome*), and others connected to these films were lauded for their Australian resourcefulness, cultural pride, innovative spirit, and commercial savvy—a fine legacy indeed that kept avid audience interest locally and worldwide throughout the next thirty years in anticipation of the release of *Fury Road*.

Mad Max: Fury Road

The worldwide commercial success and high visibility of *Mad Max: Fury Road* reinforced the formidable reputation of the *Max* series, as well as the standing and renown of co-writer/director Miller, along with co-writers Brendan McCarthy and Nick Lathouris, in addition to KMM Productions, ensuring the future production of at least two sequels currently in the works (as noted earlier). *Fury Road* was one of the first high-profile films to kick off the summer season in North America, opening in mid-May 2015 after its earlier debut at Cannes, accumulating box office grosses of US$154.1 million in the United States and Canada. Internationally, with runs in eighty countries, the film grossed US$375 million. The Australian box office was equally successful, at approximately $21.8 million. *Fury Road* boldly and confidently competed with other blockbuster summer releases from Hollywood: *Furious 7* of the *Fast and Furious* franchise (released April 10) and *Mission Impossible: Rogue Nation* (released July 31).

Deviating from the light-hearted tone of *Thunderdome*, and consistent with the somber milieu and outback menace of *Mad Max: Fury Road* focuses on the serious business of survival in yet another perilous, post-apocalyptic wilderness. A new crisis looms, not dwindling energy resources as in *Max II* and *Thunderdome*, but precious water, horded by a ferocious, fascist-style leader, Immortan Joe (Hugh Keays-Byrne), who reigns at his "castle," the Citadel, a huge towering fortress in the desert. Blood is also a valued commodity, and early on in the film, Max (played by a new actor, Tom Hardy), still the nomad, is captured to keep a blood supply readily available for Joe's henchmen—his "war boys." Hardy wears Max's trademark worn black leather jacket and pants, and he takes on Mel Gibson's world-weary stance as a warrior–survivor. Taller and more muscular than Gibson, and slightly hunched over, this Max, like his precursor, is always on alert, demonstrating his keen eyesight and rapid-fire reflexes. For example, in an early scene after his capture and escape, and pursued by Joe's boys through the caverns of the Citadel, Max runs swiftly and nimbly, like a large cat, engaging in fierce, hand-to-hand combat with them. He punches and claws his captors, tears himself away from them, then jumps on and dangles from a swinging pulley, which he turns into a pendulum battering ram.

Fury Road showcases and escalates the flamboyant and often violent spectacle of high-speed, exhilarating chases, streamlined into a grand-scale road film narrative—clearly Miller's preferred component of the gothic. Throughout the film, the mise en scène vibrates with kinetic energy, pulsating with flying metal and bodies, as well as sudden fiery explosions that all but burst through the screen. The war cry, "Fang it!" an Australian expression which roughly translates to "punch the accelerator," punctuates several high-velocity scenes, acting like a whip to a spirited horse. Essentially a round-trip chase, *Fury Road* captures and reboots the vitality, excitement, and daring, which made the action and stunts in *Mad Max* and especially *Max II* so ground-breaking and captivating. Throughout *Fury Road*, the filmmakers demonstrate and dramatize their Australian ingenuity, craft, and innovative skills in three major areas.

First of all, with respect to the film's lead, *Fury Road* features an original and formidable female warrior protagonist, Furiosa Imperator, as portrayed by the versatile Charlize Theron. Her character is a breakthrough for a series that has consistently privileged males. "Imperator" is an apt name, as it refers to the ancient Roman rank of Commander-in-Chief. Furiosa confidently and aggressively displays a sure-footed strut and a defiant posture, her penetrating eyes circled by black axle grease; she is always ready for combat.

Given Furiosa's prominence and centrality, *Fury Road* could easily be named *Furiosa Road*. As Diana Sandars notes, Furiosa is "an accomplished fighter, marksman, mechanic, strategist and driver" (Sandars, 2019, 321). Furiosa clearly deviates from earlier representations of women in the first three *Max* films—innocent victims and minor characters, with the exception of the whip-smart and intrepid Auntie Entity from *Thunderdome*. Furiosa is unflinching, strong, and valiant, driving the narrative (pun intended), and is an essential character in this "new text" (to recall Lotman's Stage 4 from his cultural transfer theory). Just as *Max II* established a unique prototype, the "crash and burn" genre featuring a newly forged Australian hero, so does *Fury Road* stand prominently as another Australian original: a new structural model featuring its "center of gravity," Furiosa.

Furiosa fits appropriately, as Sandars argues, into the legacy of the "disruptive daughter" from classic Australian cinema during the early sound era in the 1930s, in particular, films by Ken G. Hall (2019, 317) as well as contemporary female protagonist daughters, including those featured in *Rabbit Proof Fence* (2002) and *The Dressmaker*. Sandars further notes that a disruptive daughter is a "strong independent woman who dominates her male companions and counterparts … [Such] daughters are aligned with an outback defined by discourses of fearless determination, struggle and unorthodox roles … from which the daughters derive a level of self-determination" (Sandars, 2019, 317, 318). Furiosa was kidnapped as a child by Joe and his henchmen from her mother, who belonged to the "Many Mother's Tribe" in a remote land called "The Green Place." She was enslaved for nineteen years. Throughout the film, and audaciously challenging her former prisoner status, Furiosa proves to be a tough and resilient combatant, almost out-wrestling and overpowering Max, for example, in an early hand-to-hand combat struggle before they join forces. Furiosa's noticeably missing left arm has been replaced by an artificial forearm and hand forged of steel and cable. Hardly a handicap, this synthetic limb seems to energize her in many battles, thus creating a powerful force field. At one point, she rescues Max, who is tumbling over the side of her rig and in danger of being crushed by the wheels. With her prosthetic arm, she grabs and holds on to Max's arm, exerting enough force to be able to pull him up and land him safely into the cab. Moreover, Furiosa is an inspiration for her rescued charges, the frightened young women, whom Joe casually and condescendingly refers to as his "prize breeders." They initially hide in her rig upon their escape from the Citadel. Furiosa's model of fearlessness and audacity spurs the young women to become assertive and able fighters, some choosing to arm themselves with heavy weapons, bravely taking on Joe's war boys one by one, inside as well as outside the rig.

Secondly, Furiosa's bond with Max is a unique and vital component of the film. Their initial encounters are contentious as he is a self-serving loner; each is wary of the other. Through his growing partnership with Furiosa, however, Max transforms into a different kind of *rōnin* or bodyguard than depicted in earlier versions in the *Max* series. This marks a critical new dimension for the series, as well as for the gothic genre in general (at least with respect to the films discussed in this chapter): a close working bond of trust—not without affection and tenderness—between a female protagonist and a male protagonist. To the filmmakers' credit, *Fury Road* opens up and explores this new facet of Max, enriching his character and enhancing the series mythology, further reinforcing the evolution of *Fury Road* as an innovative new text. But first, Max must earn Furiosa's respect and faith. He needs to prove himself as an ally, not a wasteland rogue who could steal her rig and disappear (as she first perceives him). Accordingly, Max demonstrates his support for Furiosa, rising to the occasion, for example, during a crucial scene during her escape from the Citadel, where a broken hydraulic hose on her rig threatens to explode and incinerate everyone aboard. Rather than using this development as an opportunity to escape, Max quickly sizes up this emergency situation, jumps onto the side of the vehicle, and devises a sturdy repair mechanism from spare parts, all while the rig is travelling at a high speed. All are saved. Later, with only minutes to prepare as Joe's war boys are fast approaching, he puts into place a clever defense of Furiosa's rig. He embeds firing platforms in the sand with motion sensors that explode just as the marauders threaten to ambush. Threat diminished.

The demands and challenges of the road create opportunities for an unexpected mateship between Max and Furiosa, these moments serving as "grace notes" amidst the grand-scale "nuts and bolts" of the chases. For example, when Max cuts his hand, Furiosa carefully bandages it; later, he lends her his shoulder to steady her shotgun. Moreover, they increasingly communicate with a relay of glances and nods. Before their return trip to the Citadel, and with genuine concern, Max earnestly reaches out to Furiosa, clearly worried about her safety, as well as the security of the others. He gently convinces her to take the shortest route back through the canyon, clearly communicating his commitment to protect Furiosa, as well as the women, young and old (the latter from the clan of The Green Place inhabitants), from attacks by Joe and his forces. Max's pledge to Furiosa is displayed and validated when he saves her life not once, but twice. First, he instinctively grabs onto her when she tumbles from the rig. Without his assistance, she would have certainly been crushed under the rig's wheels or run over by one of the vehicles of the war boys. Secondly, at a crucial turning point in the return chase toward the end of the film, when Furiosa, Max, and the women have outrun Joe's men (not without some casualties), Furiosa is close to death from a critical bayonet wound. Max summons all of his skills in a tense, yet tender and deeply touching scene, where he saves her life by pumping air into her lungs, then quickly assembling a makeshift tube and drawing needle that transfuses his own blood into her veins while she lies unconscious. His face and body language convey genuine compassion.

Their close interaction, especially during the second half of the film, is dramatized in close, medium, and full shots, playing out within the larger framework of the grand, epic-style spectacle of the chase, the dynamics of which are captured in long, extreme long, ground-level, and bird's-eye shots, duly enhanced by a wide screen 2.39:1 format. This deft balance of styles comprises the third area, the film's dazzling visuals, choreography, and editing. For his production design, Colin Gibson received an Academy Award, and Margaret Sixel was also honored by the Academy for editing, accolades in these areas also recognized by the British Academy of Film and Television Arts (BAFTA)—a high point for both in their distinguished careers in Australia. Throughout the film, chases and desert battles feature high-velocity vehicles (also created by Colin Gibson). In addition to super turbo-charged vintage cars, lightweight high dune buggies and motorcycles are oversized "monster trucks" created by stacked car frames welded together and mounted on oversized tires for maximum height and attack leverage from Joe's war boys. Some of the vehicles have voluminous tankers attached for the long haul through the outback, others sport elongated rigs and hoists, and still others are equipped with grappling hooks and/or mounted flamethrowers. For example, Joe's customized vehicle, his 1,200-horsepower "Gigahorse," is built from two classic Cadillac Coupe de Ville frames layered on top of an extended truck flatbed, with elongated, trombone-like exhaust pipes on each side. Furiosa's unique "War Rig" is a huge double long tanker, and looks like a massive locomotive engine, sporting huge struts in front to protect the cab and its occupants as it thunders down the dirt road. With a nod to *The Cars That Ate Paris*, some cars are covered with elongated spikes and look like ancient stegosauruses—a detail which enhances the primal sweep of the clashes during the chase scenes.

In addition to its myriad of vehicles, *Fury Road* flaunts world-class stunt work devised and designed by Australian veteran stuntman and coordinator, Guy Norris (a member of the stunt team for *Max II*). His stunning maneuvers are clearly intended to surpass those in prior *Max* films. For example, in a particularly daring scene shot via an overhead camera from a helicopter or drone, one of the war boys on a fast-moving monster truck is shot by an arrow through his skull; it lodges in one of his eye sockets. He rolls his head, screaming in pain, his body wracked with rage as he searches to see who attacked him.

As a suicidal payback, he leaps off the truck, falling 10 to 15 feet through the air, plunging onto a dune buggy with saber-like spikes, just as one of his mates unknowingly aims a flamethrower at the buggy. The buggy explodes into a massive fireball. Another innovation by Norris for the battle scenes are clusters of long, flexible, white poles planted in fast-moving vehicles maneuvered by a gang of Joe's special elite forces, the "pole-cats." The men sway gracefully yet forcefully and menacingly through the air, as the poles catapult them for maximum attack power. In one particularly audacious scene, a war boy grapples with Max while both are clutching the end of one pole, each trying to knock the other to the ground below. They sway back and forth, using gravitational force for clout.

With *Fury Road*, Miller has reinforced Australia's presence firmly on the global cinematic map with a steady and confident hand, flaunting Australian creativity and daring, firmly maintaining his and KMM's reputation as savvy and resourceful filmmakers. Miller was subsequently honored by the Australian Academy of Cinema and Television Arts (AACTA), receiving Best Picture and Best Director awards. He and his partners have successfully cultivated and advanced the Max saga, infusing it with new blood (pun intended), driving it in a fresh direction, taking the adventure of the road picture to new heights, commandeered by an original female warrior, Furiosa Imperator, who leads with intelligence and valor along with her comrade-in-arms, Max, also an Australian original. The two have established a firm bond that promises to mature and flourish in future *Max* films.

Over forty years ago, *Mad Max*, a deliberate exploitation film, tapped into a seductive gothic sensibility; a fascination with malevolence and menace leveled at innocent victims—women and a child—as well as the police who returned in kind against the cruel and avenging bikers amidst the decay of civilization. In the wake of the popularity of *Mad Max*, Miller and partner Byron Kennedy honed a sequel with their "crash and burn" prototype, *Mad Max II*, which advanced the Max saga with unique, captivating, and formidable characters engaged in wild and thrilling chases on the post-apocalyptic outback. As with *Mad Max*, *Max II* sported Australian gusto and brazenness, cleverly drawing on the country's cultural specificity, including love of fast cars unleashed on the open road— the bigger the vehicle the better—defiance of any kind of authority, ripping masculinity, thus sparking avid viewer attention and a loyal following locally and abroad, prompting the filmmakers to create two more sequels in an evolving, high-profile series. *Fury Road* caps off a successful fourth installment which has resonated worldwide, leaving audiences hungry for more. What does the future hold for the series? Forthcoming is, first of all, *Furiosa*, in pre-production at the time of this writing and scheduled for a May 2024 release. This film is a "prequel," again featuring Furiosa, and dramatizing her early years before the time frame of *Fury Road*, with the title role played by British–American actress Anya Taylor-Joy. The sixth film in development for the series is entitled *Mad Max: The Wasteland*, with the probable return of Tom Hardy as Max.

Fury Road preserves and reinforces the gothic fascination with evil and the monstrous in many incarnations upon a land of peril: a combat zone where neo-primitive factions battle for survival via high-speed chases and where all-purpose road vehicles race, clash, and crash. The unleashed might of treacherous weapons and powerful machines is linked to the shocking horror of sudden death and unimaginable destruction. Miller and his team adroitly incorporate actual global conditions and events: petrol shortages (*Max II, Beyond Thunderdome*), the scarcity of water within blighted areas in the midst of climate change (*Fury Road*), the threat of nuclear war, the event itself, and the holocaust (all the *Max* films). Road rage and free-wheeling joyriding go all the way back to the nihilistic *The Cars That Ate Paris*, in many ways a precursor to *Mad Max*, if not an inspiration, wherein Arthur and Max became as vicious as those who attacked them. To its credit, however, *Fury Road* accentuates and reinforces humanity's higher and more noble qualities—heroism, camaraderie, and sacrifice through Max, Furiosa, and others—attributes rekindled in Max as dramatized in *Max II* and *Beyond Thunderdome*, and enacted in full triumphant glory in *Fury Road*. Fellow warriors Furiosa and Max solidify this legacy, giving this latest gothic rendition an aura of guarded optimism.

Fury Road is not the last word on Australian Gothic, of course, as other filmmakers, many in the new millennium, have chosen to work in this protean format. Earlier examples include *Chopper* (2000, Andrew Dominick), based on the adult life of one of Australia's most notorious modern criminals, Mark "Chopper" Read, so named because of his alleged propensity for chopping off the toes of his enemies. As opposed to the outback settings in the *Max* films, *Chopper*'s environs include murky urban streets, seedy bars, and dangerous, claustrophobic prisons. *Wolf Creek* (2005) and its sequel *Wolf Creek 2* (2013, both directed by Greg McLean) feature a vicious predatory psychopath, Mick, who traps, tortures, and kills young hikers. (McLean was influenced by the Ivan Milat serial killings in the 1990s.) Both *Wolf Creek* films draw on the tradition of the horror film, featuring a new breed of monster, who reinforces the perils of the outback so vividly dramatized in the *Max* films.

More recently, *The Dressmaker* is also noteworthy. This film is a deft balance of melodrama and satire, laced with black comedy, as deaths, past and present, haunt and permeate the town, veering into the gothic in arresting, even shocking ways. *The Dressmaker* returns the focus of the gothic to female protagonists in insular communities, the milieu of *Shirley Thompson Versus the Aliens* and *The Night the Prowler*. Tilly (Kate Winslet), in her late twenties, and a woman with a hidden vengeance, visits her home town (the time frame is the 1950s) to reconnect with her eccentric and feisty mother, Molly (Judy Davis). She has been banished since childhood from this remote bush settlement, having been accused of the death of a classmate, wrongly, as we discover. Nevertheless, Tilly garners favor by designing spectacular attire for the local women. Her gowns, made of silk, satin, and other luxurious fabrics in an array of radiant pastels, are worn proudly by the women at local events. As the narrative evolves, however, *The Dressmaker* becomes increasingly morbid and gruesome in light of a multitude of deaths: Tilly's short-term, but heartfelt lover is suddenly killed by a fall in the grain elevator. A woman stabs her philandering husband multiple times and leaves him to die. An incompetent and apathetic doctor deserts Molly, suffering from a stroke, who later collapses in the street and dies. Finally, Tilly's flashbacks reveal that the bully who abused and beat her up for so long killed himself accidentally when he charged into the side of their school building; he intended to head-butt her. Tilly soon realizes that the majority of the townspeople are still small-minded and unscrupulous: nothing has changed from earlier years. Disgusted and fraught by the deaths of her lover and mother, Tilly decides to leave, but not before her revenge is enacted. She sets fire to the town's buildings, the encroaching flames threatening to engulf the inhabitants. Triumphant and proud, Tilly departs for good.

Gothic films are edgy cultural representations: alluring yet terrifying, groundbreaking yet reactionary, pleasurable yet unnerving. In many ways, they serve as "pressure valves," clever and inspired approaches to confront, alleviate, and perhaps overcome fears, anxieties, and insecurities, while also giving vicarious thrills. As Dermody and Jacka have noted, there is "an enjoyable whiff of danger in this process" (Dermody and Jacka, 1988, 239).

Notes

1 Not all of Australia was a penal colony. The primary locations of prisoner sites were on the East Coast in the states of New South Wales, Queensland, as well as Van Diemen's Land, which was renamed Tasmania in 1856.

2 In 1975 Jim Sharman directed the cult classic *The Rocky Horror Picture Show* (British/American produced). He directed its "sequel" *Shock Treatment* in 1981 (American produced), later settling into a directing career with live theater in Sydney.

3 Mrs. Bannister releases her own sexual repression and frustration through violent sexual fantasies. For example, she plays the victim in a rape scenario, suggesting that this kind of sex is a tonic and thrill for the bored housewife who finds her husband a complete turn-off.

Sources

Bishop, Rod and Fiona Mackie (1980), "Loneliness and Alienation," in Scott Murray (ed.), *The New Australian Cinema*, London: Elm Tree Books, 153–65.

Campbell, Joseph (1972), *The Hero with a Thousand Faces*, Princeton, NJ: Princeton University Press.

Cohan, Steven and Ina Rae Hark, eds (1997), *The Road Movie Book*, London: Routledge.

Corrigan, Timothy (1991), *A Cinema without Walls: Movies and Culture after Vietnam*, New Brunswick, NJ: Rutgers University Press.

Cunningham, Stuart (1985), "Hollywood Genres, American Movies," in Albert Moran and Tom O'Regan (eds), *An Australian Film Reader*, Sydney: Currency Press, 235–41.

Dermody, Susan (1980), "Action and Adventure," in Scott Murray (ed.), *The New Australian Cinema*, London: Elm Tree Books, 79–95.

Dermody, Susan and Elizabeth Jacka (1988), *The Screening of Australia*, Volume II, Sydney: Currency Press.

Falconer, Delia (1997), "We Don't Need to Know the Way Home: The Disappearance of the Road in the Mad Max Trilogy," in Steven Cohan and Ina Rae Hark (eds), *The Road Movie Book*, London: Routledge, 249–70.

Gelder, Ken (2012), *New Companion to Gothic*, Hoboken, NJ: Wiley-Blackwell.

Gibson, Ross (1992), *South of the West: Postcolonialism and the Narrative Construction of Australia*, Bloomington and Indianapolis: Indiana University Press.

Hughes, William (2013), *Historical Dictionary of Gothic Literature*, Lanham, UK: Scarecrow Press.

Jancovich, Mark (1996), *Rational Fears: American Horror in the 50s*, London: Manchester University Press.

Jewell, Richard (1983), "Road Warrior: A Neoteric Western," Unpublished paper.

Kawin, Bruce F. (2012), "Children of the Light," in Barry Keith Grant (ed.), *Film Genre IV*, Austin: University of Texas Press, 360–81.

Lotman, Yuri (1990), *Universe of the Mind: A Semiotic Theory of Culture*, trans. Ann Shukman, Bloomington and Indianapolis: Indiana University Press.

Lukhurst, Roger (2021), *Gothic: An Illustrated History*, New Jersey: Princeton University Press.

Maddox, Garry (2015), "On the Set of Mad Max Fury Road with director George Miller," *Sydney Morning Herald*, April 25. http://www.smh.com.au/entertainment/movies/on-the-set-of-mad-max-fury-road-with-director-george-miller-20150423-1mhimu.html (accessed June 1, 2015).

Martin, Adrian (2003), *The Mad Max Movies*, Sydney: Currency Press in association with Screen Sound.

Mathews, Sue (1984), *35 MM Dreams: Conservations with Five Directors about the Australian Film Revival*, Melbourne: Penguin.

Mathieson, Craig (2015), "Mad Max Fury Road Review: A Thundering Thrilling Blockbuster," *Sydney Morning Herald*, May 17. http://www.smh.com.au/entertainment/movies/mad-max-fury-road-review-a-thundering-thrilling-blockbuster-20150511-ggz5g1.html (accessed May 30, 2015).

O'Regan, Tom (1996), *Australian National Cinema*, London: Routledge.

Sandars, Diana (2019), "Disruptive Daughters: The Heroine's Journey in Four Films," in Felicity Collins, Jane Landman and Susan Bye (eds), *A Companion to Australian Cinema*, Hoboken, NJ: Wiley-Blackwell, 321.

Sharrett, Christopher (1985), "Myth, Male Fantasy, and Simulacra in Mad Max and The Road Warrior," *Journal of Popular Film and Television*, 13 (2).

Thomas, David and Garry Gillard (2003), "Threads of Resemblance in New Australian Gothic Cinema," *Metro*, 136: 36–43.

Thomas, David and Garry Gillard (2007), "Chapter 9: Gothic: Ten Types of Australian Film," http://garrygillard.net/writing/tentypes/gothic.html (accessed April 10, 2016).

Turcotte, Gerry (1998), "Australian Gothic," in Marie Mulvey-Roberts (ed.), *The Handbook to Gothic Literature*, Basingstoke: Macmillan, 10–19. http://ro.uow.edu.au/cgi/viewcontent.cgi?article-1060&context-artspapers (accessed April 10, 2016).

Van Hise, J. (1983), "Interview with George Miller," *Starlog*, August: 30–4.

Wood, Robin (1986), *Hollywood from Vietnam to Reagan*, New York: Columbia University Press.

Wood, Robin ([1986] 2003), *Hollywood from Vietnam to Reagan and Beyond*, rev. edn, New York: Columbia University Press.

Index

abjection 134–5, 141
Aboriginal and Torres Strait Islander Commission (ATSIC) 171
Aboriginal communities 6, 15–16, 26–7, 38, 65, 142–143 nn.10–13, 145, 182, 198 n.14. *See also* Indigenous
  assimilation of mixed-race children 147, 159, 172, 174, 182–95
  Council for Aboriginal Reconciliation Act 171–2
  Dreamtime/Dreamings depiction 145–6, 150–2, 156–7, 189, 198 n.16
  Howard government 172–3
  land and 145–6
  Mabo decision 38, 42, 168, 171–2
  and Torres Strait Islander peoples 42, 147–8, 167–8, 171–2, 194–5
Aboriginal Land Rights Act 148
Academy Awards 13–14
  Foreign Language film 29–30
Acker, Elizabeth van 69 n.3
activists 2–4, 48, 171
Adams, Brian 155
Adams, Phillip 3, 225
adolescent life 36, 40, 67, 72, 89, 102, 123, 185
  pain and disappointments of 80–90
  travelers 191
The Adventures of Barry McKenzie (Beresford) 3, 6, 40, 45, 47–8, 63, 195 n.1
  Barry (character) 50–1
  Edna Everage (character) 51
  representations of women vis ocker males 50–1
The Adventures of Priscilla, Queen of the Desert (Elliott) 17–18, 40, 47, 50, 56, 195 n.1, 219
  Adam (character) 62–3, 65–7
  attitude toward women 63–4
  Bernadette (character) 62–5
  Cynthia (character) 63–6
  family values 66
  heterosexuality 62
  masculinity 64
  Ol' Shirl (character) 63–4
  racism 63
  Tick (character) 62–7
Alvin Purple (Burstall) 40. 45, 47, 50, 65, 67, 69 n.2
  Graeme Blundell (character) 52–4
  Liz Sort (character) 53
  motherhood 54
  representations of women vis ocker males 52–4
  Tina (character) 54
American Academy of Motion Picture Arts and Sciences 4
American company Group W 46
Amores Perros 20
Amy 122
Andrews, Munya 151
Animal Kingdom (Michod) 24
animated films 10
Another Country (Reynolds) 26
Archer, Jeffrey 172
Armstrong, Gillian 6, 11, 13, 58, 90 n.5, 104, 121, 141 n.1
assimilation 16, 138–9
  of mixed-race children 147, 159, 172, 174, 182–95
Associated R&R Films 7
Aussie battlers 18–19
Australia (Luhrmann) 21
Australian Academy of Cinema and Television Arts (AACTA) 4, 25, 28, 248
Australian Cinema (Murray) 35–7
Australian Cinema after Mabo (Collins and Davis) 38
Australian Cinema in the 1990s (Craven) 33
Australian company NLT 46
Australian Film and Television School 6

Australian Film Commission (AFC) 5–8, 23, 46, 68, 93–4, 208
Australian Film Development Corporation (AFDC) 3–5, 45–7, 93, 208
Australian Film Institute (AFI), award 4–5, 10–11, 14–16, 20, 29, 225, 238
Australian films 1–2, 16, 18, 36, 46, 72, 118 n.1, 122, 240, 242
  fathers role in 72
  government funding 2–3, 93, 224
  land/landscape/bush 93, 95
  local audiences 2–3, 5–9
  road films 195 n.1
Australian Gothic 24, 42–3, 46, 203–8
  budgets 208
  The Cars That Ate Paris 5, 42, 47, 146, 157, 203–5, 213–17
  censorship 203
  The Dressmaker 208
  evolution of 205
  filmmakers 204
  Imperial/colonial hegemony 206
  Mad Max 10, 24, 35, 38–9, 72, 146, 157, 203, 205–7, 217–28
  Mad Max Beyond Thunderdome 10, 146, 203, 205–7, 240–3
  Mad Max: Fury Road 39, 42, 146, 203, 205–7, 243–50
  Mad Max II 10, 35, 39, 146, 157, 203, 205–7, 228–40
  The Night the Prowler 42–3, 146, 203–7, 211–13
  post-Second World War period 204
  sensationalist presentation 206
  Shirley Thompson Versus the Aliens 42–3, 146, 203–4, 207, 209–11
Australian masculinity 11, 89–90, 208, 227
Australian National Cinema (O'Regan) 39
Australian Production Screen Incentive 22–42
Australian Rules (Goldman) 196 n.8
The Australian Screen (Moran and O'Regan) 35–6
Ayres, Tony 29

Babadook (Kent) 25
Babe (Miller) 18
Babe (Noonan) 10, 239
Babel 20
Backlash 195 n.2
Backroads (Noyce) 42, 68, 145–6, 162–6, 194
  cross-racial relationship 146–7, 162–6
  Gary (character) 162–6
  Jack (character) 162–6
  Jean-Claude (character) 164
  joyriding in stolen car 162–6
Bakaitus, Helmut 209
Barry, John 158
Baynton, Barbara 205
Beneath Clouds (Sen) 42, 190–4
Beresford, Bruce 6, 13, 15, 47, 55, 57, 68, 99
Berger, John 154
Bergman, Ingmar 72
Besson, Luc 239
Between Wars (Thornhill) 4, 7, 47, 71, 93
  Edward Trenbow (character) 71, 90 n.2
Blackfellas (Ricketson) 196 n.8
Blundell, Graeme 52, 61
Bond, Edward 149–50, 196 n.4
Bovell, Andrew 15, 20
box office gross 238, 242, 243
Breaker Morant (Beresford) 6–7, 9, 49, 56, 67–8, 71, 93
Brett, Judith 199 n.22
Brierley, Saroo 31
Bringing Them Home (Pilkington-Garimara) 172–3
British Academy of Film and Television Arts (BAFTA) 13, 247
British Independent Film Award 13, 20
Bulbeck, Pip 23
Bunuel, Luis 72
Burstall, Tim 48, 51, 52
bushman 37, 114–15
Bye, Susan 34
Byrnes, Paul 128

Caddie (Crombie) 2, 6–7, 68, 122
Callahan, David 42, 65
Cameron, James 77–8, 239
Campbell, Joseph 228, 232, 234–5
Campion, Jane 10–11, 34, 115, 117
Cannes screenings 5–6, 13, 18

Caputo, Raffaele 91 n.7
The Cars That Ate Paris (Weir) 5, 42,
    47, 146, 157, 203–7, 213–19, 238,
    247, 249
  Arthur (character) 216–17
  budgets 208
  car wreckage 214
  Charlie (character) 214–15
  mayor (character) 215–17
  Midvale (character) 214–15
  road pictures 216–17
  violence and killing 215–16
The Castle (Sitch) 18
Celia 122
censorship 4, 10, 45, 203
The Chant of Jimmie Blacksmith (Schepisi)
    2, 6–7, 15, 37, 68, 143 n.12, 145–6,
    164–5, 196 n.8, 198 n.15, 199 n.21
  Gilda (character) 158
  Graf (character) 159–60
  Harry Edwards (character) 161
  Healey (character) 160–1
  Jimmie Blacksmith (character) 158–66
  McCreadie (character) 161
  Mort (character) 162
  Neville (character) 159
  Newby (character) 159–61
  relationship of Aboriginal men and
    non-Indigenous women 146,
    158–66
Chapman, Penny 10
Charlie's Country (de Heer) 26, 34
Chauvel, Charles 8, 195 n.3
chauvinism 40, 47
  racism 62–7
  representation of women 49
  zealous patriotism 47–9
Chopper (Dominick) 19–20, 249
Cinesound 43 n.1
Clark, Marcus 205
Coad, Peter 176
Cohan, Steven 216, 219
Collins, Felicity 16, 34, 38, 105, 174, 188,
    190, 198 n.18
colonialism 7, 17, 19, 25, 27, 30, 147–8, 150,
    171, 174, 184–5, 189–90, 194, 206
Companion to Australian Cinema (Collins,
    Landman, and Bye) 34

Connolly, Robert 34
Conomos, John 14
Contemporary Australian Cinema
    (Raynor) 35
Cook, Kenneth 46
Corman, Roger 220, 227
Corrigan, Timothy 217, 219, 238
Costner, Kevin 239
Council for Aboriginal Reconciliation Act
    171–2
Cowan, James 150–1
Cox, Paul 11, 14, 17, 26, 36, 40, 67, 72–3,
    77–8, 80, 89–90
  alternative masculinities 71
  films by 71–2
  Man of Flowers 67, 73–7
  marriage life 78
  My First Wife 67, 77–80
Crash 20
Creed, Barbara 50, 129, 142 n.3
criminal themes 19–20, 24, 249
*Crisis Cinema: The Apocalyptic Idea in
    Postmodern Narrative Cinema*
    (Sharrett) 39
"Crocodile" Dundee (Faiman) 9, 19, 40–1,
    68, 95, 112, 195 n.1
  bushman 114–15
  Mick Dundee (character) 114–15
Crofts, Stephen 48, 130, 132, 142 n.4
Crombie, Donald 6
cultural cringe 7, 19, 20, 48, 226

Dark City (Proyas) 22
Davies, Luke 31
Davies, Piers 213
Davis, Therese 16, 38, 174, 188, 190, 198
    n.18
Dead Calm (Noyce) 10, 239
Dead End Drive-In 195 n.1
Dead Heart (Parsons) 196 n.8
Death in Brunswick (John Ruane) 14
de Heer, Rolf 13, 16–17, 25–6, 174, 176–7,
    180, 196 n.8, 197 n.13, 198 n.15
Department of Aboriginal Affairs (DAA)
    148, 171
Dermody, Susan 34–7, 47, 53, 57, 93–4,
    160, 165, 203, 210, 214, 216, 228,
    232, 238, 250

Diasporas of Australian Cinema (Simpson, Murawska and Lambert) 34
diasporic hybridity 34
The Directory of World Cinema: Australia and New Zealand, volume 3 (Goldsmith and Leland) 33–4
The Directory of World Cinema: Australia and New Zealand, volume 19 (Goldsmith, Ryan, and Leland) 33–4
disabilities/vulnerable bodies model 36, 94–6, 115–18, 118 n.1, 119 n.7
The Dish (Sitch) 20–1
The Dismissal 239
diversity 14–15, 62, 68, 118, 219
Djigirr, Peter 25–6
Docklands Studios 21
Don's Party (Beresford) 40, 45, 47, 67–8
    Cooley (character) 56–7, 60
    Don (character) 56–62
    Evan (character) 56, 60
    Jenny (character) 56, 58–9, 61–2
    Jody (character) 56–7, 60–1
    Kath (character) 56–7
    Kerry (character) 56–7, 60
    Mack (character) 56–7, 59–61
    Mal (character) 56–62
    middle-class lives 55
    ocker genre film 56
    Simon (character) 56–7, 60–1
    Susan (character) 56–8
    tradition and comedy 55
Dreamtime/Dreamings depiction 145–6, 150–2, 156–7, 189, 198 n.16
The Dressmaker 208, 245, 249–50
Duigan, John 10, 36, 40–1, 69 n.2, 71, 80–1, 91 n.8
    alternative masculinities 71
    films by 71–2
    Flirting 10, 36, 40–1, 71, 84–90, 239
    The Year My Voice Broke 10, 36, 40–1, 71, 80–4, 239
Dunne, Frank 228

Elliott, Stephan 13, 62
Ellis, Bob 73–5, 77, 90 n.4
Emery, John 162, 165
employment 11, 148, 166, 192
Experimental Film Fund 45

Falconer, Delia 8, 39, 223–5, 241
Farrell, Constable 159, 161
Fast and Furious 239, 243
The Fatal Shore 19
Fear of the Dark (Young) 185
Federation Ballroom Dancing 17
Federation of Australia 7, 93, 158
female protagonists 93–5, 118, 124, 147, 204, 250
feminine/femininity 37, 95, 97–8
    feminized landscape 104–13
Ferrier, Liz 36–7, 94–6, 100, 102, 104, 116, 118 n.1, 119 n.7
fetishism 74–5
Film Finance Corporation (FCC) 12–22, 63
    Aussie battlers 18–19
    criminal themes 19–20
    ethnic diversity 13–14
    films/filmmakers 13
    financed scripts 13–14
    glitter cycle 17–18
    Indigenous 14–16
    loans 12–13
    significant Australian content 12
Film in Australia: An Introduction (Moran and Vieth) 35
filmmakers/filmmaking 7–8, 11–13, 46, 71, 93–4, 129, 135, 149, 190, 194, 197 n.12, 203–6, 218–19, 222, 226–7, 232, 248–9
First Nations Peoples 147–8. *See also* Aboriginal communities; Indigenous; Torres Strait Islander peoples
Fischer, Lucy 129, 133
Fitzpatrick, Peter 56
Flirting (Duigan) 10, 36, 40–1, 71, 84–90, 239
    Bourke (character) 84–90
    boxing match 88–9
    Danny Embling (character) 80, 84–90
    relationship with young African woman 84–90
    schools 85–90, 91 n.8
    Thandiwe (character) 80, 84–90
Foley, Gary 162, 167
Follow the Rabbit Proof Fence (Pilkington-Garimara) 182

Ford, John 222–3
Foster, Stephen 184
Fox Studios 21
Fran 11, 36, 41
    Cynthia (character) 123, 126–8
    foster care system 126
    Fran (character) 123–8
    Jeff (character) 125–8
    Lisa (character) 123–6
    Mike (character) 125–6
    mother-daughter relationships 121–8
    sexual abuse 123
    Tommy (character) 123–8
franchise films 32
Fraser, Malcolm 8
French, Lisa 12
The Fringe Dwellers (Beresford) 15, 68
funding 2–3, 21–2, 46–7, 93, 190, 208, 224
The Furnace (MacKay) 31

Gallipoli (Weir) 6–7, 9, 49, 67–8, 71, 93, 207, 224, 228
Gardiner, Lizzie 17
gay 17, 52, 62–7
The Getting of Wisdom (Beresford) 6, 37, 41, 49, 68, 93, 99–104
    bush and environment 93, 95, 99–104
    Evelyn (character) 101–2
    Gurley (character) 100
    imagination power 99–100, 103
    Laura (character) 99–104
    Lilith (character) 100
    mother-daughter relationships 122
    Strachey (character) 101
Gibson, Colin 247
Gillard, Garry 159
Girls' Own Stories: Australia and New Zealand Women's Film (Robson and Zalcock) 37
Goldman, Paul 196 n.8
Goldsmith, Ben 33–4
Gorton, John 3
Gothic: An Illustrated History (Lukhurst) 228
government funding 2–3, 93, 224
Gow, Keith 213

The Great Gatsby (Luhrmann) 32
Greenwood, Margaret 74
Gulpilil, David 16–17, 26, 34, 149–50, 174–5, 186

Haebich, Anna 170
Hall, Ken G. 8
Hambly, Glenda 11, 121
Handcock, Peter 227–8
Hannam, Ken 6
Hannant, Brian 228
Hanson, Pauline 172
Hanson, Philip 147
Happy Feet (Miller) 10, 239
Happy Feet II (Miller) 10
Hark, Ina Rae 216
Harley, Ruth 23
Hawke, Bob 171
Hayes, Terry 228, 240, 243
Hayward, Susan 75
Head On (Kokkinos) 14–15
Hearn, Matt 22
The Heartbreak Kid (Jenkins) 14
Helfgott, David 18–19
The Hero with a Thousand Faces (Campbell) 228
Herzog, Werner 72
Hicks, Scott 13
High Ground (Johnson) 26–8
High Tide (Armstrong) 11, 36, 41
    Ally (character) 128–33, 142 n.6
    Bet (character) 128–32, 142 n.6
    Col (character) 130–1
    feminist melodrama 129
    figure of love 129, 131–3
    Lilli (character) 128–33, 142 n.6
    Mick (character) 131–2
    mother-daughter relationships 121–3, 128–33
"History Wars" (Macintyre and Clark) 173
Hodge, Bob 151, 182–3
Hogan, P. J. 13, 69 n.2
Holden, Stephen 199 n.20
Homesdale 214
Home Song Stories (Ayres) 29
Hopgood, Alan 52
Hostel 24

Houston, Beverle 155
Howard government 172–3
humorous films 17, 82, 86, 231
Humphries, Barry 47, 51
hypnosis 82

Images of Australia: 100 Films of the New Australian Cinema (Rattigan) 35
The Imaginary Industry: Australian Film in the Late 80's (Dermody and Jacka) 34
immigrants 14, 28, 31, 34, 147, 164, 219
Indigenous 1, 6, 14–17, 25–7, 31, 34, 37–8, 42
   band performance 166–74
   "Bringing Them Home" 173
   civil rights movement 148, 163, 174
   filmmakers 190
   genocide 183
   "History Wars" 173
   politicization 147
   Reconciliation Council 172–3
   Whitlam Labor administration 148
Indigenous road film 37–8, 42, 145–6
   Backroads 146–7, 162–6
   mechanized transportation 146
   in non-Indigenous films 146
   Rabbit Proof Fence 147, 182–95
   Radiance 134
   role of land 145–6
   The Tracker 174–82
   Walkabout 146, 149–58
   Wrong Side of the Road 147, 166–74
invisible ethnicity 65
Isaac, Graeme 166, 197 nn.11–12

Jacka, Elizabeth 34–7, 47, 53, 57, 93–4, 160, 165, 203, 210, 214, 216, 228, 232, 250
Japanese Story (Brooks) 28–9
Jennett, Christine 148, 172
Jennings, Karen 38, 147
Jindabyne (Lawrence) 20
Johnson, Stephen 26
Jones, Evan 46

Kael, Pauline 119 n.5, 130, 159
Kawin, Bruce 210–11

Keating, Paul 171, 174, 194
Keneally, Thomas 158, 160
Kennedy, Byron 10, 208, 217, 220, 224, 229, 243, 248
Kennedy Miller Productions 10, 207, 239
Kent, Jennifer 25
Kinder, Marsha 155
KMM (Kennedy Miller Mitchell) studios 10, 243, 248
Kokinos, Ana 13
Kotcheff, Ted 46
Kroenert, Tim 22
Kurosawa, Akira 228

Lambert, Anthony 34
Lander, Ned 166
land/landscape/bush 93, 95. *See also* women and bush environments
Landman, Jane 34
Land Rights Movement 15, 38, 148, 167–8, 171, 195
Langton, Marcia 163
Lantana (Lawrence) 20
Lapsley, John 225
The Last Days of Chez Nous (Armstrong) 61, 90 n.5
Last House on the Left 24
The Last Wave (Weir) 2, 15
Lathouris, Nick 243
Lawson, Henry 205
Lawson, Sylvia 171
Lealand, Geoff 33–4
Lethal Weapon 239
Lion (Davis) 30–1
Location Offset 23, 32–3
Lonely Hearts (Cox) 11, 36, 40
   Patricia (character) 73
   Peter (character) 73
Longford, Raymond 8
Long, Joan 10
A Long Way Home (Brierley) 31
Looking for Alibrandi 122
lost child films. *See Rabbit Proof Fence* (Noyce)
Lotman, Yuri 38–9, 42, 225–6, 240
Love Serenade 61
Lucas, Rose 112
Lucia Di Lammermoor (Donizetti) 74

Luhrmann, Baz 13, 18, 21
Lukhurst, Roger 228

Mabo decision 38, 42, 168, 171–2
MacKay, Roderick 31
Maddox, Garry 231
Mad Max (Miller) 10, 24, 35, 38–9, 68, 72, 146, 157, 203, 205–7, 217–28
   aggressive car culture 218–19
   bikers/cops conflict 220–1
   budgets 208
   Goose (character) 218, 220–2
   hybrid nature of 225
   Jessie (character) 220
   Johnny Boy (character) 222
   male fury and road rage 218
   Max Rockatansky (character) 218–25, 227–8
   Nightrider (character) 219
   road picture 220
   Sprog (character) 220
   Toecutter (character) 218, 220–1
   white male sensibility 218
Mad Max Beyond Thunderdome (Miller) 10, 146, 203, 205–7, 240–3
   box office gross 242
   budgets 208
   Pigkiller (character) 242
Mad Max: Fury Road (Miller) 39, 42, 146, 203, 205–7, 243–50
   box office gross 243
   budgets 208
   Furiosa Imperator (character) 244–5
   gothic fascination 249
   high-profile films 243
   Max (character) 243
Mad Max II (Miller) 10, 35, 39, 68, 146, 157, 203, 205–7, 213, 228–40
   Australian Film Institute Awards 238
   box office gross 238
   budgets 208
   driver (character) 231
   extreme outback 228
   Gyro Captain (character) 231–6
   Lord Humungus (character) 230–1
   male identity 230
   Max (character) 228–40
   Pappagallo (character) 234
   post-apocalyptic predators 229
   Wez (character) 230–1, 235–6
   winning awards 238
male ensemble film 36
male identity 37, 41, 50, 95, 115, 146, 223, 229, 231. *See also* masculinity
   high-powered mechanical vehicles and 146
The Man from Snowy River (Miller) 9, 20, 41, 68, 72, 113–14, 119 n.8
   Harrison (character) 113–14
   Jessica (character) 113–14
   Jim Craig (character) 113–14
   woman to wildlife 113–14
Manganinnie 195 n.2
Man of Flowers (Cox) 11, 36, 40, 71, 73–7
   Charles (character) 72–7
   David (character) 72–3, 75–6
   father/mother role 73–4
   fetishism 75
   Lisa (character) 72–7
   male-female relationships in 72
   voyeurism 74–5
Mao's Last Dancer (Beresford) 29
market values 8–9. *See also* box office gross
marriage 107–9, 116–17
Marshall, James Vance 149
Martin, Adrian 195 n.1, 230–1, 239
masculinity 9, 11, 13, 18, 37, 50, 64, 223, 229. *See also* male identity
   alternative 71
   Australian 89–90
   bush and 112–13
   threats to 51
Matchbox Pictures 34
maternal figure 36, 40, 50, 52, 54, 66–7, 72, 77, 79, 101, 127, 188
maternal omnipotence 97–8
The Matrix 22
Matrix Reloaded 22
Matrix Revolutions 22
Mayer, Geoff 35
Maynard, John 10
McCarthy, Brendan 243
McCausland, James 217–18, 226
McFarlane, Brian 35, 55, 60, 101, 105
McGirr, Leah 61, 72

McNiven, Liz 192
men and mountain scape 113–14
Metal Skin 195 n.1
Michod, David 24
Midnite Spares (Trenchard-Smith) 12, 195 n.1
Miller, George 10, 18, 38, 72, 207, 216–29, 232–3, 235–44, 248–9
Mishra, Vijay 151, 182–3
Mission Impossible 2 22
mixed-race 1, 134, 146–7, 159, 172, 174, 183–6, 191
Monkey Grip 61
Moorhouse, Frank 4
Moorhouse, Jocelyn 13
Moran, Albert 34–6
Morant, Harry 227–8
Morris, Meaghan 48–9, 97, 163
mother-daughter relationships
    Fran 121–8
    High Tide 121–3, 128–33
    Radiance 121–3, 133–41
motherhood 11, 50, 54, 121–2
Moulin Rouge! (Luhrmann) 18
mountain scape 113–14
Mulvey, Laura 75
Murawska, Renata 34
Murdoch, Rupert 7
Muriel's Wedding (Hogan) 18, 95, 115–18
    disabilities and difference 115–16
    mother-daughter relationships 122
    Muriel (character) 116–17
Murray, John B. 52
Murray, Scott 35
My Brilliant Career (Armstrong) 2, 6–7, 37, 41, 49, 93, 99, 104–13, 119 n.6, 122
    bush as inspirational place 104, 107–13
    feminized landscape 93, 95, 104–13
    Frank Hawdon (character) 104
    Gussie (character) 106
    Harry Beecham (character) 104–13
    Helen (character) 107
    intellectual/creativity 108
    marriage interruption 107–9, 116–17
    McSwatt (character) 105
    mother-daughter relationships 122
    period films 94
    self-expression 107
    societal constraints 105
    Sybylla (character) 104–13, 119 n.5
    writing skills 105–6
My First Wife (Cox) 11, 36, 40, 68, 71, 77–80
    Helen (character) 72, 77–80
    Hilary (character) 79
    John (character) 72, 77–80
    Lucy (character) 79–80
    male-female relationships in 72
    mother's role 77–8
    Tom (character) 78–9
My Name Is Gulpilil (Reynolds) 26

The Naked Bunyip (Murray) 52
Nazism 185
Ned Kelly (Jordan) 19–20, 22
New Australian Cinema: Sources and Parallels in American and British Film (McFarlane and Mayer) 35
The New Barbarians 238–9
Newsfront (Noyce) 68
The Nightingale (Kent) 25
The Night the Prowler (Sharman) 42–3, 203–4, 211–13, 217, 224, 250
    Bannister (character) 211–13, 251 n.3
    budgets 208
    family in crisis 211
    Felicity Bannister (character) 211–13
Nolan, Marguerite 134–5, 137, 139
Nowra, Louis 121, 196 n.4
Noyce, Phillip 6, 13, 16, 162, 165, 182–3, 197 n.9
nudity 4, 10, 49, 55, 79, 86, 154
    and sexuality 10, 45, 49, 52–3

ocker 3–4, 10, 36, 40
    The Adventures of Barry McKenzie 3, 6, 40, 45, 47, 50–1
    The Adventures of Priscilla, Queen of the Desert 17–18, 40, 47, 56, 62–9
    Alvin Purple 40. 45, 47, 52–4
    characters in films 47
    chauvinism 47
    cultural nationalism 48
    depiction of women 10, 45, 49, 52–3

Don's Party 40, 45, 47, 55–62
   genre 45–7, 195 n.1
   male 36, 40, 47, 49–50
   nudity and sexuality in 10, 45, 49, 52–3, 87
   Petersen 3, 40, 45, 48, 54–5
   Stork 3–4, 40, 45, 47, 51–2
   success of 68
The Odd Angry Shot 56
Oedipal 40, 54–5, 66–7
   dramas 72–4
   pre-Oedipal bond 50–1, 77, 79–80, 97–8, 104, 118, 138
Ogilvie, George 203, 240
Olsen, Christine 16, 182, 199 n.19
One Nation Party 172
One Night the Moon (Perkins) 42, 122, 190–1, 194
O'Regan, Tom 35–6, 39, 45–6, 52, 206, 219, 221, 225–6
O'Shaughnessy, Michael 158
overseas-based productions 22–4, 32–3
Oxley, Harry 45

Palmer, Dave 159
PDV Offset 22–3
Peake, Catherine 169
period films 36, 93–4
Perkins, Rachel 13, 15–16, 41, 142 n.8, 190
Petersen (Burstall) 3, 40, 45, 48
   view of women 54–5
Peterson, Nicolas 148–9
Pettitt, Lance 161–2
Peyton Place 212
Pharlap 68
Phar Lap (Wincer) 9–10
Picnic at Hanging Rock (Weir) 2, 5–7, 15, 37, 41, 47–8, 93, 207
   Albert (character) 97, 118 n.2
   Appleyard (character) 96, 99
   disabilities 95–9
   Edith (character) 95
   feminine/femininity 95, 97–8
   Irma (character) 95–7
   Marion (character) 95–8
   Michael (character) 97, 118 n.2
   Miranda (character) 95–8
   pre-Oedipal mother as bush 97–8
   Sara (character) 95–7
   women and bush environments 93, 95–9
Pilkington-Garimara, Doris 16, 182–3, 185, 198 n.17
Pirates of the Caribbean: Dead Men Tell No Tales 32
The Postman 239
post-Second World War period 1–2, 7
pre-Oedipal role 50–1, 77, 79–80, 97–8, 104, 118, 138
Primrose, Ian 151
Probyn-Rapsey, Fiona 195
Producer Offset 22–3, 32
Proof (Moorhouse) 14–15
The Proposition (Hillcoat) 20
Puberty Blues (Beresford) 11, 68

Rabbit Proof Fence (Noyce) 16, 22, 26, 37–8, 122, 147, 167, 170, 174, 182–95, 199 n.21, 245
   assimilation of mixed-race children 182–95
   Daisy (character) 183, 185–9
   Frinda (character) 188
   Gracie (character) 183, 185–8
   male-dominated road picture 147
   Maude (character) 188–9
   Molly Craig (character) 183–9
   Moodoo (character) 186–8
   Neville (character) 184–8
Racial Discrimination Act 148, 219
racism 14, 27–8, 63, 162–6
Radiance (Perkins) 15–16, 41, 133–41
   Cressy (character) 134–40
   Mae (character) 134–40, 142 n.9
   mother-daughter relationships 121–3, 133–41
   negligent/abject mother 134–5, 141
   Nona (character) 134–9, 140
   sexual danger 133–41
Rattigan, Neil 35, 37, 94
Raynor, Jonathan 35–6
Red Dog (Stenders) 32
"Restating the Cultural Framework: Kay Schaffer's Women and the Bush and Jane Campion's *Sweetie*" (Strain) 117–18

Reynolds, Henry 173
Reynolds, Molly 25–6
Ricketson, James 196 n.8
Roach, Archie 181
The Road Movie Book 39
Robertson, Mira 15
Robertson, Pamela 65
Robo Cop 238–9
Robson, Jocelyn 37
Robson, Lloyd 173
The Rocket (Mordaunt) 30
The Rocky Horror Picture Show (Sharman) 43, 251 n.2
Roeg, Nicolas 6, 146, 149–52, 154–6, 196 n.4, 196 n.6
Romeril, John 190
Romper Stomper (Wright) 14, 63, 219
Rosen, Brian 23
The Rover (Michod) 24
Ruane, John 13
Rudd, Kevin 194
Rush, Geoffrey 19
Rustin, Emily 65, 116–17
Ryan, Lyndall 173
Ryan, Mark David 33–4
Ryan, Tom 119 n.6

Samson and Delilah (Thornton) 26, 42, 190–2
San Andreas 32
Sandars, Diana 244–5
The Sapphires (Blair) 26
Schaffer, Kay 37, 94–5, 97–8, 112–13
Scheckter, John 175
Schepisi, Fred 6, 13, 15, 158, 196 n.8, 198 n.15
Screen Australia (SA) 12, 208
   Asia-Pacific connection 28–32
   crime and gothic films 24–5
   funding 23
   guidelines 23–4
   Indigenous cinema 25–7
   overseas productions 33
The Screening of Australia: Anatomy of a Film Industry (Dermody and Jacka) 34
The Searchers 222–3
self-determination 7, 37, 148, 171

Sen, Ivan 190
sexual/sexuality 4, 36, 40, 54, 74, 82, 213, 251 n.3
   danger 133–41
   desires 186
   female 40, 57, 85, 87, 206
   nudity and 10, 45, 49, 52–3
   violence 137–8, 203, 211, 216
Shame (Jodress) 142 n.3
Shane (George) 228
Shang-Chi and the Legend of the Ten Rings 32
Sharman, Jim 43, 207–9, 211, 213, 251 n.2
Sharrett, Christopher 39, 216, 222, 227
Shine (Hicks) 18–19
Shirley, Graham 155
Shirley Thompson Versus the Aliens (Sharman) 42–3, 203–4, 207, 209–11, 213, 224, 250
   budgets 208
   home environment 209–10
   Mr. Thompson (character) 210
   Shirley (character) 209–11
Shortland, Cate 142 n.2
Significant Australian Content (SAC) guidelines 22
Simmons, Gary 185
Simpson, Catherine 34, 124, 142 n.11
Sisters, McDonagh 8
Sixel, Margaret 247
Smaill, Belinda 175
social realism 142 n.4
Soft Fruit 122
Somersault (Shortland) 142 n.2
Spark, Ceridwen 142 n.10
Spence, Nigel 61, 72
Spiderman: No Way Home 32
The Square (Edgerton) 20
Star Wars: Episode II-Attack of the Clones 22
Star Wars Episode III: Revenge of the Sith 22
Steel Dawn 239
Stigwood, Robert 7
Still Our Country (Reynolds) 26
Stolen Generations 16, 42, 134, 141, 145, 167, 172–3, 183, 194–5
Stork (Burstall) 3–4, 40, 45, 47, 51–2, 55, 59
   Anna (character) 51–2

representations of women vis ocker males 51–2
Stork (character) 51–2
Storm Boy 68
Strain, Ellen 117–18
Stratton, David 6, 225
Strictly Ballroom (Luhrmann) 14, 17–18, 56
"Suburban Subversions: Women's Negotiation of Suburban Space in Australian Cinema" (Simpson) 124
Sunday Too Far Away (Hannam) 2, 4, 7, 60, 68
Superman Returns 22
Sweet Country (Thornton) 26–8
Sweetie (Campion) 10–11, 36, 95, 115–16
   bush in 117
   disabilities and difference 115–16
   Kay (character) 117
   Sweetie (character) 116–18

Tanna (Butler and Dean) 30
10BA period 8–12, 35–6, 141, 208, 224
Ten Canoes (de Heer) 16, 17, 26
The Terminator 239
The New Nationalism 2
Thornhill, Michael 4, 47
Thornton, Warwick 26, 190–3
Tilson, Alison 29
Toro, Guillermo del 239
Torres Strait Islander peoples 42, 147–8, 167–8, 171–2, 194–5
The Tracker (de Heer) 16, 26, 38, 42, 145, 147, 165, 170, 174–82, 184, 187, 191, 194, 196 n.8, 197 n.13, 198 n.15, 199 n.21
   Fanatic (character) 174–82
   murders of Aboriginal Peoples 147
   Tracker (character) 175–82
transportation 19, 146, 219, 232
tribes/communities of Indigenous Australians. *See* Aboriginal communities; Indigenous
Turcotte, Gerry 205–6
Turkey Shoot (Masters) 12
Turner, Graeme 2, 94
Twelve Canoes (de Heer and Reynolds) 25–6
Two Hands (Jordan) 19

Un Certain Regard (Cox) 14, 17–18, 26, 29
Uncivilised (Chauvel) 195 n.3

Vieth, Errol 35
Vietnam 239
Visions of Australia 3
voyeurism 60, 74–5
Vulnerable Bodies: Creative Disabilities in Contemporary Australian Film (Ferrier) 36–7, 94
vulnerable bodies model 36, 94–6, 118 n.1

Wake in Fright (Kotcheff) 5–6, 46, 68, 207–8
Walkabout 5–6, 143 n.12, 145–6, 174–5, 177, 181, 190–1, 196 n.7
   David Gulpilil (character) 149–50
   Dreamtime/Dreamings 145–6, 150–2
   racism 150, 155
   relationship of Aboriginal men and non-Indigenous women 146, 149–58
Warner Center/Village Roadshow Studios 21
Warrick, Steve 130–1
Waterworld 239
Ways of Seeing (Berger) 154
Weir, Peter 4–6, 13, 15, 47, 207, 213–16, 218–19
Western Australian Department of Community Welfare 121
Wheels of Fire 239
White, Patrick 211
Whitlam, Gough 3, 56, 148, 171, 218
Whitlam Labor administration 148
The Wild Angels (Corman) 220, 227
Williamson, David 51, 55–7, 68
Wincer, Simon 9
Wish You Were Here (Darcy-Smith) 29
Wolf Creek (McLean) 22, 24–5, 249
Wolf Creek 2 (McLean) 24–5
Wolverine (Mangold) 32
A Woman's Tale (Cox) 142 n.3
women and bush environments 9, 18, 37, 41, 93
   in *"Crocodile" Dundee* 114–15
   The Getting of Wisdom 99–104
   as inspirational place 104, 107–13

in *My Brilliant Career* 104–13
in *Picnic at Hanging Rock* 95–9
pre-Oedipal mother 97–8
in *Sweetie* 117
to wildlife 113–14
Women and the Bush: Forces of Desire in the Australian Cultural Tradition (Schaffer) 37, 94
women/womanhood 41–2, 66, 122, 158, 211
   in Australian society 56
   and bush/nature environments 93, 95–9, 114–15
   independence of 49
   in ocker films 36, 47, 49–50
Wood, Robin 212, 214
Wright, Geoffrey 13–14, 63
Wrong Side of the Road (Lander) 37, 42, 145, 147, 165–74, 190, 194, 197 n.12
   Aboriginal music performance 147
   Indigenous bands 166–74

Les (character) 167–9
Ron (character) 167–70
Veronika (character) 169–70

The Year My Voice Broke (Duigan) 10, 36, 40–1, 71, 239
   adolescent life 80–4
   Danny Embling (character) 80–4, 90 n.6
   Freya (character) 80–4, 90 n.6
   hypnosis 82
   Jonah (character) 81, 83, 90 n.6
   sexual intimacy 82
   spirits 83–4, 90 n.6
   Trevor (character) 81–4
The Year of Living Dangerously 68
Yojimbo (Kurosawa) 228, 232–4
Young, Lola 86, 185

Zalcock, Beverley 37
zealous patriotism, chauvinist 47

www.ingramcontent.com/pod-product-compliance
Lightning Source LLC
Chambersburg PA
CBHW062123300426
44115CB00012BA/1786